Copyright and Popular Media

Also by Trajce Cvetkovski
THE POLITICAL ECONOMY OF THE MUSIC INDUSTRY

Copyright and Popular Media

Liberal Villains and Technological Change

Trajce Cvetkovski
University of Queensland, Australia

palgrave
macmillan

First published 2013 by
PALGRAVE MACMILLAN

Palgrave Macmillan in the UK is an imprint of Macmillan Publishers Limited, registered in England, company number 785998, of Houndmills, Basingstoke, Hampshire RG21 6XS.

Palgrave Macmillan in the US is a division of St Martin's Press LLC, 175 Fifth Avenue, New York, NY 10010.

Palgrave Macmillan is the global academic imprint of the above companies and has companies and representatives throughout the world.

Palgrave® and Macmillan® are registered trademarks in the United States, the United Kingdom, Europe and other countries.

ISBN 978–0–230–36847–7

This book is printed on paper suitable for recycling and made from fully managed and sustained forest sources. Logging, pulping and manufacturing processes are expected to conform to the environmental regulations of the country of origin.

A catalogue record for this book is available from the British Library.

A catalog record for this book is available from the Library of Congress.

10   9   8   7   6   5   4   3   2   1
22   21   20   19   18   17   16   15   14   13

Printed and bound in the United States of America

For Steven

'Everything that rises must converge'
(title used extensively throughout popular media)

Contents

List of Tables and Figures

Tables

Figure

xi

Author's Note

I have always possessed a voracious appetite for popular media. I especially love music. I recall in 1975, at the age of seven, being given AUD$5 in order to go to the record shop to 'independently' purchase my very own new-release vinyl for AUD$4.99. An equivalent new-release CD is now, more or less, AUD$10. In 35 years the price has doubled, but little did I know that, back then, minimum wages were seven times less than they are now! I still have that weathered item, and am grateful to my parents for regularly allowing such luxuries. They did indeed pay a dear price for me to indulge in my passion for popular media. My view on how popular media should be consumed remains ambivalent. I trust this investigation into media consumption will assist in situating the debate beyond the black and white.

Acknowledgements

My family, through their unconditional love and support, enabled me to write this book. They are, however, disappointed that Captain Jack Sparrow did not get a mention. I thank Lars Brandle (*Billboard*) for his expert knowledge, and my friends and students who offered me updates and opinions. It seems *everyone* I meet has a view on popular culture, piracy, copyright law and the consumption of popular media. I thank Geraldine Matthews for solving my maths problems and for proofreading generally, and Tui Andersen for her corrections and suggestions. I especially thank Felicity Plester at Palgrave Macmillan for her constant guidance. Catherine Mitchell's administrative support is also acknowledged. Naturally, I assume responsibility for the text.

Abbreviations

AACP	Alliance Against Counterfeiting and Piracy
ACCC	Australian Competition and Consumer Commission
AFACT	Australian Federation Against Copyright Theft
AMCOS	Australian Mechanical Copyright Owners Society
APRA	Australasian Performing Right Association
ARIA	Australian Recording Industry Association
Art.	Article
Arts.	Articles
AVI	audio-video interleave
BIRPI	United International Bureau for the Protection of Intellectual Property
BMG	Bertelsmann Group
BPI	British Phonographic Industry
CC	copy controlled technology
CCG	Copyright Convergence Group
CCL	creative commons licences
CD	compact disc
CD-R	compact disc – recordable
DAT	digital audio tape
DEA	Digital Economy Act (2010) (UK)
DIY	do-it-yourself
DMCA	Digital Millennium Copyright Act 1998 (US)
DRM	digital rights management
DSB	Dispute Settlement Board
DVD	digital versatile disc (earlier name: digital video disc)
EC	European Community
ESA	Entertainment Software Association (US)
email	electronic mail
EU	European Union
FTC	Federal Trade Commission (US)

GDP	gross domestic product
IFPI	International Federation of the Phonographic Industry
IIPA	International Intellectual Property Alliance
IPRs	intellectual property rights
ISP	Internet service provider
IT	information technologies
M&C	music & copyright
MD	mini disc
MPEG	Moving Picture Experts Group
Mi2N	Music Industry News Network
MIPI	Music Industry Piracy Investigations (Australia)
MPAA	Motion Picture Association of America
MP3	Motion Picture Experts Group – 1 audio layer 3
OECD	Organization for Economic Co-operation and Development
OFT	Office of Fair Trading (UK)
P2P	peer-to-peer
PC	personal computer
PPCA	Phonographic Performance Company of Australia
PPD	published price to dealers/published dealer price
PPL	Phonographic Performance Ltd (UK)
PR	public relations
PRS	Performing Right Society (UK)
RIAA	Recording Industry Association of America
RRP	recommended retail price
RRS	really simple syndication
s.	section
ss	sections
telcos	telecommunication industry services
TPMs	technical protection measures
TRIPS	Agreement on Trade-Related Aspects of Intellectual Property Rights
UK	United Kingdom
US	United States
USB	universal serial bus (port)

VCR	videocassette recorder
VHS	video home system
WCT	WIPO Copyright Treaty (1996)
WIPO	World Intellectual Property Organization
WPPT	World Intellectual Property Organization Performances and Phonograms Treaty (1996)
WTO	World Trade Organization
WWW	World Wide Web

Cases

A&M Records, Inc. v Napster, Inc. (2000) USDC ND Cal, 114 F. Supp. 2d 896 (*Napster*)

Adelaide Corporation v Australasian Performing Right Association Ltd (1928) Ltd [1928] HCA 10

Arista Records LLC v Lime Group LLC 715 F. Supp. 2d 481 (2010) (*LimeWire*)

Atari Europe S.A.S.U. v Rapidshare AG (OLG Dusseldorf, Judgment (22 March 2010, Az I-20 U 166/09, unreported) (*Rapidshare*)

Australian Tape Manufacturers Association Ltd v Commonwealth (1993) 176 CLR 480

Australian Capital Television v Commonwealth (1992) 177 CLR 106

Australian Competition and Consumer Commission v Universal Music Australia Pty Ltd (formerly known as PolyGram Pty Ltd) and Others (N925 of 1999) 201 ALR 502

Australian Competition & Consumer Commission v Universal Music Australia Pty Limited (No 2) [2002] FCA 192

Australasian Performing Right Association Limited v Jain (1990) 26 FCR 53

Australasian Performing Right Association Limited v Monster Communications Pty Limited [2006] FCA 1806

Autodesk Australia Pty Ltd v Cheung (1990) 94 ALR 472

Autodesk Inc v Yee (1996) 139 ALR 735

Boosey v Purday (1849) 4 Ex. 145

Broadcast Music, Inc. v Columbia Broadcasting System, Inc. 441 U.S. 1 (1979)

CBS Inc v Ames and Records and Tapes Ltd [1982] Ch 91

CBS Songs Ltd v Amstrad Consumer Electronics PLC [1988] 2 All ER 484

Chappell & Co Ltd v Nestle Co Ltd [1960] AC 87

Columbia Broadcasting System Inc and Columbia Record Club, Inc., Petitioners, v Federal Trade Commission, No. 16492 United States Court of Appeals Seventh Circuit June 26, 1969, 414 F.2d 974

Columbia Picture Industries Inc v Luckins (1996) 34 IPR 504

Cooper v Universal Music Australia Pty Ltd [2006] FCAFC 187

D'Almaine v Boosey (1835) 1 Y & C Ex 288

Dispute Settlement Board Finding WT/DS362/7 (2009)

Legislation (Statutes, Regulations, Codes, Ratified Treaties, Instruments and other formal International Obligations)

Act for the Encouragement of Literature and Genius, Connecticut Copyright Statute, Connecticut (1783)

Australian Constitution

Agreement between the United Nations and World Intellectual Property Organization WIPO Publication No. 111 (1975)

Agreement on Trade-Related Aspects of Intellectual Property Rights (1994)

Australian Competition and Consumer Act 2010 (formerly Trade Practices Act 1974)

Australian Industries Preservation Act 1906 (Cth)

Berne Convention for the Protection of Literary and Artistic Works (1886)

Berne Convention Implementation Act of 1988 (App. II to the United States Code (Title 17) (US)

Broadcasting Legislation Amendment (Digital Television) Act 2006 (Cth)

Bubble Act 1720 (Great Britain) (Royal Exchange and London Assurance Corporation Act 1719)

Clayton Antitrust Act of 1914 (US)

Companies Clauses Consolidation Act 1845

Competition Act 1998 (UK)

Competition and Consumer Act 2010 (Cth)

Convention Establishing the World Intellectual Property Organization (1967)

Copyright (World Trade Organization Amendments) Act 1994 (Australia)

Copyright Act 1842 (UK)

Copyright Act 1911 (UK)

Copyright Act 1912 (Cth)

Copyright Act 1956 (UK)

Copyright Act 1968 (Cth)

xxii *Legislation*

The Constitution of the Republic of Rwanda (2003) confirmed by Supreme Court Ruling 772/14.06/2003)

Trade Practices Act 1974 (Cth)

Treaty of Rome (1957)

US Free Trade Implementation Act 2004 (Cth)

WIPO Copyright Treaty (1996)

WIPO Performances and Phonograms Treaty (1996)

Copyright Designs and Patents Act 1988 (UK)

Copyright Amendment (Digital Agenda Act) 2000 (Digital Agenda Amendments (Cth))

Copyright Regulations 1969 (Cth)

Copyright, Designs and Patent Act 1988 (UK)

Copyright Term Extension Act of 1998 (US)

Corporations Act 2001 (Cth)

Crimes Act 1909 (Cth)

Criminal Code 1995 (Cth)

Digital Economy Act 2010 (UK)

Digital Millennium Copyright Act of 1998 (US) amending the Copyright Act of 1976 (US)

Copyright Term Extension Act 1998 (US)

Directive on the Harmonisation of Certain Aspects of Copyright and Related Rights in the Information Society, Directive 2001/29 of the European Parliament and Council, May 22, 2001 (EU Copyright Directive)

Directive/2006/116/EC of the European Parliament and of the Council, 12 December 2006 on the term of protection of copyright and certain related rights (codified version)

European Convention on Human Rights and Fundamental Freedoms (1950)

Federal Trade Commission Act (US)

Implementation Act of 1988 1914 (as amended) (US)

Industries Preservation Act 1906 (Cth)

International Convention on the Protection of Literary and Artistic Works (1886)

Lobbying Disclosure Act of 1995 (US)

No Electronic Theft Act of 1997 (US)

Obscene Publications Act 1959 (UK)

Robinson-Patman Act of 1936 (US)

Rome Convention for the Protection of Performers, Producers of Phonograms and Broadcasting Organizations (1961)

Sherman Act 1890 (US)

Statute of Anne 1709/10 (UK)

Telecommunications Act 1997 (as amended) (Cth)

Part I
Setting the Scene

1
Liberalism, Realism, Convergence, Consumption and Tensions between Technological and Legal Change

A short parable on copyright

Mark Twain believed in copyright law. An international author, prolific writer and social commentator, he was most vociferous on the issue of copyright regulation for public interest reasons, and extolled the virtues of greater protection of authors' rights. Twain publicly expressed these imperatives well before world trade organizations politicized the need for international governance in the twentieth century.

But Mark Twain was very disappointed in how copyright was regulated in the West. He declared in 1903: 'Only one thing is impossible for God: to find any sense in any copyright law on the planet. Whenever a copyright law is to be made or altered, then the idiots assemble' (1935, pp. 381–382). Twain was frustrated by the disorganizational effects of piracy. As a successful author, he was acutely aware of how copyright law worked in its natural state, and the hazards for authors[1] presented by pirates who sought to plunder the fruits of creative labour.[1]

Indeed, Twain detested pirates, and also blamed the legislature for the weak response to proper copyright regulation and protection. He was fed up with those armed with new and emerging technologies copying his works for free, and worried for the future of his children (as reported in *The New York Times* on Christmas Eve 1908). He looked upon piracy as 'pure robbery'. In 1906, *The New York Times* also published an article on how Mark Twain, prolific writer and self-appointed unsalaried copyright reform lobbyist, intended to 'put pirates to rout'. Despite his best efforts to improve the copyright regime, favourable legislative change was beyond his control.

Twain's views have always been shared by copyright owners – so why is this small bit of history important for an understanding of the political economy of popular media today? They are relevant because the media pirates in Twain's world were not the pirates the reader might have in mind. They were not necessarily the opportunistic backstreet peddlers found in alleyways or, in the modern context, organized commercial pirates in large counterfeiting warehouses or rogue Internet operators (the Napsteresque copycats, the wilfully disobedient 'Kazaariers', the cyber-vigilantes and the rapscallion Pirate Bayers). Would they have been the morally derelict teen-age downloaders, university student uploaders, holidaymakers returning with pirated goods, and the entire broad spectrum of illegal consumers (parents and children alike)?

Ironically, the pirates Twain was referring to were the publishers (publishing companies) – the legitimate artificial citizens who take things that aren't theirs. Twain considered publishers (the prototypes of the current übercopyright owners and para-copyright dealers) with their new technologies and means of production as pirates because they *profited* from the authors. They profited from something that was not theirs because of the weak copyright framework. His purpose to reform copyright, therefore, was based on a distrust of publishers for they were not altruistic. They were the opportunistic beneficiaries of copyright law.

How preposterous must Twain's interpretation of publishers as pirates sound in today's normative and discursive world of copyright governance? Surely the real pirates are those unlicensed copiers and illegal consumers – not the entrepreneurial publishers. Are these new pirates the natural citizens who voted for the 15 members of The Pirate Party, which was comfortably elected into the German Parliament in Berlin on 20 September 2011 (as reported in *The Sydney Morning Herald*)? It was also reported that this party now joins the several 'pirate parties' in parliaments of other European Union (EU) states, which have been democratically elected to represent constituents (presumably with piratical ideologies). Indeed piracy is a slippery term, and so it must be asked, who are the real pirates? If Twain's perspective appears odd, then the current copyright governance paradigm is nothing short of Kafkaesque.

Twain's dilemma is even more significant today because it suggests the political economy of popular media, historically, has been an ongoing site of struggle for the ownership of popular culture, communication and information dissemination. Copyright as a form of dialectical legal realism continues to present its perpetual unresolved issues.

Whilst Twain's hyperbole about publishers as ungodly robbers may sound absurd or at least unfair, his observation about the futility of any attempt by God to make sense of copyright law is not. It is this level of confusion in contemporary society that makes the identification of the real liberal villains that much more challenging.

Overview: setting the tone, establishing the terms and providing the scope of this book

The intention of this book is to examine developments in popular media and copyright in the light of the challenges, namely piracy and illegal consumption. The central question guiding this book asks: what will be the effect of emerging technologies on the future organization of copyright? This question is historically relevant in that, since the inception of modern copyright legislation in 1709 (and the subsequent common law recognition of media piracy as far back as 1769), the flow of illegal consumption over the past three centuries has not been stemmed. The argument raised is that media piracy is illustrative of a plurality of media consumption within a converging legal, technological, economic and ideological universe. If convergence means the union of these various sectors within capitalist society, then copyright is anything but harmonious. And this has led to a crisis in popular media consumption.

This investigation is primarily concerned with technology, copyright and popular media in Western nations[2] where liberalism underpins societies as the dominant political ideology. Of interest is the fact that modern conceptions of liberalism, copyright laws, popular media and technology have evolved concurrently, but not necessarily harmoniously. And in the past century when mass production of modern popular culture (especially various audio-visual media) became a dominant mode of advanced capitalist cultural production, both the organizational and disorganizational effects of technology on copyright law became apparent.

One fundamental tenet of liberalism that is important for understanding popular media is that liberalism is concerned with ensuring individuals are able make their own choices rather than having them imposed on them by society, the state or corporate citizens. Specifically, liberalism places emphasis on personal autonomy and individualism (a natural state of being). It follows that a laissez-faire approach to the manner in which popular media products are consumed by individuals should be encouraged in liberal societies. Indeed, the initial substantive conceptions of copyright under common law also encapsulated a somewhat laissez-faire, non-interventionist or residual institutional approach because copyright as a private, personal and natural legal right was originally designed to restrain use *only* if matter had never been published. Writing about the circumstances prior to 1842 in Britain, Slater (1939, p. 206) states, '[i]f the author once gave it to the world, he had no remedy against the one who chose to pirate it'.

It is fair to observe that liberalism, common law copyright and laissez-faire economics are natural states. Conversely, it will be argued in terms of popular media governance – institutions and associations involved in business and corporate activity – that the role of government and the enactment of statutes for the regulation of copyright and corporations are seen as unnatural since they purport to change, control or otherwise limit the behaviour of individuals.

What lies at the heart of the issue is that liberalism encourages freedom of expression and freedom from interference. Liberals traditionaily resist absolutism and challenge centralized control. Consumption of popular culture is regarded as a personal or individualistic experience, irrespective of the fact the bulk of popular culture has been mass-produced by a dominant handful of corporate media players over the past century. That is, while popular media might be described as the consumption of intrinsically personal pleasures, these pleasures traditionally and historically have been technologically determined and legally controlled, both cumulatively and conjunctively, by large corporations (state or privately owned).

Cultural consolidation by corporations is a feature of the status quo in advanced capitalist societies. It is argued that unquestioned and unchallenged control of popular media appears to be ideologically at cross purposes with notions of personal liberty and the pursuit of freedom of expression. The tension that arises is the result of centralized or dominant control of popular media by unnatural or artificial citizens.

Focus is on the two established major popular entertainment media industries, film and popular music ('pop'). To a lesser extent the computer games industry will also be considered because it falls under this broader digital audio-visual entertainment media rubric. These industries are culturally relevant for three interconnected reasons. The first is multinational corporations control these dominant modes of cultural production, and the subsequent copyrights attached to the products (hence the term 'copyright industries' to describe these industries). Second, new technologies, namely the Internet and file-sharing software, are inextricably linked to the manner in which these products are currently being consumed. The third reason for limiting the scope of these popular media is that the bulk of media piracy (and the alleged subsequent loss in revenue) is sustained by these copyright industries. In relation to these three reasons, the literature supports the general presumption that as the major players control the bulk of commercially available entertainment media, then it stands to reason that most of the financial harm is being experienced by these comptrollers of popular culture in the West.

Given the above contextual setting, the central argument is that technology has significantly influenced the organization of popular media in their commodified forms. This book expands on this basic proposition by presenting a comprehensive analysis of the interaction between the politico-economic and legal issues and the underlying political ideological environment in which popular media are consumed. It argues that problems between advancement and copyright law in liberal democratic capitalist societies have always existed because emerging technologies are a double-edged sword. And when conditions become unpredictable or unstable (as in the current phase involving omnipotent digital products as opposed to analogue or mechanical devices), a fragile tension in the relationship between innovation and consumption is formed. Indeed, digitalization has in recent years effectively threatened any positive relationship corporate media enjoyed with technological advancement. It is suggested this will continue to undermine any successful maintenance of copyright that dominant players have enjoyed for exclusive and perpetual revenue generation.

What flows from this assertion is the need to examine the practical, or rather, *real* effects of the manner in which major popular media copyright controllers are organizing their products. This broad focus is important as the doctrinal evidence supports the contention that recent universally accessible digital technologies have raised questions about future legal preservation and protection of copyright in an era of highly advanced digital piracy and universal consumption.

Copyright protection mechanisms and supervision processes are highly integrated. They focus on sophisticated (and aggressive) management of intellectual property for repeated exploitation for decades after acquisition. Yet consumption (legal, quasi-legal or illegal) is a relatively simple process. The film, pop and computer game industries provide excellent case studies for such centralized protectionist behaviour in an era where basic free or low-cost access to products is easily provided. Recent doctrinal developments and empirical data concerning these media industries suggest overall maintenance of copyright has become generally disjointed, ad hoc and relatively inconsistent. In short, there is no cogent evidence to suggest that modern copyright protection can successfully prevail over innovative change.

An objective analysis of the actual *success* of copyright supervision and subsequent protection remains underdeveloped in the literature. Furthermore, substantive literature on the combined disorganizational effects of innovation for illegitimate and legitimate consumption is virtually non-existent. Significant recent developments in the case law are identified as the literature is not conclusive in terms of explaining recent developments. In particular, the interaction between copyright, product protection and consumer behaviour has not been comprehensively developed. Existing research is focused on stemming and controlling illegitimate consumption, namely piracy. The literature does not adequately explain the reasons for the decline in success rates for the prevention of further copyright disorganization. This book remedies this deficiency by proposing that several legal and technological factors in liberal democratic society are affecting the political economy of popular media industries and their respective capacity to control illegal consumption.

It is suggested that some of these factors are beyond the control of specific industry and regulatory regimes because: (a) not all challenges are illegal, and (b) consumers do not necessarily deem unapproved consumption as deviant behaviour. In particular, Internet service providers (ISPs) by virtue of their business or undertaking are hollowing out or diluting any potency that copyright laws technically possess. This is occurring through a range of concurrent convergence developments, including legislative incompatibility between technology laws and copyright laws (the neighbouring laws and digital rights debate), and current digital products legitimately available to law-abiding individual citizens (consumers freely accessing the Internet and enabling software). The recent Hollywood film industry case against iiNet provides clear and unequivocal evidence for these propositions.[3]

For the first time in legal and innovation history, independently evolving products, namely file management, replication devices, social networking and related protocols via the Internet, and related computer hardware have concurrently affected traditional modes of media access and consumption. En masse illegal peer-to-peer (P2P) consumption can hardly be construed as deviant or antisocial behaviour in any strict criminal or even quasi-criminal context simply by virtue of the number of media consumers online engaging in such behaviour. And it would be an infinitely futile task to profile a typical illegal downloader given the broad-spectrum antecedents of illegal consumers. It is argued, given the decentralized and somewhat atomistic process of file-sharing, that these recent modes of media consumption are consistent with classic liberal behaviour.

Despite the generally negative publicity and adverse inferences cast on replicating devices, some of these effects are positive or enabling. The first significant observation is that many of these technologies are perfectly legal and have developed free from any popular media influence imposed by the major players. Innovation has universally enabled consumers to explore media products freely and without corporate influence. Recent technologies have affected the status quo. It will be asserted that when corporations restrict access to cultural products they are acting as cultural gatekeepers. They are effectively censoring, or rather dictating and limiting, what an individual may wish to watch or listen to. Similarly, where the deletion of a back catalogue occurs due to a lack of commercial viability, or one film is promoted over another for commercial reasons, then these actions might be construed as fundamental restrictions on an individual's right to choose from a wide range of media. This crisis of liberty leads to a quest for self-sufficiency through self-determination via enabling technologies. The Internet is the most ideal forum for news, information and links to various sources of legal and illegal access to popular media. It appears quite rational for individuals to source products beyond the cultural gate if limitations are perpetually placed on them as consumers. In other words, consumers might feel compelled to defend their natural right to choose freely in the face of a corporate ruling elite that refuses to make products available for economic or other reasons. Any subsequent duplicitous behaviour appears to prima facie co-exist with legitimate use. I argue that the rationale for purported illegal consumption extends beyond the obvious legal or illegal dichotomy.

The dilemma is that when an individual explores cultural products that are outside traditional modes of supply access or consumption, she or he is deemed to have committed a technical breach of statutory copyright law by infringing the rights of the copyright owner (as no permission was sought). In advanced capitalist states where copyright laws are particularly complex, those rights are generally not vested in natural or ordinary citizens, but rather in artificial corporate entities. The sheer volume of illegal consumption suggests consumers of popular media – that is, multinational, transglobal citizens enjoying a near perfect monopoly – struggle with the concept that popular media industries might suffer harm. It will be argued that in some instances ordinary citizens, as consumers, generally do not construe their infringing behaviour as deviant or antisocial and do not see their actions as harmful or detrimental in the ordinary sense of the word. If they do, then it is contended that prosecutorial action combined with educational policies and anti-piracy technology ought to have completely curbed, or at least substantially minimized, illegal consumption in this current climate of technological change and enlightened state of information and entertainment consumption. Liberal attitudes and beliefs held by individuals in the West correctly represent actual conceptions of popular media consumption and transcend beyond corporate conceptions of copyright and popular culture as an industry.

Technology's democratizing effects have blurred the boundaries between illegal and legal consumption. The interaction between these two modes of convergence of both illegal and legal consumption has not been fully addressed in the literature in any politico-economic and legal context. The positive and negative impacts of emerging technologies have together created a serious dilemma in terms of product commodification for the major controllers of media. The ultimate diminishing effect for copyright as a (lucrative) form of intangible property is the significant decrease in its intrinsic value; in other words, combined developments that have led to consumer disorientation and copyright industry disorganization.

The unresolved issues elaborated in the following chapters focus on whether traditional and legal modes of media consumption can be reconciled with illegal consumption, apropos media piracy, as a core feature in the consumption of popular media. If this is correct, then illegal consumption can hardly be construed as subversive or counter-cultural. An extreme liberal view might even suggest that such innovation is liberating because of its emancipatory potential.

To test these propositions, the research behind this book is doctrinally and empirically grounded. The inferences drawn and conclusions reached attempt to determine to what extent different technologies can be regarded as the primary catalysts to challenge the corporate control of the media. If the dominant few intend to identify and manage these changes in terms of their corporate model, then they must understand the dynamic nature of interacting technologies.

The relevance of the study of political economy to copyright in popular media

The application of political economy to copyright is useful for various reasons. Firstly, it provides a broad and unifying disciplinary framework for any multidisciplinary approach that requires an examination of several interacting subjects involving consumer behaviour (organizational studies), corporate control of popular media (communications), law (legal studies), policy and governance (political science) and popular culture generally (sociology). Secondly, using political economy to study of the production and consumption of popular media is also politically relevant because its roots, like liberalism, are firmly embedded in nineteenth-century notions of individuality, morality and liberty. Thirdly, it underscores various interrelated traditional disciplines, namely political science, law and economics. It is therefore the most appropriate field in which to analyse the interaction between corporate citizens and individuals in a world of digitalization and convergence. The themes and definitions situate the debate within this field of study.

Therefore, the book's framework is an analysis of the interaction of the fundamental ideals of liberalism and the principles of legal realism and are set out as follows:

- convergent consumption (cultural products in popular media industries and the nature of sociocultural shifts, including changing audience habits, attitudes and beliefs about consumption),
- copyright and digital legislation convergence (copyright laws and digital rights management policies, copyright governance and the organization of popular media industries as copyright industries, including national and international legal and regulatory change),
- convergent corporate media industry (influence on competition law and policy, globalized corporate governance, and the corporate response to copyright developments), and
- technological convergence (economic development and advancement in an era of digitalization).

Political theme: liberalism, consumers and copyright

It is important to acknowledge at the outset that liberalism and primary notions of copyright are relatively compatible. Indeed it is fair to state that freedom and copyright are both founded on natural rights. In 1690 the father of liberalism recognized that 'every man has a property in his person. This no body has any right to but himself. The labour of his body, and the work of his hands, we may say, are properly his' (John Locke, 1967, sec. 27).

The tenet of liberalism that is important for understanding popular media and consumption is the emphasis on freedom (also known as negative or individualistic freedom). The modern sense of this freedom from interference ideology may be traced back to John Stuart Mill's nineteenth-century principle of harm and Isaiah Berlin's *Four Essays on Liberty* (1969) where these nineteenth-century principles lay the foundations for modern liberalism. Liberalism is concerned with limiting the extent to which entities and institutions regulate individual behaviour.

The state, through the legal system, sets the limits on interference by establishing the principle that the only end for which it is legitimate to interfere with the liberty of an individual is to prevent harm to others by way of a *morally* driven legal code (for example, preventing acts of criminality against persons or property or any form of physical or financial harm). Limits to interference also apply to all artificial agencies including corporations: 'The defects, therefore, of government management, do not seem to be necessarily much greater, if necessarily greater at all, than those of management by joint-stock [company]' (J. S. Mill, 1982, p. 11).

Specifically, liberalism places reliance on personal autonomy because of this natural right. Individuals are understood to enter into an implicit social contract by which they sanction the activities of governments that protect their life, liberty and property. The idea that individuals exist in a natural state prior to being a part of society implies that the activities of individuals are natural. As a consequence, business and corporate activity and the processes of government are seen as unnatural because they change, control or otherwise limit the behaviour of individuals. In other words, entities are veiled by artificial corporate structures, and their moral attitudes and beliefs (if any) are unclear or at least different to natural conceptions of morality. This is not to suggest that artificial citizens' corporate executives and delegated representatives are devoid of morality. Indeed, personal attitudes and beliefs may differ from those of the corporation as an organically whole organism. But companies duly incorporated under corporation laws reflect corporate citizenship, and it follows therefore that entities are governed as persons with distinct legal rights. Copyright governance is one such arena where the elevation of artificial citizenship over natural citizenship is clear. Historically, humans have been bound buy a moral code. Unnatural behaviour (for example, criminal conduct) has been largely constrained by informal and formal traditions, norms, customs, cultural practices, religion and laws – some of which remain unchanged (for example, capital punishment and imprisonment as a form of deterrence). Whilst terms such as corporate governance and corporate social responsibility suggest, at least on a formal level, that a moral code could be applied to artificial citizens, the practical reality is that a comparable natural moral code cannot be applied to artificial citizens when comparing their behaviour with that of individuals. (Entities can never be imprisoned for any deterrent effect.) Artificial citizens therefore exist in an unnatural setting because it is impossible to measure whether they possess a moral code. These fundamental differences in citizenship lay the foundations for tensions in the copyright governance framework.

In this context it must be asked how individualistic attitudes are expressed in atomistic settings such as the World Wide Web. Liberalism as an ideology appears to thrive in digitalized environments, or rather, virtual environments, given the degree of consumer anonymity compared to that in traditional transactional spaces.

Of particular importance to this book is that this individualistic behaviour typically represents the conduct of ordinary citizens in classic liberal democratic societies where negative freedoms (freedom of choice) prevail. In the case of popular media, corporations have become arbiters of the modes in which products are consumed and prices are set. Empirical data suggests that consumers are relatively informed about how to consume popular media and do not necessarily view illegal consumption of popular media as harmful behaviour. (Individual consumption or one-off illegal transactions must clearly be distinguished from illegal production for profit or some form of pecuniary advantage.) If one, conceptually only, accepts Robert Nozick's (1974) notions of 'night watchman' and 'minimal interference', then a desire to choose illegal or legal consumption of popular culture in a convergent environment might be viewed as a rational choice provided individuals do not derogate from traditional notions of the harm principle.

Legal theme: realism, consumerism and copyright

Legal realism requires an acceptance of the fact that there is a range of non-legal factors that influence legal outcomes. Jones (1961, p. 801) poses the question whether legal realism 'has something unique to offer on the age-old jurisprudential problem of the role of moral ideas in the functioning of law in society'. By introducing morality to the question of whether a prima facie illegal act is right or wrong, legal realism challenges formal conceptions of the law and the dominant positivist position that the law is interpreted in a neutral and objective manner. According to Jones (ibid., pp. 802, 808), legal realism, 'with its emphasis on the inevitability of choice and discretion' and 'emphasis on the tensions that exist in law administration between the demands of the prescriptive rule-formulation and the appeal of the concrete problem situation', is essentially an attack on the formalist account of legal reasoning. The realist view therefore considers social influences and social norms when determining how the status quo ought to be shaped in a particular arena by exposing the political, social and economic influences supporting strict legal formalism.

Such an approach in the field of copyright governance would be concerned with the practical legal question of how popular culture should be consumed in a copyright governance environment clearly dominated by the dominant few. This is important in understanding copyright governance as conceptually it includes a broader definition of copyright that recognizes non-legal influences, such as corporate power and domination in capitalist society, the judicialization of politics, consumer behaviour and morality, politics, policy and even the prejudices of individuals as consumers including attitudes towards copyright law.

Legal realism was particularly influential from the 1920s to the 1940s in the West. Interestingly, during this phase of jurisprudential evolution, two substantive politico-legal developments also occurred. Firstly, this was an era of rapid corporate consolidation in the popular music and film industries. It was characterized by weak competition policy and corporate regulation (thereby situating Hollywood at the epicentre (Moran, 1993)). For at least three decades major corporations have dominated popular film and music, both vertically and horizontally, because of weak anticompetition policies (antitrust or trade policies) and legislation, and policies generally, in the Western world (see Gomery, 1986; Balio, 1990). This weak regulatory national and transnational environment assisted in the creation of omnipotent international market oligopolies well before meaningful domestic laws were enacted to monitor and review corporate citizens in the marketplace.

Secondly, corporate interest groups and associations remain influential in the legislative arena in the West. This is evident because the period for the duration of copyright in popular media products has been extended due to forceful petitions by the corporate lobby to increase copyright monopolies. Even in the past few decades, after proper competition policy implementation, this economic landscape has remained largely unchanged.

It follows that governance devices (the machinery for influencing how copyright laws and policy are to be shaped and created) have become politicized in that corporate copyright owners have become the most powerful voice in the copyright governance arena. Applying legal realism to the facts of the political economy of copyright enables the exposure of the exclusive and monopolistic tendencies in which corporate copyright industries thrive. The fact that this dominant position did not change throughout the twentieth century exposes the artificiality of formalist legal rules purporting to provide a balance in the copyright paradigm.

Importantly, a critical realist legal theory underscores the political nature of copyright law. This can be used to justify the continuation of existing power relations in the organization of these industries. It emphasizes the legitimizing function of the law. The relationship between the powerful few who own the copyright vested in popular media and the evolution of copyright laws constitutes this ideology of law.

Legal realism recognizes the artificiality of corporations. They are not tangible beings like humans. It is difficult to imagine how policies might be implemented so as to enforce proper moral or ethical values on such 'citizens'. This research advances this basic proposition by suggesting that as corporate citizens can only distinguish between legal and illegal they have no capacity to distinguish the complexity of consumer behaviour in a digital environment. The lack of pragmatism on the part of corporate entities is evident in popular media.

The objective of a realistic approach to understanding the current problems is to accept the practical realities of how copyright evolved, and the political and economic influences shaping those laws. Applying realism to the study of the political economy of copyright in popular media means a theoretical or rather positivist definition of the concept of copyright law, and that a formalistic understanding of copyright law is not enough to explain the disorganizational effects. In other words, practical things, not formal copyright law, determine the manner in which popular media products are organized, or disorganized as the case may be.

Laws are legitimized through the processes of responsible government and the rule of law. These gives laws the appearance of neutrality and objectivity. But a realist view of copyright laws is that they are hegemonic in that they reinforce the structures by which the powerful dominate subordinate groups. In theory, consumers in liberal societies accept and support the structures that dominate them if they take on the appearance of being value free, objective and fair. For individual consumers, this usually translates to consumption of products that are deemed to be fairly priced, easily or readily accessible in several formats and free from interference or coercion.

However, consumption of popular media in reality is quite complex because, on the one hand, popular media are dominated by a few major actors who have created a distinct set of legal principles yet, on the other hand, consumers possess different or competing values. This creates a divergence that produces different outcomes for consumers and creates an alternative set of legal principles and values. This has led to conflicting issues between copyright law and other legal doctrines and policies.

Convergent consumption

This book is concerned with technology and contemporary popular media in Western society because popular media represent the bulwark of advanced commercial exploitation in advanced capitalist societies. In addition to the description of the typological scope and legal and political themes, further definitions are required to establish the framework for the following chapters. In particular, it is important to define 'popular media' and 'consumption' in the context of a copyright industry overwhelmingly dominated by a handful of multinational corporate citizens. Research relating to the political economy of copyright is a study of the political economy of the consumption of popular culture. In this context it might be convenient to describe the popular media industry and the copyright industry as a synergy of sorts where the embedded component of the intellectual property is attached to the finished tangible product for the purposes of commercial exploitation.

Popular media, for the purpose of this research, is defined as contemporarily influential Western culture capable of being commercially exploited for the *express* purpose of commodification. It becomes popular not by its capacity to become labelled or genre laden,[4] but by virtue of its commercial

potential as entertainment value. This mode of cultural production dominates the entire global industry.[5]
    There is already a substantial body of literature on the sociology of cul-
tural production and notions of 'legitimate culture' (Bourdieu and Passeron
1977) and 'cultural capital' (Bourdieu 1984) in the West. Bourdieu's concept
of capital as a *resource* is particularly useful because it incorporates both
financial and non-financial elements of culture (the tangible and intangible forms of cultural capital). Bourdieu's works on cultural production,
reproduction and legitimization are acknowledged as key sociological concepts in the analysis of power relations in the fields of artistic and literary
production.
    More specifically, substantive works exist on the political economy of
cultural production and notions of 'cultural dependency' (Schiller 1969) and
'cultural industries' (Garnham 1984, 1990). Schiller's works on American
corporate power and monopolization in the communications and media
industries and the consequent influence on popular culture assist in contextualizing the debate in two ways: first, Western notions of popular culture
have dominated the entire globe; and, second, the United States is by far the
most influential nation in popular culture (see generally Schiller 1969, 2000).
It may have been appropriated as a lucrative economic resource for corporations, but capital as a cultural resource instrumental in facilitating individual
freedom and expression is equally identifiable (Bourdieu, 1984; Bourdieu and
Eagleton, 1991).
    Garnham's work (1990) in relation to ownership concentration and the
multinational dimension of cultural industries is particularly helpful when
conceptualizing media industries. Furthermore, Petersen and Annand's works
(2004) (including works on pop music and pop culture generally (Peterson
and Berger, 1990)) on the production of culture and its nexus with technology, law, industry structure and organization is important. These significant
contributions in the broader field of popular culture assist in situating the
debate about how popular culture is produced, developed and expressed – or,
in other words, popular culture's system of organization. Beyond the broader
theoretical and sociological framework exists a large body of literature solely
concerned with specific elements of the popular media entertainment industries. Issues intersecting technology, copyright and popular media form the
core of the investigation into these specific industries.
    The forms of popular media examined here are those typically described
as multimedia products capable of being digitized, disseminated and played
by electronic audio-visual devices, computers and related consoles. They
fall under a broader entertainment media rubric and comprise the bulk
of popular culture. They are best described as entertainment products (as
opposed to those media products associated with critical artistic merit or
knowledge value (including newsworthiness)). Mass media products are
popular, standardized and generally devoid of 'the pursuit of knowledge'

(Leet, 2004, p. 11). In this group the most relevant popular entertainment media are film, music and game software.[6] These products are significant because most media piracy and copyright infringement considerations relate to these media. These media form the best case study for an inquiry into piracy. Favourable price-setting, format control, protectionist regulation and copyright control are the essential ingredients in the creation of a corporate-controlled, oligopolistic media market. The justification for limiting the research to these three types of popular media is apparent because the multinational majors who own most of the copyright in film, music and games products experience the bulk of the loss.

Another reason for examining these three modes of cultural capital is that the physical or tangible formats – the content and the devices by which the products are made available to consumers – are almost exclusively owned and controlled by the major players. Leavis (1933) first observed how monopolistic economic power was exercised by anticompetitive popular culture corporations. Adorno and Horkeheimer (1997) went further by arguing the purpose of mass culture was to ensure smoothness in the 'unity of individual and society' (ibid., p. 131) and smoothness in the running of the 'supply' chain of mass-produced lines (ibid., p. 135) thereby enabling 'obedience to the social hierarchy' (ibid., p. 131). In short, these form key elements in the manner in which popular culture is unified for the purpose of commodification. While technological developments will be the subject of discussion in subsequent chapters, it is important to highlight that, until the end of the twentieth century, entertainment media formats were centrally controlled by the major music companies (the 'majors') that controlled the bulk of copyright in popular media. In this respect, vinyl records, cassettes, compact discs (CDs), digital video discs (DVDs) and their respective players are all products (and devices) of the majors. The cultural material embedded in the media products has, traditionally, been retained and owned by the same organizations. These products have been distributed through well-established channels (retail outlets) allied to the major players. Put simply, the makers of playing devices are makers of formats and are the exclusive ultimate proprietors of property vested in commodified cultural products for consumption.

The horizontal and vertical integration of popular media through ownership and control of all technologies has ensured homogenized cultural commodification for a handful of dominant players in each industry. It is apparent that the majors, who own the bulk of intellectual property in these cultural productions, unequivocally control the bulk of popular media in their commodified form.

There are three interconnected reasons for focusing on developments in the West. The most obvious reason is that the available statutory and doctrinal information is generally concerned with illegal consumption in Western (liberal or social) democracies. Copyright laws were developed in Europe (under English common law principles and subsequently under French codes). Consequently the first media piracy cases were reported in the Western world. These developments have provided a rich source of information capable of being substantiated and, where necessary, corroborated using accurate data. This is in stark contrast to the relatively underdeveloped empirical data and legal developments in non-Western jurisdictions where primary sources are less capable of adequate scrutiny or validation.

The second reason is that liberalism, as a dominant political ideology, also developed in the West (again, especially under English, French and American influences). This political relationship with the law is important as this investigation explores the politico-legal tensions in popular media in advanced capitalist society.

The third reason is that as the bulk of media products (including previous formats) have been controlled by a handful of Western-influenced multinational corporations, namely corporations from the US, UK, France, Germany and Japan, with subsidiary interests in non-Western jurisdictions, it stands to reason that consumer behaviour in those non-Western nations might largely reflect behaviour elsewhere due to the fact the products are identical. By way of illustration, a CD purchased in Australia, manufactured and issued by Sony Music (Australia), bears no material distinguishing features from the identical CD supplied by Sony Music (Indonesia) (pursuant to the parallel importation amendments to the Copyright Act 1968 (Australia)). The products are internationally standardized and it would be wrong to suggest the legitimate Indonesian product is inferior.

Copyright laws in Indonesia are relatively underdeveloped, but where non-Western developments could add probative value is in terms of understanding the relationship between piracy and Western consumers in emerging economies (the subject of Chapter 7). A brief examination concerning the intersection between non-Western individuals' attitudes – the dominant political ideologies of which are not founded on liberalism – and Western consumers' attitudes is therefore relevant given that so much illegal activity occurs in these jurisdictions.[7]

Who is a consumer and what is consumption? Fornäs, et al. (2007, p. 42) narrowly define consumption as 'that specific kind of interaction whereby people exchange money for goods in an act of purchase, and then use these acquired goods'. The essential factual elements in the consumption process appear include selection, purchase and use (renting, buying and then consuming the products (ibid., p. 43)). Emphasis is clearly placed on financial exchange. Individual producers and consumers are involved in a perfectly rational, private, legal and economic process (a sale) in an organized marketplace.

Convergence in consumption implies *consumption by communication* on the part of consumers, in that the element of *purchase* is subordinated, subsumed, subverted, omitted, partially omitted or otherwise diverted by the primary act of communication. The element of *use* remains static, but the process is not a simple private commercial transaction. It becomes blurred. In this transaction, popular media is freely exchanged over space and time without a sense of finality (offer, acceptance and other commercial transaction qualities). Not paying simply means illegal consumption. In a convergent world, popular media exchanges occur concurrently in a legal and illegal capacity – with or without the exchange of money. Traditional boundaries essential in financial transactions thus become blurred thereby complicating the acts of communication and consumption.

Conceptions of mass media are broad spectrum in the sense they include all aspects of cultural consumption (from cinema and live-music attendance to purchasing products or participating in illegal consumption). This definition is narrower than the general notions of mass media as espoused in the literature – it is solely concerned with commodified products capable of being replicated and subsequently consumed gratis (namely recorded formats). Media piracy as a component of consumption convergence involves the consumption, possession, receipt, interference and conversion of copyrighted materials without permission or authorization, be it with or without financial gain. In short, anyone who consumes media illegally is deemed to be a pirate. Popular media piracy is the replication of film, music and game media using non-traditional methods (namely, digital copying tools).

Nowhere is such consumption more pervasive than online. The Internet is not a physical environment and online formats are regarded as virtual. File-sharing with the aid of P2P is not an invention devised, promoted or supported by the major players. In this realm the majors have no desire to pursue file-sharing to commodification. P2P and other related technologies have evolved independently, uniquely and in relative compatibility with the telecommunication industry services (telcos) because of customers' needs for fast and large data usage plans. Not surprisingly, telcos work independently of the popular media industry. For obvious reasons the major entertainment players (especially Hollywood and the music majors) have removed themselves from P2P development.

Given the commercial imperative, it is important to consider to what extent attitudes have changed from pay-to-play to play-for-free through convergence in regulation and technological changes in the West.

Copyright and digital legislation convergence

By definition, copyright laws in liberal democratic societies are designed to encourage and reward the production of creative works, which include literature, art, music, dramatic works, films, videos, broadcasts, sound recordings and computer programs. Copyright is concerned with the protection of the *expression* of the idea. But there are two fundamental misconceptions about the relevance of copyright in the modern corporate-citizenship setting.

The first relates to the class of copyright that is the specific topic of debate; and the second is about the alleged actual loss of value attributed to copyright abuse.

Copyrights have no manifest material form, notwithstanding that they are capable of being trapped in material form (CD, DVD, book and any other physical or tangible format). Until ideas become realized, copyright remains nothing more than a theoretical construct.

Copyrights are not corporeal chattels (choses in possession). A music album in the form of a CD is a 'thing' as it is in a material form. The copyrights embedded in the album are incorporeal chattels (choses in action) and are intangible. Once copyright moves from the virtual realm (idea) to an actual realm (material world in the form a recording), it is represented as a chose in action rather than a chose in possession. When it is co-mingled with the recorded format and is purchased for good consideration, it has been presented to the consumer in the form of a hybrid incorporeal and corporeal chattel, along with the usual copyright warnings and infringement notices affixed to the packaging. The original creator is the author or composer, but the actual owner of the commodified form (along with the copyrights) who is presenting the CD to the consumer will undoubtedly be the recording company.

What is problematic is that after purchase the material *item* is legally possessed by an individual who quite naturally might think she or he owns the entire item, rights included. These rights might be thought to include the freedom to share, swap, enhance and otherwise interfere with the intellectual property contained in the product. This intermixture has caused a dilemma for individuals, as well as owners of copyright in liberal societies. This attitude or belief pertaining to the relationship between ownership and control requires examination because, as Bourdieu and Eagleton (1991, pp. 115–116) argue, the relations between the individual, culture and production have shifted. The individual as a self-interested consumer has shifted to the centre thereby creating a new social reality.

What is not in dispute is that copyright principles are embedded in the core principles espoused by liberalism, namely freedom from interference in the natural rights of all property possessed by individuals. Copyright is akin to liberty because copyright owners possess exclusive rights to allow the replication of their intellectual property. Authority for this proposition can be found in J. S. Mill's, *Principles of Political Economy with Some of Their Applications to Social Philosophy* (2004, pp. 271–272) where he explains:

[B]ut in this case, as well as in the closely analogous one of *Copyright*, it would be a gross immorality in the law to set everybody free to use a person's work without his consent, and without giving him an equivalent. I have seen with real alarm several recent attempts, in quarters carrying some authority, to impugn the principle of patents altogether; attempts which, if practically successful, would enthrone free stealing under the prostituted name of free trade, and make the men of brains, still more than at present, the needy retainers and dependents of the men of money-bags.

Originally a common law doctrine, the principles and values accorded to copyright were derived from classical liberal thought where very minimal state intervention was preferred so as to encourage individuals' freedoms. Common law notions of copyright have done nothing more than map out basic rights.

Modern copyright law no longer displays common law attributes. Mill's observation is important because it relates to protecting individuals' works from greedy behaviour ('men of money-bags'). It is interesting to note that individuals have accused corporate owners of popular media of displaying monopolistic and greedy tendencies.

Copyrights commence as personal rights. One of the most important rights of the owner of the copyright is the right to reproduce the created works (that is, copy the works). Consider the following passage from Slater (1939, p. 206):

> At common law there was no copyright in literary productions after publication, though there was before. The result was that if a person produced a work of imagination or reasoning, he could refrain another from publishing it, if by any chance that other happened to become acquainted with it, but if the author once gave it to the world he had no remedy against anyone who chose to pirate it.

In the modern context classically liberal mid-nineteenth-century common law copyright seems implausible. The modern day consumer might be forgiven for being quite liberal with popular media given the manner in which copyright has evolved. However, a radical politico-economic shift occurred, and these prima facie legal presumptions became the subject of a reverse onus during a period of great industrial transition in the mid-nineteenth century. This era witnessed a rapid consolidation of statute-based copyright laws that emphasized the creation of near perfect monopolies upon publication in conjunction with the birth of the modern corporation.

Unlike early-nineteenth-century legal conceptions of common law copyright, statute-enshrined copyright laws are codified and invariably prescriptive in that they prescribe how obligations are discharged and rights imposed through various legislative, judicial and executive instruments. Natural laws are not prescriptive (rules imposed by the government authority). These are new customs and traditions. That is, the old, liberal copyright customs that once reflected natural, personal rights have been subsumed under a broader modern copyright custom in which behaviour and conduct are imposed on individuals. In this modern universe, copyrights have been consolidated through international customs and conventions and imposed on natural citizens. Modern approaches are corporatist approaches, and largely reflect the wishes of the controlling elite rather than individuals. But they run contrary to international laws. In any politico-economic setting where prescriptive laws are imposed it is inevitable that tensions will arise. These issues may lie dormant or at least be successfully controlled over time, but when significant technological changes are introduced, the differences between old and new customs become clear. Digitalization has provided the most recent catalyst for challenges to prescriptive modes embedded in copyright legislation. Copyright obligations are absolute and exclusive (subject to exceptions such as obtaining a license and 'fair use'). Modern copyright laws are no longer natural rights, but virtual monopolistic rights. In *Jeffery v Boosey* (1854) it was held at 935–936:

> Weighing all the argument on both sides, and looking to the authorities up to the present time, the conclusion I have arrived at is, that copyright is altogether an artificial right, not naturally and necessarily arising out of the social rules that ought to prevail among mankind assembled in communities, but is a creature of the municipal law of each country, to be enjoyed for such time and under such regulations as the law of each State may direct, and has no existence by the common law of England. It would follow from this that copyright in this country depends altogether on the statutes which have been passed on this subject.

With the advent of emerging technologies in the fields of book and music publishing, copyright was one such proprietary right where a series of statutes were passed so that by 1842 the Copyright Act in Britain restrained those who chose to be liberal with literary works.

What should be acknowledged is that common law copyright (as opposed to codified copyright laws) and liberalism were related because of the emphasis placed on individual autonomy. As a private right, this principle still remains. Validation for this proposition can be found in *Roadshow Films Pty Ltd v iiNet Limited* (2010) (*iiNet*) where it was held (per Cowdury at para. 492) that:

> There is no legal obligation or duty on any person to protect the copyright of a third party. There is only a legal prohibition on doing an act composed in the copyright without the license of the owner or exclusive licensee of that copyright or authorizing another to do that copyright infringing act. Consequently, merely being indifferent or inactive in the knowledge that copyright infringement is occurring cannot possibly constitute authorisation.

But as mentioned, by the mid-nineteenth century internationalization of agreed copyright principles through governance ensured copyright conformed to the process of codification. These purposes were originally reflected in the Berne Convention for the Protection of Literary and Artistic Works 1886. The consolidation, or rather politicization, of copyright in the latter part of that century largely reflects the general consensus in the Western world. Schwarzschild (2006, p. 218) correctly notes that:

> [i]n the twentieth century – the age of statutes – by contrast, a variety of doctrines and political forces challenged free market liberalism and denigrated it as retrograde, sometimes with great political success.

The rapid legal developments, which are the subject of detailed examination in subsequent chapters, are also consistent with innovative change experienced during the mid-point of the Industrial Revolution.

In Britain, not long after the start of the twentieth century, the Copyright Act (1911) unified the common law into a single coherent system in the form of a wide-ranging statute. By the early twentieth century, the developed nations continued the debate about the relevance of a robust international copyright governance framework and became signatories in a bid to universally unify copyright laws. The first of these was the Berne Convention for the Protection of Literary and Artistic Works 1886, and it was the Berne Convention (1908), and Rome Convention (1968) that included agenda items pertaining to recorded music, and the protection of the copyright in the recorded works. The 1956 Copyright Act (UK) 'attempted to keep pace with international and technological developments' (Edenborough, 1997, p. 11). In response to further international and technical developments, new legislation in the form of the Copyright, Designs and Patents Act (1988) was enacted. Throughout this almost 100-year period, Parliament constantly modified its copyright laws in a bid to keep abreast of new types of copyrights being created in order to ensure protection for the owners. As will be discussed in the following chapters, corporate citizens were the primary drivers in the bid to expand copyright and its administration.

Corporate copyright (corporate ownership of copyright) is fundamentally different to individual or beneficial copyright. Its objective is purely for commercial endeavour and thus should be described as an exclusive entrepreneurial copyright. Because of limitations in protection periods thereby limiting exclusivity whereby copyrights automatically revert into the public domain, it is only partially correct to describe corporate copyright as a quasi-monopoly.

It is argued, in terms of popular culture, that corporate copyright ownership displays true monopolistic behaviour because the impetus in copyright ownership is to preserve and protect copyright embedded in a particular product for as long as possible if it is deemed commercially viable.

Corporations, not individuals (natural citizens), have become the main beneficiaries of modern copyright protection. Corporate citizens are devoid of natural rights possessed by individual citizens. Such rights as enshrined in corporation laws are artificial. Attali (1985, p. 52) remarks, '[c]opyright established a monopoly over reproduction, not protection for the composition or control over representations of it'. This observation is further elaborated by Whale (1970, p. 18):

> Copyright for some 150 years was quite simply the right to copy and, except for the implied right to publish, nothing else. It was accordingly not an author's right but a publisher's right, and indeed it was the booksellers (publishers) who created this right for themselves as a necessary protection for their business ... and although under the statute the author became entitled to hold copyright, the right protected was still essentially the publisher's right to copy.

Corporate influence over favourable conditions and legislative change was a core feature during industrialization. An interesting concurrent development in nineteenth-century Britain was that significant changes in a related legal arena also occurred. In 1825, the Bubble Act 1720 (England) was repealed thereby ending a 105-year ban on corporations. (This Act, curiously, was enacted shortly after the Statute of Anne (UK) was enacted in 1709. The Bubble Act was enacted after the Royal Exchange and London Assurance Corporation Act 1719 because the specific companies the Bubble Act related to were incorporated under the Corporation Act of 1719. The Acts are referred to concurrently because the Bubble Act was the result of a legislative response to the South Sea Bubble stock market crash.) Bakan (2005, p. 7) explains: 'in 1720, Parliament passed the Bubble Act which made it a criminal offense to create a company presuming to be a corporate body.' The main reason for the virtual carte blanche ban on associations of individuals possessing a common goal to pursue profit was that the British Parliament was 'fed up with the epidemic of corporate high jinks' (Bakan, 2004, p. 6).

The Companies Clauses Consolidation Act 1845 statutorily paved the way for a second chance for these corporate citizens (just three years after copyright laws were significantly changed). By 1929 the Companies Act in Britain was responsible for giving rise to the modern corporation (which was also the same time that copyright had become robustly consolidated and regulated through international custom and convention). By coincidence or design, modern copyright legislation and corporate rules commenced a congruent path to mutualism. The rise of corporate copyright consolidation will be discussed in the following chapters.

Given the above observation about entrepreneurial elements of modern day corporate copyright, it is important to recognize that copyright has evolved in three material stages: primary (basic), secondary (intermediate) and tertiary (advanced). The first two stages are concerned with individuals or groups of individuals directly, whilst the last stage represents the status quo of modern copyright (corporations as the relevant rights-holders assigning and licensing rights without individual interaction or consent). That is, the primary phase is closely associated with this natural state of ownership (where the original copyright owner retains control in his or her property). The next (secondary) stage and the final or late stage of copyright development are problematic and difficult to reconcile with notions of classic liberalism. In these later stages, natural copyright owners (namely creators) usually relinquish their rights in copyright as exploitable property by way of assignment – and in many cases perpetually. The difference in the second and the third stage is that in the latter, assignment is invariably to a large firm, whereas in the secondary stage, the transaction is between the natural owner of copyright and a minor player. The advanced stage creates the so-called entrepreneurial or corporate copyright in advanced capitalist society. The divergence of consumer and corporate attitudes stems from this final stage.

In relation to copyright as a natural, common law right, Justice Willes in *Millar v Taylor* (1769, p. 220) stated: 'It is certainly not agreeable to natural justice that a stranger should reap the beneficial pecuniary produce of another man's work.' In other words, a copyright owner has a right to profit from the proprietary right vested in a work. Gaining a pecuniary advantage through piracy would be akin to, say, trespassing onto property and fishing in a river on that property and where a license or royalties may be required. I do not cavil with this basic proposition. But whether consumers perceive downloading cultural products for personal consumption as harmful to corporate citizens is specifically open to debate.

It is suggested that when modern copyright developed, the notion of 'harm' did not extend to acts of media piracy against corporate ownership because corporations are artificial or unnatural constructs. Alternatively, recognition by individuals that illegal media consumption creates harm per se has remained unrecognized during the evolution of liberalism. The primary reasons for a perceived lack of recognition in the modern context are twofold:

- individuals appear not to recognize illegal consumption as harmful to corporate citizens when compared to obvious or literal acts constituting harm; and
- individuals in liberal society are naturally suspicious of dominant institutions, and regard the state, large corporations and their associate organizations as entities that actively interfere in *negative freedom*.

Any harm felt by corporations in terms of copyright infringement might be regarded as artificial or pseudo-harm when compared to individuals' general notions of harm (for example, physical harm or property harm against the person). Obviously, this is not to suggest copyright corporations are not legally entitled to damages for financial loss. It will be asserted that corporate harm, for example, losses allegedly sustained through piracy, might be perceived differently to losses caused to a composer in the eyes of consumers. In this regard, it is more difficult to conceptualize stealing an opportunity to make a profit as a loss of sorts and in a natural sense, compared to, say, the theft of a CD, which is easily measured in terms of harm.

The artificiality and unnatural state of corporations can be contrasted to the natural right of individuals and the natural rights vested in primary notions of copyright. In the corporate realm, the individual in the natural sense is lost and the effect of capital-raising by way of shares is a formidable instrument for large-scale investment. The corporation is not accountable to natural persons, but rather shareholders who possess corporate citizenship rather than natural rights. In this artificial universe, the bulk of incorporeal popular media copyrights are parked.

It is, therefore, not surprising that individuals find it difficult to contextualize how unauthorized use of invisible rights vested in artificial corporate entities might constitute harm. Copyright transcends basic notions and becomes complex by virtue of the manner in which it is dealt with through intricate intangible permutations and combinations exercised by corporations. Once copyright becomes assigned to and subsumed by corporations, compatibility between liberalism and modern copyright becomes less obvious.

Convergent corporate media industry

This typology is concerned with corporate governance in an era of globalization in late capitalism. Anticompetitive behaviour in an arena where a small group of majors control the playing field is evident. This form of aggressive corporate behaviour is completely natural for firms where the core of their existence solely rests on preservation and exploitation of primary copyrights.

The reasons for this assertion are based on the fact that naturally occurring copyright monopolies in popular media complement the manner in which products are organized. While it is difficult to define precisely the term 'natural monopoly', copyright industries are good examples. Like other monopolists, the owner of a copyright is able to use its monopoly position to theoretically charge higher prices and derive monopoly profits at the expense of consumers and economic efficiency.

Thus conditions typically associated with anticompetitive behaviour in popular media industries include:

- discriminatory pricing and artificial regional barriers (for example, regional viewing and gaming zones and subsequent resistance to parallel importation (e.g., music industry));

- general hindrance to direct free market access for consumers; and
- restricted entry for new or independent participants (independent participants and other secondary or meso-level players).

Corporate consolidation of popular media has created a monopoly over content and delivery. In reality, competition governance and copyright governance are not very symbiotic or mutualistic in liberal democratic societies (and recent case law is analysed in following chapters to support this contention).

The concentration of market share should remain a concern for competition law and policy. This is because there seems to be an obvious connection between concentration and market power (Leavis, 1933; Schiller, 1969; Petersen and Annand, 2005). Market power, of course, can arise not just by acquisitions, but also through a range of contractual relationships between parties. A merger is, in a sense, just another contract. Sometimes it is difficult to know where to draw the line between contractual relationships and mergers. Popular media industries flourish in a variety of horizontally collaborative environments that incorporate remarkable elements of mutualism and cooperation. In these settings, dominant players create predictable economic exchanges and maintain consistent product information and commercial exchanges. These behaviours are mimicked by each corporate entity as competitors follow each other (film and music are typical of this type of behaviour). For example, consistencies in sales and marketing and broadcast media promotion through 'top-forty'-style chart systems work in the favour of the dominant few. This level of standardization has enabled unprecedented cooperation amongst the major players. This raises concerns about market coercion and undue influence (examples are provided in Chapter 3 to support this assertion).

The rationale for the implementation of anticompetition legislation is to protect society and promote economic efficiency (see generally, Burgess, 1989). In a situation where a dominant market player with substantial influence refuses to comply and this ultimately leads to a reduction in competition, this player could be deemed to be abusing its power. This conduct is detrimental to the retailer and the consumer.

Hausman (2008) argues fairness in the marketplace is best achieved when neither no individual firm (or group of firms) is exercising significant market power nor is the price above the competitive price.[8] Popular media industries have traditionally displayed these unattractive characteristics.

Where naturally occurring temporary monopolies (such as those found in copyright industries) are created, it is in the best public interest to ensure these industries do not abuse their position of control. The question about such behaviour on the part of corporate citizens is squarely concerned with societal benefits overriding private interests related to profitably and efficiency. This relates to the implementation of effective competition that enhances the welfare of individual citizens through the promotion of competition.

In the West, unfair monopolistic practices have been addressed by legislatures in a bid to control and minimize sharp or unfair trading practices. Recent notable cases before US, EU and Australian courts highlight the particular issues. The observation made here is that media piracy and anti-competition cases dovetail the respective arenas because of the internationalization of copyright governance. When investigating agencies conduct an assessment of potential exclusionary conduct or complaints of anticompetitive behaviour, tests including the effect of narrow competition for the public as a benefit and the detriment to smaller market participants are considered. Allegations usually centre on issues such as a substantial degree of power in a market, taking advantage of that power by preventing the entry of a person into that or any other market, and deterring competition. The consequential flow is obvious in that consumers suffer both in terms of product choice and pricing. The object of anticompetition legislation is to enhance the rights of consumers through the promotion of competition and fair trading (consumer protection and consumerism). But the success of such formal measures is open to conjecture.

Synonymous with the preservation of copyright control is copyright protection against piracy. Corporate governance ensures cohesive copyright maintenance. When disruptive events such as illegitimate consumption occur, corporations react in a predictable manner. As discussed in detail in Chapter 6, corporations reactively assess the cost of illegal consumption and implement several control measures in a bid to stem the flow of piracy. The preventative strategies generally include technological protection, legal action and education.

The law provides for penalties and subsequent retributive justice to ensure general deterrence in order to control recidivism. Yet why do consumers continue to defy the law in the West? One explanation might be that on a moral level, copyright interference, including computer fraud, hacking into financial data, tax evasion and other classes of 'white collar crime', is not viewed as negatively as, say, actual property interference (that is, of tangible or physical property). Copyright interference as a form of trespass to intellectual property is broadly illegal and deemed harmful according to law. This dichotomy of morality has not been adequately explored in the literature, and an account of these attitudes is not only desirable, but essential for any proper debate about global media piracy.

The conclusion reached is that regulation of monopolistic behaviour has not ensured quality of outcome for consumers in terms of consumer welfare (namely fair pricing and service). Consumers have reacted to this imbalance in various ways. Media piracy behaviour could be described as the alternative regulation of anticompetitive behaviour. As such, it is the subject of debate in that context.

Technological convergence

The final typology is concerned with innovation and economic development. Technological change predetermines popular media consumption in
the modern setting through digitalization and convergence. This is because,
unlike analogue devices, popular media digitized products are broad spectrum, accessible and generally pervasive in terms of popular culture products
because of their ease of use and consumption (see Flew, 2005). Digitalization
is a simple but effective utilitarian form of communication and information
exchange that empowers individuals who wish to derive affective pleasure
from popular media products without interference from an intermediary.
In terms of consumption, digitalization complicates matters whether or not
these pleasures are to be derived in an unfettered mode.

It is important to re-emphasize that popular media technologies – which
are analysed in detail in Chapter 3 – have traditionally been controlled by a
few dominant corporations throughout the twentieth century (see Longhurst,
1995; Negus, 1992). These industries constitute nothing more than a highly
concentrated, horizontally integrated organization (see generally Canterbury
and Marvasti, 2001).

Mandel (1975) identifies concentrated control by transglobal corporations
as a fundamental tenet of late capitalism. Indeed, those who control the media
industry are traditionally obsessed with discoveries, namely in the fields of
electronics, communications, entertainment, and the further acquisition
in these fields. It is argued that carte blanche control is the ultimate aim of
corporate owners in the popular media industry. The rationale for having
vested interests in a variety of related industries is obvious. Vertical integration allows for complete control and maintenance of the product from start
to finish – a flow of production from raw materials (including intellectual
property) to sales (Peterson and Berger, 1990, p. 143).

Globalization and technology also complement the rise of the corporation
and the advent of innovation and consolidation of intellectual property, and
together these elements form the core of advanced capitalist production and
development. In *Late Capitalism*, Mandel's goal is 'to provide an explanation
of the capitalist mode of production in the twentieth century' (Mandel,
1975, p. 9). Mandel was particularly interested in how capitalism had recon-
structed itself as consumer capitalism. Consumer capitalism is concerned
with the accelerated use of technology as fixed capital, and the implications
of the emergence of technology and intellectual property. A study of popular
media should therefore include an examination of the interaction between
technology, commodification, the creation of surplus value through copyright acquisition and the subsequent control of tangible and intangible
products in capitalist society. In the Foucauldian sense, the imperative
by corporate citizens to subsume popular media represents *power* (corporate control of popular media), *knowledge* (technological determination)

and *truth* (legal owners of copyright in popular media asserting their rights through formalist conceptions of copyright governance).

For Adorno, popular culture became consolidated through recorded formats that inevitably changed the way in which musical and artistic expression was perceived. By recording moments, records permanently created fragments of time. By inventing various formats, companies ensured that these products were capable of being recreated and thus repeated identically at any given time (and in any given space). Adorno (1990, p. 60) stressed that records themselves were not an expression of art, but as they were part of a 'breakthrough', records were able to 'transform the most recent sound of old feelings into an archaic text of knowledge to come'. In other words (ibid., p. 61):

> Ultimately the phonograph records are not artworks but the black seals on the missives that are rushing towards us from all sides in the traffic with technology; missives whose formulations capture the sounds of creation, the first and last sounds, judgment upon life and messages about that which may come thereafter.

Frith (1983, pp. 44–45) has stressed the importance of Adorno's contribution to the sociology of popular media:

> Adorno's is the most systematic and most searing analysis of mass culture and the most challenging for anyone claiming even a scrap of value for the products that come churning out of the music industry. His argument ... is that modern capital is burdened by the problem of overproduction. Markets can only be stimulated by creating needs ... needs which are the result of capital rather than human logic and therefore, inevitably, false. The culture industry is the central agency in contemporary capitalism for the production and satisfaction of false needs.

As principal controllers of finished products, corporate players are directly responsible for influencing the mass cultural landscape. In short, these multinationals set the entertainment standard and have standardized the norm for consumers. As Burnett (1995, p. 43) writes:

> The vertical and horizontal integration of the music, film and television production, publishing industries, and alignment of technology development and ownership that is coupled to production and distribution control, has never been more closely linked to the power centres of media and electronics industries in America, Europe and Japan.

Not surprisingly, the major players have become powerful primarily by a process of consolidation through mergers and acquisitions (including corporate raiding), and by controlling innovative change or development through joint-venture research and technological development (see especially Negus, 1992; Brown, 1997; Longhurst, 1995). In essence, media corporations are the epitome of what Mandel (1975, pp. 310–311, 342) described as 'late capitalism' – an aggressive and pressurized advanced form of capitalism premised on increasing levels of market internationalization, or, in other words, globalization in conjunction with the acquisition of intellectual property rights (IPRs). Andrews (1997, p. 143) succinctly describes Mandel's thesis as follows:

> It explains the emergence of technology and intellectual property ... as the most valuable forms of capital. In this accelerating process old distinctions between fixed capital and circulating capital disappear. This leads to further specialization in labour to develop and manage technology and intellectual property.

The behaviour of the majors in film and television – especially in the last 50 years – fits the above description. Indeed since 1910, the core interrelated entertainment industries within popular music have witnessed a series of acquisitions. The industry has continued to be dominated by a few corporations from either side of the Atlantic (Negus, 1992, p. 3). During this period eight companies regularly accounted for between 83 and 85 per cent of the revenue in recorded media (see especially Chappel and Garafalo, 1977). Over the course of the past 100 years, the popular media industry has come to be characterized by three major factors:

- heavy concentration,
- organizational integration, and
- acceptance of specific technology.

Generally, these factors accurately reflect the state of play throughout the twentieth century. Within this broad corporate environment, technology in popular media was subsumed and thereby controlled.

Historically, the subsumption of innovative advancement by popular media corporations has provided for controlled synergistic developments between product creation and delivery. The same observation cannot be made for the period commencing this millennium. The most intriguing aspect of technology for the purposes of this discussion is its capacity to change and become double-edged in a relatively short space of time. Frith (1986, p. 286) is correct in maintaining that electronic advancement undermines the idea of fixed objects on which copyright, the essential legal safeguard of art as property, rests. Reference here is made to ('pirate-friendly') inventions for legitimate replication. Once the domain of industry professionals and elite consumers, in less than 40 years reasonably high and ultimately very good quality replicating technologies have become universally accessible to consumers. In this environment the challenges to the status quo are evident, and it is perfectly understandable why media industries are so obsessed about curtailing the carte blanche free use of their property in the twenty-first century. In this climate, individuals freely utilize external discoveries to consume popular media products and do so without the need for popular corporate media direction. In the current world of digitalization where quality is not an issue, the evolution of enabling technologies has not only created a legal crisis for industries delivering entertainment, communications and new technologies, but a moral dilemma for consumers. These issues are not new, but in this era the cause for concern is at its greatest.

By way of illustration, the Internet is like no other media protocol/device in that it connects individuals' computers worldwide by using access connection tools and an ISP. Communication devices (mainly computers) are able to access the Internet in remote locations or public places (where Wi-Fi services are available, and by 'leeching' from neighbours and those in close proximity). It is a virtual tool, but codependent on actual interconnected devices. Digital data is sent and received as 'packets' from one address to another. Modems and related signal and carrier devices enable people to subscribe to ISPs (telcos) for Internet plans where the user is afforded fast access and download rates for a relatively small fee.

In this environment, P2P developments thrive. BitTorrent was described in the *iiNet* case as a scheme for a highly efficient and decentralized means of distributing data across the Internet. As a form of software for accessing popular media it is exceptional in that it can be used for legal and illegal means concurrently. For the purpose of copyright infringement, P2P is an almost universal, ad hoc and free form of digitalized consumption because a successful download of any media involves several computers working online, communicating with one another.

Several users may be using computer protocols to swarm around one title, participating in simultaneous uploads and downloads of specific items or parts of a packet of data so that a complete file is made, shared and otherwise redistributed. Computers might be working in peer groups across the World Wide Web sharing in the production of a complete file. Each 'bit' makes a unique part. For example, clusters of persons in Australia may contribute 33 per cent of the bits to a movie, another person or persons in Bolivia may have another 33 per cent, whilst another in Canada might have yet another 33 per cent. Finally a person in, say, Denmark may have the remaining 1 per cent. Together, these uploaders have created a complete file as seeders and peers.

The material contained in the file is the subject of copyright control and restrictions. However the tools utilized may not be, and the proprietors and services providers are invariably pursued by copyright owners. BitTorrent's omnipotence as a legal and legitimate form of multimedia software is unprecedented. In the past ten years consumers have been able to progress from downloading P2P small files (equivalent to individual songs à la Napster) to downloading larger files (for example, albums with artwork) with the use of BitTorrent. Highly individuated behaviour in social forums has become a show case arena for the owners of the economic capital in popular culture.

This heightened state of corporate concern stems from the combined effect of burning, ripping and file-swapping – protocols, add-ons, application and devices generally standard in all computer hardware. Downloading and uploading means the loss of control of a lucrative mode of centralized cultural control. Innovation has provided a radically new mode of entertainment. The Internet is a way of communicative life. It intimates a true era of digitalization and convergence, and it is difficult to imagine how education and policing can subsume this paradigm shift.

In practical terms, copying perfect or near perfect recordings is a very standard task. It is suggested this behaviour might also be construed as socially acceptable behaviour despite the industry's strict prosecutorial stance. As mentioned above, P2P is heavily used for both legitimate and illegitimate means. As a form of software/protocol for accessing popular media it is extraordinarily fluid, and by virtue of its enabling properties it also possesses the positive aspects of individual behaviour in a civilized liberal society, namely:

- self-determination (freedom of choice) through the Internet (without corporate or government coercion); and
- self-reliance (the emergence of a type of social Darwinism) and the capacity for individuals to evolve naturally, free from organizational influence and interference in new or different settings (see Heywood, 2003, pp. 55–56).

These processes are inherently private and self-regulating.

It is argued that freedom from interference in the exchange of information is a natural desire for citizens in liberal societies. Famous literary works, in particular those of Shakespeare, provide interesting examples of liberal values throughout history.[9] Schwarzschild (2006, p. 217) identifies the relationship between individuality and voluntary exchange: 'They ensure a degree of moral independence from other people; they are also an indispensible counterweight to government power and the force of social conformity.' Not all innovation in popular media has been subsumed by corporations. Consumers' attitudes towards emerging digital technologies reflect nineteenth-century ideals in the form of a more liberal approach by individuals towards media piracy.

If it is acknowledged that any freedom expressed by individuals in the twenty-first century in relation to advancement (especially replicating tools and P2P software) is more consistent with classic liberal attitudes, then it is difficult to accept natural citizens have become morally derelict in their duty towards corporate citizens. Independently evolving developments epitomize emancipatory concepts as espoused by early liberal thinkers, such J. S. Mill, who argued for individual independence and autonomy when there 'were growing pressures to conform which inhibited individual spontaneity and cultural diversity. Without the space for individual experimentation with life the human potential would be thwarted and society would stagnate' (Eccleshall, 2003, p. 35). When conditions allow for liberal expression, problems between the individual and authoritative control are created. The issues between individuality and opportunism, corporate control, government regulation and legal instruments are briefly discussed below and are the themes for the chapters to follow.

Tensions between liberalism, realism, copyright control and technological change

The *iiNet* case is unusual in that it demonstrates the capacity for challenges to a strict and formal application of statutory copyright legislation when assessing technological impact on copyright. The differences between innovative change and (copyright) statutory interpretation are summarized at the outset of the case (per Cowdury J at para. 19):

> The result of this proceeding will disappoint the applicants. The evidence establishes that copyright infringement of the applicants' films is occurring on a large scale, and I infer that such infringements are occurring worldwide. However, such fact does not necessitate or compel, and can never necessitate or compel, a finding of authorisation, merely because it is felt that 'something must be done' to stop the infringements. An ISP such as iiNet provides a legitimate communication facility which is neither intended nor designed to infringe copyright. It is only by means of the application of the BitTorrent system that copyright infringements are enabled, although it must be recognized that the BitTorrent system can be used for legitimate purposes as well. iiNet is not responsible if an iiNet user chooses to make use of that system to bring about copyright infringement.

Fragile tension has probably always existed in finished copyrighted products due to the process involved in blending incorporeal chattels within actual objects. The heavily protected copyrights possess no intrinsic worth to the consumer, but the products give affective pleasure to the individual. As individualism and personal autonomy are deeply embedded in classical liberal thought, emerging digitalization has called legal and technological divisions into question.

Convergence in popular media has fused the boundaries between a legal understanding of exclusive copyrights as private rights and a common understanding of public rights. This has led to a misguided perception by consumers about access rights in popular media. It is argued that individuals rank their own rights, including the right to choose without influence or control, higher than the holders of the exclusive copyrights. If so, then the effect of statutory interpretation of copyright is being affected. Convergence in popular media has affected copyright governance frameworks because it potentially undermines the stability of copyright laws and challenges corporate control. It is argued that such change is capable of destabilizing popular media industries as a consequence of individualistic, self-determining behaviour. This development creates omnipotent opportunities in liberal society. The most unprecedented private-to-public tool capable of destabilizing the balance of power is the Internet – something regulated by laws *other* than copyright legislation.

It was affirmed in the *iiNet* case there is no compulsion (under liberalism) on any person to protect the copyright of another. It was held that: 'The law only recognizes a prohibition on the doing of copyright acts without the license of the copyright owner or exclusive licensee, or the authorisation of those acts … it is impossible to conclude that *iiNet* has authorized copyright infringement' (per Cowdury J at para. 20).

Liberalism is the very political ideology that underpins US, UK, Australian and other significant English-speaking common law copyright jurisdictions including Canada and New Zealand.[10] Drahos (1998, p. 2) correctly observes that 'property in expression (copyright) conflicts with freedom of expression'. Herein lies the point of contention between the right to unconditionally utilize information via convergence in popular media and the right to preserve proprietary interests.

Prior to the mid-1800s, copyright was regarded as a creature of the common law and not statute. Modern common law copyright regimes are now completely codified. Common law, English-speaking nations (especially the US and UK) are extremely influential in terms of media commodification and consumption. They are therefore of particular interest because several notable cases concerned with legal and illegal consumption have been heard in those jurisdictions. But more notably, liberalism as an important political ideology evolved alongside copyright laws in these two important common law jurisdictions.

Yet the purpose of copyright in the modern sense, however, is not to preserve a natural state of freedom. Rather it is a mode of complex intangible property and its purpose is to protect an environment that to a large extent has allowed a consolidation of property into the hands of a few powerful players who are cultural and copyright gatekeepers.

It is important to acknowledge this because a fundamental shift has meant the Internet is now probably the major cultural gatekeeping forum. Nonetheless, it is trite law to state that copyright protection exists in cyberspace. The issues remain unresolved, and Lyman (1995, pp. 33–35) correctly summarizes the ongoing dilemmas:

> [N]et-culture – if that isn't an oxymoron – has become hostile to the concept of intellectual property … [and] although the Internet has become more sociologically diverse, it still reflects the academic view that knowledge is properly governed by a gift culture in which each of us gives away what we know for free, and takes what we know for free.

The political and legal reality seems to be that on any objective assessment of media piracy, digitalization and convergence are occurring on multidimensional level.

Illegal consumption combined with unresolved neighbouring laws issues are material to these developments. In Chapter 8 the impact made on copyright governance by the advent of personal websites and social networking sites such as YouTube, Facebook and Myspace is discussed. It is quite clear the Internet has become the new forum – a new marketplace where money is not necessarily exchanged. Instead, exchanges are represented by a populist-created commons movement. In simple terms, the act of purchasing a song in the form of a CD single at the local shopping mall for $5 or even by mail order is now lost in a milieu of exchange – legal downloads, illegal torrent uploads and downloads, and streaming. This low-level regulatory environment has made it difficult to successfully monitor, review and implement protection against piracy.

Methods: why empirical and doctrinal literature should be examined concurrently

The approach adopted for the theoretical insight relevant to this study combines case law, legislation and literature. Research into the political economy of popular media does not usually take into account doctrinal developments. However, the information contained in the cases extends beyond the law. Decisions, submissions and related legal extrinsic materials also provide a fertile source of empirical data. These are often ignored in popular media studies, which is curious in itself given the inextricable link between copyright and popular media products. This book remedies any deficiencies in the existing literature by including significant legal, politico-economic and cultural developments. A concurrent application of primary and secondary sources is not only preferable when examining the tangible and intangible dimension of popular media products, but essential. By providing an examination of doctrinal and statutory developments in the subsequent chapters, the methodological framework for interpreting, understanding and characterizing digitalization and convergence becomes firmly grounded in both legal and empirical reality. Given the litigious nature of the film, music and gaming industries, the law provides the best source of contemporary primary evidence in the form of forensic data and judicial reasoning. It is highly desirable to cross-reference the data and literature with statutory change vis-à-vis significant court decisions. A *substantive* position rather than a formal discursive approach is adopted in relation to the legal concerns raised in the case law and literature. Emphasis is placed on recent cases and recent legislative change where the central consideration has been the management of digital rights in an age of broad-spectrum file-sharing and -swapping.

Building on existing literature with empirical insights and primary legal data, this study enables a more robust examination of the state of disorganization in popular media. Reliance is also placed on quantitative data provided by various powerful industry associations. In many respects, the case law provides a form of triangulation in a bid to overcome subjectivity and bias on the part of industry representatives.

Legal insights are also useful because in terms of the formal separation of powers in a democratic liberal society, the judiciary (as opposed to the executive and legislature) is the most independent arm of responsible government (both in terms of formal and informal governance structures). Consideration of judicial reasoning based on forensic evidence helps to assess positive theory about popular media and media piracy and corporate behaviour, the empirical reality of consumer behaviour and corporate control in popular culture, and the normative dimension of copyright governance in terms of digitalization and convergence.

The methodology adopted asks questions that ultimately assist in conceptualizing a framework for the purpose of developing a new perspective that enables a multidisciplinary approach. And despite some excellent debates in the literature and case law relating to media piracy, the consequences of the measures and strategies adopted by the ruling corporate elite have not been critically analysed.

Outline of chapters

In addition to introducing the themes, and setting the scene, Chapter 1 also examines the governance of copyright, and the creation of a globalized and consolidated popular media industry.

Chapter 2 addresses international copyright governance and the manner in which the popular media industries are controlled and supervised. The modern copyright industry framework in popular media comprises various vertically and horizontally integrated local and international institutions. Copyright is a social-interest-based concept created to enable, promote and otherwise encourage innovation for the greater public good and benefit. Its development reflects significant economic changes in the West, which also shape prevailing socio-economic rules and public policy.

Copyright was transformed into an entrepreneurial proprietary right by companies for the purpose of perpetual commercial exploitation. This transformation occurred at the time significant replicating advancements were made. Accordingly, lobbying was required to assist in alerting Parliament to the need to create a framework that has by and large facilitated the creation of the current status quo (Barnett, 2004, p. 10). In short, the development of modern copyright regimes was a reaction to the prevailing politico-economic changes.

Chapter 2 examines how copyright in popular media became politicized, That is, it became politicized in the sense the laws were created to primarily protect and preserve corporate interests in the West. It is asserted that the current international legislative and regulatory framework overwhelmingly supports and protects the interests of only the most powerful actors. The implications for the organizational framework for copyright are obvious to the extent that copyright has become politicized by moving from an individual rights-based concept to an internationalized and statutorily codified process for the preservation of power in the hands of a limited number of multinational corporations. This can be described as the transition to corporatized copyright control in advanced stages of capitalism.

The chapter also provides a case study on pressures imposed by Western nations in the face of flagrant piracy. The literature is dominated by reports of the excesses of piratical conduct in nations less developed politically and economically (and legally). The conclusion is that in this modern copyright setting several legal and illegal factors affect global copyright governance through emerging digital communications, namely the Internet. The chapter builds on the unusual idea that individuals' natural rights and corporate copyright owners' rights in popular media industries are incompatible. It supports the proposition made in Chapter 1 that copyright is a policy or instrument of social control.

Chapter 3 analyses the corporate control of popular culture and the manner in which products are organized. The governance of competition policy in popular media intersects with traditional or established activities including trade, commerce, corporate regulation, administration of associations and organizations, and copyright. The chapter argues that centralized corporate control of copyright law in popular media constitutes obvious anticompetitive behaviour because the concept of copyright promoting innovation has been usurped by the desire of corporate citizens to control intangible property to the extent that it remains in their exclusive possession. If such objectives are deemed anticompetitive then such conduct is not in the best social interest.

The chapter also charts the rise corporate of media citizenship through transglobal capitalism in the light of competition policy, regulation and its governance framework. The consolidation of standardized technologies (tangible products in the form of industry-endorsed formats) and copyrights (intangible property) is identified. The creation of an exclusive copyright club comprising a dominant few is also identified. The chapter determines the point at which corporations subsumed copyright and effectively became copyright industry controllers.

Competition policy in popular media industries is a dynamic concept driven by a desire to regulate copyright and influence modes of delivery. This is also historically relevant because popular media is correctly particularized as an arena traditionally concentrated in power both in terms of copyright ownership and technological control. This was certainly the state of play until the end of the twentieth century. Accordingly, the nature of anticompetitive behaviour in popular media industries is identified and the effectiveness of competition policy is assessed in the light of potential market power abuse.

Chapter 3 argues that because popular media industries exhibit natural monopoly characteristics they are in conflict with concepts of social interest. It re-emphasizes that the phenomenon of the globalization of popular media products should not be viewed as merely a global consolidation of popular culture per se, but rather as exclusive international and domestic appropriation of copyrights contained in finished products (commodification). In other words, when popular media corporations merge and become more centralized, the impact is twofold: cultural control of the commodities and capacity to exploit these commodities in the future (the intellectual property component).

The concentration of market share has long been a concern of competition law and policy. This is because there is an obvious connection between concentration and market power. Market power, of course, can arise not just by acquisitions, but also through a range of contractual relationships between parties.

Competitor collaboration in popular media is also identified. In recent years the main reason for an interest in competition governance in popular media industries is that one of the more dynamic features of popular media controllers is the capacity to enter into various semi-permanent or arm's length commercial arrangements (joint ventures, mutual benefit agreements and other more fluid arrangements). Due to the exclusive nature of copyright, the potential for naturally occurring monopolies to flourish in media industries exists. This is because the exclusive ownership and proprietorship embedded in the products is controlled by the owners of the means of production. That is, traditionally the technologies used to mine these rights have also remained the property of the dominant few. Combined, these elements form the essential ingredients for the existence of natural monopolies.

The chapter develops the argument that the music, film and games industries (in that order) are extremely centralized and represent some of the most anticompetitive forms of commercial enterprise in advanced capitalist societies. Misconceptions about popular media industries are also identified in this chapter. The assumption that media firms always, or usually, behave in an economically rational manner (especially when exposed to media piracy) is questioned. The conclusion sets the scene for the next Part where an analysis of the challenges to centralized control is presented.

The chapters in Part II make a case for the creation of a new structure in governance arrangements to enable socio-economic rather than economic regulation. Part II also assesses challenges to the dominant position of the major corporations in popular media. Chapters 4, 5, 6 and 7 highlight the interconnected problems facing the major actors. They consider connected, but unresolved rights issues, and the illegal threats facing popular media industries. Chapter 4 draws on the legal principles established in Chapter 2 and provides a concurrent examination of legislative developments and relevant case law. These developments highlight the complexities in the changes currently being experienced in neighbouring legal arenas. These changes have clearly impinged on the structure of copyright industries in a world of digitalization. This legislative impact is referred to as an external or horizontally integrated legal challenge.

Neighbouring laws in digital arenas refer to the statutorily and jurisdictionally separate and distinct set of technology-driven statutes that have been enacted without the necessary direct consideration of the copyright regime and its myriad exclusions and limitations. In light of this legal convergence, reconciliatory digitalization initiatives, namely law harmonization protocols between copyright telecommunications industry frameworks, are examined in order to assess the impact.

It is trite to assert that primary infringements of copyright become prevalent once copyright owners make products available online to the public, or once members of the public make products, primarily ones that infringe copyright, available online (P2P). Illegal consumption of copyrighted products is a hazard, as is the risk of illegal use of copyrighted products. Concern should not just be about copyright infringement per se, but rather about individuals participating in all forms of copyrighted products.

Chapter 4 analyses the disorganizational and reorganizational effects currently being experienced in popular media industries that are materially reliant on the maintenance and preservation of copyright on the one hand, but have become increasingly reliant on emerging but externally dominant technologies located in the telecommunications arena. The commercial value of the copyright industries is being diluted in the digitalized world by these concurrent developments. In the digitalized world, copyright industries appear to be experiencing disjointed, but incrementally negative effects capable of diluting or diminishing the commercial value of copyright industries. The obvious negative effects include piracy, but residual effects in the form of consumer interest in other popular forms of entertainment such as social networking must also be viewed as destabilizing because they distract consumers from traditional modes of commodification. The chapter stresses the need to recognize that the commercial value attributed to copyright by the major players is being hollowed out by various interconnected factors, including competing legal interests, changing business models and especially through individuals' changing attitudes.

Chapter 4's analysis is limited to copyright legislation in the West, and the respective digital agendas and telecommunications laws in those jurisdictions. Reference will also be made to international obligations and specific jurisdictions where relevant. The laws will be scrutinized in light of the most significant recent cases. These cases demonstrate popular attitudes and beliefs in liberal society. Common themes in these decisions raise concerns about how consumers' overall attitudes towards copyright have been shaped by emerging technologies.

In the light of emerging technologies, several significant cases over the last decade have attempted to deal with the problem of digital media piracy (by way of example, and most notably, *A&M Records, Inc. v Napster, Inc.* (*Napster*) (US, 2000), *Universal Music Australia Pty Limited v Sharman License Holdings Ltd* (*Kazaa*) (Australia, 2005), *Cooper v Universal Music Australia Pty Ltd* (*Cooper*) (Australia, 2005), *Neij, Svartholm, Sunde, Lundstrom* (*The Pirate Bay*) (Sweden, 2009) and, most recently, *iiNet* (Australia, 2011); these examples are purely for introductory purposes, several other important cases are addressed in following chapters). In addition, there is liability-limiting legislation. So-called telco acts, for example, consider the implications of Digital Millennium Copyright Act 1998 (US), the Telecommunications Act 1996 (US) or Telecommunications Act 1997 (Australia), limit obligations, liabilities and remedies available against ISPs (pursuant to 'safe harbour' provisions). What becomes clear is the existence of unresolved matters between copyright and telco/ISP legislation through convergence.

The cases analysed suggest copyright and telecommunications industries do not make good neighbours in legislative arenas. The long-established popular media industries continue to elevate their concerns to the highest level on the political calendar thus rendering digital harmonization problematic. The issues explicated in the case law are technically complex and highly contestable, and the case law demonstrates divergent views.

Obviously in some cases the findings are less vexing (for example, the *Kazaa* case or the recent settlement in *Arista Records LLC v Lime Group LLC* (2010) (*LimeWire*)). It is argued that contrary to the misguided view held by industry representatives, applying identical legal principles to very different factual circumstances is not possible. Indeed contrary to the views expressed by copyright industries, digitalization is not simply about copyright. Whether media piracy debates should focus solely on the narrow issue of copyright infringement as opposed to forming a component of a broader topic concerned with emerging consumption patterns requires greater consideration in the literature. That is, whilst consumption in the general economic sense requires the elements of a financial transaction, individuals engaged in these transactions are also capable of participating in discrete forms of infinite communication and transmission. These consumption patterns are unique when one reflects on other goods and services in the marketplace (for example, the purchase of finite items such as food or urban utilities).

This leads to the legislative dilemma that was exposed in the *iiNet* case. Major international motion picture studios initiated proceedings against the ISP based on the undisputed fact that a number of *iiNet* customers were downloading films. Yet while it was found that certain iiNet users infringed copyright, the ISP was not found to have authorized BitTorrent downloads of films. But it was very plain from the evidence that iiNet, as an ISP, possessed the relevant technical capacity to stop illegal downloads. Why then is it so difficult for telco and copyright industries to form workable memoranda of understanding? It is argued that the legal jurisdictions in which these industries reside are at cross-purposes and not capable of being reconciled in this current climate. One practical illustration is the spurious aspersion cast on ISPs by Hollywood that large ISP customer download plans attract more illegal activity. This correlation might be apparent from the view of a dominant few, but it does not account for large volumes of legitimate Internet traffic in the form of social networking. Online game sites, for example, require a very large amount of data, and YouTube demands extensive usage.

The conclusion is that these externalities have challenged the rigid control once exercised by copyright controllers because conditions in the digital environment are not necessarily determined by developments in copyright governance. Take the example of safe harbour provisions that operate as a defence. They provide a defence to actions against copyright infringement brought against an ISP (for example, the Digital Millennium Copyright Act and the respective mirror laws throughout the West). Due diligence is one way an ISP will discharge its obligations in relation to actions against copyright infringement brought against it. Prima facie certainty against impunity has been provided to carriers and ISPs over the last ten years. To date (2012), ISPs have largely relied on good faith and reasonable and best endeavours principles to minimize liability. Yet whilst the safe harbour defence was raised by iiNet, the Court did not need to discuss it because infringement had not been established. The *iiNet* case is one of the recent authorities examining issues of remoteness in terms of causation and a general lack of interconnectedness between copyright owners, ISPs and consumers in the world of digitalization. The case demonstrates how an ISP might protect itself from legal action without even relying on statutory defences. The defendant was able to argue successfully that through telecommunications industry best practices and other semi-regulated compliance initiatives, such as codes of good conduct, it had met its legal requirements to both the aggrieved parties. The dilemmas for copyright owners remain unresolved because, at best, if third-party (customers) infringement is proved to have occurred, but due diligence has been performed, then the ISP is deemed to have taken reasonable and practicable steps and cannot be accused of failure to prevent piracy or other forms of illegal behaviour. At worst, if a court rules infringement did not occur and that an ISP was a 'mere conduit', then a defendant may have a complete defence. The remedies are therefore limited given the robustness of the defence provisions. Good neighbour fences appear to have been erected by competing industries, or rather externalities have encroached upon the uneven playing field once exclusively enjoyed by corporate popular media industries as copyright owners.

Chapter 5 is concerned with recent developments in innovation and format change in an era of digitalization. It provides a historic account of liberal attitudes to illegal access via new technologies.

The chapter also presents significant developments in media consumption. Its main focus is the rise of digitalization and, in particular, universal accessibility to replicating devices. It provides a historical examination to demonstrate the fact that illegal consumption is not a new phenomenon. Three centuries of copyright development in common law nations has provided a fertile source of technology-versus-copyright-style cases. By analysing the case law and literature specifically concerned with innovation, the chapter attempts to situate the debate about the rise of centralized corporate control of popular media through technological consolidation.

By way of background, the first section of Chapter 5 briefly charts the evolution of popular media products, including the transition from analogue to digital reproduction. This is significant because while media piracy has existed for over three centuries, near perfect replication is a relatively new development. The section describes popular media devices (including their replicating potential) and revisits the argument that the system of copyright control that emerged in the mid-nineteenth century was designed for corporations as the financial controllers of popular media, and whose priorities rested with copyright as an entrepreneurial right. From book pressing to universally popular audio file format extension known simply as MP3 (motion picture experts group – 1 audio layer 3), to a raft of other subsequently developed audio and visual file formats with high-quality compression rates, a direct correlation has always existed between developing technologies and the desire to consume products in new formats, legally or otherwise.

The inextricable relationship between popular media's corporate control of intangible property and tangible products is examined in the light of technologies directly and indirectly related to popular copyright industries. It is argued these technologies are double edged in the sense they have positive and negative effects. The next section of Chapter 5 identifies several concerns. External developments in the form of MP3 or BitTorrent are clearly capable of facilitating pirated media. But internal technologies directly manufactured by different arms of copyright industries are also specifically capable of facilitating pirated media (for example, Sony's replicating and storage media and devices (blank CDs and PlayStation)) enable illegal activity as freely as other non-industry standards (namely MP3).

The second form of innovation is usually unrelated to any media industry developments, lacks governance and appears to evolve organically (without any apparent economic incentive in some cases) – but is nevertheless unequivocally empowering. These are so-called freeware products (BitTorrent and other P2P). The definition of copyright is rigidly connected to the concept of mechanical reproduction (and subsequent manufacture). Historically, the rationale for the implementation of copyright was to protect economic interests in intellectual property. Modern copyright law developed to complement advances in the mechanical reproduction of works. Accordingly, Chapter 5 maps the significant reactions by corporate citizens when copyrights are threatened.

Chapter 5 examines the tension between innovation and copyright law. This tension is a double-edged sword because it enables optimal exploitation of copyright in a commodified form. However it also emancipates individuals who illegally use copyrighted products. One conclusion is that while copyright law is an instrument of social control, the problems it faces are technologically determined. Since the advent of digitalization the quality of illegal products has been remarkable given the capacity to replicate perfect or near perfect copies.

Internet-based P2P file-sharing networks also differ significantly from physical digital media because of the social networking dimension. P2P sharing is more problematic. It follows that omnipresent digitalization channels have empowered consumers because they are free to consume popular media products independently and in any manner and form. That is, where consumers were once limited to a small range of prescribed hard formats, exploration into new forms has created several discrete avenues.

What becomes apparent from the case law is the *reactionary*, not the *anticipatory*, approach adopted by corporate citizens. To claim, as some corporate citizens do, that users of perfectly legitimate social networking and file-sharing tools are somehow complicit in acts of copyright infringement is blatantly unfair. Yet corporate citizens continue to initiate proceedings against innovators of new technologies, which is incongruous with the fundamental tenets of economic liberalism and, in legal terms, would border on the vexatious. Several cases demonstrate the fact the controllers of popular media are exceptionally litigious towards parties (natural or artificial) that pose a threat to the status quo through their use of emerging technologies.

An analysis of case law shows that, for substantive and procedural evidentiary reasons, it is becoming increasingly futile for corporate copyright industries to resist change. The fact that it was revealed in the *iiNet* case that iiNet (the third largest ISP in Australia) received allegations of infringement involving in excess of 5,000 Internet Protocol (IP) addresses over a seven-week period indicates that media piracy is more than an illegal act. It is a popular social act. The popular nature of media piracy is also expressed on the forums of BitTorrent sites where downloaders and uploaders brazenly exchange opinions on the quality of the illegally sourced items. In other words, the infringement notices suggest groups of like-minded individuals are exchanging information as if they were in some form of book club for piracy. (And it leads one to wonder just how many complaints are received by the largest telcos in Australia (Telstra and Optus)). Given the scope of the problem, it would be no more than a daydream to suggest that successful legal action against an inordinate number of downloaders and uploaders is in the best public interest. Civil, quasi-criminal and criminal copyright infringement cases are costly given the complexities of intellectual property. While corporate citizens continue to feel aggrieved, governments would hardly justify the significant expense that would be incurred in terms of court resources.

Drawing on the problems revealed in Chapter 4, it is argued that ISPs have made available online (pursuant to copyright legislation) copyrighted material capable of being manipulated by humans through computers. The act of making something available en masse is an unprecedented development, and it is argued that the sequence of actions to download a file and leave popular media available to, say, BitTorrent users in a P2P environment is beyond copyright industries' control for various interlocking reasons.

The conclusion is that, historically, new technologies for legitimate and illegitimate consumption have always coexisted. Furthermore, despite aggressive attempts by artificial citizens to stunt the advancement of technologies in direct competition with their own internal technologies, the case law supports the proposition that external enabling devices are perfectly reconcilable with conceptions of liberalism, but some incompatibility exists with corporate copyright models. The cases explicate the fact that ongoing incompatibility continues to exist with corporate copyright models. At worst, digitalization promotes illegal consumption and, at best (through P2P filesharing), it offers external models where popular media copyright holders have no option other than to license their products to third parties on less favourable terms (for example, Apple iTunes stores). In either scenario, soft formats are beyond the control of corporate popular media industries.

Adopting a legal realism perspective, Chapters 6 and 7 substantively examine the illegitimate attacks on the organization of copyright, namely acts of piracy. 'Organization' means the interrelationships between emerging technologies and copyright law in the core popular media industries affected by media piracy.

How effectively have corporate entities in popular entertainment media pursued copyright protection and management in the light of attacks on the position of the dominant status quo? Chapter 6 provides a detailed assessment of the corporate and political response to illegal consumption.

It addresses the legal and politico-economic approach to piracy by analysing the success of the current regulatory regime, prosecutorial policies and civil and criminal legal action. It considers the response by the major stakeholders, namely the corporations.

Chapter 6 provides an empirically grounded assessment of the methods implemented by popular media corporations in the war against illegal consumption. It evaluates the overall success of the anti-piracy policies implemented by these copyright industry stakeholders. It examines first-, second- and third-line strategies (technological, legal and educational measures). These strategies are deployed concurrently, cumulatively and conjunctively in the sense they attempt to reduce illegal activity through campaigns designed to create formalized consumer awareness, modify behaviours and ensure that consumers comply with the law. The first is described as primary in the sense that research and development departments have been established by copyright owners to help make piracy technically challenging. The second quite simply relates to legal sanctions whilst the third is used to consciously appeal to individuals to refrain from consuming products illegally. These measures are described as corrective processes, and will be discussed in Chapter 6. The aggregate rate of the norms displayed by many consumers shows a lag in the actual success of these stages. If anything, these strategies have been the subject of ridicule and contempt by citizens in liberal democratized societies. The guiding question is: what is the overall effectiveness of these preventative steps?

The chapter is concerned with the multidimensional corporate response to media piracy. It is posited that legal sanctions and copyright preservation remain core strategic business positions and solutions adopted by the major actors. It maps out legislative, procedural and substantive difficulties. Significant legal obstacles in copyright enforcement are identified, including why the state does not deem copyright infringement a high priority in the overall public safety enforcement framework. The level of enforcement adopted by investigating agencies specifically devoted to copyright regulation is comparably minimal when one considers the resources devoted to tangible offences against property and persons in the form of policing, taxation, border security, and customs. This is reflected in the low rates of court activity involving copyright breaches. The nature of penalties in successful cases is also considered.

The impracticalities of pursuing individual pirates are examined. Substantive litigation is aimed at ISPs and software design pioneers (as in the *Napster*, *Kazaa* and *UMG Recordings, Inc. v. MP3.com, Inc* (2000) (*MP3.com*) cases), but the *iiNet* case demonstrates that emerging technologies cannot necessarily be limited by legal action.

Despite these general observations, the current environment in which anti-piracy policies are implemented is of particular interest and concern because the literature shows that the key actors have traditionally adopted both *reactive* and *anticipatory* policies in order to ebb the flow of illegal consumption. This tends to suggest these policies have produced mixed results despite the fact the industry is combating the damage to copyright property more strenuously than it ever has before.

Chapter 6 also attempts to reconcile the doctrinal developments raised in previous chapters by focusing on both the general and specific deterrent values (if any) of the more well-known cases. Accordingly, emphasis is placed on the capacity of statutory regimes to control P2P behaviour (especially BitTorrent file-swapping practices). These decisions demonstrate an inherent weakness in the ability of copyright legislation and legal action to restrict the capacity of individuals to consume products illegally.

Notwithstanding the limited number of cases that are or have been before courts and copyright tribunals, the legal-political response by the major players has been to take the stance that unauthorized use is more than illegal – it is criminal or quasi-criminal and therefore punishable according to law. Criminal behaviour relating to financial loss is also gauged by societal norms and values that are largely shaped and influenced by powerful groups in society. For example, copyright infractions are generally deemed by corporate copyright industries as an opportunity loss because of the potential for interference with the primary commercial imperative that is associated with copyright exploitation. While traditional, formal conceptions of justice define illegal behaviours as crimes, substantive conceptions adopting critical legal perspectives broaden the scope facilitating norms, values and even morals. Media piracy for non-financial gain should not be ranked equally with piracy for commercial gain in the form of racketeers or site administrators in any criminological sense. Chapter 6 assesses the moral dimensions of illegal consumption in the light of the literature concerned with deviance and anti-social behaviour in Western society.

It is contended that many citizens in liberal democratic societies (and probably elsewhere) do not equate downloading a movie or CD without paying in the same light as walking into a store and stealing a DVD or CD from the store shelf. Downloading is embedded in notions of soft or quasi-immoral conduct whereas stealing is immoral behaviour. Furthermore, the movie downloader who occasionally consumes a show must clearly be distinguished from the commercial operator who procures the media and passes it on for favourable consideration. Commercial operators might be described as robbers, but not individual consumers, as uploaders and downloaders, because of the aggravated nature of the activity. That is, profit obtained through illegal means is akin to proceeds of crime, but performing illegal activity for personal consumption or even swapping for some altruistic reason (for example, expressing fondness for an artist's work by disseminating an illegally recorded concert on YouTube) must be viewed as morally distinct – notwithstanding both acts are illegal. Legal realism allows for an examination of these activities.

What is important to note is that rarely are end-users found to have committed aggravating offences. Although, legislatures deem copyright infringement to be a serious matter, judiciaries do not place the same weight or value on acts that would objectively create the elements of a serious offence. When one thinks of subjectivity involved in elementizing fault in terms of *mens rea*, one thinks of malice in relation to actual criminal offences against property and persons. These ordinarily include stealing objects, destruction of property or reckless acts of violence. The perpetrator and victim are objectively easy to identify. In all these scenarios, a person cannot be said to be lawfully excused from his or actions in any objective sense. File-swapping cases demonstrate, however, that consumers engaging in illegal activity as uploaders and downloaders are inextricably linked across various sites offering conduit services, and to the ISPs acting as the primary enablers of information exchange. Proving the elements of any copyright offence is problematic because inbuilt into this complex communicative process are several discrete avenues for all the respective parties in distancing one another from liability. Strict liability or even absolute liability actions are rendered meaningless if the aggrieved parties cannot even establish causation. Even if courts did, there is little empirical evidence to support the proposition that offenders (infringers) are strenuously pursued by prosecutors in Western society.

The current literature and case law suggests combating media piracy can, at best, be described as incrementally disjointed. Chapter 6 contributes to the debate by analysing the effects of piracy prevention. Any analysis in the academic literature that extends the dimension of technology and law might be construed as relatively underdeveloped as recent contributions do not provide a wide and comprehensive range of substantive normative works relating to the measure of actual success of current piracy protection strategies. Chapter 6 attempts to remedy some of these deficiencies.

Copyright laws are generally flouted by both consumers and pirates in a synergistic process, both in the West and emerging economies. Chapters 1 to 6 focus on consumption patterns from within Western nations. Chapter 7 considers the relationship between Western consumers and emerging economies in the light of moral and altruistic considerations. The chapter also analyses the inherent structural weaknesses that preclude a substantive governance framework in emerging/developing nations and lead to a façade of regulation – an appearance that something is being done. The West repose to piracy is a thinly disguised threat that trade sanctions and embargoes will be imposed if universal (Western) notions of copyright fail to be imposed. It is argued that any objective blameworthiness on the part of emerging nations should be viewed, at least in part, as due to Western influences.

Chapters 2 to 6 highlight the strong emphasis in the literature on media piracy as a one-dimensional issue based purely on legal transgression. An examination of the statistical data proffered by the industries' associations confirms this. But there has been no comprehensive consideration of why consumers find illegal consumption so desirable. One explanation is obvious, and this is reflected in the play-for-free attitude. But this simple observation does not explain individual uploaders' motives as altruistic consumers who risk legal action. Acts of bravado and rebellion have been identified to some extent in the literature and cases, but those without malice or political motivation are largely ignored in the literature. For example, what possible benefit may an uploader who subscribes to a cable service have in uploading a TV show for the benefit of viewers who are not subscribers? By way of analogy, these particular acts are reminiscent of free-love movements – and are consistent with liberalism. The anarchical dimension of illegal consumption therefore requires examination.

Part III focuses on cultural convergence matters, such as the mode of consumption and its effects on copyright policy. Chapter 8 introduces a parallel theme to the debate by suggesting consumer discontent is also inextricably linked to modern illegitimate consumption. It explores whether there is any causal nexus between P2P file-sharing (and other modes of file exchange) and a genuine lack of consumer discontent vis-á-vis the manner in which popular media is offered by the major players. Has the Internet (and allied software products) emancipated consumers to the point that they no longer accept at face value the monetary value placed on cultural products owned by major firms? In other words, does this independent behaviour constitute some form of protest?

Chapter 8 revisits the political and legal themes raised in Chapter 1 by arguing that consumers empowered by change have undermined the concentrated corporate status quo in the sense that consumption patterns have significantly decentralized in the past decade. And despite some initial denial on the part of corporate controllers that external technology could seriously challenge the dominant position, the fact the dominant popular media industries have entered into external joint ventures with allied and unallied industries suggests that consumers are not responding to the traditional entrenched business model. There are significant socio-economic reasons for the denial that the concentrated status quo was capable of being disturbed, including consumer discontent about how popular media markets products for consumption, as well as more 'interesting' or exciting modes of cultural exchange competing with popular media. In addition to pricing and perceived value for money, issues also relate to choice, range and mode of delivery of commodified popular culture. How these issues are juxtaposed in terms of social networking developments are discussed in Chapter 8.

As stated in Chapters 3 and 5, corporate citizens act as powerful gatekeepers in relation to popular culture. But as new technologies have evolved independently of any entertainment media industry involvement, consumers have become less influenced or controlled by these major companies in terms of how products should be consumed. Similarly, consumers have become less interested in the traditional products and prefer to surf the 'net for entertainment. The Internet has enabled consumers to listen, watch and play entertainment media without the need to access main industry channels.

Social networking provides the best case study about these challenges. Change or, rather, a shift in power from centralized to decentralized modes of control has created a *revolution* of sorts. This development suggests some form of biopolitical struggle, in the Foucauldian sense. The conflict is concerned with the struggle for legitimacy of copyright and not the illegitimate consumption of copyright. The integrity and superiority of major players is questioned by consumers who appear to resist this norm of discipline (Foucault, 1991b, p. 223). That is, through innovation, consumers have questioned the following corporate-driven norms:

- the monetary value of media products,
- the format of products, and
- the manner in which products are disseminated.

Consumers utilizing external or alternative technologies through social networking in the pursuit of entertainment have called into question established norms in traditional modes of media consumption. This has caused a reflexive reaction in popular media. The cause-and-effect relationships established through file-sharing have encouraged consumers to use social networking as an alternative source of entertainment. This behaviour is also described as viral consumption patterns where value, format, and manner of dissemination are subordinated by a sense of immediacy. For example, corporate channels dictate the commodification processes from the input to the output end for the creation of a finished product, say a live film clip taken from a concert. Yet the same subject matter is instantly uploaded for social networking purposes by a devout fan who was at the concert (presumably for a fee). It is irrelevant when (or in many cases, if) the infringing material is taken down by, say, YouTube – the product has been consumed in what might be described as in a transreflexive fashion between consumers acting as virtual automatons. However, social networking has exacerbated the issues of copyright infringement. The combined effects of convergent consumption patterns reflect a sense of biopolitical power which leads to a disconnect between law and compliance on the one hand, and moral behaviour on the other hand. In other words, does indifference towards copyright necessarily constitute recklessness?

In Foucauldian terms, the rise of corporate popular media as a genealogy of power – the power of corporate control through copyright to normalize individuals. In other words, the genealogy of technology and copyright historically represents corporate knowledge in terms of what is right and what is wrong. Traditional business models remain the primary focus of copyright industries notwithstanding the fact that hybrid business models have (reluctantly) been considered and implemented by the major players. But in any event, newer corporatized models have also been significantly challenged because neighbouring laws developments and consumer behaviour (including divergent attitudes to traditional consumption and delinquent conduct) have penetrated the heart of copyright industries. Whilst it makes no economic sense to fall behind the IT revolution, the desire to preserve a lucrative monopoly makes perfect sense. The music industry in particular is a good case study about such falling behind and eventual reaction.

Of significant consequence is that consumers have not become increasingly benign or malevolent, but rather ambivalent in relation to copyright and subsequent infringement. This attitude is consistent with the fundamental tenets of liberalism and basic liberal values in advanced capitalist society. The most compelling case study to support this proposition in the past decade is the music industry and the rise of the MP3 format as the dominant mode of product delivery. This decade of disorganization has also been significantly experienced in film and gaming industries.

Chapter 8 also acknowledges the impact of other forms of entertainment (namely social media) on the historical significance of popular media products in the West in terms of traditional modes of commodification and consumption. The fact that live-music and cinema attendance and pricing appear to be unaffected by innovative change suggests that traditionally commodified popular media products are at risk of being less influential as modes of popular culture. That is, from an affective perspective, physical attendance at a concert can never be replaced. Yet popular culture in a commodified form is now consumed in convergent ways. Flexible approaches to popular media reflect attitudes that are firmly embedded in liberalism and shape the current modes of consumer behaviour. Recent developments such as corporate social networking where corporations have established Facebook and Twitter sites suggest radical changes in the majors' business models. The corporations are 'tweeting', 'twittering' and otherwise following the followers in a bid to gain a following. The level of self-reflexivity on the part of corporate citizens in a world of digitalization is remarkable.

The increasing play-for-free attitude in the context of private use must not be ignored. Chapter 8 concludes that the Internet has created a market environment that encourages forms of socio-economic reciprocity on an unprecedented scale. This is an extension of social media network behaviour free from control or intervention. Consumers freely exchange views, opinions, ideas and material (popular culture) without intervention or control from cultural gatekeepers. For example, a CD or TV show may have been legitimately purchased, but is uploaded so that others may benefit from the experience. The behaviour is mutualistic in the sense that the uploader may rely on reciprocity at some later time. The perception that consumers are providing a community good through media exchange has not been identified in the literature. Digitalization of popular media transcends traditional ownership boundaries that were clear in the pre-digital era.

It is also asserted that consumers have not only become suspicious of those who control copyright industries, but they are also generally discontented with those who act as cultural gatekeepers. This observation leads to the conclusion that if the value of copyrighted goods is reduced, then there will probably be a reduction in the rate of illegal consumption; but if the value is significantly diminished, then this is hardly a positive outcome for corporate controllers of popular media products.

Chapter 9 asks whether emerging technologies are difficult to reconcile with modern copyright laws. One conclusion is that popular media corporations must now compete in a decentralized entertainment arena. This means direct interaction with software, telecommunications and other allied external industries. Where once copyright governance existed in an unfettered, one-dimensional environment, it now must conform to a combined machinery of copyright and telecommunications governance. Modern day popular media industries are underpinned by copyright at the substructural level, but at the superstructural level the playing field has been altered substantially. Digital rights management and protection were problematic until recently. These developments have caused irreconcilable shifts in the balance of power between the various stakeholders at the superstructual (horizontal) level.

Chapter 9 remarks about a growing sense of futility and perpetual frustration by industry controllers, fittingly, given the competing or incompatible paradigms concerning consumer attitudes and perceptions. Governance, in the light of convergence, and approaches about the best way forward for copyright remain unresolved. On the matter of copyright preservation, the doctrinal evidence and empirical data suggest prima facie illegal consumption is too complex and multidimensional for copyright to provide any meaningful protection.

The chapter argues that there appears to be less room for copyright recognition where specific new technologies have assisted in emancipating those who previously could not consume popular media. The general impact these new technologies have had on copyright controllers is evident simply by a cursory Internet search. Currently, several discrete opportunities to engage in discreet consumption exist for media consumers. These must be viewed as *negative* and debilitating for the owners of copyright because of the loss in control, but *positive* for those who believe in the democratization (or rather, emancipation) of popular media consumption. The significance is that consumers have become disorientated in a state of market disorganization while the major owners of copyright continue to experience reorganizational effects.

The old business models based on monopoly power have been directly affected to the extent that rapid decentralization is causing dilution of

copyright to a 'commons content' sphere. The products, services and participants all appear to be experiencing reorganizational effects.

Corporate strategies have not taken into consideration the democratizing effects of new technologies. The Internet might be deemed the catalyst
capable of reorganizing delivery of popular media. Should this approach
proliferate, it is argued that the traditional industry will become less concentrated as the parameters concerning copyright control must also change.
In this environment, large-scale acquisition of future entrepreneurial copyrights would diminish, creating a decentralized convergent pluralist popular
media industry as opposed to the current situation where the dominant few
maintain the status quo.

2
Global Governance: Regulation of Copyright Law and Policy in Popular Media Copyright Industries

> Copyright is one of the great balancing acts of the law. Many balls are in play and many interests are in conflict.
> (Ricketson, 2001, p. 154)

The global copyright governance regime: background and brief history

As Ricketson suggests, the regulation of copyright law and the administration of policy requires the juggling of interests of various interacting parties across society. Copyright law encompasses a diverse range of legal measures. It allows for a most advanced form of governance as it uniformly transcends national and international regulatory boundaries. Its level of complexity stems from the fact that copyright transcends the intangible realm by inextricably binding tangible products through various modes of rights management (including digital, replication and synchronization rights management). As copyright has no tangible form it only exists in the form of popular media products and services. Furthermore, its complex regulation is only matched by the aggressive enforcement of protection undertaken by its legal owners.

Yet it is tempting to view copyright law in a narrow sense as simply a legal discourse guided by the language of law and the interpretation of various statutes, regulations and other codified principles. The law (in total, not just copyright law) as a discipline is generally taught in the normative sense where the objective is to ensure the student learns how to identify the law, state the legal principles, apply the facts and then reach a conclusion. Rarely is the 'politics of law' or the 'governance of law' considered as inherently relevant in the discourse of law, let alone copyright law. Yet the practical legal reality in which the legislature, executive and judiciary intersect is manifestly considered within the politicization of copyright legal principles – or in this case, the political economy of copyright law.

In the proceeding chapters, a significant general observation about the intersection between modern copyright and corporations, and regulatory frameworks in highly advanced capitalist states is made. That is, respective legislative regimes purportedly aim to promote innovation and encourage competition for the benefit of both commercial exploitation and individual consumption. Theoretically, these are the basic tenets of free market capitalism.

The next two chapters, however, suggest there is quite an imbalance when copyright-related industries involved in the delivery of popular media products become subsumed under a broader corporate rubric. The reality is that popular media industries are anything but 'free' and competitive. That is, copyright governance is as much linked to monopolistic tendencies as is the anticompetitive nature of the dominant corporations that exploit copyright in popular media industries. The relationship is therefore somewhat mutualistic. Efficient, economically feasible copyright exploitation by major players connotes large private profitability returns and vested corporate interests.

The central argument in this chapter is that copyright law should, primarily, be viewed as protection implemented to preserve the rights of those whose business it is to exploit copyright as a form of intangible property. Whilst creators are also dependent on legal protection, the major benefactors of copyright legislation are the key corporate players in the popular media; and despite some progress in terms of moral rights for creators, copyright exploitation solely relates to generating surplus value and protecting profits and future economic interests. White (1987, p. 171) is correct when he contends that 'copyright law appears to have been heavily weighted in favor of protecting the interests of publishers against financial loss rather than the authors, and has led to interesting examples of exploitation of musicians by music publishers'.

This argument is based on the observation that the 'law' of the market and not the 'law' of altruism or common good dictates that copyright protection is ranked higher than social considerations – the economic factors have subsumed all social and cultural considerations (despite the perception of a balanced approach). Accessibility and dissemination of creativity should be encouraged – provided externalities (namely piracy or any other mode of consumption that does not fit into the current framework) do not interfere with the market mechanism. This remains the international basis for copyright governance – even in a convergent digital environment.

The first four sections of this chapter reaffirm the position that copyright governance is a highly integrated and complex process that centres on uniform management of primary, secondary and tertiary levels of copyright. In principle, the 'meta-governor' of political administration, the World Intellectual Property Organization (WIPO) claims to represent all copyright stakeholders. But when one considers the interaction with the Agreement on Trade Related Aspects of Intellectual Property Rights) (1994) (TRIPS) mandated by the World Trade Organization (WTO), it becomes quite apparent the protection of commercial or advanced modes copyright exploitation is the main focus.[1] As set out below, the purpose of such agencies is to internationally implement collaborative regulatory agreements and thereby monitor and review the impact of emerging technologies – namely digitalization – on the globalization of copyright. Copyright governance is achieved through multilayered protective measures. In short, global perspectives assist in the harmonization of copyright industries across members of WIPO for the purposes of promoting trade.

But what of WIPO member nations with substantively divergent views? How are they managed by the custodians of Western conceptions of copyright? The sixth section of the chapter (Legal realism strikes back: a case of China and the crouching paper tiger) presents a compelling case study on actual outcomes of, rather than theoretical perspectives on, copyright governance. The case exposes the façade of copyright neutrality, and the 'artificial prism'[2] in which copyright exists. The conclusion of this chapter is that media piracy and emerging technologies generally interrupt the efficiency of the harmonizing and streamlining processes characteristic of copyright governance thereby making copyright unstable from a corporate private rights perspective (but not necessarily from a societal perspective). It follows that copyright governance is probably somewhat narrower in scope than its terms of reference currently suggest.

Copyright: historical relevance and rationale

England's Statute of Anne 1709 was an 'Act for the Encouragement of Learning, by vesting the Copies of printed Books in the Authors or Purchasers of such Copies, during the Times therein mentioned' (Preamble). Espousing the basic principles of liberalism, this law recognized the significance of individual authors (as primary controllers of copyright) for the purpose of *learning* and *enlightenment*, and purchasers (consumers) as the recipients of these virtues.

Over time, starting in the 1850s, emphasis on those seeking to preserve copyrights by way of extension has not been placed on individual original copyright owners or consumers, but rather on 'music sellers' and book publishers – the corporate citizens who act as copyright controllers and cultural gatekeepers in popular media. The development, a transition from personal to corporate copyright, reflects significant economic changes in the West, which also shaped the prevailing socio-economic rules and public policy. Through legislative intervention, copyright was transformed into a proprietary right (chose in action) by companies (corporations) for the purpose of perpetual commercial exploitation. This transformation started at or about the time when significant technological advancements took place towards the end of the nineteenth century and continued throughout the twentieth century. The development of modern copyright law regimes was a reaction to the prevailing politico-economic changes in the face of emerging technologies. This observation is historically situated, but is particularly relevant for the twentieth and twenty-first centuries (see Table 2.1).

By way of background, the Convention Establishing the World Intellectual Property Organization (1967) formally established the objectives, functions and membership of the organization. The various rights ordinarily found in popular media industries are reflected in Article 2. One of the most important features of the Convention is the recognition of the need to enforce remedies relating to infringement, including the need to deter through criminal sanctions. Given the fact that most, if not all, copyright ownership is transferred to major players, then it is fair to infer such provisions are directly aimed to benefit the corporate owners.[3]

WIPO's predecessor, the United International Bureau for the Protection of Intellectual Property (or BIRPI) was established in 1893. One of its earliest functions was to recognize the Berne Convention for the Protection of Literary and Artistic Works (1886). At that time, scientific discoveries were being made at a remarkable rate. For example, in the entertainment arena, Thomas Edison built on Leon Scott's early 1800s experimentations with sound recordings, and invented a playback gramophone. And Alexander Bell similarly improved on Edison's discovery in the late 1800s, and by the turn of the twentieth century Emile Berliner realized the potential for home entertainment and mass production with cheap vinyl record pressing as a viable format for mass consumption. By then the economic rationale for an effective patents system was evident to the West. It is fair to observe that such organizations commenced as politico-economic organizations for the advancement of Western conceptions of intellectual power during a time of great European expansion, nationalism and imperialism, the last for the exploitation of indigenous natural resources from non-Western lands. For example, if the preposterously absurd doctrine of *terra nullius* (no one's land) validated the claim for land grabs and subsequent settlement in Australia (tangible colonialization),[4] then it would not be hard to imagine, based on Eurocentric legal discourse and policies, the possibility of intellectual exploitation and Western appropriation of indigenous know-how. Just as natural resources were formally subsumed by Europeans, and justified by the Lockean concept of hard toil and labour bearing fruit, indigenous customary intellectual practices and cultural materials were Westernized in terms of formal conceptions of copyright regulation (attribution to specific authors, materialization of the works in a prescribed form, and the standing of the authority in the territory). In Australia these conceptions were substantially different from indigenous cultural practices, which were not recognized in a formal sense. For example, the façade of Western legal policy in Australia was particularly evident when the doctrine of *terra nullius* was shamelessly formally applied in 1835. That is, not only had the land been deemed unoccupied and therefore uninhabited, but Aboriginal cultural law with its own customary traditional codes and practices remained generally unrecognized by virtue of the common law interpretation that Australia had been devoid of civilization. Commodification and commercial exploitation of 'dreamtime' as folklore was impossible. Economic development was the main ingredient in colonial Western paradigms. Indigenous identity in the form of art, music, song, dance, poetry, storytelling and ceremonious application of general know-how had been spiritually embedded in the form of communal cultural heritage. It had also been in existence since time immemorial. This was clearly incompatible with notions of individualism and liberalism. Under Western conceptions of copyright governance, indigenous intellectual property became commercial 'fruits' ripe for picking in the Lockean sense. The connection between the colonial past of Western nations (including Japan, in a Westernized economic sense) and the subsequent domination of the physical world and the current 'imperialization' of the intangible world of popular media by a few Western corporations is worth noting. Organizations such as WIPO were created by a handful of powerful nations with Eurocentric agendas. While membership grew significantly over the past 100 years, Anglo and Eurocentric member nations (especially the US) still largely dictate the terms for copyright policy implementation. Other member nations, many of whom were colonized, are symbolic members because the terms of membership are dictated by the more influential nations under 'transposition' provisions for the purposes of harmonization and compliance. But, as demonstrated below, not all powerful WIPO members share the same American, Anglo and Eurocentric political views.

The film and music industries, in particular, boomed from the 1950s to 1990s when the primary recorded formats were vinyl and magnetic cassette tapes. Hollywood and record companies prospered whilst becoming increasingly concerned about copyright protection. As Edenborough (1997, p. 17) states, 'major commercial pressures that led to a review of the law of copyright as a whole'.

The last 125 years of copyright governance in the West reflect internationalization of copyright governance and compliance with the relevant statutory conditions and schemes administered by the WIPO Copyright Treaty (WCT), and regional administration of international WIPO protocols through nation state legislative schemes. In the European Union (EU), copyright governance is achieved through Directives implemented at the national level for reasonably harmonious application by other Member States (refer to EU Directive 2001/29).

WIPO does not mandate and impose change as a superior body over inferior bodies in a hierarchical fashion. Each member state is expected to administer meaningful management systems according to its sovereign position and membership. A WIPO member must show how it discharges its obligation in various stated ways (namely local laws and customs). This mode of co-decision-making was initiated to suggest harmonization at the formal level, but it is fair to acknowledge that the more powerful trading nations initiate protocols for legal consideration at the domestic level. For example, the main current international instruments for copyright protection stem from the Berne Convention, the Universal Copyright Convention, the Rome Convention, the TRIPS Agreement and the 1996 WIPO treaties. Once a protocol is adopted, a contracting party is responsible for enforcing the obligations by way of a statutory instrument at the domestic level. The relationship between the dominant nations and the below-mentioned international organizations therefore is somewhat osmotic, or at least, diffuse.

That is, once a community-based directive is implemented in the national setting, it is technically a law that is supreme over a conflicting domestic law (in the event of inconsistency). But the concept sovereignty of nations allows for domestic legal administration of procedural and substantive outcomes. In other words, an Italian approach to piracy risk minimization may differ substantially from a German initiative. This two-tiered approach in Europe is called subsidiarity. Hanlon (1998, p. 10) explains: 'This means decisions should be made at the lowest level where possible. If an adequate solution cannot be made by a Member State, there is no reason why that decision should be taken by a Community institution.' In other words, incompatibilities between national court processes and outcomes and community laws expose weaknesses in transnational governance structures.

The US, for example, passed the US Digital Millennium Copyright Act (DMCA) (1998) so that, through WIPO, digitalization rights are transnationally coordinated. This high level of cooperation is achievable because whilst there are some procedural differences and conflicts of laws between jurisdictions in the West, the substantive conceptions of copyright regulation have remained largely uniform within the jurisdictions of the original handful of Western WIPO members – many of whom have been instrumental in globally governing copyright since the late nineteenth century.[5]

The aim of the Berne Convention for the Protection of Literary and Artistic Works (1886) was to help nationals of signatory states obtain international protection of their right to control and receive payment for the use of their creative works. In 1893, the administrative functions for the management of copyright protection established by Berne Convention and the Paris Convention were merged. The merged administrative function became the template for WIPO. Other universal copyright conventions and protocols followed (see Table 2.1), and in 1974 WIPO was integrated into the United Nations (UN). The agreement between the UN and WIPO recognizes WIPO as the specialized agency dedicated to the promotion of intellectual activity states (Art. 1). The agreement authorizes WIPO to ventilate copyright concerns at the diplomatic level and make general enquiries about UN mandates relating to copyright issues on behalf of WIPO members. The UN General Assembly as a forum is a significantly broader political forum concerned with more humanitarian and public interest issues than the narrower WIPO General Assembly. But as an integrated specialized lead agency within the

UN, WIPO is in the best position to influence and shape attitudes in developing nations concerning international copyright governance under the guise of wider UN goals such as socio-economic and cultural development. By providing financial assistance (Art. 16), technical assistance (Art. 10) and other support services to developing countries, WIPO monitors, reviews and otherwise assesses the attitudes of member developing nations in relation to norms, practices and general conduct towards copyright regulation in developing nations – and especially those nations that have been warned by the WTO of potential sanctions as a result of allegations concerning media piracy. Arguably, the UN is the perfect political forum for advanced nations to set the standard for copyright protection in developing nations. Adopting this line of argument, it would not be unreasonable to suggest less developed sovereign nations might view WIPO as just another specialized agency for powerful nations with colonial tendencies which have substituted tangible exploitation for the intangible. After all, Australia's colonial past is a notable example of the propensity for dominant nations to subsume the tangible and intangible realms of 'others' under the cloak of legal formalism. Physical regulation by coercion or otherwise of non-Anglo and non-European lands is a thing of the past. But in a transnational world of advanced capitalism, copyright convention ratification has become a new mode of global regulation by a few powerful nations whose corporations exert great cultural, social and economic influence on the rest of the world. The 1975 agreement between the UN and WIPO symbolizes the nexus between economic and political copyright world order. That WIPO has been firmly embedded in the UN legitimizes its role in establishing an international copyright governance framework. However the US did not ratify the Berne Convention until 1988 (by way of the US Berne Conventions Implementation Act of 1988). Several legal and political reasons might explain the US trepidation about joining the Convention. These include the fact that the US insisted on preserving the display of the copyright symbol and the specific maintenance of a system of copyright registration. (Copyright registration augments the general right of recognition of copyright once created and is in material form.) The US did not entertain moral rights, and probably felt that internationalization was a Eurocentric invention. Now, in relation to the digital agenda, the US leads the way in international harmonization and global copyright governance. It is fair to say that the US is the most vociferous member and arguably the most influential actor in the identification of risks to the global copyright governance framework.

The WTO and WIPO, while they are separate organizations, are interlocking in relation to copyright. WIPO is the oldest and most experienced organization in the administration of copyright regulation but lacks dispute resolution expertise, whereas WTO TRIPS initiatives assert more pragmatic dominance because of the WTO's capacity to identify legal issues and potential disputes. The WTO is perhaps the most dynamic because it has the authority to pave the way for trade sanctions against a nation unless meaningful enforcement strategies are implemented domestically.

In 1996, WIPO entered into a cooperation agreement with the WTO. This coincided with two new Protocols to the original Berne Convention (the WCT, and the WIPO Performances and Phonograms Treaty 1996 (WPPT). Both treaties were a response to digitalization challenges – namely the Internet. The US enjoys the dominant position followed by the EU. Japan endorses these superpowers' actions because its popular media is heavily reliant on Western popular culture developments. For all intents and purposes, it is part of the US and European Union/European Community (EC) unilaterally enforced domestic measures to ensure that TRIPs standards are met by weaker nations.

Modern copyright laws work to protect the legal position of copyright owners. If there is conflict (for example, from external technologies such as the Internet and information technology), then copyright operates to simultaneously limit opportunities for users who may wish to derive benefit from technological developments if such technologies are at cross-purposes with copyright ownership.

The new hope: copyright convergence or sophisticated governance?

Digitalization convergence in terms of technological change – namely the convergence of telecommunications and broadcasting – is not a new concept (Curran, 1991, pp. 119–120). The relevant telecommunication industry services (telco) Acts and broadcasting legislation highlight the difficulties in harmonization of distinct regulatory regimes.[6] However, whilst the term 'convergence' might form part of policy debates about how digitalization has affected copyright, it does not feature in the case law, nor does it form part of the legal nomenclature.[7] Yet the term is used as if it is also somehow applicable to procedural and legal principles (see, for example, taskforce initiatives such as the Copyright Convergence Group (1994) (CCG)).

Convergence suggests broadening of scope whereas copyright legislation is essentially concerned with analysing the meaning of a provision in a more narrow sense. Take the example of the CCG terms of reference, which included a recommendation for the simplification of the copyright legislation in Australia. In 1994, a taskforce from the Australian Copyright Convergence Committee recommended 'a new, broadly defined right of transmission to the public, to replace the technology-specific rights of broadcast by wireless telegraphy and transmission to subscribers to a diffusion service' (Copyright Law Review Committee, 1999, p. 54). How is simplification of the law conceivable let alone achievable in the twenty-first century? Convergence in the technological sense might be realized, but in the legal sense it has further complicated the already intrinsically complex nature of copyright law.

Copyright legislation is a difficult concept – not least because it concerns several layers of concurrent intangible property that is joint and several, severable, and non-severable (depending on what part of the copyright in a product is being exploited). Given its characteristic complexity, it is difficult to contemplate that copyright is capable of simplification. At a time when sweeping reforms to copyright legislation were being made to cater for television broadcasting, Kaplan (1967, p. 40) observed that copyright law possessed 'maddeningly casual prolixity and imprecision'. In addition to the digital agenda reforms, mechanical, cable, satellite, television and radio broadcast licences, and public licenses generally, and the relationship with home-use licences suggest more complexities than ever before.

The 1886 Convention provides the *minimum* standards of protection for economic and moral rights and coexists with a number of the provisions in the TRIPS Agreement. An examination of WIPO's website indicates that through these concurrent, interacting treaties and agreements, global protection is administered by arrangement with WIPO member nations. Consider the WTO–WIPO arrangements for cooperation in the implementation of the WTO TRIPS Agreement. The same nations are members of both institutions, thereby facilitating horizontal integration for harmonized policy implementation for economic development. The obligations of members appear to be cumulatively and conjunctively facilitative. Otherwise, it would be difficult to conceive how global governance could be imposed on independent and sovereign nations.

It is tempting to accept at face value the rationale and objectives of WIPO, namely 'the desire to promote creativity by protecting the works of the mind' (WIPO). Its core objectives are concerned with the uniform protection of rights of authors in light of new economic, social, cultural and technological challenges. WIPO therefore recognizes the impact of the convergence of information and communication technologies, and emphasizes the 'outstanding significance of copyright protection as an incentive for literary and artistic creation' (Preamble). WIPO recognizes the 'need to maintain a balance between the rights of authors and the larger public interest' (Preamble). But when tracing the development of modern copyright laws in Britain and beyond, it is clear that economic, and not social or cultural, imperatives dominate the copyright agenda. Rose (1993, p. 142) rightly concludes:

> Copyright is not a transcendental moral idea, but a specifically modern formation produced by printing technology, market place economics, and the classic liberal culture of possessive individualism.

Copyright governance is primarily the legal-political regime that provides an institutionalized framework for the protection of economic rights vested in the owners of copyright and, at a more *residual* level, protection of the economic rights and creators' non-economic rights (moral rights of the first copyright holder). Moral rights cannot be vested in corporations for obvious reasons so it is clear that the primary obligation of copyright maintenance rests with the economic, or rather entrepreneurial, dimension of copyright. As will be discussed in the next chapter, this is because most copyright ownership (or at least the legal control of copyright) in popular media belongs to the major players.

It follows that moral and other non-commercial considerations are important philosophically but do not possess the same level of cogent urgency that commercial incentives possess. To rank non-commercial factors equally with market economics would constitute an inexact reason why copyright regulation is enforced. Any balancing act appears to be one-sided because most of the agreements implemented since the Rome Convention for the Protection of Performers, Producers of Phonograms and Broadcasting Organizations (1961) specifically relate to the preservation and protection of entrepreneurial rights (see Table 2.1). As a multilateral trading agreement TRIPS aligns all WTO members (currently 155) and sets minimum standards for the protection of copyright. But powerful nations (in particular, the US) have managed to augment TRIPS with bilateral free trade agreements that impose onerous obligations on developing nations that have fundamentally weak copyright regulatory frameworks. The influence exerted by the more powerful WTO members is probably the best indicator that economic imperatives of copyright owners prevail over other considerations in the governance regime.

Table 2.1 Snapshot of significant copyright conventions and treaties in existence, which support entrepreneurial incentives

Year	Formal instrument
1886	Berne Convention for the Protection of Literary and Artistic Works
1961	Rome Convention for the Protection of Performers, Producers of Phonograms and Broadcasting Organizations
1971	Geneva Convention, for the Protection of Producers of Phonograms Against Unauthorized Duplication of their Phonograms
1974	Brussels Convention, Relating to the Distribution of Programme-Carrying Signals Transmitted by Satellite
1996	WIPO Copyright Treaty
1996	WIPO Performances and Phonograms Treaty

Indeed, the purpose of the most recent treaties is to ensure that nations implement the necessary changes to their domestic copyright legislation so as to address the emerging digital environment, including the regulation of the circumvention of technological protection measures (digital rights management). For commercial reasons, the guiding international position stems from US law (DMCA). In Australia the Copyright Amendment (Digital Agenda) Act 2000 in essence ratified the US provisions. These developments support the observation of an increasing shift in the balance from national (individual state) media policy to an international (global) arena. The implications for the organizational framework for copyright become obvious to the extent to which it has become politicized by moving from an individual rights-based concept to an internationalized, statutorily codified process.

What can be immediately gleaned from Table 2.1 is that each period of copyright regulation is marked by a copyright challenge by a technological development. Each instrument came into force as a political reaction to a new technological threat. This might be, prima facie, an obvious statement, but the significance of these politico-economic developments is found in analyses of copyright infringement and technology cases initiated by corporate citizens. As will be discussed in the following chapter, it is important to recognize the acute resistance by dominant corporations to any change to the status quo – especially in the form of emerging technologies. Popular media industries through their alter ego, copyright governance, respond to technological challenges by lobbying for legal and administrative responses when threatened by change. Consider the line of blank audio-cassette lawsuits in the 1970s, and the Sony Betamax case of the 1980s. These cases suggest that legislation/regulation is a reaction to technological change, rather than anticipation that in light of developments, authors and creators should be protected and that, therefore, action must be taken.

In this context, the 1971 Treaty was a direct response to the proliferation of cassette duplication. It was initiated as a consequence of fierce lobbying on the part of the dominant copyright owners (the music industry majors). The dominant copyright owners in film and television broadcasting strenuously lobbied for the 1974 initiative. Changes have occurred – not because authors have urged for copyright reform but because regulatory change is implemented at the behest of the corporate copyright owners in order to preserve the dominant status quo. Any altruistic public interest considerations are residual to the primary imperative of institutionalizing copyright governance for the benefit of corporate copyright owners. The impetus for copyright governance is embedded in all levels of a neo-pluralist universe for the benefit of legitimate artificial entities. And yet, ironically, artificial corporate entities were banned until 1825 in Britain, but quickly organized themselves to lobby for the creation of international treaties and obligations within decades of being able to trade once again.

By contractual extension, the WIPO member states enter into various horizontal (lateral) trade agreements. In the era of digitalization more treaties, protocols and conventions reciprocating allegiances have been entered into than in any other period throughout the history of modern copyright. The international community, typically encouraged by the US, has approached copyright predominately from an economic viewpoint in the continued effort to assert control, exclusivity and the right to maximum profits.

Legitimacy of copyright governance structure in member nations

According to WIPO statistics, membership has grown from a few Western nations (14 in 1884 to 185 in 2012). There are currently 89 signatories to the WIPO Copyright Treaty 1996. Each member state subscribes to the following organizational model:

- international governmental organizations (*global governance*)
- national copyright administration (*statutory governance*), and
- international and national non-governmental organizations (NGOs).

As mentioned, the purpose of such integration is to enforce the treaties and maintain interaction between WIPO and WTO (and the latter with TRIPs) in order to set minimum standards for risk management and compliance. These measures are not prescriptive. They are facilitative but encourage as much protection possible. As contracting parties, member states, within the EU for example, issue Directives concerning domestic application of rules for harmonization of copyright regulation in converging digital environments.[8] Significantly, it remains a matter of national law to define the prescriptive obligations for the public – namely consumers of popular media. But, as mentioned, the principle of subsidiarity provides for significant latitude for issues to be dealt with more efficiently at a national level (Hanlon, 1998).

WIPO's objectives for copyright are therefore summarized as follows:

- harmonization of legal and regulatory procedures
- facilitation of economic management rights across member jurisdictions
- collaboration and exchange of copyright information
- creation of copyright awareness in member countries and provision of legal and technical assistance to developing countries, and
- dispute resolution services.

The rationale for WIPO's endorsement of the promotion of paracopyrights is one example of a corporate copyright imperative. The artificiality of regional/zone exclusions and the use of technologies to prevent consumers using the identical product from region to region and zone to zone is evidence of the fact that the balance is not evenly struck between competing interests. There is simply no rational, legal or moral reason to promote, or at least remain ambivalent about, unfair practices such as artificial region coding. Why an identical product purchased in another jurisdiction does not work on a device because playback is barred is demonstrative of the attitudes of the dominant corporate copyright controllers.[9] WIPO is silent on regional coding. Members of WTO are simply expected to adhere to the practice of zone/region exclusions notwithstanding the fact that regional digital rights management constitutes nothing more than sharp trading bearing in mind popular media industries have vested interests not only in media products, but in their manufacture and distribution and also in electronic devices. Transnational corporate behaviour in the current copyright governance regime is quite astonishing. International organizations such as WIPO and WTO demand uniform application of copyright governance, yet discriminatory regional zoning is ignored. Artificial barriers to consumption constitute more than an imbalance in copyright governance at the international level. They support the observation that the framework has been established by the handful of multinational corporations with vested interests in the economies of the member states of WIPO and WTO. The agenda for preserving the exclusive private rights of a few elite multinational citizens who are represented by the most advanced nations at the international level is achieved, of course, through liberal corporatism.

It appears that international organizations share one feature: they possess a monopolistic tendency that complements the structure of the dominant corporations discussed in the previous chapter. In particular, Western nations (notably the US and the EU countries) organize this model along economic market lines complemented by weak competition regulation, and have thus enjoyed an immense political and economic advantage. The sheer political clout and funding power possessed by the wealthiest members of WTO and WIPO reflect the neo-pluralist interests of corporate elites whose concerns are voiced by these organizations. The corporate agenda reflects how modern copyright is organized in both Western and developing nations. The legitimacy for adhering to Western copyright principles along commercial lines is well established. It is Eurocentric by nature because it relies on at least five fundamental Western conceptions of commercial copyright governance. These are:

- possession of the legislative authority to implement copyright laws as private economic rights and property for citizens,
- acknowledgment of the importance of copyright protection,
- enforcement of meaningful regulation for the management of private rights,
- implementation of international harmonization, and
- modification of existing regimes if existing ones not compatible with the dominant Western system.

As for the first concept, most Western nations have long-established constitutional bases by which to enforce copyright governance. Australia's rarely altered 110-year-old Constitution provides, in s. 51(xviii), that:

The Parliament shall, subject to this Constitution, have power to make laws for the peace, order, and good government of the Commonwealth with respect to ... Copyrights, patents of inventions and designs, and trademarks.

As for the balance of these principles, constitutional provisions allow for adaptation and modification through legitimate and separate arms of power.

The artificial construct in which WIPO exists is that the bulk of the weaker nations do not possess a history of seventeenth-century English-style struggles for political liberalism, the Enlightenment, and other struggles from oppression, or rather tyranny of the Crown that ultimately led to civil liberty, political rights and economic opportunity along Lockean lines.

Western copyright principles are fundamentally foreign to many developing nations. Yet WIPO insists these nations must follow established, dominant Western principles. It is doubtful that recognition of substantive copyright principles exists in these new or developing capitalist states. If it does, then at this stage the copyright principles probably represent nothing more than ad hoc, superficial reforms where provisions, articles and codes can be readily slipped into human rights bills and charters (i.e., formal or superficial recognition). By stark contrast, Western nations possess robust law, policy and governance frameworks, due, generally, to stable, separated and transparent arms of power, and due specifically to well-established, formal institutions for copyright governance dating back at least three centuries. It is difficult for non-Western and/or developing nations to accept the substantive effect of WIPO initiatives in administering international obligations. Chapter 7 provides some practical cases of the substantive shortfalls in WIPO's objectives, but the case against China (discussed below in this chapter) is equally compelling.

Corporatization of copyright: politicizing copyright

Copyright's evolution as an exclusive monopoly right has headed along one path. That is, the life of copyright has been extended by influential Western nations primarily at the behest of their influential multinational corporations. For example, in under 200 years temporary monopolies have generally increased from 14 years of exclusivity in Britain to over 70 years after the death of the author in the contemporary international setting. And it has continued to be extended in the twenty-first century (as will be seen in the following chapters) – largely at the behest of US and EU corporate copyright holders and related elites (for example, superstars and industry associations). It is worth noting that the most rapid extension of copyright occurred in recent decades, or roughly when audio-visual technologies became freely accessible to consumers. It also worth noting that copyright has never been shortened, and that on most occasions expansion is the result of rigorous lobbying on the part of industry associations for entrepreneurial reasons. The monopolization of popular culture is discussed in the next chapter, but it is important here to explore further the monopolizing effects of the statutory regime. Modern copyright laws work to protect the legal position of corporate-controlled media whilst simultaneously limiting opportunities for users of the Internet and information technology who may wish to derive the full benefits of technological developments.

In popular media, corporatism, as a corporatist copyright law model, does not only mean corporate (i.e., company) control of copyright at the macro-level. At the intermediate or meso-level, corporatism attempts to pseudo-humanize 'corporateness' in popular culture by personifying a brand or genre (for example, a pop band might be described as a typical act on a particular major label or a blockbuster movie might be described as a standard Universal studios production). At the micro-level, companies control the underlying undercopyright for the purposes of commodification. Corporate citizens therefore represent copyright control at the über (superstructural) level. There is little room for alternative modes of production in popular media. And, as will be discussed in Chapter 3, the reality is that copyright ownership is dominated by a handful of major players. For present purposes it is important to recognize corporatism as a mode of neo-pluralistic coordination and organization in terms of copyright governance. In this politico-economic corporate universe, individual consumers have no place – or standing. Corporations are represented by industry associations and representative organizations that in turn liaise with quasi-political organizations, which then interact with government agencies as relevant stakeholders. The entire process is based on the interaction of artificial citizens legitimized by two distinct areas of law – corporation law and copyright law.

Using the music industry as an example (because it is arguably the most advanced media model), the interaction between corporate actors for minimum statutory royalty-setting and product price-setting of the published price to dealers (PPD) and retailers recommended price (RRP) demonstrates the sophistication of copyright corporatism and just how it works as an effective mode of copyright governance.

For example, *Chappell & Co Ltd v Nestlé Co Ltd* (1960) is a well-known case that highlights the effects of inflating the value of a commodity. The barriers or, rather, artificiality of price-setting mechanisms created by dominant companies through their representative associations become clear when the status quo is challenged by alternative modes of production and delivery (as in this case, by legislative change (parallel importation) or external technologies). This case is also useful when assessing the extent to which copyright owners restrict the use of goods if the transaction is deemed to be on less favourable terms than the industry is used to. In this case, Nestlè was estopped from giving away records owned by corporate copyright owners because the records were being redeemed for chocolate wrappers, terms that were less favourable than those typically enjoyed. The wrappers themselves were essentially litter and, as the court observed, redeeming chocolate wrappers was hardly proof of chocolate bar purchases.

However, these special records were not standard vinyl formats, but rather thin film discs specifically produced for promotional purposes. Nestlè's agent, during the manufacture of this external, non-industry format, provided notice to the Mechanical Copyright Protection Society that it intended to make records, but the response was unfavourable given the unorthodox purpose of manufacture. In other words, the copyright owners were unhappy to receive a royalty less than the 'ordinary selling price'. Consequently, Nestlè was in breach of copyright. The majority (p. 109–110) agreed:

> Where records are sold in the ordinary way of business it can be assumed that in his own interest the manufacturer will fix a full price to cover not only the cost of production and his own profit but also the profit required by retailers. But where there is a special order and none of the records made are to be sold in the ordinary way but all are to be sold, as here, in an unusual way in order to promote a scheme for advertising quite a different business from selling records, the protection of the copyright owner is not at all secure.

Times have significantly changed in terms of value and fair price-setting, but this 50-year-old case is very important in the discussion of the political economy of popular media and copyright governance because it suggests the moment externalities are introduced, the dominant player, that is sensitive to any alternative method of doing business, reacts. In this case, the relevant amount was the price set by the industry to third parties – and not a penny less. In the *Australian Competition and Consumer Commission v Universal Music Australia Pty Limited* (*ACCC*) (2002) case, the situation was identical the moment cheaper imports were suggested.

It seems protectionism and favouritism are hallmarks of an imbalanced popular media industry. But Lord Keith of Avonholm dissented in this case. His Lordship found (at p. 112):

> [T]he Appellants' case somewhat elusive as it seems to oscillate between considering whether the sale of the record here is an ordinary retail sale and considering whether there is an ordinary retail selling price of the record.

What other industry has the benefit of enjoying a statutory minimum reserve (in this case it was 6.25 per cent) concurrently with imposing a mandate for the highest maximum price at which products are 'ordinarily to be sold to the public'? But more importantly, rejecting a venture for financial reasons demonstrates a lack of public interest consideration because persons who may ordinarily not consume music, or cannot afford to, are deprived of the opportunity to consume music at a significantly discounted price. This was not a case of clandestine production of an inferior product. The entrepreneurs were upfront with their intention to pay a reduced licence fee for a largely inferior retail product, but nevertheless a perfect promotional item. The recordings were made from flimsy material (cellulose acetate) compared to the standard vinyl formats available in retail outlets.

In this case, Nestlè offered to pay a licence for the special wrapper-for-record arrangement, but Chappell declined because there was less profit to be made. The case highlights the fact the music industry is only in the business of making as much money as it can, without considering the utility in the promotional value for the recording artist who presumably has no ownership in the recording. Once again, finding the balance evades us.

Using the recorded music industry by way of illustration again, for effective control harmonization in the international arena, the International Federation of the Phonographic Industry (IFPI) represents the interests of copyright owners at the United Nations level (WIPO) and at various trade organizations (WTO and TRIPS). Regionally, various powerful national bodies (for example the Recording Industry Association of America (RIAA), the British Phonographic Industry (BPI) and Australia's equivalent, the Australian Recording Industry Association (ARIA)) represent the interests of copyright owners at the domestic level. The most powerful members of these associations are the multinational majors who rely on these interests groups to ventilate their concerns in the appropriate forums (government (both the executive and legislature) parliamentary inquiries, the media and regulatory bodies). Industry business – price-setting, litigation and general interest group lobbying in a pluralist sense – is coordinated and conducted along corporatist lines. The charge to the High Court in the *Roadshow Films Pty Ltd v iiNet Ltd* (*iiNet*) case was not being led by Hollywood as a matter of principle, but rather by the Australian Federation Against Copyright Theft (AFACT), which is the voice of Hollywood in terms of copyright theft.[10] The major industry players, as neo-pluralistic powers, have essentially become vicarious members of WIPO. This is because reciprocal copyright protocols between the few most powerful Western nations have been established to protect specific products organized by the few most powerful corporations. Corporatism implies that popular media industries are stringently regulated and controlled on a global scale in order to maintain the status quo for the bulk of industry-controlled popular culture.

Integral to industry is the role of 'independent' collecting societies, which collect and trace (for a percentage commission) royalties on behalf of the owners of the relevant copyright. For the avoidance of any doubt, in Australia, for example, the Australian Mechanical Copyright Owners' Society (AMCOS) and the Australasian Performers' Rights Association (APRA) have enjoyed an unfettered monopolistic privilege.

These most powerful entities are statutorily enshrined and are described as not-for-profit collecting societies. In Australia, for example, music associations

such as APRA and AMCOS represent both creators (authors and composers) and publishers, whilst others such as the Phonographic Performance
Company of Australia (PPCA) focus on recordings by artists and on record
labels. The agencies are interrelated because public performance also
includes broadcasting and general public dissemination of recorded materials. These entities do more than collect royalties. PPCA clearly represents
corporate players because it is directly aligned with ARIA – a most protective
industry association. These networked entities invariably consolidate power
when, for example, unfavourable legislative issues are presented or especially
during media piracy debates. (For example, APRA was even given leave for
an *amicus curiae* presence in the *iiNet* case.) Their primary political functions
include maintenance of the dominant status quo. Therefore they do not
represent all stakeholders in a balanced manner.

One good example is the failed attempt to veto parallel importation in
Australia. Until 1998, parallel importation of popular media (namely CDs) was
successfully banned because of a statutory monopoly granted to Australian
subsidiaries of major players. Most vociferous resistance against deregulation
was ventilated in all arenas. The marketing campaigns mischievously alleged
parallel importation laws would open the floodgates to cheap imports and
pirated goods. Reasons for opposition were obvious. The 'closed shop' was being
threatened, and for associations this meant diminishing royalty-collecting
revenue from mechanical licenses that ordinarily would have been attributed
to domestic corporations. The artificiality of price-setting was scrutinized
again in the form of aggressive lobbying on the part of consumer groups and
independent retailers who were concerned about not being able to purchase
identical products from overseas suppliers. This time the corporate industry
lobby was unsuccessful and copyright laws in Australia were amended to allow
overseas products.

The associations and societies joined in the chorus of complaints, along
with corporate industry representatives. They failed – and incidentally there
were no floods of dodgy imports. This example supports the proposition that
despite attempts to diminish the power of state-sanctioned monopoly status
given to artificial entities, those entities continue to set and regulate prices
for media products for consumption. As Dunleavy and O'Leary (1987, p. 194)
correctly state, 'elite collaboration is the rule in liberal corporatism'.

It is correct to assert that associations and organizations in popular media
industries enjoy a monopoly over social interests. They are sanctioned by
statute to dictate the terms for the copyright market, and there appears to
be a lack of democratic process in these actions (for example, associations
historically have been instrumental in setting public and broadcasting rates
and collecting those rates upon the assignment of such rights). Although
the following quote relates to another dimension of copyright (paracopyrights and issues relating to anti-circumvention technologies), it is appropriate where highly integrated and well-organized corporate entities dictate

the economic conditions for the consumption of popular culture in an environment where such products are nothing more than highly elastic commodities designed to provide entertainment:

> Much modern legislation regulating an industry reflects a compromise reached between, or forced upon, powerful and competing groups in the industry whose interests are likely to be enhanced or impaired by the legislation. In such cases, what emerges from the legislative process is frequently not a law motivated solely by the public interest. It reflects wholly or partly a compromise that is the product of intensive lobbying, directly or indirectly, of Ministers and parliamentarians by groups in the industry seeking to achieve the maximum protection or advancement of their respective interests. The only purpose of the legislation or its particular provisions is to give effect to the compromise. To attempt to construe the meaning of particular provisions of such legislation not solely by reference to its text but by reference to some supposed purpose of the legislation invites error. (*Sony v Stevens* (2005), at 126, per McHugh, J)

Modern copyright has never been a utilitarian concept based on individual pursuit of self-contentment. Corporatism is deeply entrenched in the current system. Indeed the then Australian Attorney General, the Hon. Nigel Bowen QC, in his Second Reading Speech on the Copyright Bill 1968, observed these market power dynamics in the 1960s (*Parl Debs*, HR, 16 May 1968, p. 1527):

> [I]t is also necessary to have regard to those who use copyright material ... Especially in the musical field, owners of copyright have so organized, through licensing organizations, that they are in a strong bargaining position. For example, APRA claims to control the performing right in virtually all copyright music in Australia. It is thus in a position to dictate the terms on which music may be performed in public ... The present Bill recognizes that there are changes in the use of copyright material which have been brought about by changes in technology ... At the same time the Government recognizes that existing practices and existing relationships in industries which depend upon copyright material cannot be ignored. In framing this Bill, the Government has had due regard to interests which are often conflicting interests. In many cases, it has not been possible to satisfy completely all parties.

The only conclusion that can be, realistically as opposed to idealistically, reached is that copyright governance is fundamentally premised on a liberal corporatist model. Its core features are based on the notion of monopolizing intangible rights as a means to the end of securing successive exploitation.

Schmitter (1974, p. 111) describes liberal corporatism as 'the osmotic process whereby the modern state and modern interest associations seek each other out'. Corporations, 'each of which has a monopoly on the representation of particular categories' symbolize this model of organizational structure in Western democracies (Dunleavy and O'Leary, 1987, p. 193). Copyright industries, therefore, are fundamentally categorized by these traits, which are summarized as monopolies over:

- private copyrights transactions
- revenue collection for copyright (public rights)
- price-setting (public policy), and
- product delivery (socio-economic policy).

Popular media appear to be so complex that they require a broad array of closely aligned associations and companies to maintain them through a sophisticated meta-governance framework. The irony of course is that for all the complex copyright management, the product in its commodified form is quite a simple object that does nothing more than provide affective pleasure. That is, once transferred from the creator to the ultimate copyright owner, the finished product is processed through various artificial political, economic and legal layers before it is ultimately made available for consumption.

Yet copyright from simplex to complex is simply a representation of entertainment is it not? It is not! Copyright in popular media can be described as the invisible thread that binds various 'soft' and 'hard' formats. It is where the virtual and physical, the temporary and fixed, meet. For regulators, owners and industry associations, copyright is complex because it manifests itself in a variety of forms. But all that the consumer appreciates is just the actual 'thing' – a DVD, game or 'app'. The paradox of its complexity rests in the fact that it possesses a combination of complex artificial characteristics at the input end, but is converted to a simple product at the output end. As supported by observations made by the Court in *Universal Music Australia Pty Limited v Sharman License Holdings Ltd* (2005) (*Kazaa*) (see Chapter 8), it is doubtful whether the average consumer appreciates the complexity of copyright processes in the creation of popular media.

The consumer just sees a final or finished good without possibly even beginning to understand the owners' perspective of the invisible and divisible dimensions the product maintains in the marketplace. In addition, the effort needed to guard the neighbourhood of rights that exists within these products cannot be objectively appreciated by consumers. And why should they care? After all, it is a fair proposition to assert that if a person purchases a simple product for valuable consideration, then one is free to do as one wishes with that product. This is not abstract sentiment. It is important for any balanced understanding of copyright governance to acknowledge consumer sentiment, mood and other subjective psychosocial factors. In a recent landmark Australian High Court decision (*Stevens v Kabushiki Sony Computer Entertainment* (2005) (*Stevens*)), the Court looked at the balancing acts associated with proper protection against infringement of copyright and the rights of owners of chattels in the 'use and reasonable enjoyment of such chattels' when the owners are purchasers for 'personal purposes'.

The argument about the value and relevance of copyright governance might be considered on a more a level playing field that could include issues of individual rights and freedoms ordinarily acquired by sovereign citizens (consumers) who acquire chattels 'for their use as they see fit'. In addressing the corporate interests of Sony, the High Court regarded inalienable *fundamental rights* as important legal rights extending to an owner of a Sony CD-ROM and PlayStation console. The significance of this case rests on the fact that paramount considerations of copyright owners over the pursuit and enjoyment of a person's ordinary rights as an owner of chattels effectively came into question.

The governance of an abstract and ethereal concept such as copyright might be difficult for some consumers to understand. How are ordinary consumers expected to appreciate the complexity of the proposition that abstract subjectification of tangible 'things' somehow possesses a meaningful communicative and social function? Furthermore, what does exclusivity and the placement of artificial and physical restrictions on products mean to a consumer who sees the intrinsic worth in a popular media product as nothing more than an object that provides affective or perhaps altruistic pleasure (for example, sharing the love for a particular song or band)?

The short answer is that the cluster of legal rights attached to the physical incarnation of copyrighted material probably does not mean that much to consumers of popular media. Yet the rationale for the stringent regulation of copyright purports to stem from the Lockean concept that, as a result of inspiration and perspiration, the law has been developed to support, protect and promote a bundle of rights for the benefit of those who presumably 'toiled' and are now ready to reap the rewards of their labours. The spoils from the fruits of of one's own labour are one reason for setting up global governance regulatory regimes. Of course, the other, as set out above, is more realistic and accurate – that is, governance exists primarily for the protection and preservation of exclusive control vested in commercial exploiters of popular media – namely the corporations.

The need for übercopyright regulation has been made clear by corporate copyright owners (refer to the next chapter for an explanation of Kirby J's use of this term in *Stevens*). It has been demonstrated that copyright is an exclusive legal right. This unfettered right allows the owner to make copies and otherwise make known to the world works in any format. In the modern setting, 'making known' is rigidly connected to the concept of mechanical reproduction. The terms 'copyright industries' and 'popular media industries' are inextricably linked because the former represents the artificial dimensions (the intangible bundles) whilst the latter is concerned with the finished cultural product (the tangible). It follows that modern copyright law has been developed to complement technological advancement in relation to the physical exploitation of works. Its primary purpose, therefore, is to protect economic interests of those authorized to exploit it. As copyright may be dealt with similarly to any other forms of property, it would be difficult to regard the current legislation as anything else but a set of rules for the economic management of copyright for corporations that possess the increasing capacity to reproduce copyright in material form. This is the point at which copyright owners (usually corporations) subjugate copyright, and effectively become copyright industry controllers. But there cannot be a superstructure without a substructure or the underlying unter-copyright 'process'.

Copyright law is the formal protection of the rights of those whose business it is to exploit this form of intangible property. Whilst creators are also dependent on legal protection, the major benefactors of copyright legislation are the key financial players in the music industry. One simple illustration is the fact that prior to legislative reform in the last century, minimum statutory royalty rates for creators were not recognized under copyright law.[11]

Whilst copyright policy might exist in this vacuum, and indeed whilst the creation of specific pieces of copyright legislation may be politically influenced, interpretation of copyright law by the court is comparably independent. Courts identify, interpret and forensically analyse the law with established intrinsic and extrinsic materials. Examining closely the statutory text is but one part of 'der Process'. The language of the law is also analysed by reference to the historical context, precedents and other background materials.

The most intriguing aspect of copyright interpretation is the balancing act judges must perform in relation to the competing interests amongst various stakeholders and consumers of law and justice. In most Western democracies where constitutions limit the power of various heads of government particular difficulties arise. Parliaments possess the legislative authority to make laws with respect to copyright – but only within a constitutional and legal setting 'in which competing legal interests must also be upheld by the law, including, generally, free expression and the normal interest of property owners in the undisturbed enjoyment of their property' (Kirby J in *Stevens* at para. 168). The limits to power are obvious. In the absence of limiting powers, corporate elites would lobby parliament to further narrow the scope of copyright. This is most noteworthy – not least because copyright case law concerning dominant multinational corporations against ordinary citizens is comparably rare in light of sovereignty and constitutional issues. Indeed most high-profile cases are not 'David and Goliath' in proportion as they invariably involve corporations.

The substructure: *untercopyright* transition

The balancing of obligations commences at the international organizational level. The protection of copyright is a fundamental right enshrined in Article 17 of the Charter of Fundamental Rights of the European Union (2000) and Article 1 of the First Protocol of the European Convention on Human Rights (1950). But it is to be balanced against other human rights. It true that original creators of works protected by copyright, and their heirs, have certain basic rights. They hold the exclusive right to use or authorize others to use the work on agreed terms, for example. The creator of a work can prohibit or authorize:

- its reproduction in various forms, such as printed publication or sound recording,
- its public performance, as in a play or musical work,
- recordings of it, for example, in the form of compact discs, cassettes or videotapes,
- its broadcasting, by radio, cable or satellite, and
- its translation into other languages, or its adaptation, such as a novel into a screenplay.

Yet the case law overwhelmingly is concerned with corporate copyright ownership and copyright infringement matters. This is because many creative works protected by copyright require mass distribution, communication and financial investment for their dissemination (for example, publications, sound recordings and films). Hence, creators often sell the rights to their works to individuals or companies best able to market the works in return for payment. These payments are often made dependent on the actual use of the work, and are then referred to as royalties.

These economic rights have a time limit, according to the WIPO treaties. Limits enable both creators and their heirs to benefit financially for a reasonable period of time. Copyright protection also includes moral rights, which involve the right to claim authorship of a work and the right to oppose changes to it that could harm the creator's reputation. The creator – or the owner of the copyright in a work – can enforce rights, administratively and in the courts, by inspection of premises for evidence of production or possession of illegally made – 'pirated' – goods related to protected works. The owner may obtain court orders to stop such activities, as well as seek damages for loss of financial rewards and recognition (the US, UK and Australian copyright laws comprehensively reflect these legal principles).

For copyright to be administered properly in the current Western copyright governance framework, two elements must be present: monopoly and control of the intangible right, preferably through assignment (but if not, then at an absolute minimum, an exclusive license with options to renew). This is the default position. Creators of copyright usually assign copyright to corporate citizens for commercial exploitation, whilst assignment of the copyright in public performance is also given to incorporated associations (collecting societies) for royalty collection. As discussed throughout the subsequent chapters, these arrangements for the initial copyright in works are not the exception, but rather the norm.

The administrative bodies all declare that possessing the control of copyright irrefutably assists in the streamlining of doing business in copyright industries. In essence, influential corporate citizens have created a playing field where copyright is demanded from natural citizens. This is the natural order of things and is supposed to be beneficial for creators because of the ability of multinational firms and international collecting societies to communicate with one other.

But the point raised is this: if monopolization of copyright is supposed to be a positive creation or a beneficial process, why has the issue of creator exploitation been consistently raised throughout the history of modern copyright? There is so much case law and there have been so many public inquiries on the issue of copyright assignment to artificial bodies that the justification proffered by the governors of copyright is worthy of closer examination.[12]

Chapter 8 provides an examination of the actual financial worth of the original creators' work. For now it is important to accept the basic proposition that most copyright creators are exploited. And as set out in that chapter, typical author royalties in the music industries in the UK and Australia range between A$60 and A$2,500 per annum for 90 per cent of original copyright holders in a multibillion dollar industry (see the next chapter). So what happens after the creator's copyright kernel is conceived?

There are a number of ways a copyright owner can deal with the rights to creative material. Copyright is personal property and transferable. Corporate citizens have organized these basic core copyrights so that they create extraordinary surplus value for repeated exploitation decades after each copyright was acquired. Therefore most popular media contracts insist on assignment of copyright.

The organization and coordination of copyright for the purposes of commodification is a twofold process. At the micro-level or substructure, core rights are converted from a primary initial right (of the creator) to a multi-layered entrepreneurial right. This process is described as the transfer of the underlying rights (untercopyright). There is an essential common feature in all copyright industry contracts (whether they be for music, film or games). That is, there is an expectation of assignment of copyright. By way of illustration, standard clauses from two of the most popular forms of agreements in the industry, publishing and recording, are as follows:

Standard publishing agreement
Grant of Rights
Writer, as beneficial owner or authorized controller of the Compositions, hereby sells, transfers and assigns to the Publisher (and its successors

and assigns) the whole of the Writer's copyright interest in the Compositions ... subject only to the public performance right which has been
or will be assigned to APRA to exploit the Compositions, by any and all
means.

Standard recording agreement
Grant of Rights
The artist grants to the company the right to make the first recording
during the term of any songs written and/or composed by any of the
member of the artist, and consents to the use of the performances of the
members of the artist in the manufacture, distribution, promotion and
exploitation of records and videos.

The artist grants to the company an absolute and irrevocable assignment
of any rights, title and interest (including copyright) that the artist may
have in all masters of records and videos made during the term for the
life of copyright in the masters and throughout the territory.

The overriding monopolistic demands are twofold: assignment of copyrights in the private contractual sense, and the recognition of assignment
to the collecting society for the public performance rights (in this case,
the APRA).

The other clause inevitably required in a standard copyright industry
agreement is the requirement for the assignor to be appointed exclusive
attorney. This is critical for all legal, commercial and political administration
(including litigation). Rarely are these terms varied.

In other words, demanding copyright by way of assignment (or at least
exclusive license) is a natural and common sense approach – otherwise, it
is contended by the major players, there would be no popular media industry. Essentially, the monopolization of copyright is a copyright governance
imperative, and for the last 100 years WIPO has facilitated this status quo.
Global governance of copyright represents the politicization of copyright
at all levels from the top down. Once copyright is secured, exploitation
commences, and it is for this reason corporate copyright industries insist
Western governments enforce these rights transglobally.

Legal realism strikes back: a case of China and the crouching paper tiger

In certain respects, the US seems to be the primary nation to threaten trade
sanctions against any country that will not comply with international copyright standards and protocols. Multilateral trade options and variations to
international harmonization do not seem to be preferred over the dominant
unilateral and bilateral agreements urged by the US and EU. China, however, is not a small country, and has not only a disparate copyright history

to that of the West, but also a radically different modern political history in the form of a semi-colonial past.

Just how effective is WIPO as an organizational, harmonizing regulatory body given it is common ground that piracy in China is rife? If its efficiency is measured by encouraging member states from Afghanistan to Zambia to join, then its measure of success is very high.

China has been a member WIPO since 1980 and joined TRIPS in 2001 and WTO in 2002. Suffice to say, the fusion of copyright law, censorship law and cultural political elements within a centralized political regime represents the antithesis of liberalism and negative liberty. Diplomatic encouragement, on the part of Western trade partners, for China to join the list of notable trade heavyweights and world leaders (specifically the US) is indeed important for international copyright governance recognition because other non-Western nations might be influenced by China's accession to organizations such as WIPO and the WTO. But just how effective is WIPO's regulatory bureau in terms of actually minimizing economic harm from acts of carte blanche piracy? Is it fair to call the organizations and structures (WIPO, the WTO, and TRIPS) within the copyright governance framework 'paper tigers' or 'toothless tigers' when assessing whether any action against China can be meaningfully implemented and measured against the sheer political and economic might that China possesses?

The following section presents a case study of a WIPO member superpower where public administration for peace, order, and good government overrides prima facie private rights legal considerations. Freedom from international interference in domestic sovereignty is not unusual, but the 'Chinese Rule of Law' is a super-jurisdiction that has proved problematic for the West. In short, the decision of the WTO Panel in the dispute between China and the United States explicates this ad hoc, disjointed – essentially incompatible – view of copyright in China.[13] The decision, submissions, explanatory memoranda are summarized below.

By way of background, WIPO's objectives, as set out in the Convention establishing it, are to 'promote the protection of intellectual property throughout the world'. In the light of that, its first function is to 'promote the development of measures designed to facilitate the efficient protection of intellectual property throughout the world and to harmonize national legislation in this field' (see Article 4 of the Convention).

The statutory recognition of copyright in China ('copyright law') was adopted by the National People's Congress in 1990 and subsequently amended in 2001. Compare this with the fact Western nations moved to statutory recognition and harmonization in the nineteenth century. Whilst it is not the place to compare and contrast theories of the state and conflicting political ideologies between China and the US, it is important to at least recognize these fundamentally controversial differences for the purposes of copyright governance.

The ideological tensions about the organization of copyright arose in a recent dispute where the US alleged Chinese nationals were flagrantly involved in copyright abuses. Several issues arose – first, by virtue of the Chinese state's legal definition of copyright protection that was in conflict with WIPO's articles and, second, the manner by which illegal goods were disposed was in direct conflict with WIPOs terms. Given the nature of the multilayered allegations, the grievances appear to have been aimed at alleged systemic shortfalls in the Chinese system of copyright governance as it relates to copyright protection and piracy minimization based on WIPO guidelines.

In short, the attack was on the substantive provisions in China's copyright law and its procedural regulatory policy about protecting and preserving the economic rights of copyright owners. It was, in essence, about interference with entrepreneurial ownership – notably copyright vested in powerful Western corporations (see the next chapter).

The US claimed that China's copyright laws denied meaningful protection for owners of copyright. China, naturally, refuted such allegations and insisted that it grants full copyright protection by expressly incorporating into Chinese law the rights conferred under international agreements (the Berne Convention and the TRIPS Agreement).

At the material time (the dispute was filed in 2007), under its copyright law, China (like many other non-Western nations) banned from publication and dissemination such works as those that consisted entirely of unconstitutional or immoral content. Copyright recognition in China was, therefore, required to undergo a legitimization process before it could be formally recognized. This point is significant because the subjectivity of such individual customs and norms create vague parameters. These must surely complicate matters and frustrate Western enforcers of copyright. In the case of copyrighted materials, the Chinese government protects copyright where a work has been edited to pass content review. But at the time of the allegations it did not enforce copyright against unedited works or prohibited copies of an unedited, prohibited work that failed content review.

Chinese law sets out criteria of eligibility for protection (in Article 2):

> Chinese citizens, legal entities or other organizations shall enjoy copyright in their works in accordance with this Law, whether published or not.

Protection extends to foreigners under international agreements and treaties. But there are exceptions to protection (Articles 4 and 10). China therefore does not protect the copyright in unapproved works that have failed content review. There cannot be enforcement of the copyright of such works and therefore there is no infringement.

In short, if Chinese authorities find copyrighted works to be unconstitutional or immoral, then these works are not protected in China. Immorality can mean many things and in the Chinese context it extends to 'the publication or distribution of which is prohibited' because of 'unconstitutional or immoral' or 'reactionary, pornographic or superstitious' content. The West does not incorporate denial of copyright protection based on such matters because censorship is an entirely separate legal matter. China's position is, simply put, that upon successful approval of content review, protection will be afforded – but this is contingent upon administrative and legal acceptance.

It was further submitted that Chinese 'Regulations on the Administration of Publications' forbid constitutionally offensive materials. In certain respects any matter that jeopardizes the unification, sovereignty and territorial integrity of the state is deemed against the public interest. Such matters extend to state security and its 'prestige', matters that may incite hatred and discrimination among ethnic groups, harm their unity, or violate their customs and habits or that may propagate cults and superstition, disrupt public order and undermine social stability, propagate obscenity or violence, insult or slander others, or infringe upon legitimate rights and interests of others, jeopardize social ethics or fine national cultural traditions and/or other contents banned by laws, administrative regulations and provisions of the state. The ambit relating to the conditional protection of protection is very wide (Alford, 1995).

To Western observers these may appear convenient or artificial excuses, but under the Chinese system of law, copyright and copyright protection are distinguishable. Chinese authorities, and not US regulators, determine what is prohibited and what is protected under Chinese law. This is inconsistent with obligations under Article 9.1 of the TRIPS Agreement, and demonstrates the tensions that may be caused between international obligations, national sovereignty and constitutional powers.

The central point of contention for the US was that Chinese law facilitates commercial uncertainty by enabling pirates to profit at the expense of the legitimate rights holder. The US relied on Article 17 of the Berne Convention (1971), which does not permit signatories to deny copyright protection to authors.

China strenuously denied the allegations and defended its sovereign position that copyright protection is contingent upon content review. And, curiously, the US offered no evidence in support of its case, and simply relied on the text of agreements between member states (and some news articles concerning piracy). The US bore the burden of proof in the proceedings. The text of agreements between member states and some Western news articles concerning piracy were of little or no probative value. China submitted that the US offered no evidence in support of its case at all. It is hard to ignore China's submissions given the evidence presented by the US did not support the objective gravity of the allegations made by the US.

This significant case, involving the two most powerful nations in the world, demonstrates just how limited the scope and operation of WIPO's treaties are when applied in a real legal scenario involving major political players. The threat of trade sanctions aside, it appears that when the rules are seriously tested by the application of sovereign laws WIPO, WTO and TRIPS are limited. The sovereign power to prohibit works is recognized, for example in Article 17 of the Berne Convention (1971), but signatories are permitted to maintain a domestic law, for example as in the Chinese copyright law.

These domestic laws may represent nothing more than a façade of protection and copyright recognition. But it should be remembered that China's state and sovereign power within its territory is just that – supreme and ultimate. Any monopoly of power was acquired along radically different and revolutionary lines, namely Maoist interpretations of Marxism. China has never accepted colonial (Western) economic foundations. Its military struggle against capitalism since 1939 is the basis for this proposition. The Revolution of 1949 was a triumph against Western imperialism. It makes perfect sense that China might view Western ideals of übercopyright as imperialistic. In other words, why should it dilute or diminish the value of its Cultural Revolution ideals because powerful WIPO and WTO member states (and their allies – especially Australia and Canada) feel aggrieved about alternative copyright models?

Popular culture is just that – culture; and in the Chinese tradition, vigilance in safeguarding the work of the Revolution has been paramount. These political ideologies may appear at first artificial and nebulous in today's transglobal economic arena – but they are enshrined in Chinese copyright law (Alford, 1995). This point matters enormously for a nation's sovereignty and self-determination. Australia, for example, recognizes copyright in its constitution.

Another point of contention in the proceedings was that the US felt aggrieved that China permits social welfare bodies to sell infringing goods. China's right to dispose of pirated goods is in line with its legal responsibility to ensure that goods as 'donations' are used exclusively for social welfare purposes (for example, by the Red Cross Society of China). The US again construed these actions as nothing more than a vehicle through which to recycle illegal products back onto the market. These domestic directives defied international obligations and thereby caused harm to the actual copyright owners. China had never resisted the on-selling for charitable purposes allegation, but strenuously denied that goods make their way into commerce. More importantly, no evidence was proffered to support this allegation.

For the last five decades, people in China have been fed, educated and supported by a system that does its best to enforce equality among all its members; no one, including intellectuals, is supposed to profit from the work of the vanguard (Wan and Lu, 1997). Recycling products for charity is not a bizarre proposition in this ideological context given that copyright legislation and enforcement evolved from divergent ideologies. As a side issue, what if the Western artist whose copyrights have been infringed morally wishes to have his or her counterfeited goods sold to international organizations such as UNESCO for charitable reasons? There would no legal basis to allow such commercial actions where assignment or waivers have been provided. It is doubtful that WIPO would condone such actions. In any event, the case was not concerned with creators' attitudes and moral beliefs, but the entrepreneurial copyrights vested in the works.

Assume for one moment that altruism of this kind prevailed in the West. Imagine using the proceeds of illegal activity for altruistic reasons – akin to, say, Good Samaritan behaviour in the West. Suppose a warehouse in Sydney full of high-quality pirated top–20 CDs is raided or a London supplier is charged with supplying pirated R4 Card Nintendo chips used to circumvent Nintendo DS and the merchandise is seized. Different laws come into play, including copyright legislation and relevant criminal codes and statutes. The obvious fate for the high quality is certain – destruction. Yet instead of these counterfeit goods being destroyed pursuant to a destruction order, they are kept, recycled and sold on to charities for social good and humanitarian reasons in China. Imagine the corporate furore if proceeds from pirated Lady Gaga CDs went to the *Big Issue* or the sale of 'rip-off' *Shrek* DVDs were given to the Starlight Children's Foundation for sick children.

Altruists in the West who believe in a utilitarian or redistributive view of copyright would applaud such practical measures. These products are generally viewed as no different to seized illicit drugs and thereby deemed harmful in the West. Indeed, symbolically, these destruction orders are reminiscent of Beatles and Rolling Stones record-burning parties inspired by 'new moral' evangelical ministers in the US and the Thatcherite morality purges in the 1980s where police seized and successfully sought destruction orders for respectably high-selling independently released records pursuant to the Obscene Publications Act 1959.[14] But unlike illicit drugs, these popular media are not branded with the same moral turpitude, notwithstanding that piracy is an illegal act. Laws contained in provisions are breached, but concepts of Samaritanism in relation to these illegal goods are invoked. True, these goods are not proper goods and corporate social responsibility would not extend to laundering cheap rip-offs. This point matters because moral questions relating to corporate wealth gained through the creation of surplus value against charitable actions in relation to recycling illegal but functional goods must certainly cross the minds of ordinary citizens in the West.

Yet, much to the abhorrence and overall frustration of aggrieved Western nations (notably the US and various 'coalition of the willing' member states such as Australia), this is what China condones. It actions go against every modern Western copyright legal principle and legal obligation. Those actions dilute the value of destruction, injunctions and related Anton Pillar orders in some respects.

Needless to say, in advanced capitalist societies there is no balancing act when pirated popular media is involved. The goods are destroyed and costs orders made against the perpetrators. The law in the West is well settled.

The issue is not so much what to do or what not to do about pirated media, but what sovereign states do or not do. International obligations require that signatories strike a balance between social concerns, on the one hand, and the protection and preservation of copyright on the other. Article 46 of TRIPs requires that disposal of illegal goods be a 'neutral' operation for rights holders. There is no mandate placed on a signatory state. Domestic administrative bodies and local enforcement agencies cannot be compelled to destroy the goods. Indeed they may 'dispose of them outside the channels of commerce'. In this case, China allegedly donated the proceeds of infringed goods to the Red Cross. However, humanitarian donations must be qualified by a condition that seeks 'to avoid any harm caused to the rights holder'.

Another point of contention raised by the US was that China's regulatory system is currently fundamentally inadequate to deal with perpetrators (namely pirates). China's criminal law was adopted by the National People's Congress in 1979, revised by the National People's Congress in 1997 and promulgated by Order of the President of the People's Republic of China in 1997. The criminal law is divided into two parts: Part 1, sets out 'General Provisions', and Part 2, sets out 'Specific Provisions'. Part 2, Chapter III, of China's criminal law (1979) ('crimes of disrupting the order of the socialist market economy') contains both substantive and procedural laws relating to certain crimes, including copyright violations. Chapter III, section 7, relates to 'crimes of infringing upon intellectual property rights'. In section 7, Article 117 expressly relates to copyright infringement and provides for terms of imprisonment and fines by way of deterrence.

The central contention made by US and Japan was again whether the Chinese legislation had any practical and meaningful effect or whether the copyright prosecutorial policies were artificial in nature. Two issues arise. First, criminal law concerning citizens domiciled in China is expressly a national issue, and any formal reading of the criminal law would support the argument that China has adequate laws addressing copyright infringement. For example, it includes a tiered structure similar in principle to that under the Crimes Act 1909 (Australia). Second, there was no forensic evidence tendered by the US in relation to DVD piracy, or Japan in relation to games piracy, to test the strengths and weaknesses of the criminal law.

The US demonstrated very clear objective analyses of the statutory breaches and the dealing of infringed goods. Prima facie there was a case. But given the fact that in copyright cases there is no reverse onus of proof, it is up to the aggrieved party to forensically present relevant and direct evidence. Hearsay and anecdotal evidence through newspaper reports and 'stories' of wholesale piracy are not enough. But, more relevantly, the Chinese government openly admitted that its views on copyright recognition, protection and infringements substantively differ from the position in the West.

Given the unresolved copyright issues in China, what was achieved? The US did not win the dispute (in terms of the adversarial concepts of 'winning' and 'losing'). The US must have felt disappointed with the contents of the Board's report. But according to WTO, on 15 April 2009 China informed the Disputes Board that it intended to implement some of the recommendations and adopt into its domestic laws the relevant protocols (namely revision of its customs policies for the enforcement of intellectual property rights (IPRs)). There is no evidence to suggest the US is satisfied that the issues have been meaningfully resolved.

The US was not entirely unsuccessful despite the fact that there was a prima facie case against China to suggest copyright infringement occurs in China on a large scale and on a regular basis. This fascinating case brings to the fore the precarious and unresolved issues to which global copyright governance relates. It must not be forgotten that in the past China was subject to Western imperial influence. China was shamefully and brutally exploited by the Japanese in the 1930s. Mao Tse-Tung's cultural revolutionaries held dim views about Western conceptions of intellectual property and Western intelligentsia that sought to appropriate intellectual ownership and create a separate commodity (intangible rights) from combined effects of labour power. The fusion of physical and intellectual capacity of persons was based on the ideology that factory workers do not need to mark newly made 'ingots', so why should an author claim authorship?[15] Such struggles remind the Western reader that formal progress, as evidenced by ratified treaties and protocols, does not ensure substantive protection. China celebrated 30 years as a WIPO member in 2010.

What if the US challenged a Yugoslav member of WIPO?

For a successful international framework to be promoted and sustained, the preconditions must firmly be established. Take the former Yugoslav republics as an example. Slovenia, Serbia and Croatia are all member states of WIPO and, like China, are nations of interest in relation to media piracy issues. Like Mao Tse-Tung's China, Yugoslavia was also born of Marxist ideology. But Yugoslavia was unique in that Titoism and market socialism staved off Stalinism and the Kremlin's ambition to subsume it as another Eastern Bloc satellite. Firmly situated in an East–West corridor, this nation carved out very impressive trade negotiations with both the Eastern Bloc and the West during the Cold War. This was not entirely difficult because whilst it had no common law history, European civil jurisprudence and governance influenced Yugoslavia to some extent. Glenny (1996, p. 6) asserts: 'Without question, the economic traditions of Slovenia and Croatia to the west of this line have developed in closer harmony with Western ideas in the twentieth century, whereas to the east of this divide, the corrupt barter mentality of the Ottomans still dominates the rural economies of Serbia, Bulgaria, Macedonia, Bosnia, Montenegro and Albania.' It should not come as a curious surprise therefore that there was integration of reasonably similar Western corporate copyright industries (namely in Croatia and Slovenia).

Indeed, I distinctly recall visiting Yugoslavia in the 1980s and purchasing a variety of affordable quality original vinyl records and cassettes (from *Bronski Beat* to *Human League*) that proudly displayed the 'Made in Yugoslavia' sticker. The rights to manufacture were licensed from Western major record companies to private, semi-private and government-owned corporate-controlled labels and record companies such as Jugoton, Suzy and Radio Beograd.

I marvelled at the quality of the products pressed at the Makedonska 21 plant, and of the purchases made at various private and state-controlled retailers, and wondered what the word 'SOKOJ' (royalty-collecting society) meant. I compared these purchases to the cheap but good-quality pirated cassettes of Depeche Mode purchased en route in the United Arab Emirates. It is also worth noting, since the original Yugoslav ended in the mid-1990s, formal copyright governance reflecting WIPO's ideals has largely remained intact. This can probably be explained by the closer ties with the more powerful former republics (Slovenia and Croatia) and their desires to be rapidly integrated into a greater pan-European community.

It is fair to conclude that where Western conceptions of copyright governance were already established in former Communist and/or colonial regimes in Europe (including Hungary's previous socialist market), copyright governance may appear less challenging and the potential for implementation of international integration into domestic settings is far greater than in, say, China. The legal reality is that where WIPO nations with previously established principles of Western copyright might conform to this new hope for world intellectual property order, others with structurally different ideologies remain a challenge. It follows that the US or other Western nations may exert influence and thus be successful against an allegedly non-compliant nation – not because they are more powerful per se, but probably because the dominant copyright ideological framework is already firmly established. As is set out in Chapter 7, trade sanctions are ordinarily invoked in any event should there be a failure to comply with the conditions and undertakings relating to copyright governance imposed on all WIPO and WTO members concurrently aligned by agreements – namely TRIPS. These bilateral and occasionally multilateral processes ensure that duties are discharged on the domestic front. In effect, concurrent membership of copyright and trade institutions provides a form of cross-collateralization for powerful trading nations that suspect another nation's non-delegable duties might be flouted. One example is the threat of trade sanctions where a nation fails to systematically administer copyright regulation. Another example relates to action where a nation (usually the US) believes that another nation is systemically ignoring media piracy domestically. But as any sensible reader will realize, trade sanctions would be hard to impose on China. How can copyright law be anything other than political?

Conclusion: copyright governance – the artificial reality of risk minimization

In modern copyright settings, governance risk factors include global communications and related innovations sensitive to rapid innovative change. In *Dow Jones v Gutnick* (2002) the challenge to global governance by developing digital communications (namely the Internet) was identified. This High Court decision recognizes the need for different approaches for the current framework. Justice Kirby (at para. 50) summarized the issues as follows:

> To wait for legislatures or multilateral international agreements to provide solutions to the legal problems presented by the Internet would abandon those problems to 'agonizingly slow' processes of lawmaking ... The alternative, in practice, could be an institutional failure to provide effective laws in harmony, as the Internet itself is, with contemporary civil society – national and international.

Packets of external, non-neutral digitalized global technologies have arrived. Contrast the narrow scope of copyright governance to the infinitely limitless potential of digitalization, namely:

- the ability to infinitely reproduce popular media with no loss of quality (uploads and downloads);
- the ease of communication of works in more than an ephemeral form between individuals and groups (social networks);
- the reduction or removal of the burden of marginal costs of reproduction or distribution of copies (legally or illegally) (freedom of choice); and
- the ability to allow anyone with Internet access to view works (democratization).

The above list is a reflection of attitudes expressed by Western consumers about ownership of chattels vis-á-vis copyright. Coupled with the divergent cultural attitudes and domestic policy expressed by powerful non-Western members of WIPO and WTO, these developments do not support harmonious global copyright governance. Whilst a separate legal identity such as copyright possesses an economic imperative for owners, it is doubtful whether this rigid legal framework possesses the anticipatory capacity for understanding modern popular media consumption and emerging challenges. WIPO and national associations certainly react to technological change by implementing and administering treaties and international agreements.

Implemention of treaties at the national level and acceptance of the TRIPS Agreement are necessary features of WTO membership. To avoid disputes and sanctions against recalcitrant member states, TRIPS mandates modification to domestic legislative and executive branches of government; and for developing countries this must seem an onerous task given the difficulties in establishing rule of law transparency in government. Demands to develop and implement sophisticated and robust copyright governance frameworks must seem superficial to member nations such as Rwanda and other less developed member countries whose constitutions cannot be compared to Western ones. For example, Australia's 1901 Constitution (which has rarely been amended) expressly recognizes the significance of establishing nationhood powers relating to copyright.[16] Formal membership is not the same as substantive recognition and acceptance of international obligations. This is one area of weakness in international copyright governance. Convergence of national copyright laws sounds more like a political agenda than a meaningful response.

As Kirby J held in *Stevens* (2005), litigation is 'a product of a compromise agreed to, or forced upon, interest groups in the industry affected by the legislation'. The law of copyrights (enshrined in statutes and cases) seems to suggest an ongoing demerging compromise as opposed to some consolidation or convergence of the copyright regime.

Formal conceptions of harmonization might present a successful picture of international global governance. Technology-neutral language and policy implementation might be recognized and accepted for advanced WIPO member states. Assistance in transferring technology to developing nations has been formally acknowledged for some time now (see Article 10 in the Agreement between the United Nations and the World Intellectual Property Organization). But the substantive reality is that global copyright has not been achieved, and it is doubtful that it can extend beyond the façade of formalism in which it is contained.

Administering hegemonic control through the appearance of striking a balance remains the theoretical basis for copyright governance and policy implementation. Reading the Preambles of WIPO agreements relating to copyright, the reader immediately is reminded of Lockean concepts of natural rights. Locke considered that property rights arise naturally upon the application of labour. The right to ownership and exploitation are seen as justified because they have been earned by the investment of things such as time, energy and intellect. These core values certainly epitomize attributes vested in the first copyright owner.

According to Locke, the world that God created is commonly available to the person prepared to labour for the common good of creating something (naturally for reward) so that others may benefit from such fruitful labour. In this person's world there seems to be a limit to the excesses of exploitation, or at least taking more than is commonly acceptable is 'unnatural'. This view is a utilitarian view embedded in notions of 'democratic wealth'[17] as opposed to 'elite wealth' created by a dominant minority (one of the subjects of the next chapter).

3
Corporate Control of Popular Media (and Culture): Competition Law and Policy in Popular Culture

Introduction: corporations and copyright – merging or converging, controlling or uncontrolled?

You are of course aware of the recent changes to the Copyright Act 1968 which permit the direct importation into Australia, for commercial sale, of *non-infringing* copies of CDs made overseas. *Both the Australian Government and the ACCC have spent considerable time and resources explaining the so-called benefits of this new legislation to the Australian consumer, and particularly the retailer, with the emphasis on encouraging you, the retailer, to import from overseas (and not to buy locally).*

This new parallel import regime provides a *substantial opportunity for counterfeit stocks* to come into Australia. Legitimate stocks may be mixed with infringing copies, giving the already overburdened Customs Department, a virtually impossible task of detection ...

You do have an alternative. You can stop importing PolyGram repertoire from these suppliers. *We would rather have you as a customer, than as a litigant.* (at para. 77)

If you parallel import, PolyGram would also review its terms of trading and it may cease to have a trading relationship with you. *We won't look upon you with any favours if you parallel import. It's not good for the industry.* (at para. 42, emphasis added)

The above evidence was obtained by the Australian consumer 'watchdog', the Australian Competition and Consumer Commission (ACCC). This regulator investigated Universal Music Australia Pty Limited and Warner Music Australia Pty for various breaches of trade practices. They were found guilty and penalized in relation to two out of three separate breaches of the relevant legislation.[1] These corporate citizens were effectively prosecuted and sentenced, given the use of the words 'penalty', 'parity' and 'deterrence' by the judge at first instance.

The above example explicates the substantive depth of control major media companies exert on others in the marketplace. But it also highlights the potential for deceptive, misleading, threatening and aggressive attitudes displayed by dominant major players when their naturally monopolistic habitats are challenged. On appeal, the sentence (a substantial fine) was reduced, and one of the findings was overturned. But the issues of control, coercion and anticompetitive behaviour were squarely proved. Whether or not a tribunal of fact and law makes a finding of guilt (in whole or in part), the emphasized parts of the above quotes constitute marketplace harassment (akin to, say, bullying and threats in the workplace) and suggest cartel-like behaviour that only a dominant few are capable of exerting.[2]

In this light, the popular media industry is defined as an oligopolistic 'monopoly' where only a *few* participants with similar or near-identical products are substantially concentrated in the market. These major players exert more than obvious influence. They are also acutely aware of their influence over the marketplace specifically, and consumers generally. They should not be described as 'monopolistically competitive' because they purport to promote different products (through various labels or clever market-branding and genre creation). Rather, these sellers meta-govern popular media, their products are homogenized and the concentration of power therefore suggests overt market dominance. It follows that issues relating to low barriers to entry for independent players ('indies'), fair price-setting, consumer choice and other healthy elements relating to economic competition have not traditionally existed in popular media. The gaming industry, the last to be subsumed under a highly concentrated model, now tends to lead the charge in terms of barriers to entry (see generally, Williams, 2002).

Chapter 2 was concerned with international copyright organizations and the manner in which copyright is controlled and supervised for the express purpose of exploitation. The overriding theme was firmly based on the observation that a monopolized political and legal environment for the marketization of copyright (the process of bringing copyright to a market economy) exists in Western society. This chapter examines these issues in the light of the manner in which popular media products are presented to consumers. The central argument is that it is difficult to conceive how well adjusted and balanced the delivery of popular media is in the light of an overbalanced concentration of a dominant few. Providing balance, or attempting 'to strike a balance' as posited by the World Intellectual Property Organization (WIPO) and industry representatives, seems to very popular in debates concerning copyright industries and competition regulation. But the term 'balance' requires greater examination given that an imbalance in power has always existed between original copyright owners and corporate copyright owners.

Formal conceptions of competition law are premised on the ability to strike a balance between protecting consumers from unnatural business behaviour in capitalist society and ensuring fairness to all producers (great and small) – for the benefit of consumption. But realistically, how do consumers as bottom-up participants in popular media fare against the top-down organizational structure of major corporations? It was suggested in the previous chapter that the balancing act is probably not as balanced as it purports to be. Popular media industries are not a *Wirtschaftswunder* or beneficiaries of a random chance of fortune through laissez-faire economics. Instead, domination has been an absolute design through the convergence of natural and temporary monopolistic behaviour that has enabled such a bold and anticompetitive status quo.

The following sections focus on the manner in which global corporate popular media industries are organized. The consolidation of emerging technologies (tangible products) and copyrights (intangible property) is identified. Also examined is the rise of corporate media ownership through transglobal capitalism in the light of underdeveloped domestic competition policy and regulation and its weak international governance framework. The creation of an international cartel-like status quo comprising a dominant few is also reaffirmed.

In particular, the second section provides an overview of corporate behaviour in naturally occurring monopolistic environments. The relevant historical conditions for the promotion and encouragement of anticompetitive behaviour are analysed. This leads to a consideration of the extent of such behaviour in popular media given the perfect conditions established by copyright through temporary monopolies. The overwhelming concentration of power in music, film and gaming is discussed, including a brief discussion on the moral dilemma for original copyright owners who might wish to maintain some integrity from their sweat and toil in the Lockean sense, or at least dignity in their exploited corporatized works.

A discussion of copyright law and anticompetitive behaviour in popular media ownership also raises several relevant questions about convergence and digitalization. The fourth section (The extent of anticompetitive behaviour in popular media industries) assesses the impact made by emerging and external modes of consumption on the current concentrated status quo. These externalities appear to represent a reaction to the paradoxical convergence of natural and temporary monopolies (the creation of naturally occurring perpetual monopolies). This assessment is achieved by presenting a theoretical extrapolation of the possibility of challenging this natural state through alternative modes of consumption (effectively setting the scene for Chapter 8). The conclusion is that the proximate features of entrepreneurial copyright and corporate behaviour must be acknowledged. They are both borne of artificiality, abstraction, are creatures of statute, and are inclined to function in a universally exclusive and monopolistic state. The observation that corporations (like copyright) have no prima facie moral code is also made because they are legally driven purely for financial gain.

Therefore moral considerations are difficult to contextualize in this artificial setting, thereby validating and encouraging anticompetitive behaviour.

These assertions are based on the fact that naturally occurring monopolies exist in popular media. This is because corporate control of popular media has created a monopoly over content and delivery. The music and gaming industries are horizontally and vertically integrated so as to secure as much exploitable copyright as possible in order to organize it in a material form through internal technological control. This approach is not too dissimilar to the motion picture industry where it has been found that external and internal economies of scale combined with imperfect competition and vertical integration have been critical in securing concentrated power (Canterbery and Marvasti, 2001, p. 97).

The rationale for having vested interests in a variety of related industries is, therefore, obvious. As Longhurst (1995, pp. 33–34) maintains:

> For example, an artist may record in a studio owned by a company which manufactures a disc from the recording at one of its plants, which is then reviewed in a magazine owned by that company (which may also include a review of the film made by the artist for a film company owned by the same conglomerate) and sold to the public in a shop owned by the company.

Such vertical integration enables complete control and maintenance of the product from start to finish – that is production flow from raw materials (including intellectual property) to sales (Peterson and Berger, 1990, p. 143). However, competition governance and copyright governance are not symbiotic or mutualistic in liberal democratic societies.

The convergence of natural and temporary monopolies: unnatural and anticompetitive

Enjoying statutorily enshrined copyright monopolies over respective copyrighted catalogues is not uncommon in the West. As Lee (1995, p. 16) suggests, this behaviour has unequivocally assisted in the consolidation of film, television, recording, publishing, electronics, computers, advertising and talent-brokering and has resulted in a group of powerful oligopolies that broker cultural materials in much the same way as any other commodity would be sold.

For example, in the *ACCC* case this meant that prior to 1998 a retailer who wished to source a Warner product produced locally under license by Warner (Australia) was prima facie unable to source the identical product from legitimate overseas suppliers. These monopolistic practices were legally sanctioned by copyright law and, to this end, the majors through their representatives vehemently opposed any change to the Copyright Act 1968.

The aggressively jealous reaction by these corporate citizens to the parallel importation amendment was perfectly natural under the circumstances.

Popular culture sold to consumers by the dominant media industry has little to do with competition. The industry is anticompetitive because in the traditional model the media does not respond to consumer demands. On the surface, popular media industries purport to run as perfect natural monopolies as they own the dominant means of capital and production (especially the internal technologies) and are formally regulated accordingly. The creation of naturally occurring monopolies through both the control of technological means (tangible) and copyright (intangible) however creates an interesting scenario. These combined conditions enable firms to set the terms through the creation of monopolies via the control of the copyright through statutes (temporary) and through internal technological ownership (format ownership). Simultaneously, temporary monopolies and natural monopolies therefore converge. As the name suggests, temporary monopolies are supposed to disappear when copyright periods expire. But through perpetual technological innovation and subsequent exploitation through rereleases and remasters they remain, thereby creating an unnaturally anticompetitive state. In theory such an environment might formally be monitored and reviewed, but the legal reality is that substantively it is difficult to regulate.

Take the example of Sony Corporation. It is a market leader in all forms of media entertainment, and since the introduction of the Betamax videocassette in the 1970s it has dominated the home entertainment media market. It (or rather, a handful of identically organized firms) not only sets the manner and mode in which goods and services are consumed, but it establishes the price. This is a natural monopolistic state – a state that the majors largely enjoyed throughout the twentieth century. That is, successive waves of format ownership (from vinyl to cassette to CD and so on) combined with back-catalogue ownership and rights to permit covers (and other forms of zero-cost recycling) means virtually no or low interaction costs. Here is where advanced capitalist society finds a convergence of distinct monopolies as the catalyst for anticompetitive behaviour. Copyright temporary monopolies and natural monopolies are not supposed to converge because this provides a barrier to an effective and competitive economy. This is how a multinational corporate-driven industry controls popular culture.

The paradox is obvious. Despite product differentiation and fierce competition in terms of copyright acquisition, cooperation amongst the majors is remarkable. Goold and Campbell (1998, p. 134) maintain: 'in the music industry, the four leading companies will often share the same CD-manufacturing plant in countries with insufficient sales to support four separate plants.' As each product is unique, the industry's major concern is to make its value chain of production as cost effective as possible. It achieves this by ensuring a tightly knit distribution chain. It is argued that this form of commercial (almost joint-venture-like) cooperation extends beyond saving direct manufacturing or interaction costs. In 1983, Philips and Sony launched the CD, and its superior quality and convenience guaranteed the demise of the vinyl record. Philips and Sony (as electronics and format manufacturers), along with the other majors, had comprehensive artists' repertoires. These two companies focused on providing the few other majors with the opportunity to access the technology. As Torres (1999, p. 29) elaborates:

> By licensing the CD technologies to competitors at an early stage, Philips and Sony prevented them from developing alternative forms, which could have provoked a long and draining format war like the one between video formats VHS and Betamax. In short, Philips and Sony focused on expanding the market, not just their own share of it.

What is also evident is that, irrespective of label name, different major record companies are organized virtually identically in that they all adopt identical processes. Their cultural products are well differentiated, but the formats are uniform thereby facilitating the rate of acquisition, appropriation and consolidation within the music industry. The major players are remarkably fluid – provided the formats are uniform.

By way of further example, in *Australian Competition and Consumer Commission v Universal Music Australia Pty Ltd (formerly known as PolyGram Pty Ltd) and Others* (N925 of 1999) (*ACCC* case), Hill J at para. 295 (emphasis added) describes Universal's globally encompassing persona as follows:

> Similarly the operations of Universal and its affiliates globally encompass the development, production, manufacture, marketing, promotion, sales and distribution of recorded music and exploitation of copyrights in sound recordings embodying recorded music through a network of Universal subsidiaries, joint ventures and third-party licensees in 40 countries or territories around the world. Universal affiliates in each territory sign artists under agreements that *typically included an assignment* in perpetuity of the worldwide copyright in sound recordings produced by the artist. The affiliates are parties to an 'all-in-fee agreement' under which each, for a fee, licenses the worldwide copyright (outside its territory) to a central entity and receives in return a licence to exploit (within its territory) the copyright of others. Before its merger with Universal, PolyGram and its worldwide affiliates signed artists under similar agreements and were parties to a substantially identical all-in-fee agreement.

In other words, irrespective of geography, major firms have become internationally and locally integrated (formatted) in order to maintain international harmonization (for a compelling investigation on these developments in a broader pop cultural and media sense, refer generally to Schiller 1969 and 2000).

The nature of anticompetitive behaviour: rise (and rise) of the corporate *übermensch*

Anticompetitive corporate behaviour relates to allegations of unfair monopolistic behaviour (that is, conduct substantially lessening competition). In determining exclusionary or anticompetitive conduct the relevant public benefits and detriments are weighed. These allegations usually centre on offensive behaviours. The most important consideration is whether a corporation with a substantial degree of power in a market takes advantage of that power to the detriment of others in that market. This may include whether such dominance prevents others from entering any market, whether such behaviour acts as a deterrent to others who wish to engage in fair and competitive conduct in the marketplace (for example independent players) and to what extent consumers are exposed to such detriment.

In a perfectly competitive environment many participants are involved, thus moderating influence over price and range because they are effectively 'keeping each other honest'. But in a monopoly environment there is only one dominant player capable of exerting significant influence over price (and in the case of popular media, format delivery). A group of identical firms fits the dominant player category because they are effectively a monopolistic oligopoly. They have no natural predators even when participants attempt to enter the market due to low barriers to entry. That is, anyone with an idea and the technology can hypothetically record a song, produce a film and make a game for a mobile application.[3] But these modes have no significant impact on the market in the traditional sense of product commodification. Accordingly the cartel maintains anticompetitive constraints, thereby having monopoly power or significant or substantial control – despite regulation.

The West refers to unfair monopolistic practices and related anticompetitive business conduct as 'antitrust'. The US has the Sherman Act 1890, but its initial attempts to curb unfair practices were clumsy (see below). Indeed Australia – effectively a politico-economic and legal hybrid of the US and Britain – was inspired by this legislation and implemented the modest Australian Industries Preservation Act 1906. It purported to prohibit monopolies, but parts of it were declared unconstitutional by the High Court after only three years (see *Huddart Parker & Co v Moorehead* (1909)). Eventually repealed in 1965, it was largely ad hoc and substantially ineffective.

Using the Australian experience as a cross-Western example, the Australian Competition and Consumer Act 2010 (formerly the Trade Practices Act 1974 (TPA)) best summarizes the purpose of such legislation. Its Preamble reads: 'The object of this Act is to enhance the welfare of Australians through the promotion of competition and fair trading and provision for consumer protection.' The dominant purpose for the implementation of such legislation is to protect society and theoretically promote economic efficiency (see generally, Burgess, 1989).

The first observation about the significance of comprehensive protectionist laws is that they are relatively recent (compared to copyright laws and corporation laws allowing the creation of artificial citizens' governance). The policies and subsequent laws were comparably underdeveloped when corporations had a head start in creating the status quo. Laws concerning anticompetitive behaviour stem from reactive rather than anticipatory governance.

For example, Australia, the ninth largest music market in the world, did not implement comprehensive competition laws until 1974. The following quote from the Second Reading of the Bill summarizes the state of imbalance:

> [T]his is the first legislation ... which is expressly aimed at protecting and reinforcing the individual consumer's position in the market place ... I think we all know that consumers are the largest but regrettably the least organised economic group in the community ... What we are proposing in this Bill is a consumers' charter, that is, a bill of rights for Australians as consumers. (House of Representatives, *Hansard*, July 24, 1974, p. 574 per Mr Morrison (St George – Minister for Science)).

The EU's position is even less impressive. While the importance of competition policy was acknowledged in the Treaty of Rome (1957), EU nations did not commence the process of formally implementing more robust and harmonized competition laws until 1993 (Braakman and Dutilh, 1997; Van Bael, (2005); El-Agraa (2007)). It appears that in the first three to four decades after World War II in Western Europe, only ad hoc competition policies were implemented. During this period, meaningful competition initiatives were rarely formalized either by way of domestic policy implementation or EU legislation, thereby suggesting disjointedly incremental attempts towards *acquis communautaire*. Johnson and Turner (2006), El-Agraa (2007) and Kovacic (2008) comprehensively assess trans-European global business initiatives in the light of inconsistent administration across regions and region to region. Cross-border incompatibilities should not be ignored in light of significant cultural, political and economic disparities. Some of the inductees into this Euro-club are quasi-developing nations compared to the 'neo-imperial' political heavyweights. This also lends credence to Hanlon's (1998, p. 11) observation that in terms of membership, 'citizenship of the Union in any meaningful sense is largely symbolic'.

The EU system requires each Member State to enact anticompetitive regulation for robust competition governance (for example, Britain's Competition Act 1998). In the EU, issues are significantly more problematic where deregulation to encourage greater borderless cooperation and integration for operational convenience has been divested to small and often ill-equipped economies.

Some of these nations are not realistically capable of competing at an advanced regulatory level. Since 2004, therefore, the EU devolved to Member States' competition authorities concurrent responsibility for the administration of community competition law. Regulation is enforced through national courts, and emphasis is placed on the importance of effective and uniform application of the laws along with efficient supervision and simplified administration (El-Agraa, 2007).

Germany, Britain and France certainly possess the capacity to achieve substantive and robust competition regulatory frameworks. The legal histories of these common law and civil code nations provide evidence of attempts to curb profiteering through sharp trade practices (see Motta's (2004) historical assessment of German and British competition policy objectives and legislative approaches). In my view it would be an impotent political reality to accept that the 'others' could achieve the same result in any meaningful sense. But on a note of cautious optimism, nations that once formed the Czech lands and Austro-Hungarian Empire might construct a robust and effective administration for competition regulation. These nations once possessed a sophisticated tradition of German-inspired administrative systems influenced along Weberian legal-rational lines of authority, political legitimation and bureaucracy. Weber argued that in advanced societies legal-rational authority prevails because the state and citizens (including artificial citizens) are constrained by the law. Formal rational authority in Western societies is vital for capitalism, according to Weber. Such bureaucratization effectively administers competition and exchange, as well as commodification, in mass markets. Rational legitimacy constrained by a constitution assists in collective administration and deliberative planning (for example, regulating anticompetitive behaviour) (see Tucker (2002) on Weber).

Yet it is difficult to conceive how public policy governance frameworks in Member States such as Bulgaria, Romania, Turkey or Greece and other aspiring Balkan nations might substantively facilitate both copyright (piracy) regulation issues and competition policy objectives at a micro-level (domestic level), meso-level (upstream interaction at the EU level) and ultimately at a macro-level (global considerations as members of WIPO and the World Trade Organization (WTO)). Historically, these Member States have been unable to dialectically materialize transparent administration in terms of Weberian conceptions of responsible governance because of Ottoman oppression and subsequent instabilities and identity crises (Mazower, 2000, pp. 28–30, 127). The EU directives on formal governance aim at the maintenance of political stability and regional harmony. In the absence of cogent evidence, only time will tell whether substantive uniform laws can be meaningfully administered. It is doubtful because even more influential Western regulatory systems (including Japan's US-influenced anti-monopoly laws) struggle to control the rise of the firm (First and Shiraishi (2005)).

Perhaps the governments of EU Member States and Australia can explain the challenges given these laws are relatively recent. But what of the US – the most concentrated and most corporatized popular media centre on the planet? Its arms of government have been administering antitrust legislation for the benefit of its consumers since 1890. If anything, resultant monopolistic behaviour in the form of exclusive contracts, unilateral licensing arrangements, complicated price-setting and sharp trading practices generally have epitomized popular media industries – notwithstanding that the 1890 Sherman Act was augmented by the Clayton Antitrust Act in 1914 (with enforcement provisions contained in the Federal Trade Commission Act) and in turn by the Robinson-Patman Act 1936 in a bid to protect consumers and new or independent market entrants from oppressive or predatory pricing (essentially favourable price-setting).

In so far as US Federal Trade Commission (FTC) initiatives are concerned, in the 1960s regulatory action concerning overt monopolistic conduct by the media giant CBS was particularly evident.[4] The petitions and complaints against CBS, and the Reprise Records action against Capitol Records Inc. affirm the sheer power exercised by dominant firms that have had decades of unfettered consolidation enabled by ad hoc or disjointed regulation of pricing and exclusive copyright licensing systems (refer generally to the reported FTC decisions in the July to December 1967 volume). Formal recognition of the need to address anticompetitive behaviour is clearly evident, but in the US, attempts to tame the so-called anticompetitive landscape appear to be predominated by private actions and petitions based on judicial interpretation (essentially a case-by-case approach). The US system can thus be categorized as displaying weak antitrust governance.

As mentioned below, scholars such as Veblen warned of anticompetitive practices in the US and in a modern setting back in the 1920s. The rise of the corporate citizen has largely occurred in an unfettered way as a consequence of disjointed and ad hoc incremental regulation and policies premised on economic rationalism. At both national and international levels its prominence has now become so institutionally entrenched that transglobal corporate governance permeates all aspects of daily life. This is a perfectly compatible environment for copyright and corporate governance frameworks given that the bulk of exploitable copyrights are exclusively controlled by a handful of anticompetitive corporate citizens.

In more recent years, the more dynamic features of popular media controllers have demonstrated the capacity to enter into various transnational, semi-permanent commercial arrangements (joint ventures, mutual benefit agreements and other more fluid arrangements). Aggressive mergers, hostile takeovers and traditional corporate behaviour are objectively simple to identify, monitor and review compared to newer developments.

Arm's length, corporate partnering, memoranda of understanding, joint ventures and other less rigid contractual arrangements are difficult to conceptualize in terms of competition law. The spectrum can range from a single transaction to alliances of various sorts. A joint venture is a hybrid arrangement. It differs from a conventional setting and resembles firm-like behaviour where firms might substitute a permanent governance mechanism allocating control, ownership and profits for a temporary deal on price or research development outcome. It differs from complete integration through a merger in that the parties typically retain significant control over their contribution through veto rights. This popular mode of business in popular media makes competition policy regulation a vexed issue. In other words, how does one identify the relevant obligation holder for an alleged breach of competition law if there is not a specific entity exercising control?

Complaints against restrictive horizontal alliances might be explained in light of the above arrangements. Each entity will lay blame on the other if one is deemed to be anticompetitive. By way of a social Darwinist analogy: hostile corporate takeovers are easily identifiable in that that a larger entity subsumes a smaller one thereby consolidating commercial interests upstream in order to ensure survival of the fittest (that is, the largest corporation). But when a handful of large firms form alliances in the form of joint ventures, regulation of specific conduct concerning overt market dominance becomes increasingly difficult to detect. Such partnership arrangements are mutually beneficial because of the similarities shared by these entities, but are loose in the sense that it is difficult to specifically identify where obligations intersect in terms of competition regulation. Market dominance through formal mergers and acquisitions is relatively easy to identify. Fluid transnational arrangements where corporations have found conditions historically favourable for rapid consolidation have been made possible by weak or underdeveloped competition policies. Corporations in late or advanced capitalism are passive-aggressive in nature in that they represent a reaction (Mandel, 1975) to any restrictive development that may threaten the status quo in the corporate governance of popular culture (Leavis, 1933).

It is not the purpose of trade practices/antitrust legislation that is in issue, but the nature of corporate control of copyright and popular media itself that is incongruent with the ideals and objectives of such protectionist laws. Indeed, Hill J in the *ACCC* case against Universal and Warner observed (at para. 294 (emphasis added)): 'The case of a firm operating in an oligopolistic market with only 15% market share but which has, as a result of a *temporary monopoly power* over a limited number of products in that market; substantial power to exclude competitors.' That is, corporations disseminate products broadly but uniformly whilst exclusively and narrowly consolidating copyright. Consumption of popular media may be described as convergent, but so can monopolization in that corporations merge, acquire, conglomerate and mutually benefit one another at the expense of consumers.

Commenting on the empirical realities of Great Britain in the mid-nineteenth century, Marx first identified the anticompetitive nature of corporations and the economic laws under which they sought to operate. Veblen's observations in 1923 about the anticompetitive nature of corporations in the dominant US mode of capitalism also set the scene in which to cast popular media industries (1954, pp. 107–109). Checks and balances on corporate behaviour were largely symbolic according to Veblen in the early part of the twentieth century. He warned the world of dangers in placing too much reliance on unbridled artificial citizenry. (One undisputed fact preceding the Great Depression was that the so-called roaring twenties was a period in US economic policy where business was generally left to its own laissez-faire devices. It is fair to infer the possibility of a dangerous consequential flow of unchecked rapid expansion through corporate fluidity in the marketplace.) Corporations, according to Veblen, were astonishingly untouchable. But Veblen was not the first to warn the world of the omnipotence of corporate citizenship. The parliamentarians responsible for the enactment of the Bubble Act 1720 first recognized the dangers in the lack of transparency of artificial citizenship in the 1700s. Historically, it seems, the business of corporate citizens has largely been conducted in an unfettered manner.

As this observation situates the debate in light of popular media industries and corporate copyright control, it is prophetic. Take the example of Disney – the most dominant media conglomeration in the world. In 1923, Walt Disney freely and legally adapted the Grimm brothers' classic *Snow White and the Seven Dwarfs* into a blockbuster. He achieved this because this wonderful fairy tale was in the realm of copyright commons and was therefore free to be exploited because the temporary monopoly had reached the end of its natural life. The Disney empire was launched. Now fast forward to 75 years later. The copyright landscape has significantly changed in favour of corporate copyright holders who successfully persist in extending the life of assigned copyrights. The US Copyright Term Extension Act of 1998, for example, was fiercely lobbied by media magnates (namely Disney) to extend the corporate copyrights for Mickey Mouse and other Disney copyrighted characters for a further 20 years. Unlike the Grimm's copyright fairy tale, Disney's copyrights are firmly embedded in a corporate neo-pluralistic reality.

This legal reality is overwhelming. How can copyrights be regarded temporary when the life span for corporate copyright in the US is beyond any natural term? Given the fact Hollywood, the US music industry and gaming industry dominate world media through several trade agreements, this empirical and legal reality is concerning. In the 1800s, 14 years of temporary monopoly became 50, then in the 1900s, 70 years, and now it is potentially up to 120 – but solely for corporate benefit. The fallacy of temporary monopolies is best shown in the Disney example. This Act (cynically referred to as the Mickey Mouse Act or the Sonny Bono Act (see also Lessig, 2001)) accurately shows the harsh reality of political imbalance by denying competition in the marketplace. The irony – no, rather absurdity – is that the very same copyright that helped Disney freely use Grimm's copyrights for the common public good has now been privatized for the benefit of a few. It was good for Walt Disney to exploit Snow White but it is illegal for others to exploit Mickey. This is indeed a convergence of moral, legal and social issues, but then again corporations are devoid of morality.

In a similar fashion, pursuant to Directive/116/EC, the EU (eight of the 27 member nations objected) extended copyright vested in music recordings from 50 to 70 years on 12 September 2011. The so-called Cliff's Law (Sir Cliff Richard was the spokesperson on behalf of interest groups, namely the International Federation of the Phonographic Industry (IFPI), and major recording stars (Smirke, 2011)) purports to afford protection to performers by 'acknowledging their creative artistic contributions' (see the EU's official statement on the Directive). A new fund for session musicians will be created in addition to other safety nets. The law (which is to be implemented by Member States within two years) also purports to provide other incentives in order to strike a fairer balance between artists and the record companies.

But like the situation of Mickey Mouse and other Disney characters, it must not be forgotten that copyrights in major recordings are vested in corporate copyright ownership. This new law simply affirms the fallacy of modern copyrights as being temporary monopolies. It has been largely touted as an equitable outcome for artists. This is very hard to validate. Putting the imbalanced negotiation position between majors and creators argument aside, there is no credible evidence to suggest that creators will be better off.

What should not be denied is that only a tiny percentage of traditional creators actually make a living from full-time music creation. The reality is that most musicians support themselves by other means. On the issue of distribution of composition royalties by the UK royalty collection society Phonographic Performance Ltd (PPL), Towse (2000, p. 14) calculated that the median individual payment was up to US$190 per annum throughout the 1990s. This is an important observation because that era preceded the doom and gloom portrayed by the majors as a result of digital media piracy. The perception generated by the associations and lobbyists suggests that the already elaborate and sophisticated royalty-tracking techniques combined with these new laws will ensure that *all* relevant copyright holders are compensated. However the stark reality is that this simply does not occur. Alternatively, if it does, then equitable redistribution is not reflected.

Dolfsma (2000) concurs with Towse and acknowledges that authors' incomes from copyrights are mostly negligible. Dolfsma (ibid., p. 7) argues that some authors earn vast amounts of money thanks to copyright, but 90 per cent of Performing Right Society (PRS) (broadcast and performance royalties) authors in the UK earned less than US$2,500 per annum. Specifically on the issue of authors' rights distribution, Towse (1997, p. 42) calculated that of this 90 per cent group of members, 31 per cent received less than US$60 annually. This fact supports the argument that it is the elite few (majors and superstars) who benefit from the current system. Performance or recording artists who do not own any intellectual property rights (IPRs) in the works are in a similar position because if the music is not exposed publicly, sales are probably not being made.

Creative persons should not be surprised that in relation to actual people the wealth is usually reserved for the few elite superstars (Kretschmer, et al., 2010). The argument that artists will be better lacks empirical foundation. In one of the most comprehensive discussions on the relationship between copyright and contracts, Kretschmer, et al. (ibid., p. 23) say:

> [i]t is worthwhile pointing out that ... most authors actually earn rather little from copyright royalty contracts. For example, Conolley and Krueger (2006) find that in average over the 35 top musical acts that toured during 2002, less than 10% of the income was generated by recordings (i.e. copyright royalty income) while some 73% was due to concert earnings.

This imbalance is not a recent phenomenon. Murphy (1995, p. 431) explains that in 1981–1982, 'only 5% of professional writers received more than $6,000 from royalties and advances'. This inability to redistribute on equitable terms suggests the corporate copyright model is not based on copyright as a public good, but rather copyright as a corporate profit maximization imperative.

As mentioned above, the major reason for the gross revenue concentration is because the majors dictate the contractual terms in all respects, and consequently retain the bulk of the revenue. So how can there be extra funds for the struggling median majority in this century given the fear of a less prosperous industry? IFPI (2011a, p. 7), the voice of the industry, explains: 'Global recorded music trade revenues totaled US$15.9 billion in 2010, a decline of 8.4% compared to 2009. Physical format sales fell by 14.2%.' In other words, the majors, along with Sirs Cliff Richard, Elton John, Bob Geldof, Mick Jagger and Paul McCartney and company, might be the handful of superstars who will benefit from copyright extension, but as Yates (2004, p. 25) explains: 'the entire music industry is full of people eking out a living from a relatively small number of clever, creative people.' There is no economic basis to suggest these struggling artists will be better off.

In the light of the above observation, and given the corporate super-structure, it is very hard to accept that copyright laws aim to strike a balance between exclusivity and common good for the benefit of members of society. The corporatization of copyrights supports the proposition that, after many decades, combined technological and copyright control has created a reality in which anticompetitive participants 'manipulate and persuade the population to buy unnecessary and trivial commodities' (Dowd, 1979, p. 29) at an inflated price or on rigid terms. The fact that 'price cuts' and 'better consumer orientation' have been identified in extensive studies concerning music file–sharing is empirical evidence of this issue (Bauxman, et al., 2005, p. 8)

It is argued that throughout the twentieth century, and with or without antitrust legislation, film and music have always been concentrated in four to eight majors dominating the field (see Longhurst 1995 and Negus 1992). Eliminating competition in media consumption through majority control of technologies and copyrights in popular culture creates an artificial environment by a handful of so-called business rivals who dominate the marketplace. Ironically, as anticompetitive governance evolved to recognize the rights of consumers, the marketplace has become more concentrated than ever. This paradox lends support to the notion that there is a regulatory struggle in deterring corporate behaviour within copyright industries.

This evolution is unnatural because popular media firms have risen to prominence in a capitalistic environment that is not supposed to exist without competition and rivalry in the marketplace. It is evident that corporations thrive in a highly organized, anticompetitive environment contrary to economic theories first identified by Adam Smith (1907/1759) in his conceptions of a competitive economic free world. It may not make economic sense, but from a political economic perspective these developments are obviously connected to favourable political conditions and underdeveloped competition regulation in a global governance environment.

Take the example of Sony again. In terms of direct copyright industries, globally it owns a significant portion of copyright and receives significant revenue from the sale of music, film and games. In terms of allied copyright industries (electronic devices and related hardware) it is the major supplier. It is fair to suggest that this corporate citizen does not need to respond to the marketplace or to consumers for that matter. As mentioned, Sony along with a small handful of identically organized firms control supply in specific terms and the market place *responds* to the firms' terms. Apple is another spectacular example of a powerful firm controlling supply at horizontally and vertically integrated levels. In this context, it would be factually and legally incorrect to acknowledge that Sony, or Apple for that matter, contributes to ensuring that effective competition in popular media is promoted.

The High Court decision in *Stevens v Kaisha Sony* (2005) and the insistence by Sony that paracopyrights and related anti-circumvention technologies be enforced so as to override consumers' rights in the light of artificial regions and zones are evidence of anticompetitive behaviour. Sony simply has dominant control over supply, and not the other way around. This reality is inconsistent with the principles of a free market economy in a capitalist society.

Competition governance in popular media, therefore, is weak. At worst, competition in terms of pricing and format delivery does not appear to exist in popular media consumption because a system of pseudo-rivalry or, rather, a façade of free competition has been erected by a powerful minority of corporate players. The published price to the dealer (PPD) against the recommended retail price (RRP) has always been predetermined by industry controllers. These arbitrary price structures have been formulated by corporatized stakeholders (popular media industry and retail representatives) without any meaningful consumer representation about pricing in popular media. In Australia, for example, it was not until 1998 and the passing of parallel importation laws that consumer interest lobby groups were properly heard by way of formal submissions and meetings.

At best, competition exists at a residual level through formal conceptions of consumer justice. Dowd (1979) argues that instead of effective price competition, powerful players have created an environment of 'nonprice competition' effectively marketed through clever advertising promotion and other impressive sales tools. In doing so corporate citizens have gained 'special privileges at all levels of government' (ibid., p. 29). Whilst anticompetitive legislation is the modern day response to these concerns, it is only a relatively recent legal development compared to nearly three centuries of copyright law reform promoting monopolistic behaviour.

It is tempting to surmise, from the available literature and case law, that concerns about anticompetitiveness and the dilution and diminution of a healthy and competitive economy are relatively recent developments in late capitalism. This is partly correct given that more robust global regulation addressing these concerns is a relatively recent development. However, as mentioned above, the anticompetitive characteristics of corporations and the capacity to lean towards monopolization at the outset have not changed.

> As business came to take precedence of industry, salesmanship being a matter of business not industry, and business being a matter of salesmanship not workmanship … competition as it runs under the rule of this decayed competitive system is chiefly the competition between the business concerns that control production, on the one side, and the consuming public on the other side. (Veblen, 1954, p. 78)

If anything, corporations have mutated to a more pervasive level. Traditional merger movements and aggressive takeovers and acquisitions are just one part of the integrative process to ensure concentration of power and barriers to entry. Joint ventures, arm's-length arrangements and other so-called mutual benefit agreements have also been implemented to enable corporate citizens to expand or join forces in order to preserve the current concentration of power. These arrangements can also be regarded as conglomerate behaviour because combined horizontal and vertical merging patterns have led to a stable and remarkably cooperative oligopoly in popular media. The extent is analysed below.

The extent of anticompetitive behaviour in popular media industries

As mentioned, the overriding objectives of anticompetitive legislation are clear. For example, pursuant to the UK Competition Act 1998, the merger between EMI and Time Warner was thwarted in 2000 because of the threat of unfair market domination, as were persistent subsequent attempts to merger (Fildes, 2006, and see also, Kaiser and Stouraitis, 2001, who provide a compelling analysis of Thorn EMI's diversification ambition). In order to ensure governance arrangements for popular media industries, there must be consideration of the manner in which these industries became horizontally integrated. Competition law covering popular media industries provides for recognition of corporate behaviour within vertical structures (from top down), but recognizing that horizontal developments (namely via joint ventures) are problematic.

The conditions typically associated with anticompetitive behaviour in popular media industries are identified as follows:

- artificial regional barriers (for example, unjustifiable restrictions on regional viewing and gaming zones, resistance to parallel importation (music and film) and the insistence on paracopyrights (especially gaming)),
- discriminatory pricing and general hindrance to direct free market access for consumers, and
- restricted entry for new or independent participants.

Anticompetitiveness permeates copyright industries in all facets of popular media commodification. The music industry is an excellent example. Major record labels are affiliated with publishers from the same parent company. But this horizontal relationship is a form of trading that constitutes nothing more than restrictive trade. Schulenberg (1999, p. 9) correctly states that while there is a legal fiction that the publishing companies associated with a given record company are independent and separate, more likely than not they will have the same officers and personnel. Kretschmer, Klimis and Wallis (1999, p. 182) conclude, 'competition authorities are well advised to study this grey and rapidly growing area of transfer practices'.

This is an important observation because at para. 295 of the *ACCC* decision, Hill J acknowledged the omnipotence of the level of control (through copyright assignment) from the bottom to the top. Why are politico-economic conditions so attractive as to accommodate carte blanche control? At paras 484–85, Hill J answers these questions in no uncertain terms:

> [Warner] ... offered to supply goods on condition the retailers would not acquire non-infringing copies from a competitor of [Warner] ... Put in another way ... both Universal and Warner had market power in the wholesale market in which they operated and that they took advantage of that power to prevent a competitor coming into that market, it must follow that there would be an impact upon competition by force of their conduct.

I would find that the likely effect of the conduct of Universal and Warner would be a substantial lessening of competition ... I am of the view that the ACCC has made out its case that ... Universal and Warner contravened s. 47 of the Act.

That natural temporary monopolies tend to be exclusionary in popular media is the subject of discussion in the next section. In this sense the same product cannot be duplicated (there can only ever be one *Stars Wars*, one George Lucas original screenplay or one *Thriller* album performed by Michael Jackson). Exclusivity peculiarly rests with copyright ownership. The next observation is that like other monopolists, the owner of the copyright is able to use its monopoly position to charge higher prices and derive monopoly profits at the expense of consumers and economic efficiency. Oligarchic monopolies are thus formed through collaborative behaviour.

Competitive collaboration – popular media industry domination and horizontal collusion (the nexus between a natural monopoly and oligarchy)

Traditionally, popular media (as copyright industries) comprise integrated firms. The purpose of this arrangement is to ensure absolute control of the intangible property in order to maximize products of the finished goods (for example, acquisition of copyright by way of complete assignment for perpetual exploitation, ownership of masters, ownership of manufacturing arms, control of distribution chain, and so on). The anticompetitive nature stems not only from this complete control of all the interactive processes, but also from the fact that only a handful of similarly organized major corporate citizens control the bulk of the popular media industry. This is consistent with the previously mentioned economic theory of a natural monopoly, which takes into account the ability of the firm to expand the relevant output with minimal reinvestment (Kaysen and Turner (1959), and Posner (1999)). Popular media industries are unique in that they utilize so-called temporary monopolies created from copyright for an extended period of time.

Collecting societies are another example of natural monopolies and have been the subject of various parliamentary inquiries and litigation vis-a-vis trade practices legislation. They complement the artificial environment constructed by corporate media owners.[5] This allied monopoly environment has facilitated the subordination of copyright for commercial purposes. Associations and societies have enabled major players to control (almost in perpetuity) the 'temporary monopolies' created from copyright. In short, copyright institutions were consolidated 'at a time when there was a threat of monopolization and antitrust laws were in their infancy' (Lee, 1982, p. 225).

Temporary monopolies are supposed to disappear, for example when copyrights expire. But in terms of the creation of media stars, where there is only ever one Elvis Presley, Fred Astaire, Mickey Mouse or Super Mario, these temporary monopolies are recycled and copyrights are renewed (digitally remastered, repackaged, remixed and so on). These superstars of music, film and gaming live on through the perpetual recreation of temporary monopolies. The fallacy of temporary monopolies being 'temporary' in an allegedly competitive economy where power is heavily concentrated is that technologies and copyrights remain temporary in a state of perpetuity. That is, the intellectual property vested in the format changes rests with the majors, the hardware used to play entertainment rests with the majors and the copyright used to create these stars remains with the majors.

The legal reality of temporary monopolies in popular media is that they are naturally occurring. The tension that exists between a naturally occurring temporary monopoly and consumers' interests rests upon the fact copyright and competition governance do not adequately take into account net social benefits in terms of how popular culture should be consumed and disseminated. Consumers are led to believe a balance between competing interests is struck.

Horizontal technological alliances might assist in homogenizing copyright products for, allegedly, antipiracy reasons (the Apple iTunes library system is tailored for the music industry), but the reality is they operate as a mechanism of monopoly governance in that they dictate and control delivery (format) and price-setting of popular media through various statutory schemes. Antitrust, competition and other trade practices regulatory bodies at the national level must recognize the one-sidedness of these customs and practices. If they have, then the tendency in the West for popular media industries is to 'price fix' commodified products (see *Chapell v Nestlè* (1960) (UK), *ACCC v Universal Music and Others* (2003) (Australia) and *Broadcast Music Inc v CBS* (1979) (US)).

It is not surprising that given media corporations' primary legal purpose is to pursue and exploit copyright for profit, a concentrated status quo exits today (generally in excess of 80 per cent across all media). On a global scale the multinational majors control most of the music entertainment industry.[6] These transnational few are also responsible for 90 per cent of the US music market and between 70 and 80 per cent of worldwide music market (Brown, 1997, p. 80) (see Table 3.1 below).[7]

These favourable political and economic conditions have ensured an unfair or unbalanced playing field for consumers and minor players (see Cvetkovski, 2007, and Hesmondhalgh, 2002). Three primary factors support this observation:

- historically favourable legislative change to copyright laws,
- historically underdeveloped competition law enabling favourable market conditions for the establishment of globally and locally well-organized firms, and
- global governance (powerful international and national associations).

In understanding what constitutes an oligarchic monopoly, determining precise ownership is not the point. The top-ten global players have interests across the world. No data are available to confirm the percentage of copyright owned by the few players mentioned above, but it is maintained that Hill J's comments at para. 295 of the decision in *ACCC* reflect the fact that the artists assign copyright.

Table 3.1   Concentration of power by multinational corporations in popular media industries as at 2010 (combined 80 per cent) (excluding independents)

Rank	Music	Film/TV ('Hollywood')	Gaming	Combined Global Media Entertainment
1	Universal Music (Vivendi)	Paramount (Viacom)	Nintendo (Nintendo Corporation)	Time Warner
2	Sony (Sony Corporation)	Warner (Time Warner)	Electronic Arts (Electronic Arts Inc.)	*Walt Disney*
3	Warner (Access Industries Inc.)	Universal (Comcast/Vivendi)	Activision (Vivendi)	*Vivendi*
4	EMI (Citigroup)	BuenaVista (Disney)	Ubisoft (Ubisoft Entertainment S.A)	Comcast
5	Independents (indies) (balance)	Sony/Columbia (Sony Corporation)	Take Two (Take Two Interactive Software Inc.)	News Corp
6	Indies	20th Cen. Fox (News Corp)	Sony (Sony Corporation)	Dentsu
7	Indies	Weinstein Company (Indie)	THQ (THQ Inc)	DirecTV
8	Indies	Relativity (Indie)	Square Enix	Toppan Printing
9	Indies	Lionsgate (Indie)	Microsoft	Dai Nippon
10	Indies	Fox Searchlight (News Corp)	Konami	Viacom

Sources: Music & Copyright, Music Industry News Network (Mi2N), Billboard, Entertainment Software Association, Fortune 500, MOJO Box Office 2010, Index to Media (2010).

Given that Table 3.1 shows ownership and control in terms of sales revenue, it reasonable to infer that the relevant bundles (the lucrative portions of copyright) are owned by these players. The fact that the music majors, Hollywood and gaming companies predominately litigate in copyright matters supports the assertion that the relevant copyrights have been assigned or at least exclusively licensed on very favourable terms so as to warrant actual control and protection.

The conclusion reached is that notions of naturally occurring monopolies in copyright industries are firmly embedded in exclusive ownership and proprietorship of copyright. Music, film and games industries (in that order) are extremely centralized and represent some of the most anticompetitive forms of commercial enterprise in advanced capitalist societies. Table 3.1 shows the level of concentration (top-ten firms) in popular media in the respective three industries.

This table reflects the bottom-dollar line in terms of traditional popular culture control and dissemination.

Legal realism and the artificiality of moral rights: a moral dilemma?

Warner, as part of the largest popular entertainment media organization across all three areas (also ranked 20 in the gaming sector), recently sold its entire music interests (publishing and recording) to Access Industries. This conglomeration has large interests in natural resources, chemicals, high-end fashion, media and telecommunications industries. The Warner Music Group acquisition does not suggest less popular-media concentration. On the contrary, upstream acquisition by a multinational corporation interested in unrelated sectors suggests greater concentration.

One observation that might be made about this development is that by buying up diverse portfolios national regulatory bodies interested in specific industry concentration might be less convinced of anticompetitive conduct in specific industries. It is acquiring virtually any business whose capital can be cannibalized and reconstituted as the reproduction of its own capital (Andrews, 1997, p. 147) that enables temporary monopolies and natural monopolies symbiotically thrive. Citigroup's ownership of EMI also suggests the same development. The core copyrights possessed in the works derived from this copyright industry are subsumed under a corporate rubric broader than one specifically located in popular media. Identifying monopolistic behaviour thus becomes a slippery exercise.

The Warner acquisition is an important development because not only does it suggest corporate control extending beyond traditional media conglomerate boundaries, it also demonstrates the fallacy of moral rights of the author vis-a-vis the corporate copyright imperative. It also exposes an inherent weakness in any WIPO-initiated moral rights protocols.

Access Industries boasts the following on its website:

> Access Industries is a privately held, US-based industrial group with long-term holdings worldwide. Our industrial focus spans three sectors:
>
> • Natural Resources and Chemicals
> • Media and Telecommunications
> • Real Estate
>
> Our holdings include a number of market-leading companies.

Its major acquisitions include significant stakes and interests in LyondellBasell, Faena Group, TNK-BP, Icon (UK operations and film distribution), the exclusive fashion label Tory Burch and, of course, the newly acquired Warner Music Group. As these interests are so diverse, they may present interesting future dilemmas for some of the artists signed to Warner or who have recorded under its labels. For example, given that Access Industries is expanding its retail, industrial, property and entertainment portfolios, imagine how a punk rock artist might feel or react if she or he perceives that her or his repertoire is associated (nevertheless indirectly) with dominant chemical companies under the Access portfolio such as LyondellBasell ('Lyondell') (formerly Lyondell Chemical and the Millennium and Equistar subsidiaries)? There may be no issue for the artist, but music fans may take issue.[8] The music business can best be described as a fickle business because of so many uncontrolled factors involved in making a hit song.

The issue of acquisition of traditional popular media and its creative aesthetics under a broader, general global corporate veil is worthy of consideration given that Lyondell and comparable entities in the fields of petroleum and aluminium production under the Access group of companies (whether previously related through joint ventures or newly acquired) are completely unrelated to popular media. The potential for a public relations crisis between industries open to criticism concerning the environment, health and safety, or related human rights violations, is possible. It is not the purpose here to assess the merits or validity of such concerns. However, LyondellBasell as one of the world's largest plastics, chemical and refining companies makes an interesting stablemate for a major music company that has historically only been involved in show business. What is also of interest is that, traditionally, popular media corporations acquire horizontally and vertically within a narrow popular culture rubric (the consolidation of games software development, music labels and film production studios, publishing houses or print media). Curious external corporate acquisitions are recent developments in popular media.

Corporate media giants have evolved closely with one another in order to form a remarkably well-integrated global industry. (This also explains the ability to harmonize regionally given the level of inter-industry cooperation through sub-publishing and licensing arrangements).

Consolidation by non-traditional conglomerates will no doubt present challenges given that popular media stars are acutely aware of their public roles as cultural ambassadors. Film and music stars are essentially the lifeblood of Hollywood and the music industry. They are not fixed or raw commodities capable of precise measure in terms of output. Their capacity to commodify creativity as fixed output is also dependant on the capacity to be recognized by their adoring and often sycophantic fans in a digitalized world by way of social media. Acquisition by industrialist entities with interests in chemicals and natural resources is thus somewhat unusual in the history of popular media. For example, how effective would planet-saving protest campaigns led by superstar elites be if fans learn through social networking that a pop star endorsing an environmental issue is signed to a label owned by a multinational conglomerate whose policies might be inconsistent with the campaign? These issues are indeed novel, and in a converging world of digitalization, social networking provides an ideal forum for the dissemination of informal information, whether accurate or otherwise. In this new digitalized world, tensions between the controlling parent group, attitudes of popular media stars signed to the entertainment arm, and fans as protestors about world issues irrespective of the legitimacy or merits of the claims made are open to speculation in the face of these broad-spectrum mergers.

How the impact of these recent developments might also affect the current copyright governance framework has not been considered in the literature. In this potentially restrictive environment, how does WIPO react to protect the moral rights of artists who might have an aversion to being indirectly associated with chemical and natural resource/mining owners? The short answer is that conscientious objectors will be powerless as there is little WIPO (as 'governor') and trade associations can do in terms of moral rights of the original copyright owner who no longer owns the rights in the recordings.

In the Warner example, assume a significant portion of the artist's recordings was under Electra (a Warner label), and Electra owns the master recordings (invariably). The primary recorded repertoire is now subsumed by a multinational corporation with diverse interests. Hypothetically, it is entirely possible that one of the Access holdings, Lyondell or TNK-BP, might use a recording for a marketing campaign. If an artist objects, the question is whether the moral rights (which cannot be assigned) of the artist could resist any corporate urge to synchronize the music to, say, a mining commercial. In the event of any conflict, the copyrights vested in Access Industries would probably subsume any moral rights possessed by the artist. Licensing of music or film rights by third parties despite objection on moral grounds is not a new concern. But in the case of wholesale acquisition, the issue of moral objection becomes irrelevant because the catalogue is now owned in-house.

Wiseman (2002, p. 308) explains that moral rights are important symbolically, but 'the limits placed upon when and how moral rights are used means that it is unlikely that the new regime will have much of an impact upon publishing practices'. So what of the integrity and honour bestowed on that original copyright owner? Moral rights work in theory, but not in reality. They exist in that nebulous ethereal realm that politically supports the contention that any balance in the copyright regime does not substantively exist.

Digitalization and convergence: monopolized controlled consumption vs anti-monopolized uncontrolled consumption

Why do individuals participate in convergent popular consumption? Consumers in a broad sense include people engaging in legal and illegal modes of consumption. It is argued that convergent consumption pathways significantly decentralize the manner and mode in which popular media products are consumed. This section identifies the concurrent legal and illegal, internal and external pathways, and the disorganizational effect being experienced by emerging technologies.

Until recently there was a succession of different in-house horizontal technology monopolies creating monopoly licenses (the license to use vinyl, CD, VHS formats, the hardware to play the formats was licensed from the manufacturing arm to the publishing arm and so on). Dynamic efficiency has ensured sustainable growth through continuing in-house innovation, and the nature of the competitive process has become irrelevant. However, as is discussed below, the advent of external 'soft' formats (namely peer-to-peer (P2P)) and virtual platforms (the World Wide Web and the Internet generally, and social networking specifically)) has forced a new paradigm, thereby significantly questioning the competitive process in these industries for the first time.

Recent modern technological developments (computers and related software especially) have presented interesting challenges to these consumption monopolies. Economic and non-economic imperatives have been responsible for the development of new modes of consumption. The Internet, for example, along with social media networks represent economic imperatives for owners and telco providers. The consumer might also regard these as non-economic or, rather, social imperatives. One genuine arena of confusion is when a consumer freely exchanges unauthorized copies of music for non-economic reasons. The act is unlawful, but because the uploader sees no harm in sharing his experience of a particular 'trivial good' with another in a social setting, the relationship between economic and non-economic motives becomes increasingly blurred through convergence. The issue of illegitimate use extends beyond the obvious legal considerations. Popular media firms would struggle to maintain anticompetitive behaviour in a converging universe where consumers – and not corporations – dictate the terms of market exchange.

It is argued that recent developments in emerging and competing high-tech industries in the twenty-first century have directly affected the status quo to an extent that competition regulation and policy can never achieve. Consumers through emerging, or rather, enabling, facilitative innovation have commenced displacing centralized market power (possibly contributing to losses currently experienced) by engaging in a form of co-societal behaviour (legal and illegal). These challenges are being experienced through the empowering phenomenon best described as convergence through digitalization.

Historically, consumption is associated with the use of finished or completed goods and services, whereby a direct or indirect transaction cost is involved in the process or exchange. Its ordinary dictionary meaning (as opposed to its strict legal or economic meaning) provides various definitional categories ranging from narrow economic meanings to broader social contexts. It follows that individuals may acquire or use goods and services for direct or actual ownership by purchasing such products (see Collins Dictionary, and Fornas et al., 2007). But according to the *Oxford English Dictionary*, one may also consume, waste, squander or destroy and use up an article produced, thereby exhausting its exchangeable value. Social networking or private-use piracy as a form of consumption would satisfy the elements of the *Oxford English Dictionary* meaning. The possibilities in a less concentrated, non-monopolistic world are wide-ranging.

Table 3.2 lists the methods by which popular media are generally consumed. It should not be forgotten that external technologies have influenced the consumption of popular culture in a very short space of time. Less than ten years ago, consumption pathways would have been very limited to two or three industry-controlled formats and modes of dissemination.

Table 3.2   Traditional modes of consumption (legal) (controlled convergence)

Internal (industry controlled) (twentieth-century model)		External (licensed) (twenty-first-century model)	
Control of media format and content	CDs, DVDs and other industry-owned technologies	**Control of media format and content**	MP3s and other non-industry technologies
Control of copyright	Ownership of assigned rights and intra-industry licensing (including inter-label assignments and sub-publishing deals)	**Control of copyright**	Licensed rights to third parties – iTunes stores and other external Internet allied industries or ISPs (bundles)
Control and influence over delivery	Traditional product commodification – control of retail distribution and online industry	**Control and influence over delivery**	BitTorrent, social networking and other unallied sources where popular media is an ancillary source of entertainment

A combination of internal and external modes has created a convergent legitimate consumption model. In popular media therefore, from input to output, the following permutations and combinations become apparent:

- control of media format and content:
  (A) internal and/or (B) external, and
- control of copyright:
  (C) retailers and in-house online sites not requiring licensing (traditional distribution channels) and/or (D) external bundles (iTunes and ISP licenses), and
- control and influence over delivery:
  (E) traditional popular media channels (popular culture organized by majors), and
  (F) social networking channels (consumers utilizing popular media in addition to the traditional channels in a world of digitalization).

In this traditional setting, A, C and E represent internal modes (the long-established lines) whereas B, D and F represent external influences and are relatively recent influences. In this environment there can only ever be 15 possible outcomes in terms of the organization of media consumption (three sets of two plus two). This is mathematically represented as follows:

$$ _nC_r = \frac{n!}{r!(n-r)!} $$

(where n as the total factorial number of product combinations = 6 and r as the coefficient = 2).

This represents a significant level of decentralization considering that less than ten years ago CDs and DVDs were the primary in-house digital formats.

Now consider the following permutations from the ones depicted above where the only variable addition is made in the second set:

- control of media format:
  (A) internal and (B) external, and/or
- control of copyright:
  (C^1) legal (store purchase or download) or (C^2) illegal (burning and copying), and/or
  (D^1) legal (iTunes or other virtual store or similar) or (D^2) (ripping, downloading, uploading (P2P participation) or similar infringement), and/or
- control and influence over delivery:
  (E) popular media or (F) social networking.

The possibilities become endless for consumers who are reliant on digitalized products in the legal and illegal arenas. The combinations and permutations increase to 28 where $_nC_r = 28$:

$$_nC_r = \frac{n!}{r!(n-r)!}$$

(where n = 8 and r = 2):

$$_8C_2 = \frac{8!}{2!(8-2)!}$$

In this scenario illegal consumption is introduced. This model accurately depicts the manner in which popular media is actually consumed. In this convergent setting, and using the three sets of two as the denominators, the outcomes are extrapolated from 15 to 28 – thus diluting centralized control exponentially. Media consumption converges in a more realistic process when the legal and illegal modes are introduced concurrently. The possibilities become more random and are not capable of being controlled by the owners of copyright. Monopolistic copyright control has been compromised in this convergent world.

Figures and statistics in the debate are overwhelming at the best (or worst) of times, but it is worth applying some empirical data to the above formula. Fraser (2010, p. 60) cites the following startling numbers:

- 1 billion songs were traded illegally in Australia alone in 2007
- some 2.8 million Australians downloaded only music in 2007 (according to the Australian Bureau of Statistics (ABS), Australia's population was 21.1 million)
- some 95 per cent of music online exchanges are illegal, and
- some 40 billion shares of music files were illegal across the globe in 2010.

Adding the 'illegal' variable creates a futile situation. The above developments suggest that convergence in terms of technology, legal reality and cultural behaviour are somehow symbiotic. Attaching a net bottom-dollar worth is very difficult in this convergent universe. In the past, consumption was strictly limited to technological and legal control, and therefore control of popular culture. *In other words natural and temporary monopolies have become diluted.*

So what occurs if these sets containing unstable variables (which is the real state of play in popular media) become permanent settings? Indeed, the Mp3 format is the external standard – replacing for the first time in-house formats. Given recent challenges to copyright, media industries have become less vertically integrated and more horizontally integrated, but still remain anticompetitive. Resistance to external pressures is predictable. Popular media industries were forced into the 'virtual world' of the twenty-first century. That is, whilst certain interactive processes have been hollowed out (manufacturing and promotions arms have been outsourced), anticompetitive joint ventures driven by emerging technologies have replaced these processes. Apple's iTunes is a good example these joint-venture horizontal alliances where each party retains its own IPRs.

Apple's products have become relatively rigid so they remain exclusive for popular media industries. The products are not engineered for multi-platform functionality with other products. Frustration might explain consumer discontent and suspicion. In response to anticompetitive practices and artificial pricing that are attached to this process, consumers are faced with the dilemma of buying the most accessible product for a higher price (the hardware), but might justify accessing the copyrighted material for free (illegally). The rationale is not absurd in the face of intellectual monopolization through corporate copyright entrepreneurship. Temporary monopolies are perceived as oppressive, and it is difficult to rationalize how they may create a level playing field. Illegal consumption is a reaction to an unhealthy, aniticompetitive capitalist market in this regard.

Conclusion

Given the propensity for market collusion, it is far from clear that regulation achieves a satisfactory result in relation to corporate behaviour in liberal societies as a general rule. There is no doubt that the major players enjoy a substantial degree of power (amounting to dominance) in the popular culture market. Historically, consumers have not had alternative avenues of access to popular culture. As consumption of popular culture is complex and extends beyond transaction costs and copyright protection, meaningful legislative schemes cannot be achieved without substantive reforms to attitudes of the owners of popular media.

Anticompetitive behaviour as displayed by Warner, Universal and recent allegations and class actions against Apple are reactions to copyright convergence and emerging consumption patterns where enlightened consumers have begun to question the status quo (*Re: Apple iPod ITunes* (2008)).

The conclusion reached is that anticompetitive conduct and monopolistic tendencies are undesirable behaviours and have been vehemently opposed in previous centuries (see the following chapters). They ought to be deemed just as undesirable as piracy, but somehow are downplayed by the media and relevant industry associations. Sharp practices might be taken up internally by corporations as form of 'soul searching' in terms of corporate social responsibility, but are never acknowledged as disempowering for consumers, or that freedom from choice in pricing is somehow detrimental. Yet somehow, consumers participating in convergent modes of consumption ranging from piracy to buying cheaper legitimate copies through parallel importation are branded as immoral and derelict. Piracy is just one aspect. If technological change is the means by which attitudes are shaped in this so-called new economy (a virtual economy guided by emerging digitalization), then consumer convergence is the end process. In popular culture these processes are interconnected in a world of digitalization. The technological 'means' and the consumption process as the 'ends' have thus converged by way of dialectical digitalization. The tensions in this world of convergence are inherently political and represent a challenge to the status quo.

This chapter has demonstrated that as popular media industries exhibit natural monopoly characteristics they conflict with concepts of social interest. Furthermore, as they also exhibit temporary monopoly characteristics, they are at odds with the natural rules of economics. Favourable market conditions that support copyright owners' interests (namely anti-competitive interests) have ensured legitimate consumer interests have been subordinated, thus reinforcing any imbalance in the commodification of popular media.

When corporations consolidate copyright and merge they become more centralized in popular media. This means cultural control of the commodities remains exclusive. It follows that corporate media behaviour is contrary to the original spirit of copyright law. This might explain the non-economic rationale for illegal consumption, creative commons and social networking as alternative routes to popular culture in music, film and gaming, and as a reaction to the consolidation of popular culture.

Part II
Problems with Neighbours – Unprecedented Challenge to Corporate Control

4
Copyright Developments in Popular Media: Doctrinal and Statutory Challenges

> [T]he statute, like its predecessors, leaves the development of fundamentals to the judges. Indeed the courts have had to be consulted at nearly every point, for the text of the statute has a maddeningly casual prolixity and imprecision throughout. (Kaplan, 1967, pp. 40–41).

Introduction

In the first part of this book, emphasis was placed on what might be described as the *politicization* of the copyright industry governance framework. It was argued that throughout the previous century, and especially from the 1920s to 2000, copyright preservation was institutionally entrenched and broadly designed to protect corporate copyright ownership. Legal formalism, as the dominant politico-legal ideology in Western society, has ensured several decades of generally unfettered copyright control. That is, legal formalism simply requires the court to give effect to the plain meaning of the words of copyright legislation without reference to political or social considerations. The approach to such legal reasoning is consistent with legal positivist attitudes adopted by mid-nineteenth- to mid-twentieth-century legislators tasked with consolidating copyright laws at an international level.

This chapter considers the *judicialization* of copyright governance in light of an emerging digital agenda where the courts, in the face of divergent views between government bodies and non-government organizations, have attempted to strike a balance between copyright preservation, emerging technologies and consumer rights. Judicialization involves actual or ostensible encroachment of judges into the public policy arena. This may occur where tensions exist within the community between divergent industries and corporate interests (that is, issues between majority control and individual rights). Popular culture is one such fragile domain. An increasing public interest in the judiciary and its role in the protection of human rights demonstrates a growing recognition of rights-based theories vis-à-vis formalism.

Freedom of communication (especially via the Internet) is one such fundamental human right. Attitudes towards digital amendment reforms are examples of the way judicial review of the law can create tension between the legislative and/or executive branch of government on the one hand and the judiciary on the other. Recent high-profile cases have explicated how judges attempt to explore contemporary issues beyond the narrow scope of formal legislative interpretation.

Some reasons are proffered to suggest why judicial activism might be at play. One clear reason is that because corporate popular media industries do not discriminate when it comes to aggressively protecting copyright, a concerted balancing act is required by an independent arm of responsible government. The lawsuits against iiNet and Mr Eddy Stevens (*Stevens v Kabushiki Kaisha Sony Computer Entertainment* (2005) (*Stevens*) support the contention that the means by which litigious pathways are taken are not distinguished where the ends mean preserving a lucrative empire built on temporary and natural monopolies.

The concern raised in the case law is that if copyright's overriding objective is to promote creativity for the public good, then why are many legitimate technologies specifically being targeted by corporate popular media in the marketplace? The case law demonstrates that litigation is met with mixed success. BitTorrent and software P2P file-sharing technologies are classed as second-class technology by the majors because they contribute to copyright infringement. But then again, blank CDs and DVDs are the 'weapon' of choice for organized pirates (the irony is these technologies were conceived by the majors). The persecution of emerging external technologies seems to stem from the empirical reality that these technologies are a decentralized form of communications based on lawful protocols. BitTorrent might facilitate a black market, but it is also de rigueur for console gamers and tech-savvy consumers. Its legitimacy has been squarely recognized in the case law (*Roadshow Films Pty Ltd v iiNet Limited* (2010) (*iiNet*) at para. 242, but see also the *RapidShare* case (Germany 2010)).

This section situates the debate in light of recent legislative 'neighbourhood' developments. Neighbouring laws (as opposed to neighbouring copyrights) refer to a separate and distinct set of technology-driven statutes concerned with harmonization of the digital environment. This has required the implementation of 'reconciliatory' digitalization agenda initiatives (law harmonization protocols between the two distinct business arenas, including safe harbour and immunity schemes).

But there appears to be a fair degree of disharmony in this artificial digital universe, and the courts have increasingly been asked to intervene. The third and fourth sections of this chapter are concerned with the developments in the case law. The chapter enables an analysis of the disorganizational and reorganizational effects currently being experienced in popular media industries and which are materially reliant on the maintenance and preservation of copyright, but have been forced to become increasingly reliant on emerging externally dominant digital know-how located in the tele-communications and Internet arena.

The impetus for these effects is innovation and changes in consumer attitudes (the topics of interest in the following chapters). A concurrent examination of legislative developments and judicial interpretation is use-ful for assessing the impact 'neighbouring' legal change has made on the structure of copyright industries. External or horizontally integrated legal challenges reminds both corporations and consumers that statutes and common law approaches to respective rights are not necessarily compatible where technology-driven laws have been comingled with copyright laws to form a digital agenda framework for copyright governance. That is, whilst reconciliation might formally address tensions, the actual effects of substan-tive externalities must be considered for any meaningful analysis.

In this virtual universe, copyright industries appear to be experiencing disjointedly incremental negative effects capable of diluting or diminishing their commercial value. This chapter emphasizes the need to recognize that the value attributed to copyright by the major players is potentially being hollowed out by various interconnected factors, including competing legal interests, changing business models and, especially, changing consumer attitudes.

Judicialization of copyright governance in popular media

In *iiNet* (2010), Cowdury J declared at the outset (at paras 3–4):

> This proceeding has attracted widespread interest both here in Australia and abroad, and both within the legal community and the general public. So much so that I understand this is the first Australian trial to be twit-tered or tweeted. I granted approval for this to occur in view of the public interest in the proceeding, and it seems rather fitting for a copyright trial involving the Internet.
>
> That this trial should have attracted such attention is unsurprising, given the subject matter. As far as I am aware, this trial, involving suit against an ISP claiming copyright infringement on its part due to alleged author-ization of the copyright infringement of its users or subscribers, is the first trial of its kind in the world to proceed to hearing and judgment.

The court felt compelled to acknowledge the tensions between these com-peting industries, the laws comprising the copyright governance framework and the potential effects on individual rights and liberties, which in turn shape such attitudes and beliefs in Western society given these recent technological developments.

Given the heightened state of community awareness, there is scope to suggest that some judges have adopted a relatively activist approach to decision-making in this arena. It is important to note that Vallinder (1995) uses the term judicialization to include the extension of judicial methods and techniques, especially the methods of legal reasoning associated with legal formalism, to non-legal areas of decision-making.

Influential remarks made by the court that hinge on public policy implications and potentially extend beyond formal legal analyses support an argument that digitalization issues concern the judiciary. In the case of *Stevens* (2005), evidence of the judicialization of copyright governance is much less subtle. Gleeson CJ, Gummow, Hayne and Heydon JJ make this point when they clearly state: 'it is important to avoid an overbroad construction which would extend the copyright monopoly' (at para. 47). Kirby J goes even further, and makes reference to the really extraordinary nature of übercopyright. Kirby J lists his concerns as follows:

- Sony would be given 'a de facto control over access to copyrighted works or materials that would permit the achievement of economic ends additional to, but different from, those ordinarily protected by copyright law' (region-coding exclusivity) (at para. 211); and
- Sony as the controller of format, console and peripheral products would affect the individual by limiting his or her rights 'in the pursuit of that person's ordinary rights as the owner of chattels' (at para. 213).

At paras 214–216, notions of liberalism and utilitarianism are enunciated:

Take, for example, the case earlier mentioned of a purchaser of a Sony CD-ROM in Japan or the United States who found, on arrival in Australia, that he or she could not play the game on a Sony PlayStation console purchased in Australia. In the case postulated, there is no obvious copyright reason why the purchaser should not be entitled to copy the CD-ROM and modify the console in such a way as to enjoy his or her lawfully acquired property without inhibition. Yet, on Sony's theory of the definition of TPM in s 10(1) of the Copyright Act, it is able to enforce its division of global markets by a device ostensibly limited to the protection of Sony against the infringement of its copyright.

Ordinary principles of statutory construction, observed by this Court since its earliest days, have construed legislation, where there is doubt, to protect the fundamental rights of the individual. The right of the individual to enjoy lawfully acquired private property (a CD-ROM game or a PlayStation console purchased in another region of the world or possibly to make a backup copy of the CD-ROM) would ordinarily be a right inherent in Australian law upon the acquisition of such a chattel. This is a further reason why s 116A of the Copyright Act and the definition of TPM in s 10(1) of that Act should be read strictly.

The subsequent paragraph (216) also expresses the rights of natural persons over artificial persons:

> The provisions of the Australian Constitution affording the power to make laws with respect to copyright operate in a constitutional and legal setting that normally upholds the rights of the individual to deal with his or her property as that individual thinks fit. In that setting, absent the provision of just terms, the individual is specifically entitled not to have such rights infringed by federal legislation in a way that amounts to an impermissible inhibition upon those rights constituting an acquisition. This is not the case in which to explore the limits that exist in the powers of the Australian Parliament, by legislation purporting to deal with the subject matter of copyright, to encumber the enjoyment of lawfully acquired chattel property in the supposed furtherance of the rights of copyright owners. However, limits there are.

Indeed, it also worth noting that Kirby J makes reference to Professor Lawrence Lessig's works at the footnote to this paragraph (not referenced here). Lessig, creator of the Copyright Commons website, founding member of the Free Culture Movement, lawyer, political activist and arguably one of the most influential open-source, pro-competition copyright activists, has been instrumental in shaping attitudes and beliefs about the 'democratization' of copyright. He has devoted significant time to actively examining anti-corporate approaches to copyright and was the primary intellectual contributor to the critically acclaimed Canadian documentary *RIP: A Remix Manifesto* (2008).

A high-profile High Court judge has referred to Lessig's influential works. Speaking in 2007 at a New South Wales Law Society function, His Honour Justice Michael Kirby J (as he was then, prior to his retirement) said:

> Professor Lawrence Lessig, for example, has frequently expressed concern about the balance that is being struck between rights to private copyright protection and rights to free expression guaranteed by the First Amendment to the United States Constitution. Although, in Australia, we have no equivalent constitutional guarantee to protect free expression generally, it is obviously important for courts to be aware of such competing values. It is the role of lawyers, particularly those with expertise in the field, to uphold an appropriate balance. (p. 12)

> [W]e have also become aware of the 'democratic deficit' that exists when the regulation ... moves from laws made by legislators to rules effectively

made by entrepreneurial corporations themselves. When the latter incorporate such rules in the technological 'Code' (to use Professor Lessig's expression), they normally do so to protect their own economic interests. They are not generally concerned, as such, to uphold social values derived by representative institutions or expressed in transparent court decisions. (p. 13)

In the academic legal arena, the importance of Professor Lessig's works has been widely referenced.[1]

Tate (1995) argues that judicialization is an instrumental value such that activist judges will tend to involve themselves in policy decisions when the political persuasions of a governing body or ruling elite (in this case, the popular media industry lobby) are pervasive or differ from their own. Vallinder (1995) suggests that courts give emphasis to negative freedoms and individual rights concerns whereas parliaments focus on general rules and majoritarian concerns. Recent case law in digital copyright developments supports this.

If judicialization is indeed occurring as a movement within the common law role of courts, then formal conceptions of justice (in particular the role of clear statutory authority) are being challenged. To this end, judicialization promotes liberalism. This is not a surprising approach given that the Australian Constitution, for example, contains very limited protection of rights and freedoms. Former Chief Justice Mason (1986, in Solomon, 1999, p. 234) also has been quite clear that it is impossible to separate values from the law:

Unfortunately, it is impossible to interpret any instrument, let alone a constitution, divorced from values. To the extent they are taken into account, they should be acknowledged and should be accepted community values rather than mere personal values. The ever-present danger is that 'strict and complete legalism' will be a cloak for undisclosed and unidentified policy values.

In *Australian Capital Television Pty Ltd v Commonwealth of Australia (No 2)* (1992) the High Court decided that legislation must not impose 'unacceptable restrictions on the democratic freedom of political comment and debate' (Blackshield, 1994, p. 23). David Solomon (1999) argues that given the nature of cases brought before it, the High Court plays a sociopolitical role.

The recent litigation between stakeholders with distinct business agendas and interests and telecommunication industry services (telco) industries in the West has attracted much political controversy (the Hollywood case against BT is the latest Internet service provider (ISP) clash (*Twentieth Century Fox and Ors v British Telecommunications* [2010] EWHC 1981 (Ch)). Community values, attitudes and beliefs are increasingly becoming ventilated as part of an organic legal process as judges become more attentive to social values (per Cowdury J's comments about 'twittering'). This must be unsettling for legal formalists and those wishing to uphold the dominant corporate status quo. In other words, the metagovernors of popular culture, who have subsumed copyright industries into a corporate, entrepreneurial (including 'paracopyright'), broad-spectrum right must also view techno-logical developments in the telco industry and greater judicial interest as a threat to the old ways of conducting business.

The tensions between copyright and telecommunications legislation are evident. In a case where a peer-to-peer (P2P) operator has authorized copy-right infringement in the legal sense, there is a defence for those persons who 'merely provide facilities' for these acts. This defence is designed to protect an ISP from being liable for copyright infringement. This is an important obser-vation because it is argued that a legislative confrontation between copyright protection and communication preservation is being fought in the public realm. On the one hand, copyright regulation has consolidated in order to preserve multinational corporate homogeneity but, on the other hand, as recent technology cases suggest, legislative change in relation to telcos has impeded copyright industry initiatives because the digital agenda surround-ing telcos does does not necessarily support the copyright industries' legal and political agenda. And whilst the telco corporate citizens acknowledge copyright protection as a component of the law, telcos' rights and obligations also rest with their respective customers (and shareholders). In this book it is argued that these corporate citizens are currently at cross-purposes.[2] Has technology created a situation where neighbours are turning on each other? The answer to that is vexed because these neighbours require synergetic business models to ensure content delivery and customer goodwill.

Digital neighbouring legislative framework: copyright and telecommunications

Against this legal backdrop is the operation of liability limitation legisla-tion. So-called Telco Acts limit obligations, liabilities and remedies avail-able against online service providers (pursuant to safe harbour schemes). Is copyright more conceptually relevant than transmission or communi-cation; and how is the balance struck pursuant to the World Intellectual Property Organization (WIPO) treaties and World Trade Organization (WTO) protocols? Definitional contradictions between copyright and telecom-munications legislation have created a dilemma in terms of apportioning responsibility for copyright infringement between the carrier (the person who owns a telecommunications network), the ISP (the person who pro-vides a service) and the ultimate end-user (either the customer of the telco ISP or the consumer of copyright products). Causationally, it is not a straight-forward process to establish the nexus between the telecommunications network carrier and the P2P network provider.

The copyright law term 'authorization' distinguishes between the provision of the 'means' of infringement and the provision of a precondition that enables infringement to occur. The decisions in *The University of New South Wales v Moorhouse and Another* (1975) (*Moorhouse*), *Cooper v Universal Music Australia Pty Ltd* (2006) (*Cooper*) and *Universal Music Australia Pty Limited v Sharman License Holdings Ltd) (2005)* (*Kazaa*) are each examples of cases in which the authorizer provided the means of infringement. It follows that telcos should be held liable. But the provision of access to the Internet is not the means of infringement. The mere use of devices is not infringement irrespective of the fact a system might be used for illegal purposes. Issues of control, responsibility, operation and authorization are a question of fact not law.

The issue of authorization remains unresolved. It is the factor most frequently contributing to disharmony between copyright and telco/ISP legislation. Napster claimed it was entitled to be the mere conduit pursuant to safe harbour rules. But Napster failed to:

- adopt and reasonably implement a policy providing for the termination of repeat infringers in appropriate circumstances upon having identified the risk,
- enforce actual instructions about copyright protection,
- provide reasonable information about alleged infringement, and
- monitor and review the consequences of infringement.

But when an ISP satisfactorily complies with such requirements, then the issue of copyright becomes exponentially problematic in terms of authorization (see *iiNet* and other cases below).

The other vexed issue is that copyright legislation is limited in scope in that if a breach of copyright takes place in relation to less than the whole of a work or other subject matter in which copyright subsists, there is no infringement unless a *substantial* part has been infringed. A feature of the BitTorrent System is that pieces obtained by a downloader are only fragments of the whole file (film, album, game or simply a song). In the *iiNet* case it was held that where only small, if regular, 'helpings are taken', there is no infringement (see also *Ice TV Pty Limited v Nine Network Australia Pty Limited* (2009)). Before an allegation of unauthorized use and/or infringement can be made in those circumstances, the whole or a substantial part of the relevant subject matter *must* be transmitted by someone. But on appeal in *iiNet* (2011) it was held whole or substantial portions of infringed material require 'discrimination' between different members of the 'swarm'[3] – who could be anywhere across the globe and/or any number of users individually utilizing an ISP either under one roof or many. Emmett J (at para. 162) said: 'It must also involve discriminating between users in Australia and users who are not in Australia.' (For full legal analysis of the technical nature of the allegations surrounding primary infringement in the *iiNet* case, see paras 149–171 of the appeal decision.) Coupled with statutorily sanctioned defences, these developments weaken the rigid control exercised by copyright controllers. Safe harbour operates as a defence by demonstrating how an ISP can discharge its obligations in relation to actions against copyright infringement brought against an ISP. Prima facie certainty against impunity has been provided to carriers and ISPs over the last ten years. Yet no such defence was even required in the *iiNet* case because it was not held responsible for even vicarious or contributory infringement. No apportionment of blame was made despite the fact consumers had been wilfully engaging in piratical conduct through wholesale file-sharing. *iiNet* is still the most recent authority on issues of remoteness and lack of sufficient nexus in the relationships amongst copyright owners, ISPs and consumers. It demonstrates how an ISP might protect itself from legal action. The issues for copyright owners, therefore, remain unresolved.

The combined effects of recognition of copyright convergence by the legislature and judiciary

The telco industry had been sanctioned by way of express legislation to pursue its legal rights within a copyright governance structure. The governance structure has created a divergent set of legal rights. As the cases suggest below, however, the 'jury' is still out for external producers of legitimate P2P-based technologies (even Cowdury J in *iiNet* accepted that BitTorrent can be used for legitimate purposes). In *iiNet* (at para. 21) it was held:

> In this proceeding, the key question is: Did iiNet authorize copyright infringement? The Court answers such question in the negative for three reasons: first because the copyright infringements occurred directly as a result of the use of the BitTorrent system, not the use of the Internet, and the respondent did not create and does not control the BitTorrent system; second because the respondent did not have a relevant power to prevent those infringements occurring; and third because the respondent did not sanction, approve or countenance copyright infringement.

This reasoning is consistent with the legislative intent. In the second reading speech for the Copyright Amendment (Digital Agenda) Act 2000, the then Australian Attorney-General commented on the anticipated challenges as follows:

> This extraordinary pace of development threatens the delicate balance which has existed between the rights of copyright owners and the rights of copyright users. (*Hansard*, 2 September 1999, p. 9748)

At p. 9750, the Attorney-General added:

> The amendments in the bill also respond to the concerns of carriers and carriage service providers, such as Internet service providers, about the uncertainty of the circumstances in which they could be liable for copyright infringements by their customers. The provisions in the bill limit and clarify the liability of carriers and Internet service providers in relation to both direct and authorisation liability

The law had always intended to typically hold that the person responsible for determining the content of copyright material online would be a web site proprietor, not a carrier or ISP. The tensions between copyright and telecommunications regulation were inevitable in the implementation of the digital agenda legislation. Amendments to copyright legislation so as to accommodate the needs of all parties have resulted in disharmony. Striking a balance between encouraging creativity, promoting the creation of copyright material, exploiting new online technologies, providing enforcement for copyright owners, promoting access to copyright material online and promoting certainty for communication and information technology have become significantly more complex than policing piracy per se.

Take another neighbouring rights example: paracopyrights (*Stevens*). Übercopyrights cannot physically prevent the tech-savvy consumer from overriding a protection feature any more than can ordinary copyright laws prevent a person from downloading or burning a movie (for example, Shrink Wrap is a freely available piece of software that easily overrides and unlocks 'keys' embedded in DVDs). *Stevens* is authority for the proposition that the court has taken a narrow view in accepting these ancillary or pseudo-copyrights notwithstanding the fact that the user is prima facie in breach of his or her contract and licence to use the copyrighted chattels.

But TPMs (technical protection measures) do not necessarily circumvent fundamental individual rights and freedoms. TPMs are not directly concerned with copyright control per se, but with product control. Infringement happens regardless of whether technical barring is adopted by Sony and other electronics giants. Anti-circumvention rules and laws supporting technological measures, including embedded copy protection features on equipment and in formats, and discriminatory coding of regions affecting playback or loading onto devices, not only aggravate consumers but expose copyright governance for what it realistically represents – a framework designed to maintain the corporate status quo.

In reality, measures like those used by Sony are about controlling use of and access to Sony PlayStation consoles. Sony's control over legitimate purchases is no different to Hollywood's over ISP protocols or others' control over consumer use of the Internet. These major players argue that the objective is to prevent piracy. But in doing so, blanket barriers such as limitations on mod-chips and P2P use also restrict legitimate use where the users have no piratical desires. The issue is more than just about piracy. Is it not also about loss of centralized control? The question of control seldom makes it to the centre of the debate.

All three arms of power under the Western liberal conception of the separation of powers have concurrently accepted that convergence through digitalization is occurring at a rapid rate. The implications of technological change are reflected in parliamentary debates and speeches. Popular media corporations were probably in denial in the early 1990s about the threat of technical challenges occurring through digitalization. But by the end of the 1990s, the shelf life of the CD and DVD became seriously shortened as P2P technologies evolved in a digital world. Digitalization is best described as a presentation of an omnipotent negative externality for the traditional industry for several reasons. Firstly, it has facilitated unprecedented piratical conduct. Secondly, it has driven the price of media products down because of associated interaction costs when entering into ventures with third parties such as Apple and telcos in order to get the products to a digital market (a market markedly different to traditional retail settings). Thirdly, in the music business especially, a loss of profit is reflected by the fact that consumers tend to download songs rather than albums and where prices for individual songs fluctuate depending on the download price reached with an online store. (In the past, pre-arranged published and retail prices for hard formats were exclusively set by industry because fixed price structures within each jurisdiction were agreed by associations representing majors.) This is in stark contrast to the digital age, however, where independent labels or unsigned artists even offer downloads for no fee in the hope consumers will purchase other merchandise or attend concerts. The digital world is an entirely different landscape given that consumers think in global rather than regional terms. Finally, social networking behaviour and sites such as YouTube and MySpace where media are easily accessible have empowered consumers to be selective in the products they are interested in rather than rely on industry recommendations. This is achieved through interaction with users communicating online. Indeed recent developments add further value to already dominant social networks. Access to unlimited libraries of works for minimal or no fee (for example, the venture between Spotify and Facebook) adds credence to the observation that negative digital externalities will continue to dilute or diminish the centralized control once enjoyed by popular media industries. Thse developments suggest that the concentrated industry power base enjoyed by the major industry players can be challenged in various ways, including by technical and legal challenges. Some of these challenges relate to legislative developments while others are situated in an illegal setting.

External challenges: lessons from the case law

The most important objective for digital agenda reforms appears to stem from the primary need to provide new enforcement measures, as well as the secondary need to strike a balance for the consumer. In order to protect its growing interests, the telco industry expressed concerns about being held liable for constructive knowledge about infringement, and whether the service provider knows the infringement is apparent. Limitation of liability for ISPs as providers of online delivery of content in the new information economy appears to be the new imperative for government in the early part of this century. Encouragement of continued investment in these crucial new online businesses and related telco infrastructure and services might explain why copyright responsibility was for the first time balanced by legislators alongside other economic imperatives in the world of digitalization. The copyright agenda is now competing with an emerging telecommunications agenda. Together these industries are converging into a so-called digital agenda. However, the transition has been far from smooth. That is, copyright laws have never had to share the legislative limelight with any other arena until recent digitalization agendas.

In *Stevens* (2005), the High Court rejected Sony's contention that the clear purpose of copyright legislation was to prevent conduct like that of Eddy Stevens and that of mod-chipping. The High Court saw the digital agenda reforms to legislation as a compromise between warring interest groups. Statutory interpretation principles about the legislative purpose were rejected in favour of the following politico-legal analysis:

> [T]he very range of the extrinsic materials, with shifting and contradictory positions taken by a range of interest holders in the legislative outcome, suggests that the legislative purpose was to express an inarticulate (or at least not publicly disclosed) compromise.
>
> ...
>
> The result is that in the present case to fix upon one 'purpose' and then bend the terms of the definition to that end risks 'picking a winner' where the legislature has stayed its hand from doing so. In the selection of a sole or dominant [legislative] 'purpose', there is a risk of unintended consequences ... (paras 32–34).

This decision was pro-consumer. However, in *Cooper* (2006), Branson J at para. 2 held:

> Although that website did not contain any music files, it was structured to allow internet users ready access to music files of numerous popular sound recordings via hyperlinks. When an internet user clicked on

a particular hyperlink, the music file in question was transmitted directly to his or her computer from a remote server. It is admitted that the overwhelming majority of the sound recordings the subject of the music files were the subject of copyright.

Mr Cooper was effectively facilitating carte blanche á la carte access to illegal consumption of music. He possessed the capacity to remove hyperlinks to prevent infringement. This case could hardly be construed as an example of the positive aspects of digitalization, however it once again affirms the opportunistic desire for consumption of popular media by users of external technologies, and reminds the reader of how little impact *A&M Records, Inc. v Napster* (2000) (*Napster*) has made on consumers of popular culture.

The *iiNet* (2010–2012) case also revolved around individual rights of consumers and the rights of ISPs as much as it was concerned with copyright infringement, approval, prohibition, conduct, criminality, offences and authorization. It also examined the intersection between illegality, control, power to prevent, privacy and disclosure under the telco legislation. As mentioned, the higher courts are very protective of democratic rights and freedoms in the Western world. This is an important observation, because in Chapters 7 and 8 of iiNet's submissions the Court was reminded that the evidence at trial revealed that iiNet received several hundred emails per day alleging copyright infringement. Indeed the appellants in the *iiNet* case alleged some 5,702 infringements occurred over a period of seven weeks in 2008 (see para. 101 of *iiNet* Appeal to Full Court per Emmett J (2011)). Subsequent action taken by iiNet as the ISP responsible for monitoring and reviewing traffic included the issuing of notices, warnings and related responses to customers alleged to have infringed copyrighted material. Clearly these measures were not enough according to the aggrieved copyright owners, but the courts consistently held a different view in that case.

One major causational nexus issue is that an IP address does not identify the user of a computer. If there is uncertainty as to the identity of the perpetrator then there must be uncertainty about the release of sensitive data without reasonable belief or probable cause. Identifying the person is the first element of any offence. Time and date of an alleged offence are flexible factors. Positive identification is a crucial element in establishing the source of infringement, yet digitalization has created legal anonymity. One or more computers connected to the Internet are indeed problematic for positive identification of actual users or potential copyright abuser because different computers used in the same location are assigned different IP addresses. Furthermore, trial evidence in *iiNet* revealed several persons within a household or others using a wireless connection nearby could be responsible for legal and/or illegal communication (see generally Chapter 2 of submissions 'Trial and Evidence' filed on behalf of iiNet). As mentioned in the iiNet submission (2010), 'users engaging in infringing conduct may be a family member, child, flatmate, employee or customer of the account holder'. In wireless environments, a neighbour may be using another account holder's wireless connectivity without the neighbour's knowledge or authority.

It is quite possible for anonymous users to clone more than one address allocated to an account holder. Imagine a café providing Wi-Fi services being sued for permitting infringement. Given the litigious nature of popular media industries and their associations, the reality is that such establishments will probably be targeted given the number of cases involving patrons benefiting from unlicensed music (see *Performing Right Society Ltd v Hawthorns Hotel (Bournemouth) Ltd* (1933) (*Bournemouth* case) and other cases in Chapter 8 and throughout). But it is doubtful such actions will succeed due to remoteness of causation and contractual relations between these places, and the anonymization of the user. Birchall (2004) comments on the futility of attempting to rationalize causation and identification for the purposes of copyright infringement in public spaces. But try, they will no doubt.

One ISP customer might obtain the whole of a film with or without sharing the same amount of data back into a swarm. But these swarms are international and involved in several exchanges over various periods of time. Evidence in relation to a single user sharing a substantial portion of data is hard to establish in terms of continuity. And given the fact most households use more than one computer, it would be difficult to conceive how a user might be identified even on a balance of probabilities test (let alone beyond any reasonable doubt).

Legal action requires specific knowledge and authorization of likely infringing activity after the data has been analysed by cross-checking each line of data for any IP address at a given time (referring to ISP databases, identifying the account to which a particular IP address was assigned at a particular time and adding identification data). And this is all based on the assumption that a user at a specific physical address can be identified as the likely offender. Providing personal data to third parties is something that must not be taken lightly. Diluting data protection and general rights in liberal democracies is a dangerous road to take. Why should consumers be exposed to privacy infringement because a corporation is not able to satisfy adequately the elements of an action? Why should a person be charged without knowing he or she has been correctly identified, yet still must answer to a faceless corporation ('John Doe' style)? These intrusions are indeed indicative of the aggressive nature of corporate copyright control.

Interestingly, it was submitted in the *iiNet* case that '[n]ot one of the applicants has applied for preliminary discovery from iiNet or any other ISP in order to identify the account to which an IP address was allocated in order to sue or warn an end-user' (Chapter 6 of Submissions). Why not? Counsel for iiNet stated: 'Presumably the applicants, who secure enormous profits from the exploitation of their copyright, are not willing to investigate individual end-users because of the cost involved' (Chapter 7). As Counsel in Chapter 5 of the decision observed:

> They add the rhetorical flourish that customer's children would also have to be sued. This is, of course, nonsense ... the commencement and scope of any subsequent litigation is completely at the discretion of that prospective applicant. The preliminary discovery process would be directed to seeking documents only from account holders, who are by definition 18 and over. No children would be sued, or served with process, unless the applicants chose to do so.

Popular media industries are very predictable, but so are consumers if they feel a sense of injustice. Corporate media entities would have more to lose from individual prosecutions in terms of product boycotts and other related protests if customers feel genuinely aggrieved. As the cases suggest, corporate popular media is not 'gun-shy', but filing applications against infringers causes public reaction. The deterrence value may not be achieved when weighed up against a prosecution 'persecution' cultural backlash. When an entire industry is built on taking cultural gambles, it is doubtful the lawsuit card would be played for too long (see Chapter 6 on litigation against consumers). Counsel for iiNet made the point in cross-examination: 'The applicants are "armed to the teeth with legal talent" or are familiar with the procedures of this Court' (Chapters 5 and 6 of the trial submissions). The focus of corporate protest rests squarely on the impact external technologies have made on an elite industry.

In *Cooper* (2006), Mr Cooper clearly flouted copyright law. His domain name, mp3s4free.net, invited people to access files at other locations by means of hyperlinks. The free, pirated music was, in other words, one click away. Cases of this nature cannot be compared to *iiNet*. It is a registered ISP (the third largest in Australia). As it is regulated by telco legislation, Cowdury J held iiNet was not obliged to take action, monitor and review the property of others or act as custodian. Cooper and Kazaa were opportunistic and illegal web-service providers inducing consumers to join a 'revolution'. These two benefited financially. iiNet did not need P2P consumers. iiNet did not encourage customers to engage in BitTorrent traffic. Most importantly, there was not a single 'bit' of evidence offered to prove the extent of BitTorrent illegal consumption.

Failure to take action by an ISP is not comparable to a P2P owner of BitTorrent protocols actively encouraging illegitimate use. To make comparisons in a legal context is erroneous, as this would mean invoking a reversal of the onus of proof – a precarious legal development usually associated with absolute liability jurisprudence. Such a development is regressive and draconian. It would mean an ISP would be liable to positively discourage infringing acts by its own customers. The law does not support this development.

It is argued that lobbying for such developments will prove difficult given the telco lobby is a serious player in the digital agenda environment. Constitutions that give the legislature power to make copyright laws represent just one element of any sociolegal governance framework. Individuals' enjoyment of freedom from interference and unwarranted corporate harassment is another fundamental legal right. As mentioned, the judiciary as the most independent arm under the separation of powers takes fundamental human rights, such as the right to enjoy property, seriously. Natural citizens – not corporations – participate in a truly representative democracy.

These are not abstract sentiments. In the previous chapter, Disney's anti-competitive behaviour was mentioned. In 2005, Sony felt aggrieved that its multinational status was being challenged because of circumvention technology (mod-chips). The double standards are spectacular. It feels aggrieved in the twenty-first century, but it was most grateful to the Supreme Court of the US which held, in *Sony Corp of America v Universal City Studios, Inc* (1984), that Sony, as the distributor and seller of the Betamax video cassette recorder, was not liable if users of that recorder infringed the copyright of others in television broadcasts. Sony was accused of copyright infringement in the twentieth century. It is now one of the largest repertoire owners in music, film and gaming. Yet some 20 years later, Mr Eddy Stevens, a citizen, consumer and owner of property, was accused of copyright infringement. The courts have indeed been forced to adopt a pragmatic approach.

In 2005, Sony felt aggrieved due to the disruptive effects of the technological impact of copyright infringement as a consequence of mod-chips, yet Sony was the cause of grief in 1984 because of its enabling technologies that were capable of copyright infringement. Consider the commonly accepted consumer practice of time-shifting (later viewing) so that a television program may be watched another time. It invariably requires storage of copyrighted material onto a format. In principle, is home-taping or Sony's Play TV digital copying of free-to-air Sony Picture's TV series *Breaking Bad* any different from home downloading the identical episodes via P2P using BitTorrent for time-shifting purposes? (Assume a fan has uploaded it from TV rather than ripping the DVD.) In relation to BitTorrent (very much an unaccepted externalized mode of consumption in so far the industry is concerned), Sony would argue copyright infringement and unlicensed or unauthorized use via the Internet despite the fact the downloader (or uploader) only intended to ensure a fan who missed an episode caught up with the series. Whether a person provides a copy on a disk or shares it online, the effect is the same. The only difference is that several leading blank formats, playing devices and associated hardware, and digital time-shift channel technologies are owned by Sony or its licensees. These technologies are within traditional modes of consumption patterns and are thus deemed legal. BitTorrent protocols and emerging P2P technologies are unacceptable modes of content dissemination. The means are different processes, but the end is the same in so far as consumption is concerned. Time-shifting was always met with fierce resistance, but is now considered fair use and has been integrated in popular media service-delivery models. BitTorrent protocols however do more than offer alternative and interpersonal modes of unauthorized service delivery. Emerging technologies challenge the status quo by empowering the consumer with format-shifting capacities that bypass the need for interaction with popular media controllers. To brand these altruistic file-sharers as piratical is unfair in the modern setting when one considers that copyright owners through their electronic arms have directly enabled and ostensibly encouraged consumers to participate in complicit behaviour by having promoted replicating technologies for decades prior to the rise of illegal file-sharing. The negative aspects of replicating technologies in the form of piracy had historically been offset by the positive aspects because the manufacturing arms benefited from a form of industrial cross-collateralization. The actions of convergent consumers in that environment where the side effects of piracy were offset by the consumption of replicating devices and media should not be ignored. In the world of digitalization, the means are different – not the end. The side effects of negative externalities cannot be harnessed by the media industries; blank disks and recording devices have been replaced by free software and unlimited streaming.

The issues again are about control – control of the consumer and individuals' rights. In the Western world, where attempts to increase the force of copyright legislation beyond its legitimacy at the expense of personal rights and freedoms, core constitutional issues arise. Courts appear to intervene where powerful players harass individuals. Copyright is supposed to be beneficial for the public good – but no more so than emerging technologies. Anti-circumvention technologies and artificial zones and barriers, for example, limit freedom and keep copyrights beyond public reach. Limiting freedom and keeping copyrights from public reach are not fundamental tenets of a healthy democracy in an advanced capitalist society. Judicialization is another response to the narrow formal view adopted by corporate elites.

In *MGM Studios v Grokster Inc.* (2005) (*Grokster*), the music and film industries brought an action against Grokster and StreamCast, distributors of P2P software, for contributory infringement. These technologies were legitimate and whilst the lower courts favoured Grokster's argument that it was not liable for copyright infringement, the ultimate court ruled in favour of the aggrieved copyright holders (along the *Napster* and *Kazaa* line of knowledge, inducement and actual encouragement).

Napster, iiNet, Cooper, Grokster and *Kazaa* affirm the fact that popular media industries feel aggrieved by any external digitalization developments. Because corporate popular media possess the legal and political clout, they overtly attempt to influence the marketplace and consumers by seeking to curb technological advancement. The evidence for this proposition lies in the case law. In the *iiNet* case it was clearly acknowledged that BitTorrent was legitimately used by gamers. This was also affirmed in the *RIAA v Diamond Multimedia Sys.* (1999) case. The case, brought by RIAA against Diamond Multimedia because of its design and subsequent promotion of MP3 devices, was nothing more than an attack on technology pioneers not working within the traditional popular media industry. The *Stevens* case (in Australia) also supports this observation. It seems that challenges to emerging technologies are instantly mounted against non-traditional modes of consumption without considering the detrimental effects that thwarting technological advancement have on consumers. Corporate citizens may view certain technologies as harmful to their proprietary interests, but the legal reality is that this view is one-dimensional (albeit powerful). That piracy as a toxic by-product requires sanitization is one dimension, but why should freedom to use emerging technologies also be affected in the purge against piracy? As with iiNet, MGM possessed the burden of proof. In *iiNet*, several broad grievances were mounted, but proof was limited. Grokster claimed it played no part in the illegal activity (as in the *iiNet* case). The case was very finely balanced, but weighing the positive encouragement arguments, the US Supreme Court then held that Grokster's unlawful objective was 'unmistakable' (at 2782). *The profit motive played a critical role in this case.* In the 1984 *Sony Corp. of America v Universal City Studios, Inc.* (*Sony Betamax*) case, the element of profit was not proved because it was accepted home-users typically used the technology for time-shifting (indirectly of course, Sony benefited from blank tapes and recorder purchases). But unlike in *Kazaa, Cooper* and *Grokster*, Sony did not encourage piracy. In *iiNet*, there was also no profit motive.

The doctrinal landscape is unsettled. However, the purpose of litigation appears obvious. Copyright owners clearly wish to eradicate *all* forms of emerging technologies that are beyond their control. In *Grokster*, the Appellants were relentless in the litigation against P2P providers. But Breyer J was concerned with the impact that such narrow approaches to emerging technologies would have on innovation (see at 2794). Indeed, a reactive and litigious pattern clearly emerges during stages of technological change. That is, once a new copying invention or external access to legitimate alternative media is provided, the major players litigate (see, for example, *CBS Inc* (1982) (UK) concerning litigation against manufacturers of cassette tapes and devices). Then, after one wave of technological concerns subside, newer threats become sensationalized by the industry (see *RIAA v Diamond Multimedia Sys.* (1999) in relation to manufacturers of MP3 players).

The ability to promote the best interests of the media industry through aggressive litigation is an example of the hegemonic dimension of corporate citizenship. Maintaining the status quo legitimizes the existing order of the manner in which popular culture ought to be commodified. Litigation reinforces the ideological role played by corporate citizens by attempting to remind the consumer that alternative approaches to media consumption inconsistent with industry practices will be dealt with aggressively. The recent P2P cases follow a long line of legal intimidation. The law as an instrument of socio-economic control in popular media is only powerful if it reinforces the structures by which elites exert influence on consumers. Technological change challenges the capacity of elites to maintain the mechanisms of control through the law.

Oppressive protection regimes impact the rights of individuals. As in the *iiNet* case, in *Grokster* the popular media industries offered sound legal arguments, but no evidence was tendered as to actual loss or harm sustained in terms of quantum and future economic loss (at 2796–2797). There was also no evidence about the harm associated with production at the input arm (creators' losses). In other words, it was submitted that there was a very real possibility of music being stopped as a result of emerging technologies. What a preposterous position to take. Culturally, the primary purpose of popular media products is to stimulate affective pleasure gained from entertainment. It should be borne in mind that music, especially as a complex form of popular communication and expression, has existed for millennia. Only its value to be recorded and sold as a commodity is relatively new. Its current politico-economic organization is less than 100 years old. The Court held in *Grokster* that 'it would be "silly" to think that music, [as] a cultural form without which no human society has existed, will go away because of P2P technology' (at 2794).

This is another reason why information from industry associations should be carefully scrutinized and tested as to cogency. And it might also explain why judicialization is becoming a growing phenomenon in the copyright governance framework. A case-by-case analysis attracts the potential for judicialization of copyright as it allows for greater substantive scrutiny by independent arbitrators of law and fact. *Stevens* and *iiNet* demonstrate this development – a development that is consistent with liberalism generally.

As was also observed in Chapter 2 in relation to the complaints against China, evidence is required for natural justice to be afforded. Being correct on legal principles is not enough. The liability of ISPs for infringing acts is then left to common law principles where the onus is placed on the accuser in matters relating to authorization and breach of copyright. This legal landscape frustrates corporate copyright holders because in the course of communicating material as a mere conduit there is some uncertainty as to liability.

Conclusion

Sony pleaded that the judges perform a balancing act when Universal Studios sued Sony as manufacturer of Betamax VCRs. Sony now is one of the largest film and music copyright owners and pleads before the judges to sue those consumers who rightfully ask that a balancing act be performed. The transition from the old copyright regime to a pluralistic copyright-digital-agenda regime has indeed commenced.

The High Court heard the *iiNet* case in 2012. The case was unsuccessfully contested by Hollywood on a matter of principle – that the Court should follow predetermined principles made some 35 years ago in the *Moorhouse* case (1975), a case that involved university library photocopiers and posted written notices.

But on 20 April 2011, the High Court in the United Kingdom ruled that laws aimed at tackling illegal file-sharing were legal and proportionate. The Digital Economy Act 2010 (UK) (DEA) is aimed at file-sharers. It too does not make ISPs liable for copyright infringement. However this development is somewhat inconsistent with the *iiNet* decision. It does not impose an obligation for ISPs to monitor and review infringement, but does cast a positive obligation on ISPs to share the burden of compliance, including information in relation to infringement. ISPs are required to notify their subscribers when a rights-holder provides evidence of an alleged copyright infringement on their account. The imperatives are economic as monitoring and reviewing costs are to be shared. It has paved the way for more formal or sanctioned blocking, from robot notices, specific notices particularizing alleged infringement and other aspects to final escalation in the form of court-approved legal action.

Telcos are the mere conduit – P2P platforms and BitTorrent protocols and related software and the Internet support acts of piracy. Telcos may aid piracy, but they are a means of communication and should not prima facie be liable. Gaining profit and inducing cultural riots (as Kazaa and Napster did) is another matter entirely. If this is the case, then Sony, Phillips and the other patent holders for cassettes, CDs, DVDs, DAT, MD and all other industry collaborated media should be held technically liable, vicariously at least, based on the argument that these corporate citizens introduced these replicating technologies to consumers. The position adopted by aggrieved popular media corporate citizens is indeed a situation that might be described as a 'pregnant negative'; that is, 'I would never use a Sony CD-R to burn a copy of my Sony Music artists so I can listen to my favourite Sony songs in the car', which is an assertion that is as ridiculous as someone attributing blame to media manufacturers for inducing and encouraging pirates to make counterfeit copies for sale. But artificial citizens do not think like natural citizens. The formal legal debate is quite circuitous, whereas examining the political dimension allows for greater critical analysis.

The New Zealand government also recently conducted a review of its copyright statutory regime, and in the light of digitalization and rapid development in piratical developments it implemented a three-strike policy in a bid to deter illegal consumption. The tiered response is to be facilitated by the relevant ISP. Curiously, the United Nations has queried this move from a human rights access to the Internet perspective (notions of freedom of expression and communication and interference with Article 19 of the Universal Declaration of Human Rights and the International Covenant on Civil and Political Rights, see Bennett (2011)). But human rights issues aside, serious procedural and substantive legal issues will be raised in any event given the manner in which proceedings are to be commenced (see Cvetkovski, cited in Brandle, 2011). It is argued that this policy will probably meet the same fate as the Recording Industry Association of America (RIAA) US lawsuits initiated against the consumer (see next chapter).

The issue of course with these proactive legislative changes at the behest of the major industry players is just how fairly these laws can be administered. Copyright enforcement is hardly an exact science. Media corporate heavy-weights are well versed in the art of sensationalizing doom and gloom the moment the status quo is disturbed (see discussions about *WEA Records Pty Ltd & Ors* (1983) in the proceeding chapters, resistance to parallel importa-tion laws, and the *Universal Music Australia Pty Limited; Warner Music Australia Pty Limited & Others v Australian Competition & Consumer Commission* (2003) (*ACCC*) case generally).

The judiciary is empowered to enforce copyright law within the tradi-tional judicial system. This allows for judicial interpretation of the manner in which the balance is struck between copyright owners and consumers. WIPO meta-governance and domestic regulation do not exist in a vacuum. It must be accepted that there is nothing neutral or balanced about the political economy of copyright, emerging technologies and consumer atti-tudes. This might explain why not only is the legislation unsettled in this public policy arena, but judicial reasoning is also disparate. Again this sug-gests the political economy of copyright is a landscape riddled with tension and unresolved issues.

The conclusion of this chapter is that recent developments and judicial interpretation have challenged the rigid control once exercised by copyright controllers. First, safe harbour provides a defence to actions against copyright infringement brought against an ISP. Tensions between communication and copyright are therefore evident. It is interesting to observe that the term 'copyright' appears in s. 51(viii) of the Australian Constitution, but does not appear in the US Constitution. Yet freedom of speech provisions are not enshrined in the Australian constitution, but the US First Amendment states: 'Congress shall make no law ... abridging the freedom of speech, or of the press.' Freedom of speech as a negative liberty (communication) naturally conflicts with modern copyright because it is a negative right (exclusionary). This is mentioned in the context that WIPO attempts to impose wholesale copyright meta-governance on a sovereign and independent nation, yet the judiciary attempts to strike a balance in these laws.

Safe harbours, non-disclosure privacy, confidentiality considerations and other human rights considerations for the preservation of data involving individuals, and related telco defences have indeed proved problematic for corporate copyright owners. The current approach appears to be heading towards compelling telcos to, first, acknowledge that their customers are infringing copyright, second, accept some responsibility without admitting liability, and, third, contribute to losses sustained. In short, ISPs are being asked to provide further assistance than that statutorily required of them. The issues remain unresolved.

In Chapter 2 it was stressed that harmonization of copyright laws through internationalization protocols was more than desirable – it was essential. But it was also stressed that tensions at the domestic sovereign level are clearly evident when these obligations are transplanted. Telco legislative developments reveal an attack on copyright governance from 'left field'. Harmonizing telco legislation, it is argued, will prove to be a most challenging task because of human rights considerations. One nation's interpretation of the telco industry's indifference to infringement or the legitimacy of BitTorrent protocols may appear radically different to another's. Harmonizing complex data and technology laws will concern content digital rights management. As the cases have demonstrated, there is nothing simple about the P2P process of downloading popular media.

Drawing on Star Wars trilogy euphemisms again, in the past there was *A New Hope* in the form of the Statute of Anne. But then it was a case of *The Empire Strikes Back* as corporations subsumed common law copyright. Now is it a case of *A Return of the Jedi* through judicialization, digitalization, neighbouring rights and consumer convergence including piracy? The subsequent chapters set the scene for this battle for freedom and copyright control in popular culture. However, the lines between the aesthetics of art and legal reality have become increasingly blurred because piracy has now firmly attached itself to its host – copyright.

5
From Printing Press to Peer-to-Peer: Centuries of 'Modern' Media Piracy and the Social Urge for Legal and Illegal Consumption

> Publication without easy access to the product would defeat the social purpose of copyright. (Kaplan, 1966, p. 74)

Introduction

One important observation about convergence and digitalization is the desire to disseminate, communicate and consume popular culture in a broad, open and unfettered atmosphere. Social networking and communication via the Internet generally support this development. Indeed the courts recognize it. The subjects of examination in Chapter 8, twittering, blogging, social networking, etc. (which are representative of the synergetic relationship formed during uploading and downloading), are essentially an end to a means that is firmly embedded in ideals associated with communicative emancipation, empowerment, facilitation, enablement and democratization generally.

History shows that individuals as consumers of popular culture have always expressed this innate, perhaps altruistic, desire to disseminate information for the benefit of others. Parallels with the current digitalized era and the Enlightenment period in sixteenth-century Europe can be drawn. Compare the act of a daring individual replicating copies of a book that questions the role of the Church or monarchy in medieval times to that of a modern peer-to-peer (P2P) or file-swapper uploading the latest, übercopyrighted, region-only, pre-released Super Mario Bros game by Nintendo for all to brazenly consume across the globe. In each case it can be assumed that the unauthorized replication was based on pure altruism (i.e., there was no commercial gain to be made). In the first instance, the risk of such a treasonous act was punishment by the cruellest death imaginable. In the modern example, the punishment is also equally destructive (contextually speaking) in the form of a ruinous seven-figure damages court order. If the punishment for piracy is so dire, the rationale for risking criminal or civil action is equally difficult to comprehend in both instances. Though not-for-profit piracy seems both pervasive and systemic.

What possessed Australian James Burt, a 24-year-old suburban gamer and family man to upload, onto the Internet, a pre-released, 'accidentally' sold version of the *Super Mario Bros* game (the game was allegedly inadvertently sold to him a week or so before its official Australian launch). In the case of *Nintendo Co Ltd v James Burt* (2010), Mr Burt reached a AUD$1.5 million settlement (plus AUD$100,000 legal costs) for this act of piracy. There was no evidence to suggest he received a pecuniary advantage. The claim was based on economic loss, and opportunity loss given the timing of the illegal act. It appears his actions were based on altruism (details of the settlement have not been disclosed so his motives are just as unknown as the actual loss and harm suffered by one of the largest gaming companies in the world) (see Fenech 2010). According to forensic evidence, the game was 'downloaded 50,000 times over a five day period' (Nettleton, Hayne and Darmopil, 2010). It effectively went 'viral', or in legal terms, the aggravation was clearly evident. It is one thing to pirate a game for the purpose of uploading it across the Internet. It is an entirely separate matter to steal the thunder of a major corporation that had not allowed the release in Australia until a week later.

Ironically, Mr Burt was not a so-called bootlegger – he was a 'fanatic gamer' according Fenech (2010). Perhaps if anything his 'cyber-Robin-Hood-type behaviour might be described as anarchistic, or at least he was recklessly disobedient (see Goldman (2003) on what 'motivates' P2P uploaders). But his actions were deemed virtually heretical by Nintendo.

It seems that the Crown's desire to limit control of publishing in Tudor England is comparable to modern media corporations' uncompromising control of tangible and intangible products in light of emerging technologies. Copyrights should therefore be regarded as 'absolutist' in that the rights vested in the owners are exclusive and private – not public. As such, copyrights place a restraint on dissemination and cultural exchanges. Prior to the reign of Queen Ann, Tudor English subjects lived in a restrictive monarchic environment fundamentally premised on supreme sovereignty and Crown censorship. It follows that censorship and copyright share common denominators – namely absolutism and elitism.[1]

It is argued that enabling inventions challenge these positions and are double-edged in the sense they deliver both positive and negative effects to both corporatized copyright owners and consumers. It seems that the desire to break the law is not simply based on the profit motive. The above spectacular modern example contains elements of altruism (albeit misguided). But does this development not also symbolize a distrust of those who have monopolized culture? Those wishing to suppress or control the flow of information must have been viewed with a fair degree of mistrust and suspicion in Tudor England. Perhaps trust and altruism are not necessarily compatible with notions of monopolization and copyright.

This short chapter sets the framework for subsequent chapters by asserting acts of piracy extend beyond the opportunistic desire to make a quick sale on the black market. The purpose of this chapter is to recognize that not only does copyright and its corporatized state exist in a dialectical continuum, but so does piracy through technological innovation.

Whilst modern media piracy has existed for over three centuries, carte blanche near-perfect digital replication is a relatively new phenomenon. A direct correlation has always existed between emerging technologies and the desire to consume products in new formats – legally or otherwise. This observation is historically relevant.[2]

The next four subsections provide a brief overview of significant developments over the past 300 to 500 years. Drawing on Hegelian concepts, the history of copyright can be divided into four dialectical stages. The four distinct but interconnected phases in the development of copyright law in the West might be described as: (i) pre-Statute of Anne (pre-1710) period (monarchic control), (ii) post-Statute of Anne (common law vs statutory period) (1710 to 1840s), (iii) early stages of corporate copyright (1840 to 1960) (entrepreneurial control), and (iv) advanced international corporate elite copyright (1970 to present) (anticompetitive multinational elite corporate control).

The sections examine the politicization of individualistic piracy as a form of expression. The debate about the transition to statutorily enshrined copyright law is usually centred around the Statute of Anne. Legal formalists may posit that copyright laws did not commence prior to that Act, but as Ringer (1974, p. 7) argues, that Act was 'a direct outgrowth of an elaborate series of monopoly grants, Star Chamber decrees, licensing acts, and a system involving mandatory registration of titles with the Stationer's Company'.

It is contended in this book that modern copyright governance commenced its evolutionary development prior to the statute-based economic imperative in 1710, eventually leading to the consolidation of a corporate copyright status quo. Its regulatory framework (which largely mirrors today's system) commenced in or about 1450 at the time of the invention of the printing press and the consequential flow of acts of piracy thereafter (see Johns 2009). The politicization of copyright and the natural propensity to engage in acts of piracy commenced at least 260 years before the current concerns about protecting copyrights from unauthorized use. Gómez-Arostegui (2010) traces the historical development of modern copyright, early calls for protection and the need to deter book-trade pirates. This examination is achieved through a compelling forensic analysis of the trial proceedings in *Tonson v Baker* (1710) C9/371/41 (Ch. 1710). The facts of the case were that a notorious publisher by the name of John Baker, who was known for 'dealing in dangerous books', printed a publication not long after the Lord Chancellor granted Mr Tonson the exclusive right to publish certain trial proceedings. Tonson, the most famous and reputable publisher in 1710, enjoyed an exclusive right to public works granted by the Lords. Baker, on the other hand, was regarded as a pirate, and shortly after the publication by Tonson, a version by Baker appeared in the marketplace. Gómez-Arostegui (ibid., p. 1249) explains: 'The dispute centred around the right to print the trial proceedings of Henry Sacherverell, Doctor of Divinity, who had been impeached by the House of Commons and tried in the House of Lords for High Crimes and Misdemeanours.'

Tonson commenced proceedings against Baker. The action was based on allegations of copyright infringement and unauthorized use in the light of an exclusive right to publish.

The legal story of *Tonson v Baker* is noteworthy because it sets the scene for the modern copyright setting. Tonson (a politically connected, influential citizen with the capacity to lobby for extended and exclusive copyrights) resembles a modern popular media industry representative and Baker resembles the outsider who defies the restrictions imposed by exclusivity in copyright laws, and who possesses opportunistic desires to disseminate works legally or illegally (ibid.). His piratical motives are consistent with the motto 'publish and be damned'.

However, as a consequence of several legal manoeuvres and compelling submissions on the part of Baker's lawyer – submissions concerned with jurisdictional issues and procedural technicalities bordering on matters relating to want of prosecution – the case ended without a finding against Baker, notwithstanding the cogent evidence against him (ibid., pp. 1284–1292). The outcome was indeed disappointing for the Claimant, but the case is not important for doctrinal reasons as it is over 300 years old. The unsatisfactory finding prompted the well-connected Mr Tonson and his associates (the equivalent of modern day corporate entities) to lobby vigorously for greater exclusivity by way of longer periods of copyright terms. The case is therefore politically and economically relevant as it symbolizes the birth of corporate influence over copyright governance frameworks.

In the subsequent centuries, copyright limitation periods were extended to benefit corporate copyright owners. But, as mentioned, the economic imperative is only partly correct. Copyright's political evolution occurred long before its statutory recognition. The political economy of copyright is firmly embedded in the dialectical process. It exists in a politico-economic state where the struggle is between prohibition through monopolization (an unnatural but legal state) and freedom of expression (capable of being natural and unnatural (illegal)).

Kaplan (1967) explains copyright's evolution from Crown law censorship and the 'jealous desire' to guard the 'secrets of the realm'. This is correct because the direct descendant of copyright under Tudor censorship was the Statute of Anne. That is, copyright was more concerned with preventing the publication of work than with replicating per se. Secrets complemented an absolutist monarchy that was able to impose restrictions on use. The parallels between this and current attitudes to modern corporate copyright industries are worth noting (for example, the *Nintendo v Burt* file is sealed as part of the court order – only the parties know the true state of play in this case). So what is equally striking about modern copyright is that traditions based on secrecy and jealously still prevail if the opportunities present themselves.

Reminders of early Crown control are evident in modern copyright law regimes. Tudor monarchs (1485–1603) introduced the printing press into England and also controlled its use. In the seventeenth century the Crown granted licences and patents by way of prerogative rights to individuals, thereby authorizing them to print or import books (Johns, 2009). Copyright was governed by the Stationers Company, which was granted a charter to act as a form of copyright regulator and granted licences to presses, censored books and generally policed the 'media industry' in search of illegal publishers dealing in works deemed to be heretical and generally at cross purposes with the monarchy (Ringer, 1974). The monopoly system via state regulation was commenced by the state. As the preservation of the Crown's status quo was paramount, the Star Chamber enforced the regime (Rose, 1993).

When observing the above arrangements, the nexus between the old and new worlds are noteworthy. The Australian Copyright Act 1968, for example in s. 8, provides that copyright does not subsist except by virtue of that Act, and pursuant to s. 8A details the 'Prerogative rights of the Crown in the nature of copyright'. Reminders of a monarchic past do not end there. Part VB of this modern Act contains provisions for collecting societies (very much monopolistic and exclusive in the same character as the Stationers Company). Part VI provides for the creation of a Copyright Tribunal (comparisons to the Star Chamber – in that this quasi-legal court is created by a copyright statute – might be drawn). That is, tribunals are not mentioned in the Constitution, are not courts of record, rules of evidence are rarely invoked, and as such, tribunals do not form part of the traditional court hierarchy (which is recognized by the Constitution). Their quasi-legal nature suggests tribunals are politico-legal in nature. One can glean from the evolution of modern copyright laws that a strong centralized past pre-dates the Statute of Anne.

It is curious to note that whilst legislatures in Australia, Canada and New Zealand had (and still have) legitimate authority to make copyright laws for their citizens, receiving British law along with Crown prerogative rights was preferred in these democratic societies (enabling both English judge-made precedents and British statutes to be subsumed into domestic law). These former English colonies and the US enjoy strong legal bonds through their inheritance of the same common law background. The inheritance of statutes was just one aspect – a pre-determined system of centralized control of copyright was the major gift bestowed on corporations in Western liberal democracies because the historical foundations of copyright governance also pre-date recent international harmonization protocols. That is, the preconditions for consolidated control of copyright had been set for artificial entities when competition laws were non-existent, thereby setting the scene for a seamless transition to corporate copyright control.

The inherited status of several laws and traditions throughout the common law West especially, and the unbridled acceptance of the Crown's prerogative rights throughout Commonwealth independent nations should come as no surprise. For example, the Australian Copyright Act 1912 in essence embodied the UK Copyright Act 1911. Notwithstanding that Australia was an independent sovereign nation with its own Constitution from 1901, it relied on a British imperial copyright governance framework.[3] For the avoidance of any doubt, s. 5(1) of the current (1968) Commonwealth (Australia) Act still states: 'This Act operates to the exclusion of the Copyright Act, 1911.'

In addition to English monarchic control of the copyright framework, a parallel road to statutory copyright was also taken by other Western nations, and was based on Roman law. France, Germany and, to some extent, Japan were influenced by a codified body of law from sixth century rules consolidated by the Byzantine emperor Justinius who had harmonized elements of Roman laws into a set of civil codes. These nations also eventually experienced the suzerainty of monarchic control over information as replicating technologies emerged. Prior to centralized control, Emmat J in *EMI Songs Australia Pty Limited v Larrikin Music Publishing Pty Limited* (2011) (at paras 30–31) provides a very useful description of the intersection between monopolies and copyrights:

30. The Romans disliked monopolies ... no-one was to be permitted to the sale of certain commodities ... [at the end of the fifth century] ... and that those venturing to fix the prices of their merchandise or bind themselves by any illegal contracts of that kind would be punished by a fine ... (see Justinian's Code, Book 4 Title 59).
31. However, the Romans recognized no exception for copyright. They recognized no monopoly in the result of literary, artistic or musical effort. Rather, the Romans were concerned only with ownership of the physical embodiment of a literary, artistic or musical work (see Justinian's Institutes, Book 2.1.33).

Modern European nations superimposed on their citizens national legal procedures and customs derived from ancient Roman law. Jurisprudential elements of ancient Roman laws were also preserved – in conjunction with the suppression of information dissemination and monopolies over print. For example, the application of unique national codified laws in France, Germany and Italy is a reflection of the Justinian Code and the desire to codify customs and practices with defined precision and an ordinate scope. Replicating technologies changed several attitudes and beliefs in England and continental Europe. It was during medieval times that printing presses became readily accessible and, as a consequence, monopolistic monarchic constraints were imposed. The lines blurred between monopolies and copyright. Control became a universal feature not only in Britain, but also in other Anglo-European countries (see especially, Ginsburgh, 1990). The Church and state made a case (through force and coercion) for the need to tame innovation. It follows that it was the growing distrust of the state that led to civil unrest in England and France, thereby paving the way for the Enlightenment and the need for the separation of powers.

By the 1700s, the common law and continental legal roads eventually ran concurrently as duplicating technologies improved. The decision in *Jefferys v Boosey* (1854) was important for two reasons. The first was that the Court (by majority) decided that common law copyright had been subsumed by the Statute of Anne, which allowed for a *limited* period of exclusivity (14 years). The second was that Boosey had not infringed copyright in foreign works. By the late 1880s, however, with the recognition of the need for universal copyright protection in light of technological advancement, the two distinct legal approaches harmonized internationally for economic reasons (see the Berne Convention and the subsequent ratification of legislation in the West).

Monarchic concerns (1450–1709)

The concept of copyrights and the body of laws regulating them stem from the fifteenth century invention of the printing press. In the 1470s, the printing press was introduced in England. It revolutionized information storage, retrieval and usage, and duplication of works became easier and more accurate. Starting in the 1500s, laws were passed requiring manuscripts to be licensed before publication in the interest of state preservation (Johns 2009 provides an engaging and in-depth examination of these exclusive arrangements leading up to enactment in 1709).

An important consideration, at least for the Crown, was the numerous dissident pathways made available through the printing press. In early modern England there were two absolutist parallel systems of press regulation: one was printing patents, based on the royal prerogative, and the other, the Stationer's Company system, based on the 'by-laws of the guild' (Rose, 1993). The objectives were to ensure obedience via security throughout the realm. Publishers acted as exclusive agents of the Crown. The grant of exclusive royal charters allowed for centralized control (Stationer's Copyright). The Star Chamber identified, assessed, monitored and generally reviewed offensive or inflammatory publications that might be considered to lead to civil unrest. The fact that the subject matter of the alleged copyright infringement in the first copyright suit pursuant to the Statute of Anne was based on restrictions on the publication of 'inflammatory sermons' proceedings is noteworthy given that the accused was an influential doctor of the High Church who published provocative sermons, was critical of the establishment, and whose works were immensely popular (Gómez-Arostegui, 2010, pp. 1258–1263). Gómez-Arostegui (ibid., p. 1259) observes that 'Sacheverell's greatest mistake was publishing the sermons ... around 40,000 of the more inflammatory sermons – The Perils of False Brethren – and subsequent printings (some of which were pirated copies) brought the total to nearly 100,000 copies in print'. The actions of the accused occurred during a period when liberalism, as a political ideology, was developing. The factual link between the desire to publish court records relating to a case where freedom of speech and rights to communicate without fear of persecution, and a case involving common law conceptions of copyright infringement being the subject of a subsequent piracy case pursuant to the first copyright act enacted be acknowledged. *Tonson v Baker* (1710) reflects the politicization of copyright that commenced during the Enlightenment. Non-economic imperatives were the political objectives for the monarchy: 'greate enormities and abuses ... dyvers conetntyous and disorlye persons professing the arte or mystere of Pryntinge or selling of books ...' (cited in Palmer, 1989, p. 267).

A Royal Charter of 1557 gave the Stationers' Company, a printers' guild that dominated all publishing in London at the time, exclusive and perpetual rights in books that were duly registered with it (ibid., p. 267). However, the rights granted by the Royal Charter had nothing to do with rewarding authors. Rather, the grants were much more concerned with the Crown's control of the press. The Charter made it clear that church and state were never to be subjected to heresy, scandal or descent. The Star Chamber – comprising a Privy of Counsellors – monitored and reviewed popular publications and issued decrees for seizure and destruction until 1643 (see Johns, 2009, and Rose 1993).

After the abolition of the Star Chamber, and in the spirit of the Enlightenment, the next five decades witnessed a series of licensing acts designed to remove the Stationers' Company's monopoly 'temporarily'. The only difference, however, was that more licences were granted thereby effectively creating a pre-capitalist oligopoly. Much like the modern day Hollywood, this powerful interest group strenuously lobbied the Crown, reminding it of the dangers of decentralization to the realm in the absence of continued monopolization of print and press. The result was that publishers enjoyed a state-sanctioned monopoly over what appeared in print. As the Company of Stationers survived until nearly the end of the seventeenth century, the political blueprint for modern copyright governance had already been predetermined – thereby avoiding need for any balance (much like the modern setting).

With the 1688 Revolution in England came debate and dissemination of texts on life, liberty, freedom of speech and rights to inalienable property.

The Stationers' Company monopoly legacy was replaced by the enactment of the Statute of Anne, and significant confusion descended on the realm. Justifying protectionism by arbitrarily denying communication to citizens was now replaced by a printing right vested to registered authors who could readily assign or license these rights to publishers (Rose, 1993, and Kaplan 1966). The rationale for monopolistic principles as embedded in modern copyright law are reflected in these developments. The intention of the copyright provisions in the Statute of Anne was to preserve a monopolistic status quo. The template for concentrated control had been set.

Statute of Anne and subsequent cases (1709–1842)

Westminster Parliament enacted this law giving the authors or their assigns the exclusive right to print and reprint books for a term of 14 years for publication of new works (or renewable once for 21 years if works were already in print). Fourteen years was also the time frame chosen by US legislators (Rudd, 1971, p. 138). Authors and publishers could also apply for registration and pay a fee. This tradition is reflected in copyright registration, which is still a central feature in Western jurisdictions, namely the US. The means of production (namely, plant and materials) have always been owned by the publishers. Ownership has always followed a line of a division of powers in terms of ownership tradition.

The Statute reflects the spirit of an era of enlightenment. Elements of striking a balance are clear in the Preamble to the Statute of Anne:

An act for the encouragement of learning, by vesting the copies of printed books in the authors or purchasers of such copies, during the times therein mentioned. Whereas printers, booksellers, and other persons have of late frequently taken the liberty of printing, reprinting, and publishing, or causing to be printed, reprinted, and published, books and other writings, without the consent of the authors or proprietors of such books and writings, to their very great detriment, and too often to the ruin of them and their families: for preventing therefore such practices for the future, and for the encouragement of learned men to compose and write useful books; may it please your Majesty, that it may be enacted, and be it enacted by the Queen's most excellent majesty, by and with the advice and consent of the lords spiritual and temporal, and commons, in this present parliament assembled, and by the authority of the same; That from and after the tenth day of April, one thousand seven hundred and ten, the author of any book or books already printed, who hath not transferred to any other the copy or copies of such book or books, share or shares thereof, or the bookseller or booksellers, printer or printers, or other person or persons, who hath or have purchased or acquired the copy or copies of any book or books, in order to print or reprint the same, shall have the sole right and liberty of printing such book and books for the term of one and twenty years, to commence from the said tenth day of April, and no longer; and that the author of any book or books already composed, and not printed and published, or that shall hereafter be composed, and his assignee or assigns, shall have the sole liberty of printing and reprinting such book and books for the term of fourteen years, to commence from the day of the first publishing the same, and no longer.

The Act was ambiguous in terms of copyright exploitation, but in any event the time period for exclusivity was remarkably short. In *Millar v Taylor* (1769) and *Donaldson v Becket* (1774) common law copyright based on the natural right of the author as the creator of a work was recognized. However, none of these early decisions was easily reached, but *Donaldson* addressed the common law versus statutory author's rights. That case found an author had a common law right of ownership which was held in perpetuity. But the Statute of Anne restrained, or pre-empted, this common law right and limited an author's rights to statutory ones. This reasoning was also followed in the US in the 1834 decision of *Wheaton v Peters* (Rudd, 1971, p. 138). Whilst copyright recognized a publisher's right to an author's right, the publisher was now the beneficiary of exclusive protection given the growing emphasis on the recognition of proprietorship of produced works.

Across the Atlantic, the General Court of Connecticut had passed an 'Act for the Encouragement of Literature and Genius' in 1783 (ibid., p. 137). National harmonization of copyright laws in the US in 1790 particularized with greater detail the purpose of the Act including respective rights for both authors and proprietors (ibid., p. 138).

In these jurisdictions, common law authors had rights to prevent unpublished works from being published, but whether authors possessed the right to restrict exploitation of their published works by third parties was subject to conjecture, statutory and doctrinal debate within the legislature, judicature and the public forum. That is, once in the public domain, should the 'fruits' of an author's 'labour' be protected from duplication or be open to the public? Publishers (as assignees of copyright and owners of hardware) and not authors capitalized on these gaps and played a pivotal part in the decades to follow.

Owning the means of production in a period of great industrialization and benefiting from the assignment of intellectual labour power (the creators' fruits), publishers effectively dominated the marketplace in this era. State control had been replaced by industrialists' centralized control.

But the aversion to monopolization was not lost on some members of parliament. In the 'Petition against a bill to amend the law relating to copyright: Which has been read a first time in the House of Commons' (1800), petitioners were warned of monopolies being a mistake of law and contrary to the 'Laws of this Realm'. Indeed, extensions of copyright, which paved the way for a monopoly in copyrights, would mean that works of vital importance to 'Moral Happiness', would be withheld for three generations (*Remarks on the Law of Copyright*, 188?, p. 9). Indeed, these petitioners recognized the potential of contra-piracy through non-extension as it was 'utterly impracticable' to prevent piracy and would only lead to fruitless litigation and expenses (ibid., p. 10). However, the Petition fell on deaf ears, and the flurry of lobbying in the 1830s might be directly attributed to the definition of copyright as being rigidly connected with the concept of mechanical reproduction (and subsequent manufacture) (see Rose, 1993).

The period commencing in the 1830s was marked by great periods of Western industrialization, as well as powerful lobbying. The invention of efficient replicating machinery and the fierce lobbying for the extension of copyrights marked the birth of modern copyright. At this time, the *D'Almaine v Boosey* (1835) and *Jeffreys v Boosey* (1854) cases signalled further subversion of authors' rights as a primary or originating and naturally occurring private right to a more statute-based public right where emphasis was placed on assigned rights. The early cases turned on essentially the same issues facing exclusive copyright owners today – exclusivity of ownership and unauthorized use of copyright. They were decided based on subsequent statutes throughout the eighteenth and nineteenth centuries when the rights to exclusivity increased and duration of copyright protection was extended. Several piecemeal statutes for different media were enacted containing provisions for greater exclusivity and copyright duration. For example, the Copyright Act (as amended) (1842) did more than recognize musical works. It was the modern precursor to the 1911 Act, and copyrights were extended to the life of the author plus seven years (and 42-year limitation period depending on what event triggered a time frame).

Modern statutes did more than simply subsume common law copyright. They preserved the conception of elite corporatism through absolute monopoly. Purges and the pathological pursuit of seditionists and peddlers of libellous material, and other forms of unauthorized consumption for the protection of the monarchy had been replaced. Now industry-driven initiatives for the preservation of the new ruling corporate elite, which enjoyed extended periods of absolutism, had been established by an amenable legislature. Corporations were given a fresh start in life after being banned for so long. Centralized control and ownership, and restriction of use (through extended copyrights) remained intact – in an era of enlightenment. The pre-conditions for tertiary or late-stage entrepreneurial copyrights had been laid.

Modern copyright statutes and piracy concerns (1842–1970)

This dialectical stage was marked by rapid consolidation of capital, a series of high-profile cases concerned with the piracy, and an ongoing corporate lobby for copyright extension and protection. Piracy was not uncommon in previous centuries (see especially Johns, 2009) but innovation during the Industrial Revolution provided tremendous opportunity for illegal acts.

In this era *Millar v Taylor* (1769) was overturned, and *Donaldson v Beckett* (1774) created the concept of authors' rights in their work. Subsequent legislative developments consolidated copyright law into an exclusive monopoly based on the premise that authors owned the first rights in their work. But the case law since the 1700s largely reflects a landscape of litigation between parties who own the capital and the means to exploit copyright into a material form. Most copyright cases involve publishers and money, or a loss of pecuniary advantage as consequence of a compromise to the monopoly rights enjoyed – usually by the assignees. Remedies for copyright infringement and piracy generally, including injunctive relief and damages, can be traced back to the seminal cases concerning the Statute of Anne (1709) (see the case summaries made by Baron LC, Baron Parke, Rolfe and Platt JJ in *Boosey v Purday* (1849)). Historically, statutes have primarily contained provisions that emphasize protection for published works, thus protecting the rights of those whose business it is to exploit works. Residual rights for authors have evolved in a residual capacity, linked to the economic agenda created by more powerful citizens (*Tonson v Baker* (1710)). Extending copyright meant that copyright would concurrently serve as an anti-piracy mechanism and anticompetitive process through exclusivity vested in the publisher via assignment (the era of endless reprints, reruns, and repackaging was positively affirmed). To this end, *D'Almaine v Boosey* (1835) merely ventilated the concerns about piracy and the meaning of 'substantial part' (a pivotal issue in the *Roadshow Films Pty Ltd v iiNet Limited* (2010) (*iiNet*) P2P case in 2011).

'Copy right' was the subject of regular debate by several MPS in the UK House of Commons in the 1800s, but by 1837 the threat of 'piracies' was added to the ongoing concerns about a cohesive national and international copyright governance framework. Sherman (1997, p. 240) refers to a particular issue about the jurisdictional limits to copyright and the consequential flow of piracy during what might be described as a crucial period for 'shaping the law that we have inherited':

> At present, not only is the literary intercourse of countries, who should form one great family, degraded into a low series of mutual piracies, not only are industry and talent deprived of their just reward, but our literature is debased in the eyes of the world, by the wretched medium through which they behold it. (Mr Sergeant Talfourd MP *HC Sitting (UK) Deb*, 18 May 1837, vol 38, cc 866–80, at 878)

> The grievances suffered by authors and their publishers from spurious publications printed in other countries, have greatly increased during the

last few years, and they have no power at present to protect themselves against the evil and loss it occasions to them. Every work written by a popular author is almost co-instantaneously reprinted in large numbers both in France, Germany and in America and this is done now with much rapidity, and at little expense. ((14 April 1837, FO/27/551), cited in Sherman, 1997, p. 258)

Piracy proliferated throughout the nineteenth century during rapid industrialization across Europe and America and in the absence of international protocols, treaties and general recognition of domestic and foreign copyrights. Technologies and new media seemed to share a commonality with illegal production and consumption. As set out in Chapter 2, a growing international movement for the need to protect copyright occurred later in this stage of development. By the late 1800s, international harmonization was being attempted by a copyright union for global protection and copyright recognition in the advent of emerging technologies. In particular, newly established music technologies created a lucrative opportunity for pirates to enjoy the exploitation of recordings by the turn of the century. But before unionization of common interests in copyright proprietorship, attempts to harmonize common ideals surrounding copyright protection in the West were already in place. Sherman (ibid.) traces the predominately Anglo-French attempts to negotiate international treaties from the 1830s to 1850s, with a view to effecting the outcome of bilateral arrangements in the form of comparable domestic laws. Sherman (ibid., p. 250) observes that 'the model of copyright law that came to the fore in the middle part of the nineteenth century gradually became more and more inflexible'.

The need for Western powers in Europe to harmonize international copyright along Eurocentric lines was an extension of the desire to maintain a colonial status quo. Colonies, especially those devoid of civilization and therefore culture, according to the doctrine *terra nullius*, were conveniently governed by a copyright governance framework that, in essence, exists to this day.[4]

The advent of new technology around the turn of the twentieth century also brought about further corporate lobbying that called for a revision of the law and resulted in the Copyright Act 1911. Lord Reid in *Chappell v Nestlè* (1960) (at paras 105–106) succinctly summarizes this significant development:

Before 1911 it had been held that the reproduction of copyright musical works by mechanical means such as rolls for player pianos was not an infringement of copyright, and gramophone records had been manufactured on a considerable scale and sold without licence or payment of royalty.

This UK Act brought all the modern provisions of copyright into one Act for the first time by revising and repealing earlier Acts. It abolished the requirement to register copyright and the common law copyright protection in unpublished works (generally) (see *HC Deb*, 28 July 1911, vol 28, cc 1911–1145). Most significantly, this more complex law set the scene for a sophisticated corporatized copyright governance framework for tertiary or late-stage copyright evolution. The successor 1956 Copyright Act (UK) introduced elaborate prescribed tests for authorization and use, royalty rates and compensation. The provisions, clearly favouring corporate copyright owners of assigned ownership of the entrepreneurial rights (namely favourable mechanical licensing rights so as to guarantee a minimum statutorily set rate of return irrespective of the price offered to consumers). The House of Lords debate on the Copyright Bill reflects this one-dimensional approach (see generally, *HL Deb*, 21 February 1956, vol 195, cc 1152–1202).

Publishing and recording companies capitalized on the copyright environment provided for by the 1911 Act that allowed for a more fluid process for international copyright exploitation. As mentioned, mandatory registration of copyrights domestically with government copyright agencies was abolished. (For a detailed debate on the rationale for abolition of registration, see *HC Deb*, 7 April 1911, vol 23, cc 2587–2663.) The removal of compulsory domestic registration, which differed throughout various jurisdictions, paved the way for international uniformity in copyright periods. One immediate effect was the introduction of the longest period of copyright in existence among signatories to the Berne Convention. Modifications to remove regional administrative obstacles, such as the non-recognition of copyright in unregistered works, were introduced at the Berlin Convention (1908) and paved the way for reciprocity for nations subscribing to international copyright governance. Copyright periods were extended over the following decades and that extension continues into the twenty-first century. The 1825 repeal of the Bubble Act (banning corporations) could not have been better timed (see Bakan, 2004).[5] The issues around piracy became a core feature in litigation initiated by publishers. In under 50 years, concerted efforts to consolidate copyright control and piracy through an international governance framework, corporate control and exclusivity converged, and the modern popular media industry was born. As Rudd (1971, p. 142) points out, in 1962 'the first of a number of stopgap measures to keep copyrights from expiring' commenced.

Whilst a stopgap measure in the US legislative arena is nothing more than a resolution, it usually signifies an amendment or passing of a bill largely framed along the measures proposed by the House and Senate. During this period, significant revisions were being considered to copyright legislation in the US. One issue was the extension of ownership of the life of copyright during a period of increasing concerns about 'trafficking in phonographic records bearing counterfeit labels' (Register of Copyrights, 1962, p. 6). The measure to extend copyright periods was passed and the law was subsequently amended. The sense of political urgency to extend as soon as practicable is noteworthy as it reflects the current corporate protectionist developments in a world of digitalization.

Any uncertainty created by the seminal piracy and common law cases such as *Donaldson v Millar* (1762), *Donaldson v Beckett* (1774) and *D'Almaine v Boosey* (1835) had certainly been laid to rest by the 1960s. Indeed, Mr Sergeant Talfourd MP provides a lucid account of the demise of perpetual common law authorship rights and the emergence of sophisticated statutory rights – the precursors to the modern copyright law governance frameworks (*Hansard, HC Deb*, 18 May 1837, vol 38, cc 866–880).

The rise of corporate copyright consolidation (1970–2012)

Post-World War II technological developments took into account further amendments to the Berne Convention. In terms of popular media piracy, both the legislature and corporate interest groups representing the popular media industry must have predicted that cassette tapes had the potential to be harmful to the majors. But according to Frith (1988, p. 21), 'the current problem of home-taping was certainly not foreseen'. If this is the case, then it is fair to suggest that the peer-to-peer (P2P) issue was unforeseen. This is probably partially correct. Piracy had always been foreseen, but the rate of innovative piracy was definitely unforeseen, or spectacularly downplayed by the majors.

Litigation ensued in this stage of popular media disorganization with corporations turning on anyone or anything capable of cannibalizing copyright control. But the means of infringement hardly constitutes an offence. In *Australian Tape Manufacturers* (1993), the High Court found (at 498) that:

> [i]t follows that manufacture and sale of articles such as blank tapes or video recorders, which have lawful uses, do not constitute authorization of infringement of copyright, even if the manufacturer or vendor knows that there is a likelihood that the articles will be used for an infringing purpose such as home taping of sound recordings, so long as the manufacturer or vendor has no control over the purchaser's use of that article.

Whether the facility provided (namely Internet access) constitutes an 'unqualified invitation' was refuted in *iiNet*. The cases support the proposition that to facilitate and enable infringement is a vexed issue because a means of infringement does not necessarily constitute an express invitation to infringe copyright. Confusion and ambiguity in copyright legislation remain common features in its governance framework.

This modern period is characterized by unprecedented *reactionary* rather than *anticipatory* approaches adopted by corporate citizens. To assert that all perfectly legitimate technologies are somehow complicit in acts of copyright infringement is blatantly biased, and such assertions are oppressive. Yet corporate citizens continue to initiate proceedings against suppliers of new devices. These actions are incongruous with the fundamental tenets of economic liberalism and, in legal terms, would border on the vexatious if an individual citizen commenced protracted litigation against legitimate technologies.

In the Sony Betamax case (1984) (Sony Corp. of America v Universal Studios, Inc.), the double-edged sword of innovation was reaffirmed. Duplication enables optimal exploitation of copyright in a commodified form, but it also provides freedom to individuals who consume copyrighted products illegally. Following the US decision, in *CBS Songs Ltd v Amstrad* (1988) the House of Lords considered an unsuccessful claim by the owners of copyright material against a manufacturer of high-fidelity sound recording equipment. These devices allowed users to make recordings using blank audiocassette tapes. The case is another example of reactive rather than anticipatory responses to technological change where lawsuits are directed at anyone threatening the status quo as if he, she or it were in the business of compromising copyrights for some 'filthy lucre'.

In the twenty-first century the industry turned to MP3 manufacturers (*RIAA v Diamond Multimedia Sys.* (1999)). The transition to exclusive economic rights was significantly extended as the corporation rose to prominence. Time limits have since been exponentially extended so that the corporate copyright time frame practically reflects a pre-Statute of Anne period of perpetual control. Is it surprising that piracy also proliferated in the light of these restraints, given that the level of copyright extension resembles that of a pre-statute draconian era?

Technological enlightenment and format unrest: the natural urge to disseminate

The historical development of copyright protection suggests that piracy is more political than economic in nature. It is argued that the desire to disseminate and communicate is just as important for pirates as any *mens rea* that might be attached to racketeers (the non-commercial desire first – followed by deceptive pecuniary behaviour). In a Hegelian sense, the ideology of piracy cannot be understood simply along economic rational lines. Consider the statement 'bootlegging is piracy' (Soetendorp, 2003, p. 2). The International Federation of the Phonographic Industry (IFPI) and the respective industry representatives view any form of unauthorized copying as illegal – irrespective of whether a pecuniary advantage is gained. The principle that 'piracy as theft' (ibid., p. 3) or that it is an extension of the concept of stealing, and is thus associated with thievery, has been squarely framed by corporate citizens and is analysed in Chapter 6.

Consumers engaging in the act of piracy are conveniently lumped into a 'bootleg industry' (Melton, 1991, pp. 15–16) by the majors without any great definitional consideration. In the context of bootlegging as a 'product of performance piracy' (live show copying) and 'personal piracy' (home-taping), Melton (ibid., p. 17) explains: 'Thus, both audio and video personal piracy presumes the basic intention of avoiding purchase of an original item.' Melton describes these acts as illegal, yet he uses the term 'to avoid', which for example in taxation jurisprudence does not denote an illegal act. To 'evade' certainly imputes a sense of illegality. This is an important distinction because in Australia, until amendments to the Copyright Act in 1996, unauthorized copies of live recordings (so-called bootlegs) were legal. Bootleggers of performance pirates were hardly pirates in the legal sense therefore. Similarly, the case law surrounding home-taping and time-shifting also supports this observation. Yet, ironically, until very recently in Australia (and soon in the UK), personal piracy in the form of making back-up copies of popular media was deemed illegal. Piracy is a most vexed term because it is open to debate as to whether a consumer is avoiding or evading copyright laws. By way of analogy, take the example of taxation law because, like copyright law, it too is prescriptive in nature. Piratical conduct in the context of tax evasion is obviously construed as illegal. But like the avoidance of taxation, the avoidance of copyright laws suggests another set of human values. In terms of legal realism, if people think laws such as copyright are unfair or oppressive, then piratical conduct might be construed in a different light to that of positivist legal perspective.

Edenborough (1997, p. 17) explains:

> The development of smaller and more sensitive recording equipment has allowed the unauthorized recording of musical performances and films to be easily achieved. These illicit recordings can then be sold to the general public at a large profit to the person who has made the recording. This practice of making, and then selling, illicit recording is called 'bootlegging'.

The reality is that modern bootleggers can be traced back to the 1930s (notwithstanding the fact bootlegging has existed for centuries (Johns, 2009)). For example, music piracy became a major issue in the 1970s with the advent of cassette piracy, and as a consequence pirate bootleg-runners peddled in illegal wares.

In the West, the term 'bootlegging' is more appropriately used to describe the prohibited activity of alcohol consumption (and the on-the-sly liquor trade) in the US (and other common law nations), especially during the period 1920 to 1930. An unsuccessful sociopolitical and moral experiment, prohibition was infamously associated with organized crime gangs bootlegging 'moonshine' and other forms of 'sly grog'.[6]

Though the term has been used interchangeably as a description for the act of media piracy, 'bootlegging' (not counterfeiting) technically stems from the prohibition period. Its ordinary and legal meaning would include elements such as the act of forbidding or preventing manufacture, possession, transportation, supply or otherwise distribution for sale or otherwise of a banned, prohibited substance (namely alcohol or drugs).

Non-media bootlegging differs from media piracy in the sense the latter is rooted in moral attitudes and behaviours concerned with freedom of expression in the pursuit of promulgating knowledge and awareness for the greater good. This explains why prohibiting piracy was, historically, based on political reasons. Piracy is thus related to dissemination and communication where profit or commerciality is not necessarily a factual ingredient, but might form an element of the offence. Bootlegging, therefore, is not piracy.

It is technically incorrect to classify media piracy as bootlegging because bootleggers are prohibited persons engaged in specific acts of entrepreneurial piracy. Bootleggers as a sinister mob (perhaps as those portrayed in the US *Boardwalk Empire* television series) do not involve themselves in current P2P developments. Yet the sheer aggression displayed in the *iiNet* action was squarely aimed at individual users and highlights the acrimony displayed by popular media industries that portray users as a morally derelict mob.

If comparing these two 'evils' by way of a tax law analogy, bootlegging might be akin to evasion, but piracy should be likened to avoidance (the lesser of the two tax evils). The former turns on 'prohibition' whilst the latter is concerned with use in an unauthorized manner. The differences are subtle but distinguishable. No distinction is made by copyright industries in popular media – even though it should be made. The hyperbole used by the movie industry's senior legal representatives to describe iiNet's defence in the litigation includes 'curious', 'misconceived', 'untenable', 'nonsense', 'absurd', 'hopeless' and 'desperate'. iiNet responded by accusing the applicants of viewing the proceedings through an 'artificial prism' and possessing 'narcissistic' tendencies. The case was litigated as if it were a case about bootlegging. The evidence demonstrated it was about the convergence of consumption in which piracy plays a role. Empowering technologies and externalities should not be condemned because they challenge centuries-old monopoly systems. As mentioned, the *iiNet* case was fought on principle in the High Court.

Like copyright, piracy does not exist in a vacuum. It too is technologically determined. The typical business model for any Internet service provider (ISP) incorporates a service whereby users download, upload or stream copyright material with or without infringement. Even the availability of extra data is considered as an inducement or enticement because it is opined by the major players that law-abiding citizens who would otherwise not act in a way that infringes copyright might be tempted. Are the majors suggesting temperance in a techno-hedonistic era? Romanticism is so easily substituted for realism in ideological struggles. The control of popular media is one such political arena.

Conclusion

The desire to disseminate information legally and illegally is technologically and culturally determined. Applying a legal realism perspective, if it is accepted that piracy is embedded in basic human behaviours, it becomes apparent that moral choices, ranging from altruistic piracy participation to black-market racketeering, are made by consumers. (In Chapter 7, the symbiotic relationship between pirates in developing nations and 'law-abiding' Western citizens is examined.) The issue does not concern legal choice, for the law of copyright is prescriptive and infringements are punishable (as shall be discussed in the next chapter). Jones (1961, p. 808) explains: 'on the old issue of the compete analytical separateness of the law that *is* from the law that *ought* to be.' He (ibid., p. 802) maintains that 'legal realism, with its emphasis on the tensions that exist in law administration between the demands of the prescriptive rule-formulation and the appeal of the concrete problem situation, is not the irrational philosophy that it seems to those of its critics who would find all the answers to law's moral problems in higher law precepts, or in the general concepts of analytical jurisprudence'. Convergent consumption patterns in popular media highlight the moral and legal dilemmas where ordinary citizens make reasoned choices.

Adopting a legal realism perspective, altruistic piracy coincides with black-market racketeers. The illegitimate challenges to the organization of copyright are complicated. Interrelational effects between technological advancement and copyright law in popular media (copyright) have proved difficult to reconcile. One conclusion is that as copyright laws represent instruments of social control, individuals in Western democracies see this as a threat to freedom or enlightenment.

There is more to media piracy than bootlegging. The Crown prerogative to ensure civil obedience through the control of literature has been replaced by a corporate copyright imperative to control popular culture. For example, Weatherall (2004, p. 637) correctly identifies one aspect of problems associated in a converging digitalized world:

The definition of 'technological protection measure' is a compromise, which was neither as restrictive as some copyright users had hoped, nor as broad as copyright owners sought – and parts of the legislative history are opaque.

Drawing on the tensions revealed in the previous chapter, it is argued that ISPs have made available online (pursuant to copyright legislation) copyrighted material capable of being manipulated by humans through computers. The act of making something available for use en masse is an unprecedented development. This has led to moral and legal controversies which are inherently political conflicts because the practical effects of large-scale illegal consumption disrupts the rationale for preserving formal conceptions of copyright governance. The sequence of actions taken to download a file and leave popular media available to, say, BitTorrent users in a P2P environment is beyond the control of copyright industries.

Media piracy is no longer about multiple copying – it is a social form of networking where the primary objective is to make things available online. Mr Burt learnt a very powerful lesson in his quest to 'altruistically enlighten' others by uploading *Super Mario Bros*. In this setting, people have become members of swarms in a symbiotic relationship with each other for mutualistic benefit. Consumers have organized themselves as de-identified users in an anonymized swarm of activity – by switching on or off a computer or dropping in or out of connection to the Internet. A user of the Internet searches for a 'torrent file' so as to download popular media so that 100 per cent of that commodified item is eventually copied to that user's hard drive. This may or may not be achieved so the consumer moves on to another product and may not return to the original file searched. Fragmented consumption through BitTorrent Protocol online might constitute infringing communication if the consumption is substantial enough that the user has created an infringing copy – but that is a question of fact. These new approaches symbolize something more than just acts of piracy and behaviours associated with illegal consumption. The mood transcends prohibition, bootlegging or making a quick sale. Suzerainic monopolists continue to purge heretics who defy the organized control of popular culture. *Auf Wiedersehen* common law copyright sense.

6
A Three-Front War on Piracy: Technological Protection, Legal Action and Education Programmes – *Null Bock Haltung?*

Introduction

Pirata est hostis humani generis
(A pirate is an enemy of the human race)

(in Lely, 1883, p. 628)

Lely's seventh Edition of *Wharton's Laws* was a most useful compendium for English lawyers and other Commonwealth legal practitioners at the time. The expression is a reference to actual sea pirates whose acts were punishable by death upon a finding of guilt. Piracy is defined as:

> [t]he commission of those acts of robbery and violence upon the sea, which if committed upon land would amount to felony. Pirates hold no commission or delegated authority from any sovereign or state empowering them to attack others. They can therefore only be regarded in the light of robbers. They are as Cicero has truly stated, the common enemies of all (*communes hostes oninium*); and the law of nations gives to everyone the right to pursue and exterminate them ... but it is not allowed to kill them without trial ... By the ancient common law of England, piracy ... was held to be species of treason. (*Wharton's Laws*, p. 627)

The penalties for actual sea pirates were indeed as severe as for those who were found guilty of murder. To this day such pirates are severely dealt with and their treasonous acts are akin to terrorism. And to this end, symbolically, but certainly not legally, comparisons are made between the modern-day organized media pirates and sea pirates.

Are individuals who participate in unauthorized consumption that constitutes copyright infringement just as parasitic, and therefore deserving of being labelled common enemies? The motivation for commercial pirates is obvious. But what about those devious little uploaders, the anarchist BitTorrent hosts and other related Internet users; are they part of the *null bock* cyberpunk generation who could not care less? What is their motivation? The media campaigns promulgated by the International Federation of the Phonographic Industry (IFPI), the Motion Picture Association of America (MPAA), the Entertainment Software Association (ESA) and the Australian Federation Against Copyright Theft (AFACT) suggest that there is no distinction between the two types of pirates where hazards flows from *any* illegal activity because these acts are harmful.

This chapter discusses the multidimensional corporate response to media piracy. The core strategic business positions and solutions adopted by the major players, however, present several legal and moral difficulties. Significant legal obstacles in copyright enforcement are identified, including why the state does not generally deem copyright infringement a high priority in the overall public safety enforcement framework. Accordingly, the level of formal enforcement utilized to achieve substantive outcomes is also considered. The conclusion of this chapter is that the war against piracy is difficult to conceptualize and is becoming increasingly futile because battle lines in the intangible realm are difficult if not impossible to draw.

Despite this substantive legal reality, the three arms of legitimate state power nonetheless accept that even altruistic piracy is recognized as harmful because of the potential for loss of profits and opportunity by copyright owners. Unlicensed dealing of copyright works, namely trading in illegal popular media, providing the tools to engage in illegal consumption,[1] uploading, downloading and any combination of these illegal acts, is therefore tantamount to piracy. 'Piracy is theft' (Gillespie, 2011, p. 218) ergo 'though shalt not steal'.

This chapter specifically explores the intersection between law enforcement, technology, copyright infringement, the mutualistic, or rather, symbiotic relationship between pirates and consumers, and the profiling of consumers as criminals or, at the very least, civil wrongdoers and moral derelicts. It aims to assess the implications of the corporate response to media piracy in the light of a convergence of consumption.

In the commercial setting one might be able to extend the traditional concepts of theft to media piracy, but it is difficult to apply the ordinary dictionary meanings of media piracy as theft in relation to individual P2P use. This section examines the misnomers contained in the legal nomenclature, while the following sections provide an assessment of the methods implemented by popular media corporations in the war against illegal consumption. It evaluates the overall success of the anti-piracy policies implemented by these copyright industry stakeholders. 'The war effort' section examines first-, second- and third-line strategies (technological, legal and educational measures). The guiding question is: what is the overall effectiveness of these preventative steps?

In light of the above, the proposition raised in this chapter is that as copyrights are intangible, the only dimension capable of being lost is the opportunity contained therein. Physical objects (CDs and cash) are tangible. Theft of items generally includes the physical act of committing a crime (for example, shoplifting or teller-machine skimming). The ordinary meaning of the term 'theft' would also extend to cyber-theft (hacking into accounts and email scams where cash deposits are extorted). Copyright infringement, however, is tantamount to opportunity theft. In other words, file-swappers when exchanging libraries are trading in missed opportunities of sale because there is no proof that those swappers would have actually purchased those files.

Take the example of a CD that is stolen and then converted for a specific amount at the local pawnshop. It is then purchased for good consideration for AUD$5. In the intangible realm, the same CD is uploaded by the owner, and the CD is completely downloaded 100 times. What are the damages? Is the opportunity lost valued at AUD$500, or at a greater figure given the artificial price attached as a new item pursuant to the published price to dealer, or less because it is cheaper to download it on iTunes or as part of an Internet service provider (ISP) bundled package? Perhaps the opportunity lost is zero because the downloaders would never have purchased the music on the CD in the first place. Perhaps the opportunity lost is zero because the 500 downloaders would never have purchased the music on the CD. This loss can only ever be described as theoretical or speculative. The same consumers who illegally acquired the music would still attend a performance and therefore presumably pay the admission price as concert fans. Measuring non-attendance at a concert as an actual loss is considerably easier to achieve.

Indeed what if the symbiotic illegal activity was positive? Navissi, Naiker and Upson (2005, pp. 170, 183), in a study on Napster, reported that whilst 'gross capital loss was in excess of $18 billion', 'capital gain in response to pro-Napster events was $9 billion' (via stimulation of music purchases), thereby not only suggesting both enabling and disenabling effects, but also exposing the artificiality of the allegations of actual sustained loss. Were all these people bad consumers including the ones who may have purchased concert tickets (for which a performance license fee must be paid by the venue and duly collected by the exclusive royalty collecting association)? This is difficult to accept as Navissi, Naiker and Upson (ibid., p. 182) calculated the total market capitalization for the sample firms to be US$101 billion at the time of Napster.

It follows that the objective elements of the offence of piracy are founded on subjective notions that pirates possess evil tendencies and are the scourge of civilization. But considering the above definitional parameters and subjective assessment of piratical harm, the precise symbiotic nature between the legal and the illegal requires greater scrutiny.

The above-mentioned campaigns appear to elevate the status of individual file-swappers to that of a common enemy. Lawsuits against individuals are evidence of this. But it is argued that consumers privately participating in downloading, ripping and burning should not be lumped into the same unsavoury genus as organized criminals. *Wharton's* (1883, pp. 627–628) provides a less dramatic definition of media pirates:

> 'Piracy of Works' [is] [a]n offence against the law of copyright or an author's right to his works, which consists in an exclusive right to the sequence of the words as they stand; and if anyone else reprint these without addition, subtraction, or transcription, it is an inroad on the author's right. But on one hand, the sentences and words may be so rearranged, that, although nothing be added or taken from them they give a substantially new idea to the public, and therefore no infringement of the law. And on the other hand, although parts may be omitted, and new passages introduced, yet if these alterations be merely colourable, and it is really an attempt to profit by taking the ideas of another, the publication is piracy.

Much has changed to make this old definition of piracy redundant. The label of piracy has now been extended to those consumers participating in legal and illegal consumption where these behaviours have converged. That is, some of these consumers who display piratical urges might also be good consumers because they may stimulate interest in the same media content – but in another forum. Consumption has indeed become complex and problematic.

General observations and legal misnomers

The setting for the introduction of a modern-day test for piracy (namely lack of authorization and substantive copying) was made at the turn of the nineteenth century. It still exists. However, peer-to-peer (P2P) file-sharing is the most recent of example of how simple acts of downloading and uploading 'bits' of data do not necessarily satisfy the test for infringement. Indeed, one century later, *Osborn's Concise Law Dictionary* defines copyright infringement as a form of interference with or violation of the right of another. Recovery of damage caused or profits made is the only remedy.

Popular media industries, however, promote these infringements as piratical acts – which symbolically represent one of the lowest forms of human behaviour. We know that to be a false and misguided depiction of citizens in liberal democracies. The branding of consumers as pirates in the media campaigns is nothing more than marketing propaganda.

There is no mention of evil or villainy in these definitions, but a key element is gaining a pecuniary advantage. Profit is obviously the motive. Larceny or misdemeanour might best describe the offence of stealing (as the terms relate to tangible goods, including money). The concept of personal use as 'piracy of works' being tantamount to theft is a relatively recent extension. Defining individual consumers who participate in file-sharing as pirates is problematic as copyright piracy is associated with profit (or loss thereof) – but not necessarily theft. The rationale is simple. It is argued that robbery and actual physical acts of piracy are interchangeable because of the level of violence. Violence or a perception of violence is usually associated with harm (and this would extend to harm caused by cyber-attacks – online 'virtual robbery').

To brand the act of illegitimate consumption for no financial gain as an act of piracy is indeed confusing and ambiguous. This is not to suggest that the act of copyright piracy is to be condoned, but it appears to be a modern construct mythologized by artificial corporate copyright-owning citizens in order to equate theoretical loss, loss of profit and future economic loss to that of *actual harm* sustained by natural citizens as victims of physical property offences. Kahan (1997, p. 358) observes: 'Most individuals regard compliance with law to be morally appropriate. But most also loathe being taken advantage of.' When reflecting on Veblen's 1923 observations about the corporation's rise to prominence and ultimate cultural dominance, and when considering popular media industries, there is some force in Veblen's (1954, p. 107) later statement:

> The industrial arts are a matter of tangible performance directed to work that is designed to be of material use to man ... arts of business are arts of bargaining, effrontery, sales-manship, make-believe, and are directed to the gain of the business man at the cost of the community at large and in detail. Neither tangible performance nor the common good is a business proposition. Any material use which his traffic may serve is quite beside the business man's purpose, except indirectly, in so far as it may serve to influence his clientele to his advantage.

One wonders whether the popular media industries actually reflect on how consumers perceive these shock advertising campaigns. Take a nonsensical example from one of the anti-taping cases in the 1970s and 1980s. In 1982 in one of its advertising campaigns the Australian Recording Industry Association (ARIA) alleged:

> HOME TAPING COSTS GOVERNMENT $100 MILLION P.A. HOME TAPING COSTS RECORD INDUSTRY $440 MILLION P.A.

> ... there is no way any Government or the Copyright Owners could hope to police the copyright infringement involved every time someone uses a blank tape to record music.

> ... most Australians are not even aware they are breaking the law. Half of all home taping is direct from the radio ... The situation is that for every pre-recorded disc or tape sold in Australia, another two are home taped ... This is having a very serious effect on employment, sales and profits

in the record industry in Australia. One plant has closed down in Sydney and one in Melbourne and employment is falling off generally in other record companies. Each time a home tape is made our own Artists and Composers lose a legitimate royalty. *Another effect is that the record companies have less risk capital to invest in up-and-coming Australian Artists and Composers, and they will tend to stick with the established big names.* (WEA case, p. 135 (1983) (emphasis added))

As in the *Australian Competition & Consumer Commission v Universal Music Australia Pty Limited (No 2)* (2002) *(ACCC)*, preposterous assertions were made in the *WEA Records Pty Ltd v Stereo FM Pty Ltd* (1983) *(WEA)* case. Plants closing down, job losses and capital investments have more to do with business cycles and economic downturn than anything else. As mentioned in previous chapters, most artists are unable to survive on royalties, and reinvestment into domestic markets has nothing to do with piracy.

In the 1990s, virtually the same campaigns were rolled out in relation to CDs and parallel importation. Yet the music industry thrived. Consumers are far from dim – but they clearly take a dim view if they feel have been taken advantage of (see below) or when they are relentlessly pursued because they have purportedly caused loss and upset to an artificial citizen. The anti-piracy parodies are evidence of this protest.

Tradition, customs, culture and change

What came first – the desire to consume popular media illegally, or the urge to socialize illegal consumption? This question is circular given piracy's historical developments in the light of technological change. But is not the desire to consume information or knowledge and culture generally an innately human need based on enlightenment? As a taboo, consciously consuming pirated works requires a trigger of a unique moral code based on a sliding scale of acceptability and mutualism (P2P users rely on a laissez-faire mutual benefit as do the hagglers and tourists in the bazaars).

The high rate of piracy suggests the moral threshold is low for consumers. Experiencing popular media is one of those omnipotent and instantly self-satisfying desires (especially in the world of digitalization). Technological innovation indeed facilitates affective pleasure derived from popular culture. For millions it seems it matters not whether popular media is gained legally or otherwise, as long as it consumed. There is no literature that suggests consumers of illegally obtained popular media express feelings of shame, guilt or remorse from the sin of consuming pirated media.

Indeed there is no significant historical reference point to support the contention that copyright piracy has always been deemed a social taboo or immoral act. This is because illegal consumption is a relatively recent invention. Formal sanctions for the combined effects of consuming illegal popular media and engaging in commercial media piracy evolved in the late nineteenth century. As mentioned in the previous chapter, copyright piracy was not recognized under codified Justinian rule. Johns (2009, p. 39) also comments on the Roman legal structure recognizing the need to deter piracy as espoused by Cicero. There is no mention of 'copyright piracy = theft'. Indeed copyright was not recognized at all, yet the Romans banned monopolies as early as the sixth century (see Procopius, 2004, Chapters XX, XXV–XXVI). In such an advanced codified legal system one would have anticipated some form of protection for owners of non-tangible assets (authors, architects, artists and sculptors at least). This was not the case – only physical or tangible assets were deemed capable of protection (for a detailed examination see also *Justinian's Institutes* Book 2.1.33, cited in *Larrikin Music Publishing Pty Ltd v EMI Songs Australia Pty Limited* (2011)). Under Roman law the works created by authors and artists were regarded as intrinsically valuable as commodities; however the intangible and tangible aspects of the works were not separated. In the Justinian legal sense, copying and the subsequent consumption of works support anti-monopolistic attitudes because there is no legal requirement to seek permission by way of licence or any form of authorization. This indeed might be described as the development of a rudimentary free culture or creative commons attitude. That unauthorized consumption is morally derelict behaviour is a modern construct.

It can be observed that many of the fundamental human moral and legal boundaries as set out in Judaeo-Christian Western concepts of the Ten Commandments[2] remain intact in the twenty-first century. For example, (a) *You shall not murder*, and (b) *You shall not steal* are the primary foundations for offences concerning persons and property. Other legal customs also stem from these ten rules. Under this basic legal-moral code there is no reference to intangible assets, that is, non-monetary goods. When one thinks of 'shall not steal', one imagines tangible objects. Unlike cash and precious metals, copyrights have no physical form. They are the antithesis of money and tangible value. Copyrights, like other intangibles such as high-risk shares and debt-factoring, are very volatile investments and it is doubtful security for intangibles would readily be offered, compared to, say, land, cash or even government bonds. These mores are historically embedded in commerce and trade and exchange generally.

These basic codes are moral links to our 'ancestral environment' (Manesh, 2006, para. 54). In other words, intuitively amoral behaviours have evolved over time and, in the absence of any trigger, there is no moral response and the 'cognitive system is left to reason about the appropriate moral response' (Manesh, 2005, para. 54).

Whilst Rev. David Noebel's (1974) interconnected conspiracies that communism,[3] popular rock music, the Beatles and especially the Rolling Stones are part of a greater subversive plot to corrupt young Americans should be unequivocally dismissed, his religious observations about conceptions of 'new morality' (the Ten Commandments) might be explored in light of consumption, culture and morality. Obsessed with the purported perversion caused by 'animalistic morals' – the combined effects pop music, sex, and drugs – Noebel misses the point because the sophisticated corporate organization of popular media promotes this new morality in an hierarchically and highly advanced vertically and horizontally integrated capitalist process. But his new moral philosophy argument might have application in light of artificial citizens complaining of harm caused by the moral and legal piratical transgressions.

Consumers have been slow to accept that pirated products as illegal goods should be ignored or somehow morally vetoed.[4] Copyright is a recent artificial invention. It has not been tested over many centuries as to its legal and moral fortitude in terms of whether copyright laws are universally beneficial or not. Other norms, customs and practices are well established. At best, copyright infringement is a mixture of loss of opportunity (through profits), and the law allows for compensation in a very general and unscientific way.

Infringement of copyright might be flagrant if it is knowing and deliberate, but it is traditionally difficult for consumers to construe popular media consumption as theft. Professor Gibson (2011, p. 1, emphasis added) best epitomizes this as 'millions of United States citizens commit copyright infringement on a routine basis. Illegal downloads of movies and music number in the *tens of billions annually*'. This observation is statistically corroborated by the IFPI's recent report where it is claimed nearly a quarter of global Internet traffic infringes copyrights (IFPI, 2011a, p. 18). Is this the hallmark of an enlightened, advanced, capitalist, transnational society or the profile of a regressing civilization?

These issues are technologically and historically determined. Recognition of a need to preserve and protect intangibles was created as replicating technologies emerged when the politico-economic potential surrounding monopolized intangibles became an economic reality. By the mid-eighteenth century, copyright piracy became a recognized modern problem. It is worth providing this historical background because significant resources are devoted to educating the modern consumer that the tangible and intangible are legally separated and therefore distinguishable (Dicola, 2011). This might be the law (technically), but the empirical reality is that consumers struggle with this conceptually (just as the Roman jurists did in the sixth century).

Corporate copyright was an invention of an emerging industrialized world driven by the Western need to colonize the tangible and intangible realm. Copyright piracy is not a very old concept and, relatively speaking, not a well-recognized taboo or sin (P2P file-sharing is indicative of this and, as explicated in the *Roadshow Films Pty Ltd v iiNet Limited* (*iiNet*) case and the recent

Twentieth Century Fox Film Corp & Ors v British Telecommunications Plc (2011) case, the bulk of BitTorrent traffic is illegal). It would be preposterous to suggest these users are collectively bad, just as it would be absurd to have accused home-tapers in the 1980s of encouraging each other to break the law.

On this point, why should a CD purchased for good consideration not be copied and disseminated to others? As a telecommunications industry services (telco) customer, why should there be a ban on downloading a television programme uploaded by an anonymous user and so on? For a corporation (and its legal representatives) such questions are nonsensical, but they do hinge on liberalism and notions of self-determination for consumers. Being denied the right to share popular culture because of copyright laws is a conceptually difficult restriction for consumers (especially teenagers) (as seen in the proceeding chapter).

The publicity campaigns aimed at educating and threatening consumers with legal action suggest that piracy is not a victimless crime, but, as mentioned, calculating copyright infringement is hardly a precise and exact forensic accounting exercise (compared to, say, credit-card theft or snatching a handbag). If the music industry alone is worth several billion dollars and creators receive relatively small royalty returns (see Dolfsma, 2000), then the victims must not prima facie be the creators. In certain circumstances the assessment of damages for copyright is 'at large'. The court in many copyright cases adopts speculative methods by way of guesswork. For example, see generally, *Fenning Film Service Ltd v Wolverhampton, Walsall and District Cinemas, Limited* (1914) at 1174; *Autodesk Australia Pty Ltd v Cheung* (1990) at 477 per Wilcox J; and *Columbia Picture Industries Inc v Luckins* (1996) at 510 per Tamberlin J. These cases invariably refer to corporate citizens as defendants. What the case law suggests is that harm is based on opportunity loss endorsed by an account of profits. In other words, an artificial citizen sustains theoretical harm and a hypothetical guess is made – presumably based on a forensic report in order to determine compensation. Natural citizens are entitled to scrutinize these methods.

That the court applies a statutory discretion under copyright legislation having regard to the flagrancy of the infringement and the need to deter similar conduct is problematic in itself because the victims are not specifically identified in the eyes of the consumers. The discretion is very wide, including fees that the copyright owner (not creator) might otherwise have charged based on the market value. In other cases actual or potential loss of commercial opportunity (loss of profit or a disappointment loss because a marketing campaign has been compromised) may be calculated. The success of the current response therefore cannot be accurately measured in these terms given the relatively small number of legal actions commenced against individuals as pirates. Relying on industry data is simply not enough.

The war effort

This section examines the current three-tiered approach. Generally speaking, corporations reactively assess the cost of illegal consumption and implement the following control measures which are categorized into three distinct but interlocking areas of piracy prevention:

1. technological control and protection;
2. legal action (policing, prosecution and litigation against both natural citizens (human consumers) and artificial citizens (chiefly legitimate telcos and software manufacturers and suppliers as media pirates)); and
3. education and awareness campaigns/programs.

These are described as first-, second- and third-line measures. However, it is fair to suggest educating and campaigning complement the other two areas.

At least eight categories of identifiable illegal copyright activity exist:

1. sophisticated national and international piracy (large-scale organized crime);
2. small-scale operations (criminal activity for profit);
3. Internet services and sites (ignoring infringers' acts, encouraging piracy, supplying enabling software and receiving financial benefit (civil));
4. as in (3) above, but the civil wrong stems from *not* having received financial benefit;
5. home users burning and ripping for personal use and sharing with others (civil);
6. home users uploading and downloading via P2P technologies for personal reasons and sharing with others (civil);
7. home users downloading via P2P technologies for personal reasons and sharing with others (civil);
8. casual/curious users knowingly consuming pirated products (civil).

These categories are cumulative and conjunctive and, as such, several permutations and combinations obviously exist, but it is fair to accept the term piracy is used to describe all classes of transgressors. Having said that, substantive litigation is squarely aimed at ISPs and technology pioneers (Napster, Kazaa, MP3.com and iiNet).

The concurrent methods of deterrence listed above have been deployed to stem the flow of illegal copyright activity. In keeping with the copyright regulatory regime, the corporate response is prescriptive and firmly embedded in what seems to be a five-step risk-management process to manage copyright infringement. These processes are universal. The five steps are:

1. *identify* the risk of piracy and its sources as a commercial 'hazard';
2. *assess* the financial risks that may result because of piracy;
3. *determine* the choice of controls;
4. *implement* strategies to combat piracy; and
5. *monitor* and *review* the effectiveness of the strategies.

In terms of understanding the nature of illegal consumption, it is argued that these steps are reactive rather than anticipatory. That is, corporations dogmatically utilize the three modes of deterrence in order to properly identify the source of piracy for the purpose of minimizing it. This is a reactive approach to copyright infringement. The means of prevention are used to put an end to illegal activity (piracy). For example, during the early years of the last decade, on behalf of the music industry, IFPI and the respective national associations commenced comprehensive legal action against individuals. This was a reactive policy. It gained the immediate attention of the media, but then the legal actions slowed down and, as reported in the documentary film *RIP*, by 2008, litigation against consumers no longer became official policy (see the next section). An anticipatory approach accepts piracy as a mode of consumption, and policing and prevention are therefore limited to organized piracy (and do not extend consumers or telco neighbours).

The first line of defence is anti-piracy technology. With the threat of digitalized replication in a converging media world, various techniques, such as watermarking (Simpson, 2002) and invisible signatures (McKeogh and Stewart, 1997), were introduced throughout the 1990s with minimal effect or impact. In fact, corporate attempts to prevent CD- and DVD-copying have, generally speaking, failed over the past two decades. Take, for example, the fascinating practical attempt to discourage consumers wishing to copy CDs onto recordable CR-ROMs (CD-burning) in the 1990s. Early on it was reported that the major manufacturers of CD recording devices (Sony and Phillips, whose cultural arms also own record labels) were encouraged by the music industry lobby to create electronic devices incapable of reading cheap CD-ROMs. The devices were created so that more expensive blank CDs could only be used on the recording devices, thereby deterring potential pirates because of the cost of the blank media. (Incidentally, these popular media manufacturers also sold blank CDs.)

But this combative technique was designed with such a fundamental flaw that a loophole was published in the *Home Cinema Choice* magazine (see Fox, 1998). The 'trick' allowed for playback compatibility between copied CDs and copied CD-ROMs. Fox (2002, p. 9) reports that the futility of copyright protection stems from the fact that measures for making CDs and CD-ROMs incompatible can quite simply be sidestepped. One main reason is that the computer industry builds into its technologies the capability to read media on a macro-level through regularly upgraded software and hardware – much to the disappointment of the popular media industry. But the popular media industry should not always point the finger at external technologies. It is curious to note that Sony's PlayStation 3 has been created with two universal serial bus (USB) ports that conveniently allow movies with audio-video interleave (AVI) extensions (a popular choice for BitTorrent users) to be played. Fox is right – the task is somewhat futile because the popular media industry itself is enabling ease of illegal use. The technological deterrent effects appear to have minimal effect in a world of digitalization.

Some of the more recent examples of technological deterrence in the music industry have also failed and have done much to frustrate and estrange consumers. When EMI in association with the rest of the music industry announced in 2003 the introduction of Copy Controlled (CC) into its digitally recorded formats in a bid to stem CD piracy, the world took notice. This anti-piracy measure received a great deal of publicity but the Internet provided a perfect forum for discussion about techniques to circumvent it.[5] That is, not only were members of social networks actively promoting loopholes and complaining about incompatibility issues on forums, there were several programs freely available to assist in copying the CDs. Are these 'liberal villains' actively engaged in commercial treason or promotion of free speech? The distinction between encouragement and dissemination has become increasingly blurred as consumers rise to the challenge of circumventing the technology. Goldman (2003, pp. 406–408) notes the significance of ego, bravado and a sense of community ('kindred spirits'). These are all human traits. In an environment of open-ended, emerging technological development, it is suggested copyright protection through technological means is becoming increasingly futile – or at least problematic – because people seem to view these hurdles as challenges that must be overcome.

As for legal action and deterrence, the civil standard of proof – the balance of probabilities – is applied to defences (a lower standard of proof than the criminal standard – beyond reasonable doubt). Once a matter has been determined in favour of the aggrieved party, the critical issue of deterrence (both general and specific) must be considered. What is missing from the debates is a critical analysis of the deterrent value placed on legal outcomes (judgments) in media piracy cases. This might be because, as litigation is a second line of defence in the war against piracy, there is, as yet, insufficient empirical data to support its effectiveness. Its efficiency cannot be compared in terms of any cost–benefit analysis because litigation, arguably, is the most costly approach. Gibson (2011) suggests that it is doubtful whether prosecutorial policies have made a major impact in terms of sending a strong message. One indication is that courts rarely award exemplary damages against individual offenders for flagrant infringement. The action Nintendo pursued against Mr Burt was an unusual step and, in any event, as the precise terms of settlement were sealed by way of court order it is difficult to determine the nature of the award and the precise value of the loss.

The third line of protection is education and promotion of the concept that copying, and especially downloading, popular media is morally reprehensible. Throughout the Western world telco customer agreements emphasize the need to comply with all laws and directions by regulatory authorities, prohibit certain use, and consequently warn of restriction, suspension, disqualification and cancellation of service for any form of abuse, including copyright infringement. The warnings extend to a prohibition on encouraging third-party abuse (presumably this refers to facilitating access to others through P2P devices and protocols). Further, the warnings about copyright infringement through illegal consumption are very clear. The introduction of so-called education notices for consumers suspected of piracy suggests reorientation of consumer behaviour is factored into the anti-piracy campaign. Persistent abusers are then monitored and enforcement is graduated, or rather escalated, so as to ensure compliance and deterrence, through legal action as a last resort. Education programmes represent the 'good cop' approach whilst simultaneously reminding the illegal consumer that the 'bad cop' is in the next room waiting to be invited into the action (the legal response).

But in the face of so much prescribed regulation and policy why does the abuse continue to increase? Are all these customers thieving consumers or purveyors of popular culture in a free world? Formal conceptions of modern legal principles state the legal position; historical references assist in situating the debate; but the legal reality is copyright laws are perpetually flouted thereby questioning the effectiveness of these strategies.

Litigating against John Doe, and Fred Nurke and other armchair pirates

In 2003 the education (advertising) campaigns, copy-controlling technologies and legal action (including private prosecutions) against individual consumers of popular media converged. And thus the guns pointed at the consumer. The war against piratical terror was squarely aimed at consumers – you, me, them, we – the lovers of popular culture. In the US it commenced in September of 2003 when some 261 American music fans were sued for piracy (Electronic Frontier Foundation, 2005, p. 2). Groennings (2005b, p. 389) describes the purge best as a 'desperate move to address the P2P epidemic; the recording industry filed a first round of lawsuits against its own fans'. Legal action urged by a posse of litigators funded by vociferous associations and collecting societies continued against popular media consumers for the next five years. The antecedents of the pirates ranged from 'tweenies' (12-year-old Brianna Lahara whose mother Sylvia Torress settled for US$2,000) to septuagenarians (Durwood Pickle, a 71 year old whose computer had been used by his grandsons for illegal downloading) (Mook, 2003).

By 11 November 2004, actions were commenced against 6,200 file-sharers (see Groennings, 2005a, p. 571). By April 2007, numbers reached 18,000 and the damages ranged between US$3,000 and US$11,000 (EFF, 2007, p. 6). As McBride and Smith (2008) correctly reported in *The Wall Street Journal*, the war against the individual as an illegal consumer ended in 2008. The Recording Industry Association of America (RIAA) sent 'lawyers, guns and money' (as in the epochal title of Warren Zevon's song), but fighting consumers as pirates in an age of technological liberation does not work as the rationale behind such motives is a commercial reaction. The current war on consumers is covert in that individuals using Torrent networks are spied on and monitored for any piracy activity. How these tactics will ingratiate, rehabilitate and otherwise placate consumers in an open-source environment remains to be seen.

The logic behind the war on piracy, in relation to consumers, is based on the following moral presumption: we think that you are not bad people generally, but you do need some obvious incentives to ensure that you comply with this regulatory scheme. Therefore one would anticipate the issue of copyright infringement notices (akin to, say, traffic tickets) would suffice as a form of retribution. However, the message from the media industries during the first decade of the twenty-first became: if you 'rip' or 'burn' then you are infringing copyright because downloading a CD is like stealing a CD from a store. If you steal then you are a bad person, and you are participating in criminal behaviour. When you are caught, you will be treated like a criminal and punished as an offender because you are causing harmful losses to the industry.

But the potential for loss has always been a feature of popular media industries. When a record company commissions the recording of an album it takes a cultural gamble. If the album flops, then a poor decision was made, and it cannot be said that the company is capable of recouping losses from the recording of the album unless there are sales. If there is a profit then costs associated with production are capable of recoupment. Yet in terms of media piracy and its alleged consequential harmful effects on creativity and production, the popular media industry has remained firm in its reasons for high prices for albums and DVDs. One reason for the high price tag is based on the notion that corporations make more flops than hits. Therefore costs must be recouped, where possible, where chances or risks have been taken with cultural products. If sales do not reach expected targets then the higher price to the dealer assists in absorbing some of the associated interaction costs. This is, indeed, an elitist approach to determining how goods are to be priced for consumption. Until the advent of digitalization, higher prices were justified because of the risks taken by the corporation to physically produce the product. But when quantifying any economic loss, corporations also recoup royalties from other works by way of cross-collateralization so as to minimize future economic loss against poor sales of a subsequent album or DVD produced by the creator. This may include recoupment from future works by the same artist for example.[6] Popular media industries might acknowledge the poor performance of an album, film or game, but the loss is never presented as detrimental to the industry. For example, explanations for a 'flop' may include reasons such as consumers no longer find a style popular, or that people are time poor and simply cannot find the time to watch an entire film. The industry is quick to allege that the financial harm is the fault of the illegal participants. But responsibility for financial harm caused by making poor cultural choices or by technological change is seldom raised – unless to gain sympathy from consumers about losses sustained.

Five years after individual actions slowed down, in 2010, these issues were raised in *iiNet*. Why did Hollywood choose not to pursue individuals in this particular case? There are some answers. The first is cost mitigation. This is obvious because costs associated with pursuing an action could exceed the amount sought. The second is adverse publicity. Earlier actions against individuals received a significant amount of adverse publicity. The third reason is legal reality, in that whilst specific deterrence against an occasional and random consumer may have some effect, general deterrence in the face of millions of downloads appears to be spectacularly ineffectual. This is the fallacy of action against individuals as end-users of digital products. What *iiNet* suggests is that whilst the pursuit of individual consumers in that case was entirely possible, the option to single out the ISP was preferred. Yet from 2003 to 2008, copyright owners broadly encouraged the relentless pursuit of individual users. However, this policy whereby the end-user was depicted as the villainous consumer generally failed. Action against consumers constituted nothing more than a misguided reactive policy – not least of all because consumers of popular media are also the fans of popular culture in its commodified form.

Furthermore, in any Western jurisdiction, initiating proceedings in the lower courts is relatively cost effective (from the equivalent of US$500 to $2,000).

Proceedings would be robotic or rote in nature for experienced lawyers. And as many firms now work on speculative briefs, uplifts, no-win-no-fee bases and various debt-factoring strategies (including outsourcing to debt collection agencies), proceedings are financially and procedurally less onerous and more financially straightforward for corporations. Individual claims against consumers are templated junior-lawyer-level work, though this is not said in a flippant way.

But why did the policy change? General and specific deterrence are the best measures for determining the success of any punishment imposed for legal transgressions. Given the fact the alleged losses sustained by copyright owners are not actual physical losses (for example, a carton of games from a warehouse), but rather the loss of profits, the industry should be able to perpetually initiate countless claims largely framed on the same legal and factual bases. But in an economic sense, loss of profit claims against individuals would constitute nothing more than actions for surplus value that has been created from the profits of commodities that have traditionally been sold at high prices. In other words, it is possible for the industry to prosecute a significantly high number of individuals in a cost-effective manner, but the numbers of actual cases against individuals are comparably low.

If copyright laws generally shape consumers' perceptions about what is right and wrong, just and unjust, then they must also shape attitudes (Moohr, 2003). For example, by designating downloading as counter to the law, the law constructs this activity as 'not normal' (or antisocial or deviant). That is, in declaring piracy to be outside the boundaries of statute and common law, the law declares piracy countercultural, immoral and criminal (see Edgely, 2010). Copyright laws can be seen as an instrument of social construction because they attempt to influence the way in which members of a society see themselves and others. Copyrights as instruments of social control therefore influence peoples' views about what is right and wrong, good and bad, normal and not normal (Kahan, 1997). In this approach, the law is analysed as a discursive instrument of governance that constructs social and political relations (Edgely, 2010).

Yet general deterrence is the cornerstone of organized behaviour, customs and norms. Why is respect for copyright therefore not embedded in our moral DNA? Theoretically it is – or at least it purports to be – for citizens in Western democracies accept the rule of law. But mutualistically symbiotic P2P consumers and pirates are united in their indifference to formal copyright governance through their engagement in piratical conduct. It is difficult to accept that consumers are ignorantly unaware of the omnipresent copyright warnings affixed to popular media, or that they lack the insight that creators of popular media are deprived of income when pirated goods are consumed. The German expression *Null-Bock-Mentalität bis hin Kriminalität* (don't-care-less attitude to the point of criminality)[7] certainly best describes the attitudes and beliefs of many consumers in the current world of digitalization. The major players arrogantly fail to at least acknowledge this basic proposition.

The education campaigns are largely awareness campaigns. They are designed to appeal to the public at large (and specific age groups) in order to modify their purported criminal behaviour. But the reality is that not only are these advertisements (especially copyright infringement notices) ignored, they appear not to be taken seriously. Actors from popular comedy series even parody piracy (see *IT Crowd* Series 2 – Episode 3: Piracy Warning)[8] along with so many other casual attitudes to the campaigns. The flippant attitudes are firmly embedded in social networking culture. Piracy is thus a form of political expression that extends beyond profit and loss sustained by corporate citizens.

Farcical representations, or media piracy parodies, symbolize an emerging democratized technological 'elite' making its owned informed decisions about the seriousness of piracy – and whether technologies are subversive or not. This is not a disenfranchised Null Bock generation, as perhaps East and West German youth were perceived to be during the days of the Iron Curtain. The *IT Crowd* spoofs of piracy will invariably attract more attention than RIAA's 'True Music Fans Play by the Rules' (2006) and 'Downloading pirated films is stealing. Stealing is against the law' (text from the original 2004 AFACT commercial parodied). Cursory views of the Internet indicate that strict observance to copyright infringement liability is not obeyed (the sea of forums on BitTorrent sites (btsites.tk) and other web resources confirm this). It would be interesting to observe how cross-industry alliances (namely Alliance Against Counterfeiting and Piracy (AACP)) react to such counter-mind-set adjustment strategies. The International Intellectual Property Alliance (IIPA) is certainly silent on these developments, and one wonders how the Music Industry Piracy Investigations (MIPI) reacts to the use of social media as a tool for freedom of speech. Parodies are indeed powerful reactions to anti-piracy campaigns.

As a form of compliance regulation in copyright governance, policing policies, anti-circumvention technologies, education, procedures and regulation of the laws have not been remarkably successful in eradicating criminal behaviour. As Gusfield (1981, p. 183) remarks, 'such assurance is symbolic assurance'. Compliance as a mode of copyright governance attempts to directly impact consumer behaviour by prescribing how popular culture must be consumed, for example, by threatening consumers with legal action and appealing to their 'moral value' (ibid.). But quite the contrary has occurred in an era of digitalization. It appears that the greater the concentration of popular media control through rapid consolidation of these industries, then the greater the rate of consumer indifference about how products are consumed (Yar, 2005).

Corporate citizens take for granted the birth of the enlightened consumer – one who is capable of determining not only the manner, but also the form popular culture products might take. In this invisible marketplace it is difficult to regulate, promote and otherwise control popular media products. The current enforcement framework rests on the fact the major players envisage that deterrence and moral modification will converge to create a compliant consumer. However a theoretical analysis of the purpose of deterrence supports the proposition that the current policies fail in a world of digitalization.

Specific outcomes and the success of the current enforcement framework: issues with deterrence

Practical difficulties

An analysis of *actual* rather than *theoretical* outcomes is rarely considered in the academic literature examining the effects of piracy. Proof of *technical* rather than *substantive or material* infringement is a question of law and not fact. The evidentiary dilemmas are also exacerbated by the unreliability and inadmissibility of evidence about an infringer's involvement in the alleged acts of infringement or unauthorized use of copyright material. That is, continuity of evidence may be in issue if an infringer has only partly participated in illegal activity or is sharing a Wi-Fi connection within with several other users of the ISP. Under the common law it is not possible to establish infringement on evidence by unjustified assumption. Proper inferences must be drawn in order to establish substantial infringement. In *iiNet* (2012) it was heard that the Appellants wrote to iiNet alleging that individual 'customers were involved in multiple infringements of copyright', and went on to state that iiNet's failure to prevent the alleged infringements from occurring 'may constitute authorisation of copyright infringement by iiNet'. iiNet was asked to '[p]revent the Identified iiNet Customers from continuing to infringe' (at para. 32 of the *iiNet* High Court decision). The letters that identified infringers of the film industry's copyright were, in essence, written demands for iiNet to meet its statutory obligations, and therefore to do *something* – something more than it had already been doing – about stemming the flow of illegal BitTorrent downloads. Obviously iiNet took umbrage at accusations that it was either not meeting its obligations pursuant to the regulatory scheme or was not doing enough. The demands by the Appellants to compel iiNet to refrain individual users from infringing copyright resembled more a plaintive cry rather than a firm legal argument. The High Court held (at para. 146):

> The present case is not one where the conduct of the respondent's business was such that the primary infringements utilising BitTorrent were 'bound' to happen … iiNet only in an attenuated sense had power to 'control' the primary infringements utilising BitTorrent. It was not unreasonable for iiNet to take the view that it need not act upon the incomplete allegations of primary infringements in the AFACT Notices.

In terms of the overall aggressive approach adopted by the film industry lobby, the trial judge in the *iiNet* case (2010) remarked (per Cowdury at para. 629): 'The tone of the letter is not so much that AFACT is an agent of copyright owners, but rather seeks to imply that AFACT is some form of quasi-statutory body whose requests required compliance.' At para. 504, His Honour also remarked: 'The law recognises that favour may be implied from inaction. However, this is only so where action could or should be taken. For all the reasons discussed in this part of the judgment the respondent was not required to act and its inaction did not equal favour. It did not sanction, approve, countenance the copyright infringement of the iiNet users.'

To base assumptions of guilt relating to copyright infringement without testing evidence, or to allege neglect of duties because a copyright owner feels the prescribed reasonable steps undertaken by a service provider are inadequate are actions contrary to public policy considerations and substantive conceptions of justice in the West. In the *iiNet* case, spreadsheets of alleged downloads were tendered as exhibits. But the contents containing addresses and other information that might have been used against identifiable perpetrators were not tested in any forensic capacity. The onerous demands by the Appellants went beyond what was reasonably required of an ISP, but the film industry, naturally, is in a financial position to test these boundaries.

Criminal and quasi-criminal prosecution and civil action

Given the paucity of statistical data concerning legal actions against individuals (that is, private actions), it is appropriate to examine public (that is, criminal proceedings) and private (that is, civil actions commenced by individuals or companies) actions simultaneously. Consider, for example, the comprehensive data compiled in the 2010 annual report of the Administrative Office of the United States Courts (2011, pp. 146, 149) of the *Judicial Business of the United States Courts*, where it is shown that 2,013 copyright civil law suits were commenced in 2010 and some seven criminal and quasi-criminal prosecutions (regulatory or decriminalized) (ibid., p. 273) were initiated in the September 2010 quarter. To put into perspective the level of court business in the US dedicated to cases against intellectual property in the criminal justice system, Gibson (2011) reports convictions (including serious or flagrant matters) as totalling a mere 196 for the year ending 2010.

Now compare the above figures provided by the court and by Gibson (2011) to the 1.6 million bankruptcy applications filed in the US (Administrative Office of the United Sates Courts, 2011, p. 29) or over 12,000 fraud cases commenced (ibid., p. 23). One can appreciate the statistically negligible rates of court action in relation to intellectual property rights generally and copyright infringement specifically in the Western world's busiest jurisdiction. The paradox of course is that these crimes and civil debts cases are exceptions and not norms in terms of good citizenship. If Internet traffic constituting illegal consumption is so high, then it follows that infringers are not good people. If that is the case, then the crime rate across the board, by way of analogy, should be exponentially higher. But that is far from the sociolegal reality. The observation that millions of Western tourists engage in illegal (popular media) conduct and that there are millions of Internet illegal downloaders suggest that people do not care about the consequences of their actions, or, at the very least, are not deterred despite warnings of lawsuits. From a criminological perspective, if behavioural reorientation strategies were implemented, it is doubtful they would succeed given the already existing sheer volume of illegal traffic by individuals. These behaviours are clearly unacceptable, yet the few copyright cases before the courts suggest that illegal behaviour goes unpoliced or largely ignored.

There is no quantitative threshold for criminal liability for copyright infringement, provided unauthorized copies are made for the purposes of trade or commercial advantage. Uploaders wilfully and recklessly offering large-scale downloading opportunities (such as Mr Burt) might easily be described as participants in criminal activity, and it was for this reason that the Australian Federal Police were involved. Profiteering is but one circumstance of aggravation. Goldman correctly observes that personal criminal motives might also attract prosecutorial action. In an examination of 'warez' software trading prosecutions, Goldman (2003, pp. 406–410, emphasis added) notes:

> Warez trading is *about ego, prestige and reputation, and so long as intangible assets are fenced off, a group of enthusiasts will seek recognition for breaching the fences.* In that sense, increased criminal penalties counterproductively make warez trading more attractive by making it a little more daring and impressive.

Most consumers are not in the 'business' or eking a living from piracy. The current ministerial directions to policing agencies in the West identify terrorism, transnational and multi-jurisdictional crime, illicit drug-trafficking, organized people-smuggling, serious fraud against the state, and money-laundering as priority areas – not *copyright* infringement. Prosecutions usually proceed where, in the light of the provable facts and the whole of the surrounding circumstances, the public interest requires a prosecution to be pursued. The seriousness of the crime, mitigating or aggravating circumstances, characteristics of the alleged offender and the degree of culpability are relevant factors. The effect on public order and morale, the prevalence of the alleged offence, and the need for deterrence, both personal and general, are also important considerations. Whether any prosecution would be unduly harsh and oppressive is the final consideration.

An examination of general prosecutorial/legal action reveals that infringement notices (the lowest form of criminal sanction or penalty for copyright infringement) are used in areas where the goal of the law is compliance. These might be compared to graduated policies usually associated with revenue laws, licensing regimes, environmental protection rules, and other safety rules that extend beyond formal warnings and cautions. Protection of copyrights should fit into this hierarchy of penalty. At best, infringement notices would be the most effective form of penalty. However, the case law does not disclose many prosecutions against grass-roots users, even at the infringement notice level.

Notwithstanding the limited number of cases before courts and copyright tribunals, the legal-political response by the major players has been to press the point that unauthorized use is illegal and punishable according to law. In *Perfect 10, Inc* v *Cybernet Ventures, Inc* (2002) (at 1177) Baird J found that that '[w]hen confronted with "appropriate circumstances" however, such service providers should reasonably implement termination ... These circumstances would appear to cover, at a minimum, instances where a service provider is given sufficient evidence to create actual knowledge of blatant, repeat infringement by particular users, particularly infringement of a wilful and commercial nature.'

In the decision of *Autodesk Inc v Yee* (1996) 139 ALR 735 at 738–739 it was held that:

> An element of penalty is an accepted feature of copyright legislation. The infringer has been regarded, at least since the eighteenth century, as a 'pirate', who ought to be treated accordingly. In *Millar v Taylor* (1769) 4 Burr 2303; 98 ER 201 at Burr 2323; ER 212 reference was made to 'the whole jurisdiction exercised by the Court of Chancery since 1710, against pirates of copies'; and, in the same case (at Burr 2322; ER 211), it was said that the statute of Queen Anne of 1709, from which modern copyright law takes its origin, secures [the property of the copyright owner] by penalties.

Following this line of reasoning, the film, music and gaming industries' associations often proffer the unsubstantiated assertion that illegal downloading and illegal swapping of files are serious crimes. This proposition is difficult to substantiate and validate as most illegal downloaders are not pirates operating a business. Rather, they might be described as one-off file-swappers (albeit some are repeat swappers). Despite this legal position, flagrant-user prosecutions are reserved for exceptional cases and especially ones where a commercial benefit was derived. These are not common – despite the serious warnings provided to users.

Third parties that are capable of enabling infringement remain the primary focus in the war against piracy. Civil action often ensures restraint in the form of enforceable undertakings and damages and legal costs. These entities (usually ISPs, telcos, software developers and website owners) do not require 'educational' reorientation. It was obvious in *Universal Music Australia Pty Limited v Sharman License Holdings Ltd* (2005) (*Kazaa*) and *Cooper v Universal Music Australia Pty Ltd* (*Cooper*) that the predominant reason for P2P file-sharing was to infringe copyright. These cases were successful because, on the balance of probabilities, it was relatively easy to establish proximity and dominant use. But it becomes problematic when the plaintiff must provide evidence to support the allegation that the proportion of traffic that involves infringement of the film, music and gaming industries' copyrights is for the dominant purpose. The Court in *iiNet* took judicial notice of the fact that the Internet is increasingly the means by which the news is disseminated and created. Thus disclosure of private and sensitive personal data to third parties (including litigants) should not be given lightly.

In *iiNet* the Court accepted that graduated sanctions had been implemented by iiNet (robot notices and warnings to repeat infringers) to educate end-users. At para. 504, Cowdury J held:

> It cannot be doubted that the respondent did not do what was demanded of it by AFACT. However, this approach is not the same as approving of infringements. The applicants appear to premise their submissions on a somewhat *binary view of the world* whereby failure to do all that is requested and possible to co-operate with copyright owners to stop infringement occurring, constitutes approval of copyright infringement. Such view is not the law. (emphasis added)

iiNet was not required to punish customers by way of additional fees or charges for unauthorized use of copyrighted works or by way of legal action. In *iiNet* it was held that the Copyright Act 1968 (Australia) focuses on the actions of persons, not computers. In short, where copyright infringement is concerned, the technical process by which the connection to the Internet is effected does not render one person a repeat infringer and another a single infringer.

The significant legal hurdle is that *authorization* must flow from acts to persons, but the law is limited to acts. It is curious that the legislature is not prepared to extend infringement beyond authorization. Continuity of evidence relating to the identity of particular Internet users who make files available for sharing or who download infringed works from other users is difficult to preserve. Identification of an individual, and not simply an ISP address number, is probably is the most difficult element to establish when creating an action against individual infringers.

But even identifying an individual, for example, the account holder, as the ISP customer is still not enough. Another difficulty when trying to prove direct causal nexus between authorizations by different persons relates to identifying the one who makes material available for *primary* infringement. This individual may be a transient user, or an individual temporarily accessing the account holder's address. Furthermore, seizure of computers does not necessarily help to establish causation because the law does not recognize computers as primary infringers, but rather persons. In the case of ISPs, proving primary infringement on the part of the Internet user does not mean there was authorization to commit those acts. There seems to be little certainty other than the basic maxim that authorization is a question of fact to be decided in the particular circumstances of each case.

BitTorrent traffic as it relates to infringing material is difficult to trace because the source of the infringement is not fixed. Infringement of copyright in the virtual world is abstract and nebulous. And whilst it may be easier to prosecute BitTorrent traffic controllers (see *Kazaa* and *Cooper*) who actually promote infringement, it is extremely problematic to accuse those persons who have no causal nexus (*iiNet*). An ISP's customers may or may not participate in illegitimate consumption, but there is no evidence to suggest that the ISP could be joined in such action. It follows that action against third parties and individuals remains a vexed issue. Combined with a residual public policy towards prosecution, the current state of affairs is consistent with liberal attitudes towards copyright.

The fallacy of copyright industries as victims

The music, film and game industries are worth billions of dollars. The retail recorded-music market alone was worth US$23.4 billion in 2010 (IFPI, 2010, p. 7) (excluding publishing and performance revenue), and Mi2N estimated packaged videos generated US$42 billion globally (as at 10 July 2011), and video games contributed nearly US$5 billion dollars to the US gross domestic product (GDP) in 2009, whilst software publishing as a whole exceeded US$144 billion in revenue (Siwek, 2010, pp., 3, 7). These figures are staggering, yet industry representatives maintain the dimension of media piracy is so deep that the entire community hurts (IFPI, 2011b, p. 21).

Some consumers might be forgiven for not properly understanding how the term 'victim' extends beyond financial cost or profit loss in popular media. The most significant criminological element in consideration of 'victims of crime' is the extent of the psychological and emotional trauma and overall devastation experienced by the victim (Akers, 1994).

Property crime and especially crimes against the person are humanized in the sense they involve harm against natural persons (the shopkeeper who has been robbed, the complainant in a sexual assault or even the hacker who has transferred money from a victim's account). Invariably, the perpetrator will be an individual or a gang of offenders. Harm justification, whereby copyright infringement is broadly viewed as everyday theft and therefore causes direct harm to both industry and consumers, is not only misleading, but also legally mischievous. Harm from unauthorized use of copyrighted material is materially distinguishable from tangible notions of crimes against popular media industries or in any setting for that matter. For example, the theft of games from a warehouse (a police matter) and the seizure of pirated DVDs (a customs matter) are obvious offences, but to label consumption of illegal popular media as copyright theft is a fiction. Popular media industry educators and campaigners are unwavering in their desire to blur criminal and civil boundaries so as to reconcile the perception that all illegal use means theft and therefore the crime of media piracy is harmful.

Do consumers feel sympathy for corporations? Take the example of labour exploitation in developing nations or in powerful nations (including China) or indeed in emerging powerful nations (such as India) where labour conditions are significantly less desirable but where media piracy is rife nonetheless. Morally or socially responsible[9] consumers would find it difficult to reconcile how (allegedly) women in Bangladesh received five cents for each US$17.99 Disney shirt they sewed (Hayden and Kernaghan, 2002; see also Kopf, Boje and Torres, 2010), yet, this corporate media giant strenuously pursues individual copyright offenders. It is understandable why a crisis of morality might result. Persons not corporations experience moral dilemmas. Loyal executives, as exclusive *apparatchiks*, might be saddened, but to elevate corporate citizenship status to a higher state of consciousness constitutes nothing more than a PR exercise. Corporate citizens however possess neither moral responsibility nor social responsibility. Their only obligation is grounded in legal responsibility.

In the case of copyright infringement, however, multinational media corporations are the 'primary victims' – not the creators of the works. Despite the assertion that artists and other creative persons suffer harm as a consequence of media piracy, the true and correct legal victims are corporations – namely transnational artificial citizens. Bakan (2004, p. 60) argues that a 'corporation can neither recognize nor act upon moral reasons to refrain from harming others'. It stands to reason that consumers might not extend their moral code to artificial citizens legally sanctioned to pursue profit at the expense of social responsibility. Social responsibility in this sense might mean more affordable price structures in popular media. It appears quite rational that consumers might consider consuming popular culture in any manner or form because enlightened consumers are fully apprised of the sheer wealth of corporate media industries (Bauxman et al., 2005).

Unlike the crime against the person scenario, the element of harm to an artificial citizen in a media piracy context is perceived as not existing because, perhaps, media piracy is perceived as a victimless crime by downloaders. The advertising campaigns about media piracy as a harmful crime are diminished or diluted in value by virtue of the fact that consumers often do not view corporate citizens as victims – especially if the primary objective of the corporate citizen is to maximize profit. Corporations that sustain losses in profits because of media piracy are portrayed as victims in the same context as human beings suffering harm as victims of theft in a universal sense. Consider the script for the MPAA advertisement (the subject of the *IT Crowd* parody (MPAA, 2004)):

You wouldn't steal a car,
You wouldn't steal a handbag,
You wouldn't steal a television,
You wouldn't steal a movie,
Downloading pirated movies is stealing, stealing is against the law.
Piracy. It's a crime.

Apart from the last scene, the advertisement depicts harm being occasioned against individuals in a most serious light. In this light, the expression copyright theft is somewhat difficult to accept in a criminological sense (refer to Chapter 5 of iiNet's submissions filed in 2010, at p. 69). The message is obviously centred on conceptions of harm against humans and their physical property. The message to viewers is very personal. But how does one respect the human rights of an artificial organization when it is devoid of morality? Can sympathy be afforded to artificial citizens, for example, that are (or alleged to be) connected to labour exploitation at worst or, at best, devoid of social responsibility? The short answer is that emotional appeal to consumers cannot work because a cry for help against piracy, which in essence reflects a loss in profits by major corporations, provides no emotive response; and it is probably for this reason the campaigns are mocked. And in the absence of highly probative crime survey data or alternative sources of quantitative data on media piracy that identifies the harm – and corporations as victims – the fallacy becomes self-evident. There is no doubt that consumers are illegitimately consuming media, but the difficulty arises in calculating *actual* harm sustained. Establishing liability and proving loss are entirely separate matters. Any meaningful debate would require both parties to come the table with 'clean hands' and to identify the extent of the harm and subsequent loss.

Deterrence

In criminology the term 'deterrence theory' is commonly used to describe the process of punishing offenders within the criminal justice system (Felson, 1994). Akers (1994, p. 50) expands on this basic concept by separating general deterrence from specific deterrence as an example-setting exercise for the community. The objective is that, knowing what the punishment is, people are deterred from committing or, indeed, expressing a desire to commit a criminal act. The purpose of deterrence is for the court to express to the community at large that such acts will not be tolerated, and for any punishment to serve as warnings to others.

Specific deterrence is more narrowly defined because it relates to a specific offender (presumably a repeat offender). It targets the unlawful behaviour of an individual, and not that of a class of persons. As a theoretical model, it is connected to legal process and how the law addresses the issue of crime prevention. No longitudinal studies have been undertaken to assess the costs and benefits of either specific deterrence or general deterrence in the copyright media infringement arena or in media piracy generally. One empirical reason for little academic interest in analyzing the notion of 'copyright theft' is the paucity of reliable statistical data due to the fact that copyright matters are rarely processed in the courts (Australian Institute of Criminology, 2008, p. 60). Copyright as 'theft' is not even properly recognized in a criminological sense as a category in its own right according to the Australian Institute of Criminology (ibid., pp. 78–79). It is classified as an 'other' type of offence – a subcategory of 'theft and other related offences'. Indeed it is conceded in the Australian Institute of Criminology report that '[t]he reference to "copyright" is tantalizing, but other elements of theft such as intention permanently to deprive are presumable missing in copyright infringement' (ibid., 2008). In the *iiNet* case, the trial judge heard evidence that details about copyright infringement were referred to the police for possible action due to the plaintive cries from the film industry (see paras. 97 and 308–313 of Federal Court Appeal in *iiNet* (2011)). But the police did not take action in the form of raids, seizures, arrests or charges, or any other action that would ordinarily have resulted in the a charge. These observations alone might suggest copyright as theft is hardly worth rigorous criminological evaluation when one considers the rich body of research concerning traditional crimes.

The paradox of specific and general deterrence in popular media piracy seems, relatively speaking, obvious. Individuals remain indifferent (or at least ambivalent) about accessing popular media illegally (Madden and Lenhart, 2003). *A&M Records, Inc. v Napster* (2000) (*Napster*) provides a primary example of people's inherent desire to consume illegally at greater rates than ever before (see Easley, 2005). A ten-year historical snapshot, since the *Napster* decision in 2000, shows a picture of an overwhelming growing desire to consume popular media illegally and in large quantities and by any means. Pirate Bay and LimeWire are but recent Napsters. As the BitTorrent protocol grew in the years since its release in 2001, it became clear that legal and illegal pathways converged, thereby supporting the proposition that consumers tend to ignore any moral compass that is purportedly present in this obvious illegal activity of P2P file-sharing. According to Goldman (2003), the desire to consume popular media illegally naturally occurs when opportunities are presented (consider the illegal sites since *Napster*). This proposition is difficult to refute from either an empirical or positivist perspective. The data presented in the case law from *Napster* to *iiNet* positively affirm the observation that copyright laws are not only repeatedly violated, but are generally ignored by millions of consumers.

Nevertheless, recognizing the limits of deterrence as a theoretical approach in explaining copyright use and abuse in liberal society is useful in the explanation of community behaviour generally, and consumers' moral attitudes in particular. The lack of statistical and empirical evidence from within the justice system suggests general deterrence as a means of crime prevention is not the correct criminological approach to apply to media piracy. As mentioned, in the absence of cogent scrutiny, little probative weight should be attached to data offered by industry representatives. Veblen warns us of 'effrontery' and 'salesmanship' as promoted in PR and special-interest campaigns for monopolistic corporations wishing to maintain the status quo of concentration. The omnipotence of corporate power is demonstrated in the case law by virtue of the industry's persistently litigious nature. The disingenuous advertisement, which was nothing more than a cry for help, tendered in evidence in the *WEA* case and the evidence of overt pressure exerted on retailers in the *ACCC* case are examples of how pressure is exerted on the market, including on consumers and retailers. The sheer might of the popular media industry was recently displayed by the film industry lobby AFACT when it chose to pursue the ISP iiNet. But the ISP had never been complicit in acts pertaining to copyright infringement. Instead of pursuing individual perpetrators in the face of actual rather than constructive knowledge about individual perpetrators the film industry chose instead to test the telco industry. The above cases support the assertion that the politicization of popular is, indeed, one-dimensional.

However, deterrence as a broader non-criminological theory might be useful when analysing the behaviour of consumers. Deterrence as a sociological model might be better suited to describing consumers in a paradigm of convergence. Moral deterrence intersects social, legal and personal factors. Consumers may not perceive that they are hurting corporations, notwithstanding that the act of downloading is illegal, because they regard corporations as soulless (profit driven), exploitative (sweat shops) and devoid of human feeling. Consumers therefore weigh the probability of the following formal sanctions in the face of the three aforementioned beliefs:

- formal legal punishment (court action) (statistically low); or
- decriminalized formal action (infringement notices – akin to traffic tickets); or
- informal measures (robot notices to cease and desist, service disconnection, education and awareness and other soft measures).

Given that the use of general deterrence is low, it is fair to suggest that the perception is that the risk of legal punishment is also low. This is quite extraordinary in the face of the corporate perception that consumers might somehow be deterred by warnings and the threat of criminal and civil action. Gibson's (2011) brief observations in 'Will You Go to Jail for Copyright Infringement?' best describe the stark differences in attitudes between consumers and popular media corporations. Most consumers cannot be described as amoral beings devoid of their obligations within the social context in which they exist. Their social contract implies a level of basic cooperation and behaviour. In absolute terms, the effectiveness of formal deterrence can only be measured by determining how the minority of guilty people who are processed thorough the criminal justice system actually behave *after* they have been caught, processed and *punished* formally. As the criminal conduct of these persons is deemed antisocial, deterrence is the dominant mechanism used to prevent further crime in English-speaking jurisdictions, and especially the US (see Akers, 1994).

So where does media piracy and illegal consumption of popular media sit in a criminological or at least quasi-criminological setting? Consider the following categories:

- criminal act (prosecution of criminal offences against property and persons as opposed to private law suits);

- decriminalized act (where wrong doing is diluted or commuted to a less serious category of offence);
- civil wrong (private legal action for civil wrongdoing); and
- immoral, derelict or condemnable act

Media piracy might fall in all the above categories, but measuring rates of recidivism in a simpliciter context is a futile task given (a) the volume of P2P traffic on the Internet and (b) the paucity of empirical data on deterrence.

Media piracy is quite a unique taboo. It is formally recognized as an offence capable of attracting significant penalties, but because so few matters are, first, taken to court and, second, processed through the court system so as to generate a measurable outcome, it is not possible to measure whether any deterrence can be applied to media piracy. Individuals participate in illegal activity and if the activity is widespread the risk is low according to Kahan (1997, p. 350): 'In that circumstance, they are likely to infer that the risk of being caught for a crime is low.' The doctrinal evidence does not support the conclusion that any level of general deterrence can be measured in wrongdoing associated with media piracy. Quite conversely, consumers seem to feed off each other's attitudes toward copyright by jumping on the technological bandwagon. Law enforcement strategies are continually challenged. The concerns about media piracy are not generated by public agencies, but rather by the popular media industry lobby groups.

Popular media consumption intersects three separate and distinct, but interlocking, sociolegal codes of conduct where the formal legal realm is but one universe. That is, illegitimate consumers might subscribe to reasoning such as 'the law has been created and I must obey it, but I do not necessarily agree with it'. Consider Figure 6.1.

The commission of offences does not exist in a legal vacuum. Moral conviction, social norms and the legal consequences of actions are all at play in a given community (Kahan, 1997; Felson, 1994; Akers, 1994). The circles in the above figure represent legal, social and moral boundaries that people might apply in life generally. These boundaries are largely shaped by attitudes and beliefs and either expand or converge depending on the proximity of the parameters of behaviour between the three separate codes of legal, social and moral conduct. Applying a legal, social and moral code to different behaviours assists in determining how people might perceive whether specific acts of wrongdoing are indeed harmful. For example, the three behavioural perceptions would completely converge when individuals assess the crime of murder because any community in a civilized society condemns murder as the worst crime on the court calendar. This act of evil is simply not morally or socially permissible. The ranking of this taboo on Woods' (2000, pp. 8–9) scale of one to ten would certainly be at the highest end.

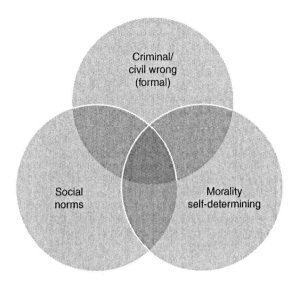

Figure 6.1 Consumers' perceptions and illegal media consumption

No law-abiding citizen would commit murder, not least of all because of the high level of retribution attached to the crime. But the level of condemnation intersects social and moral boundaries and the act is universally perceived as simply wrong in any context or meaning. Now consider a person dropping a wallet in a crowded mall. Most citizens will alert the rightful owner or perhaps surrender the wallet to the police. The impetus is again based on the above three factors.[10]

Can the same be said of illegal downloaders? The rate of P2P use suggests the same, honest, law-abiding citizens would probably download music valued at $20. He or she might participate in this activity, not necessarily because statistically they know they will not be caught, but perhaps because it is doubtful they would perceive the value of what they have obtained as being $20. Comparing the intrinsic worth of $20 in cash (or other tangible commodities) to the intangible property vested in music downloads is problematic. The dilemma for popular media industries is that the price attached to commodified products does not reflect the intrinsic value of the goods in terms of the affective pleasure derived from consumption.

This is a criticism of the way in which corporatized control of popular culture has created an unlevel playing field in the commodification of media products. Illegal consumption might be regarded as a natural response to a restriction in fair trade and fair market value. As set out in Chapter 5, if the value were fair, then, to a large extent, hordes of Westerners would not be haggling for cheap products from developing nations when they are on holidays.

The subject of the Chapter 5 – tales of bargain hunting – is repeated ad nauseam in the Western world. Price does determine attitudes and beliefs.

Organized pirates provide products that are supported by ordinary law-abiding Western citizens who appear to know right from wrong in so far as the other 'taboos' are concerned (see Bauxman et al., 2005).

Given the lack of statistical data to support the view that there is any value in pursuing illegal copyright consumers on a large scale, it is fair to conclude that perceptions of legality play a pivotal role in illegal consumption. Consumers evaluate, or rather weigh up, or are completely ignorant of the legal implications of illegal consumption. As my own experiences have shown, this is evident when second-hand MP3 players that contain the previous user's media (the content, prima facie, would be worth more than the actual device) are bought from absolute strangers. But people are acutely aware of value for money. Any consumer of popular media who has retained the 1970s and 1980s recommended retail price (RRP) stickers in his or her vinyl and/or cassette collection will be acutely aware of the historically exorbitant prices set by corporate media industries.

Consumers, perhaps with varying degrees of moral and legal conscience, evaluate the costs and benefits of legal consumption based on legal fear, threats of legal sanction and non-legal outcomes (for example, shaming or being branded a file-swapper or downloader). In the traditional criminological sense, individuals may possess varying degrees of fear based on the prospect of being caught. In a sociological sense, consumers seem to perceive the likelihood of punitive action as relatively low and appear to be less worried about such action. It appears that a combination of limited legal deterrence and low moral deterrence are the primary factors explaining illegal consumption. The former is evidenced by a lack of doctrinal legal data to corroborate the inference that legal action works, whilst the latter is empirically grounded in the fact that millions of P2P users freely exchange popular media via the Internet – void of moral conscience about corporate citizens.

In the absence of complex data with which to build models, it is not possible to determine the effects of deterrence on media piracy. It is better to conclude that deterrence has no effect. Yet the plea to deter illegal consumption still hinges on the following industry default positions:

- The media industry is hurting and jobs are being lost (IFPI, 2011a, p. 18).
- Piracy (and especially downloading) is antisocial (Gillespie, 2011, pp. 223–225).
- P2P users engage in criminal activity because copyright infringement is illegal (see the AFACT video campaign (MPAA, 2004)).

It is difficult to accept these positions. Take the following spectacular example:

Frontier Economics estimates the global economic value of counterfeiting and piracy to be US$650 billion, based on 2008 estimates (Estimating the Global Economic and Social Impacts of Counterfeiting and Piracy, February 2011). This figure is expected to escalate to US$1.8 trillion by 2015. Digitally pirated music, movies and software accounts for US$30–75 billion and is expected to rise to US$80–240 billion by 2015. (IFPI, 2011a p. 18)

Again, how one reaches figures based on calculations concerning future economic loss and the potential for loss is intriguing. Not a jot – not one scrap – of corroborated, meaningful evidence to support sustained losses was offered in the complaint against China (see Chapter 2) or in the *iiNet* case. Both cases were contested on the basis of statutory interpretation, not robust evidentiary proof. Copyright infringement cases might successfully be measured in terms of establishing liability by associations, but in terms of determining quantum, they are heavily – indeed generally – reliant on the court's discretion to be creative when awarding compensation.

Industry publications are replete with statistics that suggest gloomy forecasts due to piracy. For example, take the spectacular examples highlighted in *The Impact of Internet Piracy on the Australian Economy* (Ferrer, 2011), a report commissioned by the Australian government and heavily relied on by the popular media industry. The alarming statistics highlight the following dire state of play (ibid., p. 3):

In 2010:

- **4.7 million** Australian Internet users accessed online content illegally.
- The annual value of lost retail to Australian content industries was **$900 million.**
- Over **8,000 jobs** were lost in the content industries sector as a result of Internet piracy.
- The annual impact of Internet piracy on Commonwealth Government revenues was **$190 million.**

By 2016 (including the potential impact of the National Broadband Network (NBN)):

- **8 million** Australian Internet users will access online content illegally.
- The value of annual lost retail to the Australian content industries sector will be **$5.2 billion** – a loss of $18 billion over the period 2010–2016.
- A further **40,000 jobs** could be lost in the sector as a result of Internet piracy. Job losses due to copyright theft are projected to grow by a factor of 5.9 in less than a decade. It is also likely that, by 2016, more jobs will be lost in the sector than are created.

- The annual impact of Internet piracy on Commonwealth Government revenues will be **$1.1 billion** – a loss of $3.7 billion over the period 2010–2016.

Apart from quoting secondary sources as some form of methodological validation, the primary methodology applied to reach the above conclusions about the dangerously piratical situation in Australia was based on data collected from previous studies relating to five European nations (see ibid., pp. 8–9). Incredibly, it is reported: 'Consequently, they [Australia, France, Germany, the UK, Italy and Spain] represent a more appropriate point of comparison for the Australian context' (ibid., p. 9). It is hard to see how reliable and objective conclusions might be reached if the inferences drawn and data relied on were secondary sources from an unrelated study with its own limitations. Specifically, as no primary data were collected by the researchers in Ferrer's study, reliance was placed on secondary data from a French study in 2010 concerning job security in creative industries throughout the EU (Ferrer, 2011, p. 6). But in any event the author concedes that the 'economic impact of copyright infringement on video games was not considered' (ibid., p. 6). This makes a study on the impact made by piracy very problematic because P2P technologies are firmly embedded in gaming activities.

The main criticism however is that the epistemology and ontology of the methods adopted in the report are neither properly grounded in empiricism nor realism in so far as the findings relate to an Australian set of conditions. This is a significant weakness because the report is specifically concerned with the impact of piracy on the Australian economy, but limited data from a French study has been used. This might be acceptable for a description of the issues about media piracy generally, in order to situate the debate. But to rely on EU economic conditions to reach a conclusion on Australian job losses is methodologically unsound when spectacular projections are made, such as 40,000 jobs in popular media and allied industries will be lost, leading to a loss of AUD$18bn from 2010–2016 for creative industries (ibid., p. 3). The overgenerality of the application of the foreign demographic typologies to the Australian setting is a fundamental flaw because significant disparities exist in the politico-economic arenas of Australia, France, Germany, the UK, Italy and Spain. Spain, especially, should not be compared to Australia in terms of employment given its comparably dire, straitened financial circumstances. The report was not intended to be a cross-sectional analysis of Western jurisdictions. Those with vested interests in popular media industries commissioned the report, and subsequently the findings have been used liberally by the associations (see for example IFPI, 2011a). Objectively grounded empirical research should always be apolitical or, at the very least, neutral.

In the absence of objective empirical analysis, little weight ought to be attached reports supported by neo-pluralist meta-governors. Veblen would regard these reports as nothing more than PR exercises designed to shape and influence attitudes without real evidence to back the claims.

In the premises, there is no evidence to support the loss of jobs and other negative financial implications. The truth of the matter is that objective and impartial statistical data capable of academic scrutiny could not be obtained by industry elites and, therefore, industry-commissioned reports by industry-aligned organizations, such as AFACT or the Australian Industry Content Group, or commissioned works from established partners, such as Frontier Economics, are the only sources on offer. Because the research methods used in such reports have no theoretical framework capable of evaluation (a most fundamental factor in any empirical investigation) there is no transparent way of validating the proposition that illegitimate modes of media consumption are as devastating as popular media industries allege. At best, Ferrer's publication on the impact of piracy on the Australian economy might be described as statistical data collated to support an ideology.

Moral attitudes and beliefs are very subjective. Moral attitudes and informal sanctions are important, but the act of media piracy is as much a social activity as it is copyright infringement. There appears to be little shame or stigma attached to illegal consumption. This observation might explain why the various classes of commercial pirates, from sophisticated organized pirates to grass-roots peddlers, continue to survive. The taboo in relation to purchasing pirated media is largely kept alive due to a demand from consumers. Consumer attitudes towards pirated media are discussed in the proceeding chapters. The Piracy is Theft media campaign (that started in 2004) is still in use today and relies on the notion that consumers might cease watching a pirated movie upon discovering they were somehow regarded as ostensible or vicarious participants in illegal activity. The campaign attempts to appeal to respectable citizens as honest consumers. But a respectable person does not appear to refrain from participating in illegal activity such as watching unauthorized material. This is evidenced by the fact that illegally obtained popular media continues to thrive in various formats despite various campaigns.

It is difficult to conceive how the bulk of home users and curious users who knowingly participate in illegal consumption can be deemed as anti-social and thereby countercultural, immoral or criminal. It seems that corporate citizens are less successful in their attempts to monitor, review and perhaps understand their own attitudes towards copyright control and mechanisms in relation to grass-roots media piracy. Alternatively, corporations are acutely aware of liberal social attitudes towards copyright, but for commercial reasons refuse to accept fundamental changes in attitudes about how popular media products might be consumed in the future. Because criminal offences relating to copyright infringement are rarely prosecuted, it is fair to infer that:

- Western governments do not consider copyright infringement a prosecutorial priority (this not to suggest there are no policies in place (formally at least));
- copyright infringement is difficult to detect and stop;
- law enforcement agencies consider it not in the best public interest to prosecute piracy due to, for example, the burden of proof difficulties and other technical issues that make piracy complicated to pursue;
- deterrence requires the prosecution of a significant number of offenders, and as successful prosecutions are limited in number, such cases are unattractive to public enforcement agencies

It is an undisputed fact that much of the Internet traffic is used for illegal purposes, in so far as popular media are concerned. But the observation that can be made when considering the high rate of copyright abuse is that such behaviour cannot, by definition, be said to *deviant* (in any sociological context). Deviant behaviour is usually associated with lack of adherence to widely accepted practice and norms (antisocial behaviour). Copyright infringement is a widely accepted practice. Deterrence, as a factor that justifies ongoing prosecutorial action, fails because there is no actual risk of harm to others. Much to the disappointment of corporate citizens, this is probably a reason why prosecution will be a less attractive option for law enforcement agencies.

The challenge of illegal consumption is multidimensional and has contributed to disorganization within the industry. Several different categories of illegal consumers and pirates exist. Not many piracy cases have made it to court. It is fair to conclude the deterrent aspect of the cases is minimal. This tends to suggest these policies (that is, education and legal action) have produced mixed results despite the fact that the industry is combating the damage to copyright property more strenuously than it ever has before.

The first of the specific anti-piracy laws in the US, the No Electronic Theft Act (1997) did not deter file-swappers. *Napster* and *Kazaa* did not achieve much for the industry that would help it to mitigate its losses. The industry urged the legislature to increase penalties and introduce terms of imprisonment. But in any event, prosecutions dwindled to very low numbers in just a few years from 2003 to 2008. Seven prosecutions is not an impressive figure for any criminal justice system.

Conclusion

The fact that illegal consumption has continued as newer and faster P2P sites have proliferated, that personal lawsuits have abated, and that organized piracy has become even more sophisticated suggests that all this para-piratical activity is not hard-wired in our collective intuitive moral code, especially in the West. The five-year war showed that end-user prosecutions and civil litigation are misguided policies because they appear to have the opposite global or general deterrent effects to the ones intended. There is one agreed fact: illegal consumption is immensely popular. The patterns of illegal consumption are suggestive of the fact such behaviour – whether it be purchasing counterfeit goods in bazaars or downloading in the privacy of homes – is socially acceptable. Attempts to stem the flow of illegal consumption seem to have a reverse general deterrent effect. Specific deterrence might be achieved, but given the paucity of legal outcomes, it is not safe to conclude that warnings, threats of legal action and other soft measures are effective in relation to individual consumers.

Referring (presumably) to Voltaire's Candide,[11] in *Kazaa* Wilcox J (at 351) concluded: 'Perhaps the occasional legal proceeding might be useful *"pour encourager les autres"*... however, it is not realistic to believe legal action against individual infringers will stamp out, or even significantly reduce, file-sharing infringements of copyright.'

Whilst Chapter 8 examines consumer discontent, it is important to acknowledge that heavy-handed approaches do nothing more than estrange popular media consumers. Indeed 'technological tricks' affecting private rights also anger and annoy consumers

Corporate media citizens are aggrieved because they are unable to successfully:

- assert power against third parties who are in the position to prevent individuals from infringing in the first place;
- force third parties to implement meaningful actions to curb piracy;
- threaten legal action against third parties who rely on safe harbour provisions; and
- compel third parties to implement circumvention strategies to prevent infringement.

The law provides for penalties to enable general deterrence in order to control recidivism. Why do consumers continue to defy the law in the West? One explanation might be that on a moral level copyright interference (as a form of intangible or invisible property) is not viewed as undesirably as, say, actual (tangible or physical) property interference. Even tax evasion, in the legal sense, or tax avoidance, from a social responsibility perspective, is ranked reasonably high in terms of compliance and on a sliding scale of morality (Torgler and Schneider, 2007). In other words, in so far as copyright infringement is concerned, the question of whether it is worth complying with copyright laws seems to play a more critical role than whether punishment will be dispensed for breaking the law. A form of peer review seems to be occurring in the world of digitalization. This is evidenced by the use of P2P technologies such as BitTorrent. The use of this technology demonstrates a form of positive re-enforcement in that, because there is a lack of disapproval from peers, such behaviour is deemed to be normal. Social influences online shape attitudes more than laws ever do in the realm of copyright. This is not unusual in liberal democratic societies and it might explain the attractiveness of social media and networking as a form of omnipotent communication that allows for communication convergence. If copyright is a binary concept in the sense licensed works are right and pirated goods are wrong, then convergent consumption is ranked reasonably high on the sliding scale of morality and in terms of compliance (ibid.). References to tithing and taxes are scattered throughout the Old and New Testaments. Taxation evolved from a civilized ancestral Western past and was established several millennia before *Anno Domini*.

Focus has once again moved away from individuals, and traditional litigation against enablers and facilitators remains the primary course of action. The case against BT in the UK is a reaction to the lawlessness of convergent capabilities of digitalization. The application by Hollywood's representatives in *iiNet* for leave to appeal to Australia's highest court affirms the unresolved ongoing issues between copyright and telecommunications. It should be accepted by government groups involved in convergence issues that structural incompatibilities between these competing industries will continue to exist under any digital rights agenda until one industry subsumes the other. This seems to be the logic of late capitalism as identified by Mandel. This leads to the legislative dilemma that was exposed in the *iiNet* case. The Court found that iiNet had not authorized any breach of the applicants' copyright. That being the case, safe harbour 'indemnities' afforded to ISPs were not invoked because there was no prima facie breach on the part of iiNet. Indeed, iiNet had knowledge of infringements occurring, and did have appropriate policies in place, but the ISP did not authorize the infringements of copyright.

Individualism and principles of freedom from interference have long existed under the liberalism banner. Persons are not required to protect the rights of third parties. The *iiNet* case demonstrates that no party can compel another party to do something because that other party knows something wrong is occurring. iiNet did not have a legal responsibility to interrogate its customers on behalf of Hollywood. This is entirely consistent with the notions of negative liberty and autonomous conduct set out in Chapter 1. It was clear in the *iiNet* case that iiNet had general knowledge of copyright infringement committed by iiNet users or that infringement was likely to occur. As far back as 1928, the court recognized negative freedoms over positive freedoms in the context of copyright:

At most, it might be said that the Corporation showed itself indifferent; but ... had not the function of policing the provisions of the Copyright

Act on behalf of alleged owners of copyright. (Higgins J in *Adelaide Corporation v Australasian Performing Right Association* at 497)

Ironically, in some respects, telcos and 'liberal villains' do share one thing in common. They may appear indifferent to preserving corporate copyright in that there is no legal obligation or duty for any person to protect the copyright of a third party. But this can be distinguished from having policies in place to identify, monitor and review illegal conduct. There is obviously an obligation not to aid and abet. A legal prohibition against doing an act without the licence of the owner or exclusive licensee of that copyright or authorizing another to do that copyright-infringing act does not compel the participant in any illegal activity to intervene. Indifference is not synonymous with authorization. The popular media industry has always been particularly sensitive to technological challenges that promote unauthorized use of material, and remains resilient to those challenges. The music industry best epitomizes the compulsion to maintain the status quo.[12] Yet people still flout copyright law.

At least two centuries ago, petitioners in England warned the legislature that extending copyrights would only achieve two things: first, information for 'Moral Happiness of Mankind' and 'Religious Welfare' for those most in need would be withheld, and therefore, second, piracy would proliferate as would fruitless litigation (Remarks on the Law of Copyright, 188?, pp. 9–10).

The prophecy has been fulfilled, and yet corporate copyright owners feel victimized and aggrieved because they have failed to anticipate piracy's rabid effects in a digitalized world. Wise 'information, caution, and direction of all persons concerned in trade and commerce' was provided as far back as 1792, '[W]here the reason of the law ceases, there the law generally ceases also' (ibid., p. vi).

A wide arc of reflection allows one to draw parallels between the historical political control of information once enjoyed by institutions, such as the church and the monarchy, and elitism from the corporatization of modern copyright. The ideological dimension of copyright law in the promotion of the commercial interests of elites while purporting to strike a balance for creators and consumers under a formal copyright governance framework should be acknowledged as a product of hegemonic control in Western society. In legitimizing the existing copyright world order the dominant class exerts power on consumers and creators, thereby subordinating them economically and culturally. But technological change challenges this order irrespective of whether consumers think copyright governance is fair or not, or whether illegal consumption is right or wrong. Nevertheless, it is still entirely possible that copyright preservation might evolve to a higher state of intuitive morality in the West – perhaps through some reconciliatory third way. But can the same be said for other regions?

7
Occidental Failure: The Paradox of Transglobal Copyright Industries in Emerging Economies

> The majestic equality of the law which forbids rich and poor alike to steal bread and to sleep under bridges. (Anatole France, 1894, p. 53[1])

Introduction

This chapter examines the artificiality of copyright governance in emerging economies (also known as developing or Third World nations). Copyright laws are designed to universally protect the exclusive rights of owners of copyright by concurrently facilitating the licensing of these extensive rights, and imposing a prohibition on piracy (that is, illicit production at the input, and illegitimate consumption at the output). Interference by way of unauthorized or non-exempt dealings (especially in the commercial setting) is tantamount to theft according to the World Intellectual Property Organization (WIPO) and industry players. There are no legal distinctions between developed and developing countries in relation to copyright and no special concessions for either, and this is reflected in the formal agreements administered by the WIPO and the World Trade Organization (WTO) (an issue in the US and China case, *Dispute Settlement Board Finding* (2009)). That is, in order for nation states to be accepted internationally they must play by the prescribed rules of the 'game'. The literature overwhelmingly supports the contention that developing nations are not playing by the rules. The above quote, from novelist Anatole France's *The Red Lily*, demonstrates the absurdity in many respects of equality before formal conceptions of copyright law.

Limitations of formal conceptions of copyright governance in the developing world are apparent because the regulatory framework does not adequately take into account differences between people who are disparately divided in terms of accessing basic resources and necessities of life. It is argued that copyright governance is not embedded in legal realism in emerging economies.

How preposterous it must seem to citizens of developing nations to compare the aesthetics of copyright protection in terms of Western and non-Western economic, political and legal inequalities. Yet the West subscribes to the view that equal treatment should be applied to copyright governance and international harmonization of intellectual property generally. If economic growth can be described as the increasing capacity for a community to satisfy luxury wants (popular media products) for its consumers as opposed to basic life-sustaining wants (food, clean water, education and health care), then the empirical and legal reality of applying WIPO mandates to developing nations verges on surreal absolutism.

Furthermore, how perplexed (or unsurprised) must the local police and investigators in developing nations feel when they observe Westerners proudly haggling over counterfeited goods on market stalls. Are these consumers – liberal villains – so wretched given they are technically breaking laws mandated by their own governments, or is this the empirical reality of consumption convergence? It is argued that the answers lie in the fact that in a world of consumption convergence there are blurred boundaries between illegal and legal consumption. In the digital world this is evidenced by P2P technologies, and in the real world this is evidenced by the exchanges between Western citizens and citizens of developing nations. Is the tacit acknowledgement by the West of large-scale unacceptable Western behaviour abroad actually the paradox of the artificial prism through which Western copyright regulations are viewed by 'others'? As identified by Rousseau, the importance of social restraints imposed by copyright governance seems to be absent for those Westerners who engage in wholesale illegal consumption whilst abroad.

The argument posed in this chapter is that socio-economic limits to growth in developing nations are evident, but in this world, affluent Western consumers and socio-economically dwarfed non-Western pirate traders haggle for the best price in a codependent fashion. If Rousseau's notion of the 'noble savage' is correct in that living in a lawless realm is bad or somehow derelict, then it is something of a paradox or rather, oxymoron, that recalcitrant (but law-abiding) Westerners[2] embrace illegal behaviour without any consideration of the legal and moral consequences of their actions. The symbiotic relationship that exists between Western consumers and pirates in developing nations has not been fully considered in the literature. Indeed, the relationship lends credence to Rousseau's 'noble savage' myth in that morality exists in a natural state – beyond legal constructs and constraints.

This chapter presents a series of paradoxes that exist in universal conceptions of copyright governance. In short, piracy is 'here' with 'us' in the developed world because the dominant Western paradigm is 'there' with 'them' through transnational corporatization.

Paradox 1: piratical synergies and reflections

Emerging economies in developing nations share many common characteristics. They generally have low levels of GDP. Living conditions, quality of food and water, wage standards, education and health are substandard when compared to the standards of those members of the Organisation for Economic Co-operation and Development (OECD) with particularly advanced economies.

Developing countries have historically been referred to as Third World nations. Generally, the prospects of these nations successfully reaching the chart-topping status of the most dominant 'first world' OECD nations are quite slim.[3] Another feature of developing nations is that many of them have struggled to lift the yoke of a colonial, semi-colonial or despotic past (including undue influences from Western political ideologies or tyrannical monarchs). The era of physical colonization and imperialism has passed, but cultural and legal domination have remained. In a world where advanced capitalism prevails, these nations have emerged as fertile sites of opportunity for transglobal corporations and wealthy Western tourists alike. Access Industries (the new owner of Warner Music), Apple, Microsoft, Disney, Nike and Mattel are examples of leisure manufacturers with strong corporate presences in developing nations because of favourable economies of scale in terms of labour costs. In other words, the value of labour in developing nations is not measured as a domestic exchange in the value of the commodities produced by this cheap labour. Rather, the scale is measured transnationally by subtracting the cost of production at the input end (the labour and materials calculated domestically in a poorer nation) from the value of the goods at the output end (items for sale in Western nations). Given the disproportionately low interaction costs compared to goods produced in the West, there can never be any dis-economies of scale when relying on labour from developing nations. This rational, economic and logical exchange makes sense in late capitalism.

Not only are developing nations economically poor, many also lack the essential rule of law principles that promote transparent government and robust governance structures that are needed to create universal public wealth. The lack of transparent governance reflects the copyright regulatory frameworks of developing nations. It might explain why wholesale piracy is prevalent in developing nations.

In 2004, the Recording Industry Association of America (RIAA) identified 56 primary nations that do not place much emphasis on copyright in any realistic sense. However, on a formal level, the legal gloss of copyright governance clearly shines in many of these nations of interest.[4] Marron and Steel (2000) identify a similar 'most wanted list' in the software piracy arena for the years 1994–1997. Ironically, some of these nations are WIPO members, alongside the most economically advanced and wealthy nations.

Before analysing copyright protection in developing nations it is worth reflecting on Western attitudes as displayed by the hordes of Western tourists who flagrantly flaunt their pirated goods purchased in overseas holiday destinations. Most Westerners who have consumed popular media from developing nations have a story (or two) about purchasing, or at least being given access to, 'cheap' pirated popular media. My own recollections range from holidaymakers haggling in Kuala Lumpur's markets (in 1996)[5] for the purchase of very poor quality movies for AUD$2, and Western conference delegates in Vietnam purchasing perfect or near-perfect pirated music CDs from Saigon's street peddlers for US$1 (in 1995),[6] to a colleague walking down one of Sofia's streets (in 1998)[7] only to be accosted by a pirate, with a portable CD-burner, offering to burn a pirated copy of any compilation of top-40 music artist and to do so within 20 minutes. By way of further illustration, there are stories of Western troops, who are on peacekeeping duties in Afghanistan and Iraq,[8] purchasing pirated media from the stalls and bazaars. None of these vignettes is noteworthy because they are regular occurrences.

One particular example, however, sticks out. I recall being in the Trgovski Centre – a multilevel shopping centre in the heart of Skopje (Macedonia)[9] – in 2000 for the express purpose of purchasing Anastasia CDs.[10] In the complex was a large, modern electronic store stocking everything from white goods to popular media. When I enquired in Macedonian as to where I might find the CD aisle, he simply asked '*nashi ili zapadni*?' (local or Western?). In one aisle, legitimate, original local pressings were being sold for the dinar equivalent of US$10 while the pirated Western CDs were simultaneously being sold for US$2 in another aisle. Unlike the other scenarios, there was nothing seedy about this commercial environment. The experience was odd indeed because a clear distinction was made between illegal and legal stock in a department store.

WIPO has contracted with the above-mentioned nations to minimize the harm of flagrant copyright abuse. For example, WIPO works in collaboration with the *Minsistersvo za Pravda* (Ministry of Justice Intellectual Property Unit) in Macedonia to track Internet service provider (ISP) addresses that can be traced to persons who are domestically uploading unauthorized content. As the bulk of popular media being sourced is Western, it is clear that the main reason for collaboration is to protect Western interests (notably Hollywood), with perhaps some scope for the protection domestic popular culture. (The WIPO website has details of domestic initiatives and alliances.)

Thus the normalization process in illegal media transactions commences. In a formal legal sense, behaviours surrounding illegal consumption are clearly legal, but in a cultural sense illegal activity appears to be normal in these exchanges for value. Western consumers at bazaars, malls and stalls along streets in the developing world make purchases with a blinkered consciousness. These consumers must be cognizant, at least subconsciously, of the fact that their purchases are technically illegal. They are consuming with a blinkered consciousness because, while their purchases are technically illegal, they ignore or choose to conveniently forget about that fact during the transaction. Such conduct is normalized abroad in much the same fashion as borderless downloads occur via the Internet. Conscious or unconscious, in a Foucauldian sense, the perception by illegal consumers that copyright law as an instrument of cultural control somehow does not apply in poorer nations, or even on the Internet, is most extraordinary given concepts relating to the function of international copyright governance, its structure, and copyright regulation are not new to Westerners.

One of the few studies about people who are willing to consume counterfeit products produced some interesting results (Furnham and Valgeirsson, 2007). The first important finding was that consumers are more willing to illegally consume popular media (especially CDs, videos and music tapes) than other counterfeit goods (drugs, car parts, perfume and shoes) (ibid., p. 680). In other words, if the consumer thinks the goods are dangerous then the consumer is not likely to purchase them.

Another important finding was that value for money played a pivotal role in the transaction process (one can understand the decision to enjoy a perfect or near-perfect CD for US$1). Those who stand on the right-wing of politics are more likely to be willing to buy counterfeit goods than those on the left or in the middle. The right wing includes political ideas such as the free market (ibid., p. 684). The authors conclude these libertarian consumers 'were more likely to be willing to pay for counterfeit goods' (ibid., p. 684). That is, these consumers 'usually want fewer rules about commerce' and less 'watching' by 'authorities' in personal business transactions conducted by parties (ibid., p. 684). Western values and beliefs are firmly embedded in liberalism and conceptions of minimal interference from institutions.

Illustrations of openly brazen piracy transactions in developing nations are indicative of the fact that copyright regulation has a paradoxical impact on perceptions of how popular media should be regulated in the developing world. Economies of scale exist for pirates because they are dependent on both local consumption and Westerners' consumption patterns. When authorities choose to ignore the illegal transactions, or at least tolerate grass-roots peddling, a nation chooses to ignore the substantive issues by passively allowing the behaviour to continue. This might be construed as a political act. Doing nothing about copyright infringement (or at least superficially doing something) is, paradoxically, action in a developing nation where supply is being met by demand. Thus the local authorities that choose to ignore copyright infringement in Phuket are no different to the Western customs officers who are exposed to so much international traffic. Focus is more on illegal entry, drug trafficking and weapon smuggling than on pirated media. In Australia, for example, policies surrounding people smuggling and illegal migration gain significantly more political attention than issues surrounding media piracy. On this point, the Australia Customs and Border Protection Service website states:

Copyright piracy and trade mark counterfeiting are illegal. By buying pirated or counterfeit items, not only could you end up with a flawed product, you are supporting an illegal trade that could involve serious criminal activity.

You can play an important role in combating copyright piracy and counterfeiting of trade marks by not bringing pirated or counterfeit goods into Australia. In some circumstances pirated and counterfeit goods imported into Australia are liable to seizure by Customs and people importing such goods may be subject to civil litigation or criminal prosecution.

As mentioned in the previous chapter, there are no available data to assess whether legal action against consumers of unauthorized popular media has any deterrent effect. However, '[a] total of 906,527 items were seized, with a total retail value of over $37 million. A noticeable trend this year [2010] was the significant amount of counterfeit beer detected' (Australian Customs and Border Protection Service, 2010, p. 66).

In Chapter 6, it was noted that the relatively low rate of copyright prosecutions before the US justice system in 2010 was insignificant when compared to the rates of physical crime against the person cases (see Administrative Office of the United Sates Courts, 2011). In the US, in other common law jurisdictions and in Western nations generally, court appearances in the lower courts relate mostly to the common crimes and misdemeanours (namely assault, drugs, domestic violence and offences related to breaking, entering and stealing) where victims, recidivism and recognized deviant behaviours are clearly identified (Nesdale, 1980, pp. 176–180). In the higher courts, murders and drug trafficking trials compete with commercial trials (initiated by corporations against corporations) for court space. Copyright cases are comparably underrepresented in the court system. In 2009, Australian Customs detected 1,110 items of objectionable material and 45 cases were prosecuted, including 39 cases involving child pornography (Australian Customs and Border Protection Service, 2010, p. 66).

Western nations have established stability based on responsible government, a robust separation of powers, transparency and accountability. The same foundations cannot be said to exist in developing nations, or at least not in a substantive sense. It is fair to suggest that in developing nations regimes come and go, constitutions change overnight and Western multinational nations depart once the cost-effectiveness of the indigenous population and its resources are fully exploited. The Balkan crisis in the 1990s and the recent political crises in Iraq and Afghanistan are recent illustrations of the differences between the attitudes governing Western and non-Western conceptions of legitimate political power. Where there is not a robust rule of law, and where natural justice along with procedural fairness is not afforded to all citizens, it is impossible to imagine that the message that media piracy is illegal, or, at the least, bad or immoral, can be delivered to citizens. If copyright cases are rarely prosecuted in the West, then it would be remarkable in Venezuela and Columbia where piracy is rife – but not as remarkable as the horrifying murder rate of 52 and 38.8 per 100,000 inhabitants respectively (compared to 1.4 and 5.2 per 100,000 in the UK and US respectively) (Karaganis, 2011, p. 24). Copyright crimes might be a priority for the International Federation of the Phonographic Industry (IFPI), the Australian Federation Against Copyright Theft (AFACT) and the International Intellectual Property Alliance (IIPA), but the legal reality is that local law enforcement agencies and the judiciary struggle to cope with an unwinnable war against violent crime where resources are scarce and so are not able to tackle copyright crimes. However there is no doubt that if a Western-initiated campaign against media piracy was commenced (say a US-funded programme to purge piracy in Bolivia), then the local authorities might be able to address the issue of media piracy. But a Bolivian-initiated campaign against media piracy in a climate where resources are already scarce for the investigation of serious crimes against people would be nothing more than an impotent political daydream.

Popular media executives may ignore this substantive legal reality and it is indeed not surprising that corporate media executives view their own concerns one-dimensionally. They are not required by law to care about social issues. Unlike governments, they are devoid of social responsibility, but are legally bound to pursue profits. Piracy impedes this legal requirement. But the reality is that these concerns about the unauthorized use of popular media are probably less pressing for those in the developing world whose duty is to uphold responsible elected governments and to ensure law and order for all citizens (not just aggrieved multinational corporations' local subsidiaries) through a robust legal framework.

Paradox 2: tangibles as material needs versus intangibles as immaterial wants

A fundamental proposition is that one cannot substitute tangible for intangible goods. For example, only food (whether obtained through production, purchase or gift) can alleviate hunger, which means that substitution is not possible. But popular media can easily be substituted – legal for illegal, digital for analogue and so on. These goods are hardly scarce. Unlike food therefore, there is little value in copyright when one looks at it from a 'social scarcity' perspective. Popular media is readily available and easily accessible; even the most ardent copyright law formalist would agree that food is comparably scarce. People derive pleasure from popular media (and copyright therefore) in the form of material (and immaterial) wants, whereas food is a scarce or subsistence need.

The second paradox is based on the observation that copyright value in popular media is nothing more than transient and, once consumed, it becomes relegated to 'junk status'. It possesses some intrinsic worth and value (to the consumer, the creator and the copyright owner), but it is hardly *scarce*. It is a disposable commodity, capable of infinite reproduction and cannot be deemed physically finite (like food or food production). Food and other fundamental necessities are therefore more valuable, and positioning or rather ranking food and such necessities in a copyright paradigm in developing nations raises a number of questions. Replicating an infinite object may not necessarily be construed as stealing because any purported theft is the theft of opportunity (future economic loss). It does not necessarily follow that a person in a developing nation will (or might) perceive copyright piracy as theft just because opportunity loss is at least distinguishable from theft of tangible physical items. In this regard it is doubtful whether Western holiday-show hosts promoting Bali as a holiday destination would joke about terrorism or tangible 'dodgy' conduct, such as theft or assault by Western tourists, in the same light as intangible indiscretions, such as filling shopping bags with 'dodgy DVDs' (see endnote 1).

Food is used first to alleviate hunger and provide nourishment and then perhaps to provide taste and other culinary sensations as a form of subordinated pleasure. Its primary purpose is not to render enjoyment. Popular media transcends these basic needs by immediately producing enjoyment. In late-stage capitalism where a global economy led by dominant Western nations prevails, dealing in intangibles such as copyright is indeed quite an elitist, indulgent neo-colonial form of advanced capitalist production. Along with intellectual property rights generally, copyright in popular media products represents one of the best indicators of economic growth in advanced capitalist societies. Copyright's capacity for repeated commercial exploitation decades after its initial exploitation is unmatched in commerce when compared to the manufacture of physical goods. Copyright consolidation symbolizes the growth of an elite corporate status – one that resembles a neo-colonial environment. These copyrighted products are not necessities in developing nations. This is not to suggest that developing nations are void of their own uniquely rich and plentiful culture (on the absolute contrary!), or that citizens of developing nations do not enjoy Western culture (personal as well as commercial piracy is rife).

Commenting on the futile war in Vietnam, Marcuse (1967, p. 3) condemns the 'material veil of extravagant productivity ... [and] that in the realm of advanced capitalism the fate of man is determined by the aggressive and expansive apparatus of exploitation and the politics interwoven with it'. Copyrights may certainly be described as being aggressively protected and exploited for the purposes of extravagant productivity. In the 1990s, the rate of software piracy was estimated at between 95 and 99 per cent of software consumed in Vietnam (Marron and Steel, 2000, p. 164). This extraordinarily high percentage of illegal activity suggests that individuals and organizations in Vietnam, Bulgaria, Philippines, Indonesia, Russia and several other nations identified by the authors (nations with average rates of piracy in excess of 89 per cent) have embraced piracy as part of everyday life and activity, including commerce. Little room is left for legitimate consumption in many nations with non-Western conceptions of copyright governance, and the authors are correct in concluding that economic, institutional and cultural differences are at play (Marron and Steel, 2000, pp. 172–173). Western nations should not ignore the fact that socio-economic, political and cultural conditions are markedly different in developing nations, and the attitudes and beliefs that shape these nations are not necessarily compatible with Western conceptions of economic rationalism. Is media piracy a passive reaction to or an after-effect of US influence?

The situation is similar in Russia where in 2008 the software in the piracy market was estimated at 82 per cent of the total value of software (that is, both pirated and legitimate). Sezneva and Karaganis (in Karaganis, 2011, p. 189) explain:

> The sale of pirated goods is thus a relative privilege for people who would otherwise be—at best—part of St. Petersburg's working poor. Roughly 10% of the city's population qualifies as poor by Russian standards. The median monthly income in 2008 was 19,000 Roubles, or $770, while the estimated minimum subsistence level is 4,900 Roubles, or almost $200 (City Statistics Bureau 2008). For the many families in this category, the additional income from piracy is often the difference between simple poverty and destitution, as one working family member usually supports anywhere between two and four non-working members. The trade in pirated goods has one important further advantage: it is relatively socially acceptable and does not carry the kind of stigma associated with the drug trade, prostitution, or other forms of criminality (Ovcharova and Popova 2005, pp. 15, 28, 35).

Russian citizens, like others who have suffered at the hands of similar communist regimes (for example, Romania), are familiar with patterns of exploitation, production and consumption. In 1919, Lenin advised the Russian proletariat (presumably in St Petersburg): 'You must take advantage of bourgeois democracy ... but not for one minute must you forget the bourgeois character ... is simply a machine for the oppression of one class by another (cited in Sendy, 1968, p. 10). (No doubt citizens of former communist regimes are acutely aware of past dogmatic propaganda and rhetoric espoused by the Vanguard. But they would also be aware of the current pervasive nature of transglobal capitalism.)

Nearly 100 years after the decline of colonialism, the miserable conditions for many citizens in emerging economies remain. In an age of transnational capitalism, developing nations with differing political ideologies (e.g., communism) have not successfully embraced Western, Eurocentric liberal ideals. But the West has nonetheless economically influenced developing nations. Western nations have firmly embedded their corporate citizens in emerging economies. Given the favourable economies of scale in the developing world, corporations resemble neo-colonialists. This is not simply neo-Marxist inspired rhetoric. It is empirically grounded. According to International Labour Organization figures, minimum wage levels are unsurprisingly low. Ashenfelter and Jurajda (2001) provide an interesting practical example of minimum hourly rates compared to the price of McDonald's food products (the Big Mac Index). The study reveals that in 2000 in India, Brazil and Russia the hourly wage rates for McDonald's workers were US$0.29, $0.51 and $0.89 respectively; yet the price of a Big Mac burger was US$1.26, $1.65 and $1.07 respectively. In the US the hourly rate was US$6 and the price of a Big Mac was US$2.43.

How does the price of fast food compare to media products? Original DVDs and top-ten CDs and games in these three nations retail for between US$15 and $10 (these are 2009 prices, but prices remained relatively constant from 2000 for popular media products) (Karaganis, 2011, p. 57). Karaganis (ibid., p. i) explains: 'Relative to local incomes in Brazil, Russia ... the price of a CD, DVD, or copy of Microsoft Office is five to ten times higher than in the United States or Europe.' There is little room to reduce the cost of legitimately sourced popular media given the hourly rates of unskilled workers (presumably young people) in emerging economies vis-à-vis the price of McDonald's food and Hollywood movies.

The 1990 figures presented by Marron and Steel (2000) and the current statistical data presented by Karaganis (2011) strongly suggest overwhelming support for piratical conduct on the part of citizens in emerging economies. These figures support the observation that society accepts such piratical conduct and thus piracy has become popularized in non-Western nations. In so far as emerging economies are concerned, it is interesting to reflect on the popular Mexican revolutionary imagery of the *La Calavera* during an armed struggle against exploitation and poverty throughout the 1910s, or the traditional skull and cross bones imagery adopted by the Macedonian revolutionary Jane Sandanski during the armed struggle against the Ottoman Empire in 1908. The Jolly Roger pirate flag has always represented outcasts and illegitimate organizations. In a symbolic sense these public displays are indicative of a desire to keep the imagery of piracy alive in the world today. Dealing in counterfeit goods in developing nations is obviously a black market enterprise, but there seems to be a significant nexus between the piratical utility vested in Third World copyright infringement and the concept of otherness. Legal notions of copyright exploitation might be recognized in Western jurisdictions in a positivist sense, but 'exploitation' takes on an entirely different meaning in less wealthy nations where the connection between law, morality and culture may differ. The 'majestic' quality that international copyright governance holds in the West would certainly be lost on the street urchins peddling pirated goods in poor nations, and who are probably acutely aware of what it feels like to sleep rough. In other words, there are fundamental historical, cultural, economic and obviously political differences between how developing and developed nations view notions of copyright. Cross (2011, p. 321) considers the economic rational dimension and the feelings of self-worth from participants in the notorious Mexican[11] black market economy:

> Many vendors, in this context, saw themselves as providing a public service that the transnationals refuse to deliver. 'As someone who sells pirated goods, I screw the industry. But who am I helping?' one asked rhetorically, then answered himself: 'The people.' Another suggested: 'With the minimum [Mexican] salary [about 50 pesos or US$5 per day], it isn't possible to buy an original disc for 200 or 300 pesos. They will spend their entire weekly wage. They come here and can find the same quality ... but we can make it cheaper.' Still another added: 'The need of popular culture is to have culture that is accessible for the people. But [the industry] just makes money and more money.'

Are these modern day sentiments any different to the fundamental tenets espoused by Lenin during the period of 1918–1921? They are no different given the rationale of entrepreneurial copyright imperatives. Living standards and minimum wage issues remain unresolved in developing nations (see Primo and Lloyd's (2011, p. 99) examination of piracy in South Africa where 'some one third of the population live on less than $1 per day). Furthermore, there is a significant body of literature about labour exploitation in developing nations that suggests that citizens in those nations are acutely aware of their lot in life (see Boje and Khan, 2008; Sethi et al., 2011).

Governments enforcing unilateral copyright regulations seem to ignore cultural and economic disparities. Copyright ideology comes from a developed world where official participants impose ideals on developing nations. These Westerners reflect general attitudes about the positive and beneficial outcomes of universal copyright protection and the negative impact of piracy. The expectation is that these poorer nations will listen to the confident rhetoric of the West. But this has not been achieved because the current copyright regime is based on a secularized form of Western capitalist fundamentalism.

The stark reality is that when compared to citizens of the developed world many citizens of developing nations must grapple with issues such as poverty, crime and healthcare in addition to piracy concerns raised by the West (see the extensive research in Karaganis, 2011). Copyright policy as symbolized by American capitalism must seem preposterous to many developing states where uneducated, undernourished and/or illiterate people are expected to understand the complexities of copyright infringement and technical aspects of copyright ownership. It is fair to assume copyright ideologies have probably been ignored by many of the street urchins given the degree of absolutism and elitism attached to copyrighted products. How is this any different to the West where millions of illegal consumers demonstrate similar sentiments? If a function of the law is to create 'minimal levels of trust' between persons (Chorvat and McCabe, 2004, p. 1734), then trust – or at least respect – for copyright governance does not exist in the West. This must be seen as occidental legal and administrative failure.

Paradox 3: international copyright governance as neo-colonialism?

Describing the early stages of the industrial revolution Adam Smith marvelled at the wonders of economic growth and the potential for laissez-faire markets in the then 'developing' British world. In his *Theory of Moral Sentiments* (1761, p. 273), he remarks on the minority of rich people who are able to afford 'those baubles and trinkets ... in the economy of greatness'. Western popular media must be seen as just that – Hollywood glitter and glam – in the light of the harsh socio-economic reality of the developing world. Indeed, film producer Michael Moore's famous interlude with Nike about conditions in Indonesian factories is now virally threaded throughout the Internet:

> **Moore:** And if 12-year-olds are working in [Indonesian] factories? That's OK with you?
> **Knight:** They're not 12-year-olds working in factories ... The minimum age is 14.
> **Moore:** How about 14, then? Doesn't that bother you?
> **Knight:** No.
> (interview with Nike CEO Phil Knight and Michael Moore in a scene from *The Big One*)

In the documentary, age (and wage) conditions concerning teenage girls in Indonesian Nike factories were raised. The issues related to developments in globalization in the late 1990s – arguably a period marked by unchecked Western corporate exploitation of labour forces in developing nations. In the twenty-first century, Boje and Khan (2009) also identify Nike's corporate interests in the developing world. The authors comment on tough working conditions in Pakistan, and subsequent issues relating to child labour in Sialkot, Pakistan, which is one of the world's largest soccer ball manufacturing regions. Clearly, in so far as wages are concerned, economies of scale are favourable in developing nations for certain multinational sports companies – companies that are highly influential popular culture identities. But copyright governance, which essentially represents multinational corporate interests, presents a curious paradox in advanced capitalist states. Sporting goods (produced under relatively oppressive conditions) are accepted by Western nations, but copyrighted products from developing nations have been fiercely resisted. Popular media industries that have been, traditionally, statutorily protected with regards to minimum-price-setting, and formats that are conveniently regionally coded thereby preventing playback in some circumstances add to product obfuscation from region to region. In the popular media industry arena, one of the major concerns that industries that are historically protected, such as music, film and gaming industries, have consistently raised in the West is that parallel importation from developing nations promotes piracy and therefore inferior products. In Australia, the majors (domestically) vociferously resisted the 1998 amendments to the Australian Copyright Act 1968 against the importation of popular media (especially music CDs). Prior to 1998, because of protectionism, a CD sourced by a retailer from an internationally affiliated record label was considered illegal. One reason for this protectionist attitude was the unfounded notion that illegal goods would flood the local market should the floodgates be opened. This would not only affect sales, but consumers would suffer if inferior goods flooded the market. The fallacy in the argument that somehow copyright products should remain regionally protected is the fact that a multinational corporation with affiliations in various regions must in any event ensure quality control in each region in order to maintain its brand and reputation. For example, there is an artificial distinction between CDs manufactured in developing and developed nations because of quality assurance. It has never been substantiated that parallel importation promotes piracy through deliberate contamination of legal and illegal goods. Trade associations often raise the fear of inferior quality of imported popular media, but it is curious that there is no such concern about the quality of soccer balls produced in developing nations. The irony of course is that, like sporting goods, media goods are not inferior because they are manufactured overseas under licence. That is, a Nike shoe manufactured in Indonesia is still a Nike shoe fit for consumption in America, just as an Indonesian Sony CD is identical to the Australian-manufactured Sony CD. Until 1998 the industry lobby in Australia successfully raised the unfounded argument that imported goods promote piracy. But the legal reality is that parallel importation has neither promoted nor dissuaded media piracy in Australia. It appears that shoe and soccer ball manufacturing industries are not subject to the complexities of copyright governance where protectionism is formally defended in a globalized world. The only difference (to use Michael Moore's argument) is that Australian workers are not paid '40 cents'. (However, the cost of manufacturing a CD in the West is relatively low in any event, notwithstanding the historically high price tag.) Given the direct correlation between lower retail prices and parallel imported goods, it is fair to assume that manufacturing costs are considerably lower in developing nations. Parallel importation shows the artificiality of popular media price-setting and challenges the favourable status quo established in each Western region.

There can be no misapprehension that the entire world is acutely aware of transnational capitalism. How ironic it must seem then to enlightened Western consumers that the copyrights and trademarks that are so aggressively enforced by corporations are owned by the very same corporations that have been 'named and shamed' as promoters of sweat shops?

Beyond the safe confines of Euro- and Anglo-centric copyright laws, the balance of national copyright *lex fori* and jurisdictional considerations are spectacularly inconsistent both in substance and form (for an excellent analysis on the difficulties presented as a result of globalization, see either Goldring (2008) or King (2008)). More importantly, Brewster (2011, pp. 48–49) observes that as 'there is no inherent obligation to offer intellectual property rights' developed nations resort to the law of economic influence and political intimidation to assert their dominant status.

The use of sanctions and watch lists is a response to weak sovereign affairs. WTO agreements on Trade-Related Aspects of Intellectual Property Rights (TRIPS) that are in force worldwide remind developing nations of the significant trade obstacles they face should they not adequately identify the risk of piracy and implement WIPO rules in their respective domestic settings. A range of trade sanctions at the behest of more powerful nations has always existed in a transglobal environment. The focus of international copyright governance has been to identify developing nations with piratical tendencies and implement anti-piracy measures in those regions so as to minimize harm to corporate citizens. For example, through sheer political clout wealthier nations, such as the US, more powerful European countries and Japan consistently exert influence on developing nations to maintain international copyright governance frameworks. Brewster (2011, p. 54) explains:

> Developed states applied unilateral sanctions against developing countries regarding intellectual property protections. The US imposed import restrictions on Brazil in 1988 for its failure to respect American grants of intellectual property rights and threatened India with similar sanctions.

This ideological approach is best summarized by Brewster (ibid., p. 55) as follows:

> By creating a legal obligation to change national governmental structures, including the state's substantive laws and enforcement procedures, rights-holders hoped to use international law to change the legal culture of developing countries, embedding within them a greater respect for higher levels of intellectual property rights into the fabric of the nation's legal system.

Brewster (ibid., p. 48) also argues: 'Because the respect for intellectual property rights exists in foreign markets as a result of a political bargain between states, *there is a relationship* between intellectual property rights and other trade rules.'

The value of threatened general trade retaliation, that is, withdrawal of government subsidies to poorer nations by elite nations, should be not ignored because such measures directly influence agricultural products, textiles and core primary industries that feature prominently in poorer nations' domestic economies. Brewster's (ibid., p. 9) arguments are compelling: 'In essence, intellectual property industries in developing states have become the hostages for their government's compliance with promises of agricultural reform.' Historically, the demands and threats have been codified at the behest of the US so that recalcitrant nations face trade sanctions 'in response to intellectual property violations' (Alford, 1994, p. 13). Alford (ibid., pp. 13–14, emphasis added) describes the sanctions as a US-generated list of:

> [w]hat it unilaterally decides are offences committed against our intellectual property by our trading partners and to initiate actions – potentially in contravention ... [of] GATT and certainly contrary to its spirit – against such countries unless they make satisfactory amends *on our timetable in our way.*

Policies based on unilateral trade sanctions or, rather, one-dimensional demands at the behest of dominant nations whose major corporate citizens dominate a transglobal environment remain corporate copyright's political Zeitgeist. All nations must participate in a trade environment dominated by Western transglobalism, and weak economies' fear of trade sanctions cannot be ignored. With so much angst about promoting and consuming fair trade, does not this co-imperialist attitude constitute an ethical dilemma for powerful nations who utilize tangible threats (for example, food embargoes) because intangibles are threatened? Crean (2000, pp. 209–210) suggests that some of these ethical issues surrounding intellectual property (IP) dominance are worthy of further investigation.

Most of the recalcitrant nations listed, monitored and otherwise threatened (consider the small sample in this book) have been subjected to imperial domination and exploitation, cruel and despotic totalitarian regimes and are otherwise non-Western in many other political and ideological ways. But due to transglobal influence, our worlds have converged or in the copyright realm – collided.

Comparing the wealth of nations is hardly an exact science but by cross-referencing independently corroborated data from the International Monetary Fund and statistical data from the 2010 Legatum Prosperity Index a consensus about the wealth of a nation can be reached. Indeed, comparing the 2010 Legatum Prosperity Index against a recent study on media piracy in developing nations (*Media Piracy in Emerging Economies* (Karaganis, 2011)) leads to some significant observations. In that study, Karaganis (ibid., p. 10) cites the most recent industry-generated data concerning rates of media piracy as a percentage of the market in various emerging economies. For example, media piracy as a percentage of the film market in Russia is 81 per cent, in Brazil 48 per cent of the music market consists of pirated goods and in India some 89 per cent of the market is of pirated games. Karaganis (ibid., p. 11) is right to observe that: 'Given the relatively uniform global pricing for most media goods, a loose correlation is not surprising: the first determinant of access to media markets is income.'

Legatum uses 89 measures of wealth and well-being, including higher education, adequate food and shelter, and standard of living satisfaction, to assess a nation's state of prosperity. Brazil, Russia and India (admittedly, large and emerging economies) are in the second half of the ranking table (41–50 for Brazil and 61–110 for Russia and India[12]). The one historical bond that these three nations share is that they have been victims of oppressive colonial regimes. India and Brazil were victims of European colonists, and Russia was subjected, first, to a less enlightened – when compared to European colonial regimes – Tsarist regime where serfs were not emancipated until the 1860s, and then to Marxist dogma. Substantive copyright regulation must surely seem ethereal and esoteric given the absolute lack of connection to any copyright past. However, many developing (so-called Third World nations) are signatories to the Universal Copyright Convention and the Berne Convention, and domestic copyright laws purportedly reflect the Berne Convention on Copyrights. These nations are also usually parties to the Geneva Convention for the Protection of Rights of Producers of Phonograms and to the Universal Copyright Convention. The 'majestic equality' of formalism is patently clear.

Substantive democratic governance has not come easily to developing nations or emerging economies. All Macedonia has ever known are centuries of Ottoman oppression, followed by Balkan crises, a few decades of forming a republic under a Yugoslav banner, and only two decades of independence since 1991 (Mazower, 2000). Developed nations have enjoyed over three centuries of true separation of powers. The rule of law in countries differs as significantly as does GDP. There seems to be a very close correlation between nations with robust accountability and prosperity (see Legatum Prosperity Index (2010) for 110 nations).

Do Western consumers actually make informed decisions about illegal purchases? Morality aside, these transactions disclose the subjective nature of pricing in popular media. Illegal consumption is not necessarily the issue. Exposure to the reality that the intrinsic value placed on copyrights in popular media products is not as high as copyright owners claim is evident when considering the stark reality of daily life in emerging economies. These goods are no more than extremely elastic products – not necessities. Illegal exploitation of popular media in developing nations exposes the attitudes of citizens in developing nations. It is unlikely that a person living in abject poverty would consider it relevant to their daily existence that not purchasing a Hollywood blockbuster, such as *The Avengers*, or a Justin Bieber album was a lost opportunity. These are not essential goods – for any person, let alone those labouring in less than favourable working conditions in the developing world. The issue of street value vis-à-vis commercial continues to remain the vexed issue. The paradox is obvious. If DVDs retail for ten times the average wage in developing nations, then it follows that the value of these items has been grossly distorted. The street value (that is, the price set by pedlars of pirated goods) reflects the harsh reality of what these goods are worth in poorer nations. Pakistan, for example, is notorious for harbouring media pirates and not surprisingly has been on the US Special 301 trade watch list for some time (Ilias and Ferguson, 2011, p. 33). In terms of prosperity it ranks very low in every respect, according to 2011 figures published by the Legatum Institute. Yet according to Boje and Khan's (2009, p. 11) study, Third World nations such as Pakistan are nothing more than post-colonial domains 'where the multi-billion dollar global transnational corporations engage with penniless workers'. In their study (ibid.) they explain how, for decades, the majority of the world's soccer balls have been produced in Sialkot in Pakistan for several corporate giants (including Nike and Adidas), and where the 'great majority of children helped their parents at home who were in turn paid for the number of soccer balls rather than hours of work'. The US Trade Representative might find it possible to measure loss by measuring the potential for sales. Loss from media piracy is invariably assessed from a Western viewpoint. But it is difficult to understand how the US, for example, could measure actual economic loss through piracy in Pakistan when the domestic capacity for such a nation to participate in economic growth is so stunted due to impoverished conditions that it seems ridiculous for a Pakistani citizen to pay any price for luxury items such as popular media. For example, if a DVD is sold for US$10 in a store in Bangkok but a pirated version is haggled for US$1, then is the correct value not US$1 (given that studies show popular media to be priced at ten times more than what people can reasonably afford in emerging economies (Karaganis, 2011))?

Now extend this to the enlightened tourist who should be able to afford a US$10 original copy. She or he observes the less salubrious conditions of the local population. The transaction is completed not only because the price is low or because there is some altruistic incentive on the part of the Westerner, but also because the objective reality of over-pricing popular media is also evident. Westerners also require value for money – artificial pricings, statutory monopolies and other controls are anti-competitive. As mentioned in Chapter 6, US$20 in cash cannot equate to US$20 in music consumption because the true value of the latter cannot be determined realistically given the artificiality of price setting from region to region. This follows a reasonably sized arc of supposition that consumers loathe being taken advantage of if they suspect popular media is overpriced. It also follows that a perception that value for money is not being obtained is more than enough to cast reasonable doubt on the intrinsic worth of copyrights.

The formal conceptions of copyright governance might promote the virtue of not consuming illegal products. The paradox of transglobal business activity is that well-travelled, reasonably educated Western citizens react to copyright as a form of neo-colonialism by actively participating in a parallel economy.

Conclusion

Purchasing illegal products from the developing world is not simply a case of vigilante or protest consumption. Illegal transactions are quite rational and logical – not least because the exchange is, comparably speaking, fair given GDP (and hourly rates of pay in emerging economies, etc.) and the perception between the buyer and seller that the transaction is fair. As mentioned above, the argument that copyright holders suffer harm as a consequence of piracy in developing nations needs greater scrutiny.

WIPO agreements with developing or non-Western nations constitute a façade of unity. Western nations share a commonality. They are united in the common ideal of commercial copyright exploitation. Non-Western nations can be regarded as 'others' or at least are distinguishable because of a lack of a politico-legal past that is similar to those of Western nations. Local, not international, laws organize community values, traditions and norms. Arrangements entered between stallholders selling illegal goods and consumers are rational and economic rather than legal considerations. But this does not mean the transactions are devoid of universally moral values. Copyright industries do not include altruistic consumption as an ingredient when producing popular media products for commercial exploitation. Western conceptions of the law and compliance might formally predominate the regulation of consumption. Popular media involves so many subjective variables, including taste, mood, and even perception of value for money from deriving affective pleasure from only one song on an album, not the entire album.

The value expressed in a recommended retail price does not necessarily reflect the actual price consumers are willing to pay. Indeed this would apply to both Western and non-Western settings (see, for example, Maffioletti and Ramello's 2004 study on CD pricing, illegal consumption and opportunistic behaviour vis-à-vis the chance of being caught).

Consumers have no choice when consuming a Big Mac or purchasing a car. The price is set for the entire item, and consumers do not partly consume tangible items for a smaller fee (or free). The paradox in popular media consumption is that some or part of the item may or may not be consumed. Consumers have a choice in accepting as much or as little of the product's intrinsic worth. This reality might be reflected in consumer attitudes about their desire to pay a significantly lower price (or in many cases, nothing at all). This illegal behaviour discloses the inherent weakness in the preservation of copyright and the risk of elevating copyrights higher than the empirical reality suggests. Digitalization has done more than promote illegal consumption. Irrespective of their nationality, consumers consistently seem to devalue the value of copyright in media products by searching for significantly lower priced or free goods. This theme is universal both in the literature and the case law. Emerging technologies created the potential for an even playing field.

How should consumers answer the question of whether their activities abroad are illegal? The current state of play suggests neither a 'yes' nor a 'no' but rather a 'I don't really care'. At least in domestic and personal use this ambivalent attitude is consistent with current attitudes and beliefs. This attitude is indeed universal in the sense that Westerners and non-Westerners are united in their desire to consume popular media at a significantly lower price, even if it means illegally consuming goods. Commenting on Romanian[13] media consumers, Dwyer and Uricaru (2009, p. 52) make an interesting point about the interrelationships between technology, copyright infringement and consumption:

> Even if nowadays Romanians are ready to pay for 'quality' content ... they reserve their right to resort to piracy if the offer falls short of expectations for instance (due to regional marketing policies of global media companies), if it is prohibitively expensive or if it does not conform to Romanian tastes and standards.

Romania's past was totalitarian. But Romania too is now a member of WIPO. And it is also a member of the European Union, formally subscribing to Western notions of copyright governance. Yet the IIPA recommends it remain on the US Special 301 watch list for 2011 (IIPA, 2011c), not least because of the government's belligerence about the anti-piracy war effort. In 2007, Romania's president, Traian Basescu (during a press conference with Bill Gates) (Reuters, 2007) (cited in Karaganis, 2011, p. 55), remarked:

> Piracy helped the young generation discover computers. It set off the development of the IT industry in Romania. It helped Romanians improve their creative capacity in the IT industry, which has become famous around the world ... Ten years ago, it was an investment in Romania's friendship with Microsoft and with Bill Gates.

The Special 301 list, which is essentially an annual review by the US of nations threatening American intellectual property trade and commerce, reads like a US top-40 name and shame chart as several nations are listed, then delisted and subsequently relisted. It focuses on recalcitrant nations (including advanced welfare states such as Canada) because of their allegedly weak IP internal compliance frameworks vis-à-vis US trade imperatives. But it is somewhat of an irony that the most significant contribution to the field of consumer piracy has been the recurring invention of P2P digital piracy à la Napster.

Perhaps Romanians are not the only ones displaying vampiric tendencies. Mr Stevens, the Australian, took issue with Sony's regional übercopyright laws and did something about the digital rights management (DRM) system on his PlayStation in Australia. Sony felt threatened and alleged interference in its copyright management systems, but the High Court was very sympathetic towards Mr Stevens' rights. Post-communist Romanians, Western tourists and Western citizens all seem to accept consumption convergence.

In this context, the copyright governance framework constitutes a façade of neutrality that somehow attempts to strike a balance between copyright owners and consumers, the West and the emerging world, and the rich and the poor. Globalization of consumption deserves greater focus. Glasbeek (2002, p. 22) takes this point further: 'Law pretends to be neutral, while favoring the rich by giving corporations special treatment.' The irony – no rather, paradox – is that copyright is an artificial invention, and cannot by virtue of its composition be elevated to a scarce resource.

In the 1830s, David Urquhart Balkan, traveller (and hostage), described the terrorist brigands throughout the lawless vacuum created from Ottoman decline in the region. An Albanian pirate explained to his British captive: 'Everyone is in debt to the robber. I am sultan here, I am king of England here' (cited in Mazower, 2000, p. 32). Media piracy in the developing world reminds the West not only of its failure in promoting advanced capitalism to the rest of the world, but also of its imperialist and colonial past. The global leaders in popular media (US, Japan, German, France and the UK) have all benefited financially from industrialization and exploitation.

Much can be said about the motives of consumers and pirates in black market exchanges in emerging nations as it is presumed that both parties are aware of the illegitimacy of the transactions. Much can also be said about the consumers engaging in illegal downloads and uploads in the world of digitalization given the sheer depth of the anti-piracy campaigns in the West. Participants in illegal consumption are drawn to lawlessness in the copyright arena when it is clear the function of copyright law is to preserve and protect legitimate proprietary interests. The behaviour of many consumers in a transglobal world appears to be bound by participatory piratical culture. These transgressors as consumers and suppliers of unlicensed popular media cannot be the only pirates in existence, and so the search for a classifiable species (or probably genus) of pirate continues.

Part III
Prospects for Copyright Policy and Consumption in Popular Media

8

The Nexus between Piracy and Legitimate Consumption: Social Networking, P2P File-Sharing and Consumer Empowerment

I have no reason to believe any significant number of Kazaa users, apparently mainly teenagers and young adults, has any knowledge about, or interest in, copyright law or its application to file-sharing. Nor have I any reason to believe that any significant proportion of users would care whether or not they were infringing copyright. The 'Join the Revolution' material displayed on the Kazaa website and the 'Kazaa Revolution' T-shirt indicates the Sharman respondents perceive they might not. While I agree with the applicants that the existing warnings do not adequately convey to users what constitutes breach of copyright, *I am not persuaded it would make much difference if they did.* (Wilcox J, at [340] in *Universal Music Australia Pty Limited v Sharman License Holdings Ltd* (2005) (*Kazaa*) (emphasis added))

Introduction

The proposition presented in this chapter is that digitalization as a process of individualization and self-reflexive exploration has led to a convergence of illegitimate and legitimate behaviour in popular media consumption. Democratizing devices and protocols have equipped consumers with the relevant tools to challenge the manner and form of product delivery. Pavlov (2005, p. 657) summarizes the empirical and legal reality: 'Peer-to-peer technology has transformed music into a widely available and easily copied public good by allowing consumers to obtain music without paying royalties to copyright owners.'

Personal tastes in media are subjective, and therefore consumption has become a complicated process – not least of all because so many avenues of consumption exist. For example, it is highly likely that some consumers simultaneously access popular media legally and illegally without seriously considering the consequences of the latter. The quote from Pavlov reflects this attitude. Ignorance along with feelings that the majors are really in the business for money (obviously), and not for artistic taste or independent industry protection, are probably at play. In particular, these feelings highlight the complexities associated with consumption vis-à-vis product control and copyright maintenance and might explain the sheer volume of illegal traffic.

This chapter revisits the concerns about illegitimate consumption by focusing on cultural issues such as the use of social networking and the effects of that use on copyright policy. It introduces a parallel theme to the debate by suggesting that genuine consumer discontent is also inextricably linked to modern illegitimate consumption. It explores whether there is any causal nexus between P2P (peer-to-peer) sharing, social networking and a genuine lack of consumer interest in the manner in which popular media is offered by the major players.

Piracy is a complex term in that it includes personal users as domestic abusers of copyright – namely ordinary Western pop culture consumers who access media illegally but not for financial gain. Liberalism and notions of unfettered individualism have firmly shaped these citizens' attitudes and beliefs. This chapter builds on the argument that, in light of technological change (and especially the emergence of digitalization for compatible and interchangeable file compression formats), consumers have informed themselves about media consumption through social media peer networks. Alternatively, consumers wilfully but selectively access illegal popular media because they prefer to spend their money elsewhere.

The guiding theme of this chapter is that whilst other aspects of popular media are subject to regulation, consumer empowerment is beyond regulatory control or corporate coercion. It follows that converging technologies provide a potent challenge by arming consumers with independent tools for accessing popular culture. The questions raised in this chapter ask:

- Has the Internet and allied software emancipated consumers to the point that they no longer accept at face value the monetary value placed on cultural products owned by major firms?
- Does this independent behaviour constitute some form of protest by way of anti-absolutist consumption?
- Can these developments be described as convergent consumer behaviour signifying a challenge to the status quo?

As the above questions are answered in the affirmative, this introductory section revisits the political and legal themes raised in Chapter 1, and argues that consumers empowered by technological change have challenged the status quo in the past decade. Despite some initial denial on the part of the corporate controllers, the fact that popular media industries are entering into external joint ventures suggests that consumers are not responding to the traditionally entrenched business model.

BitTorrent file-sharing platforms (P2P) and social networking platforms (especially YouTube) bear remarkably similar characteristics – not least of all because they are entirely dependent on the Internet. Specifically situated in a virtual, digitalized telecommunications industry services (telco) realm, these two modes of popular culture consumption are neither a product of corporate popular media nor are they aligned with traditional industries. The fundamental difference between the old consumption regime and the new one is that these new platforms easily accommodate both legal and illegal possibilities (and also something in the middle) (see Chapter 3). Emerging hybrid modes of legal and illegal activity are unprecedented in that social networks demonstrate the capacity to dilate or diminish the probative value of copyright in cyberspace.

There has been no comprehensive consideration of why consumers find illegal consumption so desirable in the context of social networking. There is the potential to earn 'passive income' through banner advertisement and other syndicated forms of Internet mutual benefits. But there is no reliable data to confirm just how much money consumers are making from uploaded videos (with or without unauthorized content). For example, from a cursory examination of the named copyrights in the *Viacom v YouTube, Inc.* (2007) (*YouTube*) lawsuit, none of the illegal subject matter appears to have had advertising sponsorship.

The next section, 'Social media', examines the use of social media as a second-generation Internet tool. It determines the nexus between consumer discontent and the growing interest in digital technologies as a source of 'viral' dissemination. Why are file-sharing and mutual exchanges so popular? One suggestion is that consumers are entering into a form of mutualistic behaviour, namely a form of cultural reciprocity.

The third section, Disorder in the court, considers the interrelationship between legal and illegal consumption, including:

- reconciling attitudes of consumers in liberal societies;
- exploring the basic proposition that popular use of P2P is limited to narrow processes (copyright infringement);
- comparing artificial citizens' rights and natural citizens' conceptions of morality and freedoms.

It argues that traditional business models remain the primary focus of copyright industries notwithstanding hybrid business models have (reluctantly) been considered and implemented by the major players. Whilst it makes no economic sense to drag behind the IT revolution, the desire to preserve a lucrative, monopolistic status quo makes perfect sense. The music industry, especially, is good case study of such inaction and eventual reaction.

It is argued the dominant model remains, in that copyright enforcement is prioritized. Indeed, decentralizing and hollowing out of non-essential business has meant greater allied industry alignment with enterprises such as iTunes and Spotify, but without the need to compromise enforcement. If it is accepted that many consumers are somewhat indifferent to the legal consequences of illegal consumption, then it stands to reason that consumers might perceive the value of the current price of popular media products to be significantly less than the rates set by popular media industries. The new partnership between Spotify and FaceBook supports this observation. Whilst the correct value of popular media is hard to calculate, the evidence suggests that the price of these goods has historically always been artificially inflated. *Chappell & Co Ltd v Nestle Co Ltd (Chappell)* (1960) and the introduction of a parallel importation law in 1998 to amend the 1968 Copyright Act in Australia are evidence of this.

The industry's justification of the high price tag is based on the uncorroborated assertion that heavy risk is involved in popular culture (for example, for every one success there are so many flops). One investment is recouped cross-collaterally against another project (and so on). True interaction costs are never released by copyright industries. As was argued in Chapter 6, one explanation for historically highly priced media products is that the costs of flops are recouped from the hits. That is, the costs of a less successful release will be cross-collateralized against the revenue from a successful release. This is the justification for the high price tag. How else can the risk of taking a cultural gamble be amortized? Industry-set price tags act as 'insurance policies' for the major actors who speculate on success and loss. In other words, commercial confidence prevents disclosure of just how much the intrinsic value of popular media products is actually worth.

This section explores the impact of other forms of entertainment (namely social media) on popular media consumption. Social media as a truly democratic form of popular media consumption should be regarded as another type of external influence. Its sense of otherness stems from the fact that if popular media itself is merely the means then the mode of social communication is the ends. That is, the use of legal or illegal media is the conduit where the express purpose is to communicate in a social media context (for example, manipulating or parodying copyrighted material so that others within a social network derive pleasure from the material by way of cultural exchange). The fact that the pricing of, and attendance at, live music gigs and the cinema appear to be unaffected by technological change suggests that material, commodified, traditional popular media products are becoming less influential as a mode of popular culture. That is, people are still consuming popular media, but the value of tangible products is diminishing.

The fourth section (Consumers and respectability: a case of back to the future) revisits the recurring theme about the morality of convergent consumption. The doctrinal data support the observation that, historically, consumers placed great emphasis on enjoyment of popular media – often at the expense of the commercial value of popular media products. This leads to the observation in fifth section (The psuedopoliticization of social networks – reverse consumption) that social networking enables a mode of reverse consumption in that social networkers (as consumers) empower themselves through digitalization to freely exchange popular media for no apparent commercial reasons. That is, consumers do not consider the legal implications of their actions because they do not see their actions as a form of piratical conduct. Instead, they see their actions as the exercise of a natural right to disseminate information for free and as a form of freedom of expression. Social media networks encourage creative mutualism, and the sixth section (Creative convergence) examines the phenomenon of creative convergence that has its roots in creative commons. The democratic desire to de-monopolize popular media products is firmly embedded in social democratic phenomena such as social media and creative commons movements.

The conclusion of this chapter is that despite emerging business model synergies, the simple fact remains that, historically, consumers rank intangible property such as copyright at the bottom of the moral and strict legal observance ladder. If consumers can get away with 'free' consumption, then they probably will. This observation is historically and legally validated. The 'free concert' mentality of the 1960s, as was evidence at Woodstock, was a reflection of attitudes of consumers generally (no different to respectable restaurant patrons prepared to pay for food and accommodation but not necessarily for dinner music accompaniment, or fans making unlicensed and unauthorized remixes and compilations of their favourite bands and disseminating them to fellow fans).

Social media

In 2002, Yu suggested that copyright industries should adopt different business models instead of fighting copyright battles in order to preserve the status quo. He further argues that private and related uses should be permissible in any event. Reorientation did not occur – formally at least. But two separate issues arise. Value-added models might be considered as a viable option, including end-user Internet service provider (ISP) packages that bundle media products into the price of the Internet service, additional promotional materials for the same price (extra footage on DVDs or bonus CDs etc.), free downloads, discounted gift cards and so on. In other words, corporations have been forced to accept that the prices of marketed products were too high. There was no compulsion to review prices in 1960 when only limited formats existed (the *Chappell* case). Over the following decades, as externalities posed a threat, prices were revised. As a result, popular media prices have incrementally decreased over the past ten years.

What is also of interest is the second issue, that is, social networking's challenge to exclusivity and anticompetitive behaviour. Social media as a mode of social interaction is the process of communication and information dissemination through digitalized social interaction. The key element to this process is mutualism or reciprocity. Peer-users concurrently accessing and publishing respective information via a symbiotic process create plurality in broadcast and information dissemination. This mode of delivery bypasses traditional popular media channels. Copyright infringement issues aside, there are no distinctions between the information broadcasters and information recipients. Social networking as a mode of P2P activity possesses democratizing effects. It is in stark contradiction to the traditional mode of popular media consumption where popular media governors act as cultural gatekeepers.

What should be acknowledged is a growing 'play-for-free' attitude in the context of private use. It is no coincidence that, since 2005, technology-based companies have focused on new delivery platforms and devices supported by the Internet, mobile phones – particularly smart phones – and games consoles. Software designers and distributors continue to partner with ISPs in order to provide multiplatform broadcast and dissemination technologies that enable an ever-increasing number of value-added services for Internet customers. These include catch-up television, content on demand and access to television guides that are also linked to mobile phone applications and services, and music streaming. Spotify is one such example (see below). Social networks form an integral component in these convergent modes because many of these services are then disseminated through private channels (Facebook, MySpace and so on).

What appears to be missing in this digital environment is traditional market reciprocity between buyers and sellers. Suppose a social networker attends a live performance and uploads a video clip from the footage he or she has sourced as an attendee. The clip is then uploaded on MySpace for dissemination on the attendee's website for altruistic reasons (art for art's sake and not commercialization). The clip is clearly an unauthorized recording of a performance (but suppose the band finds it morally favourable). The unauthorized recording is an infringement of the copyrights vested in the works performed at the live performance. The unauthorized recordings are unapproved and the entrepreneurial copyright owners will insist that MySpace issues a 'take-down' notice because the unauthorized recording is a breach of copyright. Participation in illegal consumption might be construed as an act of piracy. Social networking popular media suggests that consumers have certainly not lost any interest in popular culture. Lucas (2003, quoted in Clement (2003, p. 35)) explains:

> If we do not enforce copyrights to music, will people stop writing and recording songs? ... Not likely ... If so, then protection against musical 'piracy' just comes down to protecting monopoly positions: something economists usually oppose, and with reason.

Just like personal media tastes, consumption has become a complicated process. In this regard, it is highly likely that some consumers access music both legally and illegally. This might be done at different times or intervals or perhaps simultaneously and without generally considering the consequences of the illegal access. That is, an empowered consumer could quite possibly download a game or song from the iTunes store in one part of the house whilst concurrently downloading an episode of a television series via BitTorrent in another part of the house, using different computers but the same Wi-Fi modem. The possibilities as described in Chapter 3 are indeed wide ranging. Ignorance of the law, lack of awareness and wilful disobedience might explain some of these developments.

But what about feelings of discontent? Consumer discontent is likely to breed a feeling of contempt for corporate control of popular media in relation to pricing and overall value for money. If consumers generally possess an overall feeling that the majors are in the business for money and not for artistic taste or independent industry protection then it follows that consumers may not accept the extent to which the majors purport to be sustaining loss. The major players feel aggrieved about piracy. Consumers who feel ripped off or perceive they have been treated unfairly should not be ignored in an age of emerging technologies. Digitalization gives consumers the ability to participate in unapproved conduct if they feel aggrieved. The volume of illegal traffic on the Internet supports this inference.

In a study about the brain and the law, Chorvat and McCabe (2004, p. 1731) explain that the brain reacts to an emotional desire to be treated fairly where cognitive conflict occurs. This feeling highlights the complexities associated with consumption vis-à-vis product control and copyright maintenance. Consider this finding in the light of studies concerning value for money and the rationale for illegal consumption (Furnham and Valgeirsson, 2007), and consumer behaviour in relation to infringement generally (Maffioletti and Ramello, 2004; Cvetkovski, Chapter 7 of this book) and when the 'amorality' of infringement (Manesh, 2006) argument is factored in, a case for disappointment and general consumer discontent against major players might be raised.

In recent years, allegations of unfair price-setting in popular media industries have become quite common throughout the West. Australia introduced copyright law amendments to promote more competitive pricing of popular media products through parallel importation in 1998 as a consequence of allegations concerning cooperative 'retail price maintenance' displayed by a few vertically and horizontally integrated players in the domestic marketplace. In the UK, the Office of Fair Trading (OFT) has periodically monitored and reviewed allegations of anticompetitive price-setting in popular media (see OFT391/2002). Since 2001 the EU has also considered the anticompetitive nature of cross-media price control displayed by the dominant few (see European Commission (2001)). In the US, the Federal Trade Commission examined the inherently weak competitive environment concerning the retail price of CDs. Pricing policies made by the dominant few had a direct negative impact as consumers were forced to pay higher prices for popular media due to cooperation on the part of a few similarly organized corporate entities. Combined, the US, EU and Australia comprise the top-ten markets for popular media products (excluding Japan). It is fair to conclude that a handful of multinational identities are generally responsible for determining prices and, in the absence of intervention, have historically been largely unchecked. Consumers' perceptions that corporate top-down control – from pricing to format – is not in their best interests are also reflected in the overall decline of album sales. In Australia, post the 1998 amendments to the *Copyright Act* 1968, the published price to dealers (PPD) to recommended retail price (RRP) ratio adjusted almost immediately in the new release category to reflect equitable pricing. In short, prices dropped.

The Internet has created a market environment that encourages various forms of reciprocity on an unprecedented scale. Social networking is an extension of social-hub behaviour. But it is also a reflection of consumer discontent in relation to corporate control of popular culture. Information exchange in the form of media file uploads, downloads and associated commentary occur freely without a gatekeeper and subject only to take-down notices.

Social media is pervasive and all encompassing given its purpose. RSS (really simple syndication), wiki contributions, podcasts and, especially, video-sharing sites such as YouTube (a Google subsidiary) and social network sites such as MySpace and Facebook dominate this convergent environment where communication is inextricably linked to consumption. As public profiles assume shared connections and mutual exchanges, there is very little room for corporate media intervention. Social media should be classed as an external development – completely devoid of any corporate popular media influence. It works along P2P principles in that a middle-man as content 'exhibit-keeper' is not required for content delivery or consumption.

This is not to suggest Internet-based social media has not attracted corporations. Corporations have entered into mutually beneficial arrangements – especially advertising – and have alliances with Google, YouTube, Facebook, MySpace, etc. Businesses now attempt to reach consumers in this convergent fashion. Take the example of Twitter. The judge in *Roadshow Films Pty Ltd v iiNet Limited* (*iiNet*) permitted the case to be twittered and so the case went viral. The problem with social media networking is that copyright, which is the conduit in popular media, is inherently subjugated in social media. The transient nature of social networking means it is difficult to institutionalize, that is, legitimize, the content uploaded.

Because of social media, disjointed and ad hoc fluid forms of consumption compete with traditional market models. Social media has no specific location because of its online status. Websites are registered but are not physically situated. The collection of Internet forums, blogs, wikis and podcasts that dominate this mode of decentralized consumption have proved problematic for copyright owners because working in a virtual world full of intersecting communicative pathways is the complete antithesis of a corporate, hierarchical, structured mode of delivery.

Friends become consumers in the social network setting. Membership is based on social acceptance and not financial status. A friend does not require funds to consume a product (for example a copyright-infringing video clip).

The decentralized, fragmented approach is unconventional given that the essential ingredient is interactivity. Corporations might utilize Facebook and YouTube for marketing purposes and promotion, but they are hardly substitutes for traditional media commodification processes. Imagine the absurdity of a Sony trade banner being displayed on an anti-circumvention spoof. Piracy is not a laughing matter. However the evidence to rebut that presumption suggests those libertine social networkers cannot resist the urge to mock copyright laws.

Disorder in the court

Given the plethora of anti-piracy parodies, the obvious lack of consumer concern for copyright infringement warnings and the generally disjointed approach the courts have taken, the title of the 1936 Three Stooges short film comes to mind (*Disorder in the Court*) (one of the few Three Stooges films in the public domain). The current legal position must be appear somewhat disordered for consumers who view popular media as a pervasive form of cultural expression. Indeed, millions of file-sharers are illegally engaged with social networkers in various ways through a variety of forums, links to torrent sites, as BitTorrent clients and as users of P2P software and applications. Both social networking and BitTorrent involve piracy to some extent and, consequently, both platforms are the subjects of ongoing ligation. For example, the ongoing litigation between Viacom and YouTube (2007) highlights the ambivalence about or ignorance towards copyright that social networkers share on the World Wide Web; and the decision against Lime Wire (2010) is an example of the ongoing procession of opportunistic avenues created by illegal site creators for consumption by ambivalent or ignorant individuals. BitTorrent seems to bear the brunt of adverse findings, while social networking seems to recoil behind safe harbour and conduit defences.

Take the most recent example of LimeWire (one of the world's largest P2P networks that in May 2010 suffered the same fate as Napster and Kazaa). Evidence presented to the court indicated up to '99% of the content that users requested for download through LimeWire was protected by copyright' (Heindl, 2010, p. 4). It had been actively supporting P2P technologies since June 2000. Justice Wood (in *Arista Records LLC v Lime Group LLC*, p. 7 (*LimeWire*) held:

> The evidence in the record establishes that LimeWire users infringed Plaintiff's copyright by sharing unauthorized digital copies of the Recordings through LimeWire.

According to the court, the sheer flagrancy of the copyright infringement constituted incontrovertible inducement. LimeWire, like its predecessors, was facilitating copyright abuse, enabling infringement through available software and how-to guides, marketing the illegal techniques and otherwise encouraging media piracy (along the lines of Kazaa). Furthermore, LimeWire gained a pecuniary advantage from its illegal conduct.

Just one month after the *LimeWire* decision, Viacom, one of the world's largest media conglomerates, had its US$1 billion copyright action (*Viacom v YouTube, Inc.*), based on the Data Millennium Copyright Act 1998 (DMCA), against Google's YouTube dismissed. Viacom is appealing the decision in the US. This course of action is not surprising given the developments in the *iiNet* case in Australia. Whilst these cases are materially different factually, they both turn on the issue of ISP customers as media file-sharers directly and indirectly infringing popular media copyrights. The dismissal in the *Viacom v YouTube* case largely turned on the court being satisfied by YouTube's 'prompt' take-down notice (that is, that YouTube gave notice that it would remove works immediately at a copyright-holder's request). YouTube relied on safe harbour protection. But the simple fact remains, YouTube was well aware of the copyright infringements by its social network users on its video-hosting site. For slightly different reasons (reliance on the safe harbour protection), the Court applied similar reasoning in the *iiNet* case. The DMCA's 'safe harbour' defence allows powerful intermediaries such as YouTube to thrive where they can demonstrate positive acts of compliance (as opposed to shams as in *LimeWire*). Viacom's complaint, filed in 2007, particularizes the allegations of copyright infringement as follows:

> 2. YouTube is one such entity. YouTube has harnessed technology to willfully infringe copyrights on a huge scale, depriving writers, composers and performers of the rewards they are owed for effort and innovation, reducing the incentives of America's creative industries, and profiting from the illegal conduct of others as well. Using the leverage of the Internet, YouTube appropriates the value of creative content on a massive scale for YouTube's benefit without payment or license. YouTube's brazen disregard of the intellectual property laws fundamentally threatens not just Plaintiffs, but the economic underpinnings of one of the most important sectors of the United States economy.

3. YouTube's website purports to be a forum for users to share their own original 'user generated' video content. In reality, however, a vast amount of that content consists of infringing copies of Plaintiffs' copyrighted works, including such popular (and obviously copyrighted) television programming and motion pictures as 'SpongeBob Square Pants,' 'The Daily Show with Jon Stewart,' 'The Colbert Report,' 'South Park,' 'Ren & Stimpy,' 'MTV Unplugged,' 'An Inconvenient Truth,' 'Mean Girls,' and many others. Unauthorized copies of these and other copyrighted works are posted daily on YouTube and each is viewed tens of thousands of times. As Dow Jones reported, '[i]t's no secret that millions of Internet users every day watch copyright-infringing video clips on YouTube' (Market Watch by Dow Jones, October 20, 2006). In fact, Plaintiffs have identified more than 150,000 unauthorized clips of their copyrighted programming on YouTube that had been viewed an astounding 1.5 billion times. And that is only a small fraction of the content on YouTube that infringes Plaintiffs' copyrights, because as described below, YouTube prevents copyright owners from finding on the YouTube site all of the infringing works from which YouTube profits.

30. ... Because YouTube users contribute pirated copyrighted works to YouTube by the thousands, including those owned by Plaintiffs, the videos 'deliver[ed]' by YouTube include a vast unauthorized collection of Plaintiffs' copyrighted audiovisual works.

42. ... For example, many users are sharing full-length copies of copyrighted works and stating plainly in the description 'Add me as a friend to watch.' For all these reasons, no matter how much effort and money copyright owners expend to protect their rights, there will always be a vast collection of infringing videos available on YouTube to draw users to its site.

The assertions and allegations made by the Viacom lawyers about direct and indirect active inducement, reproduction and passive infringement are correct. But the legislation does provide the requisite defence. However, the Court did not accept these submissions. Viacom may be aggressively pursuing the complaint against YouTube for several reasons notwithstanding YouTube's dominant and therefore influential social networking standing. First, its prospects of success against a corporation are better than, say, a class action against individual file-sharers. The legal blitz against music file-swappers did little to deter illegal consumption. Second, action against a well-resourced artificial citizen, as opposed to aggressive personal litigation, is better suited in terms of publicity. The media dramatized the litigation against children, their parents and the elderly, which in turn was the subject of great debate on the Internet. Third, successful litigation against telco-allied entities will send a strong message to ISPs and video-sharing websites about legal responsibility on the Internet.

So, on the one hand, the courts deem P2P platform facilitators, such as Kazaa, Napster, LimeWire, Pirate Bay, Cooper, etc., copyright abusers (that is, entities and persons classified as nothing more than opportunistic parasites living off copyright hosts). However, telcos, such as iiNet, and social network intermediaries, such as YouTube, are deemed good corporate citizens because their social networking regulatory systems are satisfactory. They are not parasitic or piratical in their business conduct, but rather 'epiphytic' because they attach themselves to the copyright host. These legal arguments and analyses are not only ambiguous and confusing, but they must appear preposterous to consumers who rely on these technologies as a form of expression.

Yet the farcical infringements continue. Take the examples of *SpongeBob*, *Beavis and Butthead*, *Ren and Stimpy* and *South Park* as averred in the particulars of the Viacom complaint. The 'YouTube Poop: The Sky Had A Weegee!', uploaded by 'Hurricoaster' on 11 November 2009 (also featuring unauthorized images of Nintendo's Mario), has been viewed more than 4.5 million times (as at October 2011). Nearly three years later in 2012 it remains for all to view. The uploader Hurricoaster in this instance is either a vicarious or direct infringer (probably both in terms of flagrancy and authorization). In the event of legal action against this individual, or more likely against YouTube, Viacom would also assert that the clip is not only a technical breach of copyrights, but a disrespectful depiction of SpongeBob and that it devalues the intellectual property rights (IPRs) vested in the character. However, what cannot be denied is that, irrespective of tastes, millions of viewers (presumably SpongeBob fans) have explored the aesthetic qualities of YouTube's 'Poop' by Hurricoaster. Indeed the several thousand positive comments and 'likes' below the YouTube link at www.youtube.com/watch?v=3MnrAw8Icfs tend to suggest SpongeBob fans approve of Hurricoaster's unauthorized samples

In recent years, legislation in the West has been amended to accept certain individual behaviours. In all there are nearly 70 exceptions to copyright infringement based on fair dealing and common law principles. Of note are the specific exceptions commonly associated with film, music and gaming (for example, the Australian Copyright Act 1968, ss109–110A and 199). It is important to note that these were relevant recent concessions by the legislature in late 2006 in Australia. But of course none of these exceptions apply to social networking and file-sharing generally or, indeed, as in the proceedings against YouTube in the US (which has always had fair use provisions in its copyright laws). Fair use via BitTorrent and P2P networks in the social setting are hardly compatible and are but one avenue for uploading and downloading copyrighted digital content. Social networks provide access beyond torrent files and so the boundaries between what constitutes fair use and infringement are becoming increasingly blurred in the world of digitalization. As social networks facilitate access to copyrighted music, movies, games and applications generally, the Internet has become one gigantic commons cataloguing resource. Currently, intermediaries such as Internet sites and software and related access tools are the primary legal targets. But imagine, for example, if the emphasis shifted not to whether BitTorrent is a facilitating tool for copyright infringements but rather whether, based on contributory or secondary liability, corporate copyright governors should target the Internet as a facilitator of indirect infringement. That is a ridiculous legal suggestion because ongoing technological change means that a generalized, sustained, global media industry war of attrition against the Internet would never end.

Such a war of attrition between the traditional industry and formidable external challenges would probably not end well for the major popular media industry (listed in Chapter 3). The only option would appear to be a merger – a truce of sorts. But for this to occur the actual commercial value in copyrights will require re-evaluation, as will the need to minimize monopolized intangible property in a digitalized environment. Litigation is a powerful tool against weaker opponents, and can be ruinous for a weaker party found at fault. But where opponents are evenly matched and matters are subject to appeal, the futility of litigation becomes increasingly apparent in the private sector.

More disorder in the court

Recently, a number of online copyright cases have been brought against those who actively provide Internet users with the ability and means to infringe copyright. Some of the better-known cases include *Neij, Svartholm, Sunde, Lundstrom (The Pirate Bay)* case in Sweden (see Chapter 9), the *Twentieth Century Fox Film Corporation and others v Newzbin Ltd (Newzbin)* (2010) case in the UK and the *GEMA v RapidShare AG (Rapidshare)* case in Germany (see www.gema.de and www.arstechnica.com). These defendants – RapidShare, Newzbin, and Pirate Bay – also share the rogues' gallery of unauthorized and flagrantly brazen enablers of copyright infringement. Whilst some file-sharing cases demonstrate facilitation of unauthorized use, the German case was overturned (eventually). RapidShare joins the ranks of iiNet and YouTube as being epiphytic, but not Pirate Bay, Newzbin and others as parasitic. The level of legal uncertainty in terms of consistency in decision-making across Western jurisdictions remains, and it is difficult to imagine how litigation and legislation will resolve the substantive technological issues.

The Digital Economy Act 2010, which came into force in the UK on 8 April 2010, is a recent attempt to aggressively pursue illegitimate file-sharers in order to permit holistic intervention against persistent offenders. Under the Act, ISPs with 400,000 subscribers or more are required to police file-sharing and introduce a 'three strikes' procedure, which should result in the reduction or termination of bandwidth for users who continually infringe copyright. The fact that two of the leading British ISPs, TalkTalk and BT, sought judicial review of the Act by the High Court to clarify whether the Act conflicts with the EU's e-commerce directive which limits the liability of ISPs is not a healthy start for the Act.

The popular media industries in Australia are lobbying for the introduction of legislation requiring ISPs to police the file-sharing activities of their users. However, because such legislation has only been introduced in other countries during the past few years, there is no evidence to indicate that these measures have any effect on the prevention or deterrence of copyright infringement.

Consumers and respectability: a case of back to the future

One needs not travel back in time to discover whether current attitudes and beliefs of consumers are respectable. The issue of respectability is nothing new. Every successive wave of innovation brings along with it moral baggage. Social networking is just the most recent socio-moral dilemma (if copyright infringement constitutes a social or moral crisis, that is). The law determines the state of legal and illegal behaviour, but not morality. Breaking the law is a question of fact; issues of respectability are not. Unlike copyright laws, technological advancement does not exist in a vacuum. Goddard LJ in *Ernest Turner Electrical Instruments Limited v Performing Right Society, Limited* (1943) summarizes the dynamics between consumers and technology as follows (at 175–176):

> [I]n selling a piece of music or a gramophone record, the owner of the copyright contemplates that it will be played, and consents to it being played, by the purchaser and he expects, not that it will be enjoyed in solitude, but that it will be heard by members of the purchaser's household and his guests.

In that case, a common sense approach was urged. Technological tools promote enjoyment as much as they incite acts of infringement. Consumers in social settings technically transgress in their legal obligations to copyright owners by sharing popular culture. In 1933, in Bournemouth (England), patrons who appeared 'respectable' paid the price at the Hawthorns Hotel for consuming meals and staying in the hotel; nonetheless, they actively *enjoyed* listening to an *unlicensed* performance by an orchestral trio playing to guests in the hotel (see *Performing Right Society Ltd v Hawthorns Hotel (Bournemouth) Ltd* (1933)).

It is highly doubtful that a single patron would have left in protest upon learning the collecting society had not been paid a fee. It would be a (legal) nonsense to suggest that restaurant patrons (already paying for the meals and service) would care about unlicensed music being played (presumably by musicians who would have negotiated a live performance fee in any event).

In 1884, in *Duck v Bates*, the Court had to consider the performance of a dramatic work at a hospital for the entertainment of nurses and others 'respectably' connected with the hospital. Admission was free for this public performance (some 170 persons attended). However, a majority of the English Court of Appeal held that the performance was not in public, but in private. Would these respectable healthcarers have blocked their ears and closed their eyes upon learning of the legalities of copyright licensing? It is highly unlikely.

A further historical legal affirmation of the decision of the English Court of Appeal was in 1927 in *Harms (Incorporated) Limited v Martans Club Limited*, in which it was held by Lord Hanworth MR (at 532–533) that:

> It appears to me that these authorities (*Planch v Braham* (1837) 4 Bing NC 17, Wall v Taylor 11 QBD 102 and *Duck v Bates*) are an abundant foundation for what Eve J has determined – namely, that the question whether there was a performance in public is largely a question of fact and to be determined by the facts of each case ... In dealing with the tests ... one must apply one's mind to see whether there has been any injury to the author ... class of persons ... whether or not the performance is a domestic one so as to exclude the notion of 'public'-domestic in the sense that it was private and domestic, a matter of family and household concern only.

The 1936 case of *Jennings v Stephens* is also good authority for contextualizing elements of authorization and common infringement as being questions of law, but the chief guide for any court is common sense. Issues about character, attitudes, relationships with the subject matter, respectability and morality are subjective and personal matters. They are not objective questions of fact.

Fast forward to the 1980s when blank-taping was the new terror for the corporations. Radio, record and cassette taping have always been a key feature of the manner in which popular culture is consumed. As with file-sharing and social networking, cassette taping is illegal. In fact, recording onto blank cassettes has traditionally been held prima facie illegal in various influential jurisdictions, especially Britain. Indeed, only in recent years has the Australian legislature allowed for limited backup (in essence, home copies). The British parliament intends to amend its copyright laws to legitimize backing-up, that is, copying for limited personal use. The reality, of course, is that copying and otherwise dealing with copyrighted material in the domestic setting – whether that is uploading, downloading files across the Internet, cassette taping, CD-ripping, DVD-burning, modifying game consoles, overriding regional coding for viewing, and all other methods of infringing copyright – has always been a feature of popular media consumption across the globe. It is remarkable that convergent consumption patterns are not recognized as the norm rather than the exception. Just as an analysis of the political economy of the popular media must take into account copyright governance so too must a consideration of concurrent consumption behaviours. These themes are interlocking because copyright is not the only thread that binds the fabric of popular culture. Liberalism, morality, technological change and consumer empowerment also bind popular media products. In 1982, the Australian music industry, through its industry body the Australian Recording Industry Association (ARIA), with the assistance of its collecting societies, the Australasian Performing Rights Association (APRA) and the Phonographic Performance Company of Australia (PPCA), demanded greater royalties for public performance because of the threat of home-taping. The demand was based on allegations that home-taping is media piracy.

Of course, none of these allegations were corroborated, substantiated or otherwise objectively assessed (see *WEA Records Pty Ltd & Ors v Stereo FM Pty Ltd* 1983 *(WEA)*). But it has always been common knowledge that people infringe copyrights. In Australia, amendments to the Copyright Act 1968 were made in 2006 to allow limited copying for home use, for example, back-ups, and the High Court recognized time-shifting (taping for later enjoyment) (see for example *Stevens v Sony* (2005)). Parliament, government and the courts, as separate arms of power under the rule of law, have reached the logical conclusion that these consumer practices generally have no commercial or financial motive. Despite the alleged losses claimed by trade lobby groups in reports and submissions made on behalf of corporations before the courts, there is little cogent evidence to suggest that corporations have sustained financial loss as a consequence of individual or, rather, personal use of copyrighted material at home. Even the curious facts in the case of Mr Burt who permitted thousands of unauthorized downloads of a pre-release copy of a Nintendo Mario game that been given to him unwittingly can never be publicly scrutinized. The data for the actual losses allegedly sustained were never forensically analysed because the evidence has been sealed by the court. As was evidenced in the *Australian Competition & Consumer Commission v Universal Music Australia Pty Limited (ACCC)* case about anticompetitive behaviour, the same fears (piracy and job losses) were peddled in the lead up to the 1998 parallel importation reforms. In *iiNet*, and now in the *Viacom v YouTube* case, the same loss of revenue complaints are raised (unsubstantiated of course).

Despite legal action and plaintive cries by corporate citizens, trade interest groups and government lobbyists, consumers continue to participate in legal and illegal modes of consumption. The pattern that emerges is that respectable citizens are acutely aware of their actions and the courts consistently insist that good common sense be applied. One indisputable fact is that corporate copyright-holders are predictably litigious. Yet the results are not always favourable to them. There are politico-economic and social costs to litigation in addition to corporate financial losses. One cost that cannot be measured is the attitude that empowered consumers might possess in the face of legal threats by dominant artificial citizens who clearly show no signs of financial impecuniosity. Spurious claims that home-taping leads to job losses or that parallel imports promote piracy and thus shrink the music and film industries do nothing but lead to a loss of respect that consumers may have for corporate citizens. Vilifying, shaming and blaming consumers for popular media market downturns is nothing new, but the relentless pursuit of consumers is a sign of an industry turning on itself. So-called common sense as proffered by the judiciary has been lost.

In the *iiNet* case, some 20 cases containing details of actual consumer infringers (iiNet account holders) were tabled (allegedly from a list of several thousand illegal downloads) (refer to Chapter 3 of Counsel's submissions). In these cases, primary infringement was positively and unequivocally identified. Yet not a single iiNet customer who had allegedly consumed illegally was prosecuted. Furthermore, customers were not subpoenaed or simply summonsed to give evidence. There was no opportunity to evaluate and assess forensically the behaviour of ordinary consumers in the absence of commercial or profit dealings. Important empirical data were sealed by the courts based on claims of professional, legal and commercial privilege (which also occurred in *Viacom v YouTube* and Nintendo's action against Mr Burt (*Nintendo Co Ltd v James Burt* (2010))).

As consumers are excluded from court proceedings because they have no legal standing, attitudes and beliefs about the legal issues are rarely recorded as primary evidence. The 20 known infringers were not joined in the proceedings in *iiNet*.

The popular media industry should make the connection that in a world of digitalized convergence there are social limits to economic growth in areas where multinational majors wish to increase the capacity for a firm to produce a satisfactory profit margin for intangible goods. Social networking is problematic in that it represents a relatively unattractive corporate copyright governance environment because commercial exploitation would require a business model that incorporates disjointed and ad hoc modes of monetized capability. Traditional bricks-and-mortar commodification is relatively simple because the relevant stakeholders are easily identifiable – there can only ever be one creator, producer and distributor. Even online distribution of physical objects or purchased downloads is workable in a world of digitalization. But social exchanges as inbuilt subscription services for little or no fee for commercial purposes are complex models. Socio-economic networking initiatives, such as the recent Swedish music-streaming initiative Spotify, where social networkers pay no initial fee or a nominal fee for an entire library of copyrighted works, are most interesting developments as they require a Facebook account and subsequent subscription (IFPI, 2012, p.12). The copyright industry's emphasis is, of course, to eradicate the scourge that is piracy by offering millions of songs for streaming for little or no direct or upfront cost to the consumer as a social network subscriber. Social networkers have embraced the service because of the nominal or no cost. But whether this à la carte, all-you-can-consume service is wholly accepted by most artists who have traditionally struggled to generate music royalty income from their creative endeavours remains to be seen. Composer/producer Benjamin Phillips observes: 'At 4.8 cents a stream no muso can make a living from this – it would take a ridiculous number of streams just to earn average wage' (quote embedded via Twitter in ABC News online – updated Wednesday 23 May 2012, 11:14am AEST). Irrespective of whether Spotify survives artist scrutiny, social network popularity and pending litigation against patent infringement (Ngak, 2011), the issue of the diminishing value of profitability of copyright remains unaddressed because the actual cost of popular media products has significantly dropped. Piracy obviously hurts creators, but low-cost, socio-economic streaming models must also disadvantage non-corporate participants whose 'fruits' are 'laboured' in popular media industries. In the past, minimum statutory rates and retail prices were centrally set with input from powerful trade associations and collecting societies who essentially dictated the terms in the market place. In the more flexible price-setting arena surrounding e-commerce, intermediaries (websites and telcos), as well as corporate copyright owners, are now also involved in determining prices. In this digitalized world, as in the earlier traditional industry era, creators and consumers are not involved in setting market prices. This is not to suggest original copyright creators and consumers should be engaged in setting business terms and conditions for consumption; however the fact that emerging technologies have equipped people with the capacity to bypass business processes in any event suggests greater community engagement might assist in resolving some of the tension created by convergent consumption.

The case law seems to indicate that the courts are able to meaningfully address the reality in the distinction between commercial and not-for-profit use of copyright material, notwithstanding that consumers who have no intention of profiting from illegal activity are committing technical breaches. However corporate copyright owners, as exclusive controllers, make no such fair use concessions based on 'common sense' observations because unauthorized use is illegal irrespective of financial gain. It is this tension between preserving individuals' private and exclusive rights that places limits on consumption and requires further examination. A convergence of law, popular culture and behaviour has existed for at least 150 years – yet the major corporations defy and deny the deference and/or indifference displayed by consumers.

In 1979, Browne-Wilkinson J (as he then was) identified the 'the character of the audience' in *Performing Right Society Ltd v Harlequin Record Shops Ltd*. It is fair to presume broad considerations robustly assessed in the light of public policy and common sense might be as important as testing the purpose of the law in a technical vacuum. In these cases, from *Duck v Bates* in the 1880s to *Performing Right Society Ltd v Hawthorns Hotel (Bournemouth) Ltd* in the 1930s to *Performing Right Society Ltd v Harlequin Record Shops Ltd* in the 1970s to the *Viacom v YouTube* case in 2007, formal interpretations of the law are challenged by the need to seek meaning and understanding as to why ordinary consumers behave the way they do. Copyright governors and legal formalists subscribing to positivist interpretations of the law label conscious infringers as pirates or persons displaying piratical tendencies. But such branding of citizens who display indifference or perhaps little interest in legal consequences of copyright preservation is more problematic. The legal reality is that copyrights probably do not determine where, how, when or even why popular culture is consumed. Non-legal factors such as technological change and the desire to consume entertainment irrespective of legal boundaries continue to challenge copyright governance. And as for copyright, it seems to be relegated to an artificial prism – ironically a prism maintained by corporations as artificial citizens.

The proper approach is to look at illegal and legal behaviour in a broad sense. Of particular importance is consideration of the character of both the unauthorized uploader or supplier of popular media and his or her audience. The monopoly owner of the copyright cannot see the exchange in any other way than as one of impropriety and indiscretion. Yet the relevant character of the audience in the exchange is that of the typical character of people throughout the years who have enjoyed unlicensed concerts, or have taped, burned, ripped and now downloaded in a private, semi-private, domestic or quasi-domestic situation. In the world of digitalization the customer feels payment has been made to the telco ISP and, given the privacy in which consumption takes place, it is quite reasonable to assume that is the end of the matter. In households where more than one computer and wireless connection is now the norm rather than the exception, it is hard to that imagine parents and legal guardians are not aware of what goes on behind closed doors with children and technology.[1]

The perception of a contradistinction between corporate expectations of how consumers must behave and how consumers actually behave is more than just a cultural issue. The character of audiences seems to be that people come together for social reasons, not for commercial exploitation. Corporations, conversely, come together for commercial reasons without considering society as a whole. As law professor Joel Bakan (2004, p. 35) forcefully asserts, '[a corporation] compels executives to prioritize the interests of their companies and shareholders above all others and forbids them from being socially responsible – at least genuinely so'. The best interests of popular media corporations are:

- to make a profit,
- to preserve and protect their dominant status quo,
- to represent corporate interests to the effect that the governance system dominates the formal structures, and
- to continue pursuing profit by minimizing in the strictest sense, and by way of forceful litigation, any obstacles to profit.

The case law as it relates to the film, music and gaming industries perfectly fits these big business criteria.

To purport to be bound to consumers (audience), creators and other non-corporate players on equal terms and by a common purpose is questionable. Liberalism and corporatism have reached a stage where the two are mutually exclusive. They always have been incompatible, but technological convergence has exposed the extent of the tensions that exists in popular media.

The psuedopoliticization of social networks – reverse consumption

Copyright governance is as concerned with resistance to alternative modes of consumption as it is with copyright protection. Copyright law is a code for setting out how copyright is to be protected and preserved, but without the usual channels for exploitation, copyright protection is artificial and pointless. Increasing indifference to, and lack of consumer interest in, traditional modes of delivery should not be dismissed as irrelevant. Lack of interest is akin to inaction, which in itself is political.

Consumers protest in various ways. Many people are generally non-confrontational, but when empowered by technology the potential exists for even the most passive to become active (through forums, blogs, tweets and email). Disgruntled consumers are powerful indeed. Stories exist about social networking being used by consumers to express discontent. Consumers express discontent directly as complaints and grievances or indirectly through parodies. Jeff Jarvis, academic, journalist and creator of the Buzz Machine Blog, provides a well-known example of consumer discontent. His 'Dell Hell' and 'Dell Sucks' stories were posted and then shared by viral Internet activity, and other consumers quickly followed to express their discontent (Jarvis, 2009, pp. 12–15).

Social networking then might be described as a form of democratic wealth akin to, say, utilitarianism along Benthamite lines. Harrod (1958) (cited in Hirsch (1977)) referred to 'oligarchic wealth' and 'democratic wealth' as an 'unbridgeable gulf'. As indicated in Chapter 3, the majors have attained oligarchic wealth through favourable copyright monopoly regimes and economic and technological consolidation. Access to the Internet, access to P2P file-sharing technologies and access to social networking sites and applications are enabling or democratic processes. Decentralized consumption is nevertheless a mode of consumption, but does not involve a direct financial transaction (of course, costs are borne indirectly by customers as they ordinarily subscribe to ISPs and buy prepaid modems – but these interaction costs are very minimal).

Kazaa's proprietors mischievously claimed 'join the revolution'. This appears to be a form of (misguided) encouragement of democratizing wealth in that Kazaa was offering redistribution of wealth created by elite media industries. But the enterprise was a democratic sham, not least of all because Kazaa was relying on income streams at the expense of the copyright owners. Nevertheless, in its altruistic form, democratizing wealth is the antithesis of oligarchic wealth (the control, command and preservation of the status quo for the purpose of maximizing commercial exploitation). Only a ribald marketing executive with allegiances to an oligopoly would put a spin on this strict and narrow mode of productivity as being anything other than exploitative.

There is nothing democratic and egalitarian about the popular music industry. The allegations of lost revenue for creative folk (see, in particular, the *WEA Records Pty Ltd v Stereo FM Pty Ltd* (1983) case and ACCC case law in previous chapters) are infused with factual errors, sweeping generalizations and inaccuracies that only a naive consumer, judge or legislator would believe. The Australian legislature certainly did not believe the hype when parallel importation was introduced into the Copyright Act in 1998. The judiciary also explicated the 'oligarchic wealth' status created by media industries through sheer political and economic clout in the *ACCC* case.

Further support for the oligarchic–democratic divide can be found in the substructure of the popular media industry, that is, the input arm of the industry where underlying copyrights initially possessed by the creators are converted to commercial copyrights. The copyright contracts between creators and the majors have proved oppressive historically (famous cases include *Panayiotou v Sony Music Entertainment (UK) Ltd* (*George Michael and Sony*) (1994) and *Schroeder v Macauley* (1974). Cumulatively, there is enough case law and literature to portray an undemocratic picture. In Western society (especially in those jurisdictions using common law principles as opposed to those using Roman law principles) only a very few creators actually make a living from full-time artistic endeavour. The waiter waiting for his big Hollywood break, the musician busking in the town square and the gaming software designer on welfare benefits working in his bedroom in his parents' house are all too familiar. Most creators have to do other things to support themselves. There have been no democratizing effects for the original copyright owners in the popular music industry.

The perception generated by neo-liberal monopolistic institutions in association with the World Intellectual Property Organization (WIPO) is that elaborate and sophisticated royalty-tracking techniques are implemented in order to ensure that *all* relevant copyright-holders are compensated. However, the stark reality is that this simply does not occur, and often those who rely on every cent are not compensated (see Kretschmer et al., 2010). The major reason for revenue concentration in the hands of the major players is because the majors dictate the terms in all respects – from copyright control to royalty distribution (refer to Kretschmer et al., 2010; and Chapter 3). Consequently the corporate elite retain most of the revenue and recent initiatives such as Spotify corroborate Kretschmer et al.'s (ibid.) observations. Oligarchic regimes rarely wish to forgo their privileged status as a rich minority. Democratizing wealth in popular media is a fallacy. In this context, as Bakan (2004, p. 37) would argue, 'corporate social responsibility is thus illegal – at least when it is genuine'.

Creative convergence

Given the critical and forensic analysis of corporate citizens and their attitudes to interference with entrepreneurial copyright, it must be asked whether creative commons licences (CCLs) support popular media reorganization. A CCL authorizes the copying, reuse, distribution and adaption of the original owner's work without additional permission. These models are popular in public-sector environments, especially in the education, research and government sectors, subject to confidentiality and Crown law copyright limitations.

This 'third-way' copyright governance mode is consistent with primary and secondary conceptions of copyright and is reminiscent of early common law copyright approaches. These licenses are not exclusive, are open-ended and generally unlimited. Because creative commons activists encourage licensing of open content from the creator of all of the materials, they are thus promoting alternative, decentralized paths to copyright governance. This third-way approach also resolves the issue of requiring licences for the publication of anonymous and orphaned works, and assists in the overall streamlining of media content in a world of digitalization and convergence. Absolute control and discretion is vested in the original owners of the works, thereby reducing the need for entrepreneurial (usually corporate) acquisition of copyright. Consistent with the Internet's borderless universe, CCLs encourage multijurisdictional access (unlike the traditional copyright model).

The online open-content movement is premised on a truly democratized communications system bypassing the need for authorization. Lessig (2001) contends that the Internet and 'continuous innovation' mutually coexist in a natural free-form state and that copyright monopolies stifle the natural desire to create and recreate an existing body of works because copyright laws represent limitations, whereas emerging technologies promote delimiting capacities.

To some extent, pseudo-creative commons, in the form of limited copyright periods, did exist in previous centuries, but copyrights in the most popular forms of media have become increasingly extended, thus limiting the potential for CCLs. Lessig (2004, p. 61, emphasis added) alleges that '*every* industry affected by copyright today is the product and beneficiary of a certain kind of piracy'. Mark Twain viewed publishers as pirates, and one wonders where would Mr Disney be if the Brothers Grimm asserted their copyright exclusivity.

There are many examples in other fields. One only need only reflect on whether rock 'n' roll would have been a mass marketing phenomenon if the current copyright restrictions had been imposed on recordings made in the early part of the twentieth century by free-spirited souls such as Muddy Waters, Little Walter, Jimmy Rodgers, Willie Dixon, Lead Belly, Son House and countless other black American musicians.

Lessig's approach focuses on the rights contained in works created by consumers as publishers in an open-content environment where the tools of the trade are universally available to all active participants in a democratic process (Lessig, 2001, p. 1072). Open-ended licenses are free and open in that users are permitted open access, but limited in the sense that the licence does not extend to redistribution rights exclusively associated with commercial copyright exploitation. The creative commons licence is limited for private or domestic use, and is premised on loose, arm's length or liberal copyright approaches more commonly associated with so-called copyleft approaches to copyright, which involve mutualistic or symbiotic input from interconnected users. From a consumer's perspective however, creative commons affords the consumer with access to content with a licence to use the media (and in some instances to distribute where permissible).

Currently, broad-spectrum creative commons avenues exist. The Project Gutenberg reminds us of just how much literature was available to the public at a time when copyright laws were less restrictive. The Internet Archive is especially interesting as it purports to provide 'universal access to all knowledge'. It indeed possesses a growing range of popular media made freely available via BitTorrent for those interested in such media for research purposes. The site is open-ended and people freely upload media for others to download (the technique is no different to any other file-sharing platform).

But even a cursory assessment of some of the content immediately raises an alarm for the lawyer. Take the example of the Depeche Mode offerings. Some of the uploads, and especially the remixes, appear to be unauthorized recordings. The issues are identical to the current YouTube/Viacom litigation. The tensions that arise between consumer attitudes and the position of corporate copyright control will become more evident in a CCL environment.

Conclusion

The primary legal question is whether BitTorrent or any other similar software is liable – based on a theory of contributory or secondary liability – for the direct infringements of its users. But a more fundamental social question is whether consumers really care (*null bock*). In the *Kazaa* case, Wilcox J (at 178) considered whether some of the advertising by Kazaa's executive team on behalf of Sharman Holdings was a form of inducement or encouragement. At para. 177 of the decision, one of the Kazaa executive members, Mr Morle, was asked about customer attitudes to the services provided. The attitude displayed by consumers was clearly that of play-for-free. That is, Mr Morle's understanding of users' perceptions was encapsulated in the following statement conducted by a focus group summary tendered as evidence: 'Kazaa is currently thought of as a free music downloading search engine.' Given the increase in illegal downloads immediately proceeding this relatively recent decision, it is fair to conclude that anti-piracy campaigns have done little to address this play-for-free attitude adopted by consumers.

THE
KAZAA
REVOLUTION
30 years of buying the music of [sic] they think you should listen to.
30 years of watching the movies they want you to see.
30 years of paying the prices they demand.
30 years of swallowing what they're shovelling.
30 years of buying crap you don't want.
30 years of being a sheep.
Over. With one a single click.
Peer 2 peer, we're sharing files.
1 by 1, we're changing the world.
Kazaa is the technology.
You are the warrior.
60 million strong. And rising.
Join the revolution
KAZAA
Share the revolution

Wilcox J found (at 405) that '[e]specially to a young audience, the "Join the Revolution" website material would have conveyed the idea that it was "cool" to defy the record companies and their stuffy reliance on their copyright'. However, the advertisement quoted above provides more than an inducement. It reflects a sense of biopolitical power that leads to a disconnect between law and compliance and consumer behaviour.

The *Cavalier's* February 1969 edition included a feature on the 'Future of Music, Travel, Newspapers and … Marihuana'. Reverend Noebel, in his most bizarre 1974 thesis on the nexus between Marxism and rock music and the moral perils presented by these 'dangerous' anti-American ideologies, alerted the reader to the *Cavalier's* feature. The *Cavalier* feature story, entitled 'Music is the Revolution', describes music's emancipatory capabilities. But Noebel is scathing of rock music's Soviet-inspired subversive agenda.[2] *Cavalier* magazine's music editors devoted the entire February 1969 edition to rock music, it being 'the revolution … it is not only subversive, it is also giving the rebelling teenager his first victory in the initial revolutionary struggle for independence and detachment from an increasingly restrictive bourgeoisie' (Rudnick and Frawley, 1969, p. 37). In Foucauldian terms, this represents a genealogy of power – the power of corporate control through copyright to 'normalize' individuals (Foucault, 1991a, pp. 101–105). That Wilcox J, *in Kaaza* (at 340), saw the influence as subtly catering to (what His Honour perceived to be) the psychology of teenagers is reinforced by his comments about the inadequacy of warnings on the Kazaa website (see quote at beginning of this chapter).

To press this point that not much has changed in terms of consumer attitudes and conceptions of morality, it is worth quoting the last paragraph of this curious *Cavalier* (Rudnick and Frawley, 1969, p. 88) article:

> The sounds of a thousand musical freaks are news bulletins of a youth revolution. It is the voice of change. As Mao once said, 'Now the cock crows, dawn breaks over the world, And from a thousand places arises a swelling music, Never were poets so inspired!'

Not surprisingly, the Reverend Noebel augments the discussion on degeneration, revolution and counter-culture with a discussion on 'Rock, Drugs, and the Beatles' – and of course 'Rock and Morals' including 'Pop Music Sex' (see pp. 72–94).

That music is revolutionary and rebelliously appealing to teenagers is an important observation despite the fact it is trite. Notwithstanding the fact that editors comment on the 'enlightened kids' with 'libertine' attitudes towards authority in the 1960s, the article is not so much about moral decay and subversion, but about the commercialization of popular culture – namely pop music. Protests concerning popular media commodification and its mode of consumption continue in late capitalism.

The 'revolution' in late capitalism is not so much concerned with morality and respectability of content, but with fairness of price and value placed on cultural products. It is therefore fair to infer that in the light of an increase in illegal consumption, the value placed on copyrights by corporate controllers seems to be well above the market value consumers are willing to pay for finished products. In the past ten years, the value of finished products in popular media has been seriously questioned (Pavlov, 2005).

Interactive technologies and consumer attitudes appear at odds with the manner and form in which major copyright industries organize their products for consumption. As to pricing, the question about to what extent the major players appreciate, accept or otherwise understand the nature of innovative change remains an unresolved and vexed issue. It is asserted that consumers have not only become suspicious of those who control copyright industries, but they are also generally discontent with those who act as price-setters and cultural gatekeepers. David and Kirkhope (2004, pp. 444–446) warn of the social effects of privacy violations at the expense of copyright preservation for a concentrated few.

Copyright laws are prescriptive in that they prescribe consumer behaviour. However, it is the consumers who choose whether to follow them or not. Freedom of choice is a liberal concept. But like P2P, social networking also displays transgressive behaviour in the marketplace. Its grass-roots communal approach is in direct opposition to a top-down copyright governance framework. Social networking is a form of communal production without authority and licensed control. It is therefore legally problematic for both copyright owners and ISPs. Sharing information (including copyrighted material) challenges exploitation because commerciality is not an element of the transaction. There may be some residual interest in gaining pecuniary advantage but the impetus is generally based on social status (getting hits and ranks) and altruism. The issue of convergent consumption where legal and illegal boundaries have blurred relates purely to value-exchange. The Internet has exposed the artificiality of price-setting by the popular media industries. This might explain the ambivalent approach to illegal consumption.

The Internet has created a market environment that encourages forms of socio-economic reciprocity on an unprecedented scale. This is an extension of social media network behaviour. Consumers are freely exchanging views, opinions, ideas and material (that is, popular culture) without intervention or control from cultural gatekeepers. For example, a legitimately purchased CD is uploaded so that others may benefit from the experience. But the behaviour is mutualistic in the sense that the uploader may rely on reciprocity at some later time; hence the enjoyable experience found in file-sharing is reciprocated.[3] The literature does not identify a perception that consumers provide a community good through media exchange. Digitalization of popular media transcends traditional ownership boundaries that were clear in the pre-digital era. Therefore, if the value of copyrighted goods is reduced, then there will probably be a reduction in the rate of illegal consumption. But if the value is significantly diminished, this is not a positive outcome for corporate controllers of popular media products.

Drawing on the Kazaa slogan, technological change or, rather, a shift in technological power from centralized to decentralized modes of control has created a revolution of sorts. The omnipotence of the advertorial rhetoric in the star-shaped Kaaza Revolution slogan suggests some form of biopolitical struggle. The legitimization of the integrity and superiority of major players has never been successfully challenged. Favourable trade and copyright governance has ensured global domination where consumers have generally accepted the terms of popular culture consumption largely on corporate terms. But there appear to be millions of enlightened consumers in a world of digitalization who appear to resist this norm by unblocking obstacles, clearing pathways and enabling freedom in a transcendental sense (Foucault, 1993, pp. 67–69). This raises questions about the substantive legitimacy of copyright. Through technological innovation, consumers have questioned the following corporate-driven norms:

- the monetary value of media products,
- the format of products, and
- the manner in which products are disseminated.

Consumption of popular media is a deeply personal experience. Consumers derive satisfaction from the popular culture embedded in the goods utilized, not the copyrights. Absolute limitations are placed on popular culture when the source is controlled. But when the source is opened, the possibilities of information exchange are limitless because there is no physical barrier to supply. Social networking, CCLs, P2P file-sharing and other digitized modes have penetrated that physical barrier by enabling access to them, thus removing any scarcity value.

The dialectical contradictions between the controlled traditional forms of popular media delivery and copyright preservation and the new modes of uncontrolled communal platforms for illegal and legal use have created an emerging set of tensions. A thesis has an antithesis creating a transcendental transformation – a synthesis or, rather, convergence of technological change.

9
Conclusion: Reconciliation or Infinite Futility?

> The administrative expedient is one that we can come to only with regret and some misgiving: for it would do away with the simplicity, one may even say the pristine innocence, of copyright law. (Kaplan, 1966, p. 847)

The conclusion of this book is that machinery of copyright governance for modern popular media industries must compete (and interact) with omnipotent externalities, that is, the Internet, software, telecommunications and other related digital external technologies. Converging challenges are new and have caused irreconcilable shifts in the balance of power between the various stakeholders at the superstructual level. Challenges have led to:

- shifts in copyright regulation from the national level to regulation at the international/global level (see Chapter 2);
- shifts in consumer attitudes toward methods of popular culture consumption in Western society, that is, a convergence of legal and illegal modes (see Chapter 8); and
- shifts in industry focus from media piracy concerns to combined media piracy and transmission and communication concerns, that is, the challenge from the 'neighbouring laws' phenomenon and other external legitimate challenges (see Chapters 4, 5, 6 and 7).

To minimize the aftereffects of unauthorized physical copying and peer-to-peer (P2P) file-sharing, corporate controllers have increased anticompetitive behaviour by extending copyright periods and by aggressive protection of copyrights. As set out in Chapters 1, 2 and 3, 'future proofing' copyright has been mainly achieved through formal governance mechanisms.

However, new technologies have created informal information exchange relationships where uploading is as important as downloading. The cases considered have provided a line of authority for the proposition that independent consumption of popular culture (free from corporate interference and personality) is emerging as a challenge to the regulated and concentrated status quo.

The uniqueness of P2P as a mode of consumption is of particular significance as P2P differs from any other development, given its social dimension and multiplatform exchange process. As mentioned in previous chapters, international 'swarms' of individuals are involved in one relatively simple transaction. Social networking has the same decentralized, anonymous and ad hoc approaches to information exchange. These developments reflect the challenges to globalized popular media industries as copyright industry custodians.

The Internet, in particular, is so invasive that it challenges conceptions of sovereignty and jurisdiction, and raises awareness about the intersubjectivity of copyright governance in terms of the 'self' and individuality in consumption. As digitalization transcends cultural, moral and legal boundaries, the (formal) traditional, key concepts have become problematic in the oligarchic popular media industry business model.

The Internet epitomizes deregulation because of its virtual composition and capacity to create borderless space in which the individual as a consumer can move. Generally unfettered, or at least fluid, information exchanges are possible because in terms of legal obligations the Internet is jurisdictionally complicated by the doctrines of *lex fori* and *lex loci* in the private international law setting (Goldring, 2008). Anonymized consumers are of little use to organizations that demand procedural order. Therefore copyright industries as protectionist regimes have historically been suited to business practices linked to tangible (bricks and mortar) businesses. In this digital age this of course extends to online stores to the same degree as it does to street stores. The horizontally integrated business practices of the twentieth century are limited in the current digital environment. The old business models based on monopoly power have been directly challenged to the extent that rapid decentralization is causing the dilution of formal copyright governance. That is, aside from a few recently enacted concessions (namely, limited fair use for research, parodies or backup), copyright use is authorized or unauthorized, licensed or unlicensed – and therefore legal or illegal. In a commons content virtual sphere where use and misuse of copyright have converged, the boundaries have become increasingly blurred. This is not only because copyright and telecommunication industry services (telco) industries are competing in the same digitalized world and experiencing compatibility issues about how business is to be conducted without encroachment, but their customers, as consumers, are invariably the same citizens. Citizens in a converging world of communications will find it difficult to navigate these interlocking but not necessarily compatible legal domains. This is because the commercial digital frontier comprises several classes of customers as consumers of digitalized products. The popular media consumer as dowloader, uploader and social networker participates in

activities in a broader telecommunications setting rather than in a traditional media one. Copyright extension lobbying and litigation against digital
neighbours and anti-piracy campaigns, generally represent a reaction to convergence and the blurring of technically legal boundaries between copyright
and telco industries. In any event it is doubtful that any meaningful digital
agenda reform might have anticipated the actual challenges presented by
ongoing technological change. The products, services, participants and
organizational structure of popular media industries have been directly challenged by legitimate and illegitimate modes of consumption. This book has
explored the blurring of the boundaries. Or, perhaps, have the boundaries
dissolved?

Popular media as commons culture: ever or never?

Chapter 8 stresses that the so-called commons culture does not subscribe to the
fundamental tenets of modern-day copyright appropriation and exploitation.
Viewed from a social media populist movement perspective, these democratized information exchanges are supported by YouTube and Myspace (and
other potent popular-media-streaming sites). Social media and open-ended
content initiatives attract attention from players on both sides. The potential to exploit via licensing arrangements is obvious (the largest collecting
agency, Broadcast Music Inc., reported positive results with external partnerships, including YouTube (Mi2N.com (2011)).

The tensions are also evident, however. Protracted litigation with these major
players over unlicensed streaming videos and songs unofficially uploaded by
consumers suggests another dynamic. This is nothing new – cassette formats
attracted cassette piracy. Copyrighted CDs, DVDs and other twentieth-century
formats were also in no small part due to the technological developments
of the manufacturing arms of the aggrieved copyright owners. All these formats attracted incessant litigation. The case law supports the argument that
emerging technologies, corporate control of media and copyright restriction
cannot reconcile these perpetually unresolved issues. In the twenty-first
century, digitalization shows just how little room there is to move in governance frameworks that have largely remained intact since the late 1800s.
Formidably opposing stakeholders (such as the telco industry) combined
with technologically empowered consumers have challenged copyright
governance. The legal reality is quite different and infinitely more complex
than the formal copyright regulation landscape. The decline of peer-to-peer
(P2P) file-sharing should have been witnessed after the collapse of some of
the largest BitTorrent sites. The heavy flow of Internet traffic should now
resemble that of a trickle, and Westerners, as enlightened liberal citizens,
should refrain from purchasing pirated copies from emerging economies.
Cheaper prices should have all but stemmed the flow of illegal traffic.

But the empirical evidence shows a spectacularly different picture. In Mi2N (2011) it was reported:

> The Motion Picture Association of America, Inc. (MPAA) issued the following statement ... regarding the release of a new report by MarkMonitor that estimates the volume of traffic to fewer than 100 websites with 'business models that are indisputably centered on the sale or distribution of counterfeit and pirated goods' at a staggering 53 billion or more annual visits, most of which are to sites peddling stolen digital content.

Because recent technological developments do not rely on corporate copyright to survive they are formidable. Users are not necessarily popular culture consumers when using the Internet. Consumers randomly accessing popular media, expressing discontent, dissatisfaction and flagrant conduct as part of a consumption process demonstrate the fact that convergence and digitalization are capable of destabilizing copyright industries. Chapter 7 explains that the issues in emerging economies are also interwoven with Western attitudes displayed by consumers. The grass-roots media piracy interaction discloses the artificiality of the copyright governance imposed by the West.

Armed with a get-tough attitude, industry controllers have (reluctantly) entered into external arrangements in a bid to sustain core business models. It should not be forgotten that the Hollywood machine, and the music majors especially, have survived for nearly a century. To adopt substantive alternative business models is exceptionally risky – externalities require too many compromises.

Popular media industries have traditional business models with traditional channels. It is too early to comment on the success of so-called business synergies, which should, at least for the moment, be dismissed as PR, marketing and sales talk. There is no doubt that revenue in the digital age is being earned (generally, iTunes and Spotify partnerships, mobile applications and Internet service provider (ISP) package deals are evidence of this). But unlike new business concepts based on e-business models, these traditional industries are not accustomed to operating at a loss in order to build brand awareness and hoping to make money at a later stage.

As Chapter 3 discusses, these industries have traditionally owned the tangible and intangible aspects of the products. The question of who pays for popular media products was easily answered in the past – the consumer. But the manner in which revenue can be recouped in this new world remains unsettled. If consumers refuse to pay upfront, then from whom does one collect royalties, and at what rate? The latter is the more significant question.

The reliance on the consumer in the actual physical realm has turned into reliance on vicarious consumers – ethereally located as artificial vessels.

Consumers with indifferent, casual or generally liberal attitudes to copyright cannot be replaced by more reliable ones who uphold the sanctity of copyright governance. Trepidation on the part of popular media industries to embrace digitalization of media products, where those products are reduced to fragmented packets of data across the World Wide Web, is entirely understandable. Popular media industries are late entries to the digitalized world. The case law since 1999 suggests that the Internet has been a technological battleground for popular media industries. In the digital world, technological innovation and advancement concerned with the consumption of media products cannot not be directly traced back to the popular media industries. In fact, since the demise of hard formats, such as CDs and DVDs, external platforms deeply rooted in information technology dominate the entertainment landscape. Where once popular media industries, as corporate governors, dominated product delivery in a highly concentrated and well-integrated manner, they must now look to striking favourable bargains with iTunes, YouTube, Facebook and highly influential Internet service providers (ISPs) and mobile phone service providers. Popular media products were once presented to the marketplace with set published prices to the dealers. Pricing was largely discriminatory. The products are now variably licensed for downloads on the Internet or as bundles for part of an inbuilt package provided to telco customers. Popular media transactions on the Internet now resemble transient or fluctuating commercial arrangements commonly associated with e-commerce. Thus, pricing structures are rarely fixed. The traditional business model built on decades of vertical and horizontal integration was eroded by a fluctuating pricing model where digital sales resemble shares (stock market) more than fixed commodities. In a world of digitalization, however, a price revaluation of these products as 'shares' has occurred through a convergence of consumption patterns. These business developments are set against a backdrop of empowered consumers who treat popular media as nothing more than a mode of disposable communicative pleasure and perhaps have some residual thought of the copyrights embedded in the products.

The popular media industry dealt with Napster using the full force of the law and a flotilla of the most prestigious blue-chip lawyers. But, as has been experienced over the past ten years, the rise of the machines and the 'new, faster, better' ideology means that the law has not provided salvation. At best, corporate copyright media remain cautiously optimistic that external digital challenges will be subjugated, for example, through litigation. Previously, consumers and popular media products were in an intersubjective state where the linkage between products and consumption was clearly identifiable. Digitalization provides no nexus between consumers and popular media industries. Instead popular media flows through legal and illegal channels, is forwarded and then forwarded on further and redistributed and reconstituted via social networks.

Suppose popular media companies enter into comprehensive service agreements with ISPs. If they do, an inference could be drawn that customers are not willing to pay (full price, that is) directly for popular media. If third parties (telcos) are substantively involved in the new business model, then the products must be offered at discounted prices (for example, bundled as an Internet package for the consumer) – not necessarily favourable terms for copyright owners. For example, in Australia, generous home Internet packages from leading providers (Telstra, Optus and iiNet) are generally affordable (on average, AUD\$50 to \$100 per month per household). However, songs on iTunes typically sell for AUD\$2. But in the digital age consumers seek to download more than music. This is evidenced by the fact most ISP subscription plans are marketed as data usage plans with associated bonuses. It follows that under a subscription model it would be difficult to charge for digitalized products per item. Unlike the traditional model and its system of fixed, usually internal, interaction costs, several entities, including software intermediaries, are included in this complex, fragmented and generally decentralized delivery system. Each new participant in this non-traditional business model imposes new interaction costs thereby potentially diluting the current value of popular media products. And all these challenges are set against an era of convergent consumption where the boundaries between the illegal and legal have blurred. In other words, the cost would have to be subsumed elsewhere and it is doubtful that telco industries would absorb the cost because, for the first time in popular media history, copyright industries do not control technological change.

In any event, popular media consumers as joint telco customers would ultimately dictate what is an acceptable price for goods in this new intangible e-commerce environment. The goods consumed become subsidized goods. Subsidized goods can never be exploited at the same rate as primary goods. Popular media in effect becomes 'bonus material' subsumed by the primary material, that is, Internet access. It then follows that this secondary material becomes simply an accessory – an 'app' rather than a unique good in its own right. In other words, it will matter not whether a specific band has a new album, but rather how many products (including new repertoires) are bundled in the ISP package. This is not to suggest that fans and the relevant artists have not engaged with one another (the relevant social media networks are used as information-update sites for releases, downloads, live events and so on). Instead, the products promoted by the major players become ancillary thereby diluting or diminishing the value of copyright in actuarial terms.

No matter what the model, the mode of delivery will be complex and the question of the relevance of copyright must be raised. In any event, products will become directly or indirectly open-content. Subsidization in the form of providing popular media as part of a package deal therefore leads to a form of market failure.

The perpetual frustration experienced by industry controllers is understandable given the competing or incompatible paradigms of consumer attitudes and perceptions. It is doubtful whether convergence of legal and illegal modes of consumption can coexist under formal conceptions of copyright laws. However, in so far as copyright governance is concerned, issues about the best way forward for the future of copyright remain unresolved. Trade representatives continue to promote education programmes and enforcement action in relation to piracy, with an emphasis on tracking and shutting down illegal websites (IFPI, 2012, pp. 24–27). Focus remains on the Internet and the issue of concurrent flow of legal and illegal traffic. But given the difficulties associated with establishing causation and the subsequent pursuite of consumers, it will be interesting to see whether copyright owners continue to focus their litigation on ISPs, search engine intermediaries, social sites and software developers in addition to the media pirates who make available unauthorized works. As mentioned in Chapter 8, action against legitimate entities will be challenging given that the media industry has only been successful against illegal enterprise. The addition of legal realism to the debate at least acknowledges the undisputable fact that the consumption of legal and illegal popular media has always coexisted – despite corporate campaigns. On the issue of copyright preservation, the doctrinal evidence and empirical data suggest that, prima facie, illegal consumption is too complex and multidimensional for copyright governance to provide any meaningful robust protection.

Whilst organized piracy, as Chapters 5 and 7 discuss, is clearly criminal behaviour, consumers purchasing pirated products (low-level individual piracy) show, at best, empirical evidence of opportunistic but morally acceptable behaviour. The implementation of 'three-strikes' quasi-criminal legislation against habitual downloaders in New Zealand and in other Western nations (both common law and European civil code nations (for example, France)) may or may not achieve the desired deterrent effect.

Whether consumers perceive low-level piracy to be objectively wrong is debatable. The reason for this is because innovative know-how has been regarded primarily as a positive, enabling and facilitative phenomenon. Innovation creates an environment where individuals utilize technology for individual expression in an autonomous environment. Under liberalism, this form of individualistic behaviour is an expression of resistance from perceived constraints and the arbitrary power of elites (the corporations and government regulators). As Chapters 4 and 6 show, in past centuries, constraints include interference with free speech, free assembly, freedom of expression and any other act tantamount to diluting liberty. Oppression of communication rights also falls under this broad rubric of interference and it matters not whether such interference is being administered by governments or corporations. Such rights are now, together, recognized as a universal or fundamental human right to communicate, but even with the recognition of formal rights by the United Nations and governments in a world of digitalization, technological change has created liberating and empowering effects regardless of formal recognition. When packets of data go viral on the Internet they do so without a gatekeeping filter. Popular media products have been subsumed under this broader communicating rubric in a world of digitalization. The empirical reality is that whilst streaming subscriptions will probably continue to gain popularity, the consumer will still enjoy physical media products (if gaming and Blu-ray discs are anything to go by). It follows that, in the digital age, people will continue to concurrently consume soft and hard formats, just as consumers did with hard formats in the twentieth century. In this century, the consumer who watches unlicensed free-to-air streamed television or catches up on a programme that has been BitTorrented will, by definition, be labelled a TV pirate. The music fan uploading unauthorized footage of a music concert will be deemed a music pirate. Technological convergence has indeed created unforeseen complexities. Adopting a realistic approach, it follows that growth of emerging delivery models must also include growth of illegal delivery models based on current retail prices. Otherwise why else would Westerners be interested in the pricing structures of black market products in emerging economies? If it is indeed not a question of perception of value for money, then the issues about the convergent consumptions must remain unresolved. In the modern context, freedom to consume popular media products in any manner, including unauthorized distribution via communicative means, would extend to copying popular (copyrighted) material. In other words, you *will* be stopped from interfering with property. Copyright law, therefore, is the political thread that has bound copyright into an exclusive design over the past 300 years.

One conclusion reached in this book is that, to date, in terms of copyright preservation, organizational action has been marginally successful. The evidence from common law (and other Western) jurisdictions is that anti-media piracy campaigns have not stemmed the flow of illegal consumption. Indeed, in certain instances, recent cases demonstrate systemic deficiencies in the attempts of corporate citizens to stem illegal consumption. This might explain why individuals are no longer aggressively pursued, and the focus is squarely on enablers. The continued litigation against P2P facilitators demonstrates the pandemic nature of BitTorrent file-sharing. Whether or not litigating against Google, BT, iiNet and other powerful external players is a sound business approach remains to be seen.

Consider the recent prosecution against those defiant pirates in *Neij, Svartholm, Sunde, Lundstrom* (2009) (*The Pirate Bay*). Ten years after Shawn Fanning's Napster was shut down, The Pirate Bay's ringleaders received comparably short terms of imprisonment (between four and ten months on appeal

in December 2010). (Prison sentences for tax evaders or rogue share-traders
tend to be considerably longer.) The ringleaders have appealed to the
Supreme Court of Sweden. The deterrent effect – the prison sentences – is
very low bearing in mind a precedent has now been set. That is, given
all the notable cases concerning illegal downloading and P2P file-sharing
since *Napster*, *The Pirate Bay* case was the first of its kind in the sense
that custodial sentences were imposed on the facilitators of illegal activity.
The case transformed the criminological landscape in terms of copyright
abuse because prison sentences were imposed (albeit relatively short sentences when one considers the alleged quantum of financial loss). These
pirates have indicated that they have no prospect of paying the damages
awarded – US$6.4 million.

The damages awarded at first instance were significant, but when compared against the comparably low prison sentences, it is difficult to determine how the sentence would have any general deterrent effect given that
the accused Pirate Bayers have no real prospect of paying the damages.
Litigation is a costly exercise and, combined with overall technological services and educational expenditure, prevention and prosecution strategies
must be considered as relatively less effective given the propensity for the
proliferation of similar sites. Indeed, the tenor of the industry's anti-piracy
campaigns and warnings highlight the threat of maximum penalties including lengthy terms of imprisonment. The hard-line approaches resemble
government campaigns that focus on serious social scourges such as drug
trafficking or violent crimes. The reality of the 'get tough' stance is difficult
to reconcile when relatively few individuals have been sentenced to a term
of imprisonment. This might also explain why anti-piracy campaigns are
openly parodied. It is not suggested that illegal consumption and piracy are
to be ignored. On the contrary, copyright infringement is illegal. However,
the current copyright governance policies require critical examination in
the light of the lack of overall success in stemming the flow of illegal consumption. Because most punishment seeks to prevent sustained or prospec-
tive illegal consumption rather than to punish the offender, it is clear that
general deterrence has not been effective in any domestic or international
context. On the domestic front, it is not possible to determine whether
three-strikes policies and other initiatives to restrict consumers' rights on
the Internet will prove effective in light of the anonymized and atomistic
manner in which consumers behave in a digitalized world. *The Pirate Bay*
case appears to be an example of intense legal action that has produced a
relatively low deterrent effect. But actions against notorious website hosts
and facilitators of illegal activity are targeted actions with limited effects
because the desired effects are temporary in that whilst the relevant rogue
sites are dismantled, others proliferate. If there were successful actions in
the future, that might support the proposition that general deterrence

works, but copyright industries run the risk of consumer estrangement if they pursue individuals as participants in P2P platforms. In light of the fact that, concurrently, millions of media files are legally and illegally consumed globally, this is based on the observation that some consumers are both legal and illegal participants in popular media exchanges. Given the ongoing concerns raised by popular media industries, the possibility of a consumer engaging in either of these activities is high.

Chapter 6 demonstrates that deterrence is contingent upon rehabilitation. Most consumers are not recidivist in any criminological sense. The issues are further complicated by the development of neighbouring telecommunications and digitalization laws created by different sets of governance policies that have separate economic agendas that are not necessarily reconcilable with copyright governance. Furthermore, developments in social media and creative commons movements have also added a level of managerial complexity to the way in which copyrights are protected because consumers are probably more confused about what is an infringeable act and at what point media-sharing becomes illegal. Consumers react to technological change in a world of digitalization by embracing it at a significantly faster rate than corporate citizens anticipate. Anti-piracy campaigns are reactive in that they attempt to address a legal problem at a certain point in time. But as technology reflects change in society, it is difficult for copyright governors to anticipate what future campaigns will need to address. For example, suppose a sharp decline in BitTorrent consumption occurred. It would be tempting to conclude that the relevant general deterrent effect had been achieved. But history has shown that a decline in the use of one technology does not necessarily mean an end to media piracy. In other words, twenty-first century technological change determines consumption patterns and not popular media industry developments. Unless corporations appropriate technological development for exclusive use in the digital age – which is a ridiculous proposition – unfettered popular media consumption patterns will remain a permanent feature in popular culture. Emerging technologies are difficult to reconcile with modern copyright laws. Copyright laws can be seen as instruments of social construction in that they attempt to influence the way in which members of society see themselves and others. They attempt to influence peoples' views about what is right and wrong, good and bad, normal and not-normal.

By positioning illegal downloading outside the realm of property law, the law constructs this activity as antisocial. Therefore, by declaring piracy to be outside the boundaries of statute and common law, the law declares piracy to be counter-cultural, immoral and criminal. In this process, the law is a discursive instrument of governance that constructs social and political relations. Yet carte blanche illegal consumption appears de rigour in every real or substantive sense.

The issue reverts back to what Chapter 1 alludes to, namely, popular media is a means to popular culture (and not the other way around). Popular culture cannot be copyright controlled. Accordingly, copyright cannot be anything other than political. Chapters 4 and 5 show the extent to which, historically, copyright has been politicized.

This book has also considered a concurrent perspective for the examination of the tangible and intangible dimensions of popular media products. It has combined existing literature with empirical insights and doctrinal developments to develop a new perspective. Where specific new technologies have assisted in emancipating those who previously could not consume popular media, there appears to be less room for traditional notions of copyright recognition. Combined anti-piracy strategies, including technological deterrence, legal action, education and consumer-awareness programmes, have not taken into consideration the democratizing effects of new technologies. It is contended that a pluralistic challenge is, generally, a silent but salient one.

Whilst organized piracy is deemed criminally inappropriate by consumers, low-level or, rather, individual piracy is, at best, opportunistic as well as morally acceptable behaviour. What advanced Western society is currently experiencing is an infinitely futile attempt to curb illegal behaviour within a new technological environment. This is because technological change has primarily been regarded as a positive, enabling facilitative phenomenon. Obviously, individuals as consumers utilize digital technologies for several reasons. One important reason is protecting personal autonomy in a transglobal world. Also, technology in the twenty-first century symbolizes individual expression, and protection from the perceived constraints and arbitrary power of the corporations and government regulators. The overwhelming interest in the Australian founder of WikiLeaks, Julian Assange, reflects one extreme example of the atomistic desire to exchange information in a digital age, but social media networking and P2P file-sharing highlight the desire for minimal interference from cultural gatekeepers such as corporate media industries.

Chapter 3 examines the nature and the anatomy of the legitimacy of corporate media industries. Chapters 2 and 4 acknowledge the proximate features of copyright and corporations. Chapters 6 and 8 show that, from a moral or natural proprietary rights perspective, media piracy is complex because individuals apply a certain rationale to the consumption of popular media obtained illegally or quasi-legally.

The conclusion of Chapter 9 is that although copyright law as a separate legal identity may have an economic imperative, it is doubtful whether the rigid legal copyright framework possesses the capacity to deal with these challenges of modern popular media consumption. The challenges squarely rest on the ongoing divisions between the laws relating to copyright preservation and evolution, and those concerned with change relating to digitalization and communication. This is reflected in the disparate judicial outcomes.

Legal reflection

Chapters 2 and 4 note that copyright laws in the West are prescriptive in nature. Copyright laws prescribe, through various statutes (including Acts, regulations and codes), how copyright is to be protected. An inordinate number of laws dictate how obligations must be discharged (technically at least) so as to ensure compliance. And once infringement is established, how declarations are sought against flagrant acts requires further sets of rules and procedures demonstrating the infinitely complex structure of copyright regulation. Cases concerning allegations of flagrant infringement that appear to be obvious on the facts seem to be burdened by what Kaplan (1966, p. 40) describes as a 'maddeningly casual prolixity and imprecision'.

Chapters 3 to 5 argue that prior to en masse digitalization (especially downloading), the centralized status quo, in terms of product creation and delivery, was preserved. The major players owned the copyright, the manufacturing arms and the formats (vinyl, cassettes, CDs, etc.). It follows that the surplus value created by copyright monopolies was unaffected because the interaction costs were minimized because costs were kept in-house. The extension of temporary copyright monopolies ensured dominant control.

However, the landscape changed. In light of these technological developments, since 2000, cases throughout the West have attempted to deal with the issue of digital media piracy (most notably *Napster*, *Kazaa*, *The Pirate Bay* and, most recently, *iiNet* and *YouTube*).

By way of historical background, Chapter 4 discusses the transition from the old copyright regime to a pluralistic copyright-digital agenda regime. Since the 1850s the emphasis on those seeking to preserve copyrights has not been placed on individual original copyright owners (authors and artists) and individual consumers, but, rather, on corporate citizens who act as copyright controllers and cultural gatekeepers in popular media.

The questions raised in this book centre on the extent of the challenges to the status quo. In other words, have emerging digitalization and other external influences (namely neighbouring legislation (for example, in relation to telecommunications) and liberal attitudes) created a democratic playing field?

The primary authorities (that is, the case law) for the proposition that safe harbour provisions introduced into copyright hinder copyright protection suggest that this is occurring; however, the anticompetitive behaviour of the dominant few suggests otherwise. The tensions between copyright and telecommunications legislation and the consumer therefore remain unresolved by the recent cases. An analysis of recent case law suggests that a transnational legislative shift is occurring in relation to everything from copyright protection to communication preservation. On the one hand, copyright regulation has been consolidated (see Chapter 2) in order to preserve multinational corporate homogeneity within separate jurisdictions; but, on the other hand, telco legislative change has impeded these initiatives. And whilst telcos acknowledge copyright protection as a component of the telecommunication laws, regulations are distinct obligations not necessarily capable of harmonization with copyright laws as part of a unified digital agenda. Convergence group predecessors have not been able to reconcile the snail-like pace of copyright change with technological change. One wonders how convergence review groups, such as the newly constituted Australian Convergence Review Committee will address the infinite complexities in balancing the business interests of traditional media industries with consumers' perceptions and expectations in a converging digitalized world. The *Convergence Review Final Report* (2012) contains recommendations for a new approach in regulation across all media platforms related to the Internet. This is probably because telco customers already expect media streaming and subscription services as part of a service package. In the absence of these services, consumers appear to search for their own supply of content. Whilst the Committee has recommended legal reform of the digital agenda, the reality is that technological change determines the digital agenda – not regulatory change – in a world of convergent digitalization. For example, does recording a live music show for personal use and then uploading it onto a social networking website, or a telco, causing 'near live' shows to be broadcast as part of an online TV Internet package, constitute infringement? It appears that reforms concerning copyright and its capacity to be harmonized under a more general digital rights platform continue to be problematic in a world of digitalization. Legal interpretation of copyright convergence highlights the infinite complexities emerging technologies create. The case law should also be considered as part of a law reform because cases assist the forensic analysis of consumer behaviours. They inevitably must be considered as part of a law reform package. But the irony, or rather paradox, is that an emerging set of technology-driven issues cannot be anticipated, thus creating a futile situation for copyright governance frameworks. It appears that Internet users are categorized in two distinct categories – popular media consumers and telco customers. These classes are not necessarily reconcilable and the struggle to satisfy consumers under different governance frameworks will be the new entertainment battleground.

This book raised the argument that these two corporate citizens – popular media industries and telcos – are currently at cross purposes because the former is attempting to preserve the status quo through copyright regulation whilst the latter has aligned itself with interactive computer and mobile technologies capable of broadcasting, rebroadcasting, downloading and uploading popular culture at speeds that inevitably result in illegal and legal activity on the part of telco customers.

Chapter 4 described the introduction of safe harbour provisions in copyright legislation. These provisions reflect free protocols in Western nations in the event of conflict between industries. For example, as the US Free Trade Implementation Act 2004 suggests, the provisions in the Australian Copyright Amendment (Digital Agenda Act) 2000 (Digital Agenda Amendments (Cth)) were influenced by US law, which had its origin in the Digital Millennium Copyright Act 1998 (DMCA)(US), amending the Copyright Act 1976 (US). Safe harbour legislation in the West has created significant obstacles to the strict interpretation of prescriptive and protectionist legislation relating to copyright. To rely on defences, such as being the mere conduit for those carrying the communication of others, for example, consumers participating in illegal activity, is a central pillar in any defence where copyright owners claim direct or vicarious infringement. Telcos rely on this defence as matter of course even if the defence is not required (as was evidenced in *iiNet*). Napster unsuccessfully attempted to invoke conduit-esque defences. Yet ten years after the DMCA was passed (calling for international trade agreements to be domestically observed pursuant to the WIPO Copyright Treaty and the WIPO Performances and Phonograms Treaty), digitalization has proved very problematic. In the digital law arena, defences that are directed at shifting blame to others are also being used by site operators such as Google's YouTube. That is, conduit and safe harbour defences or simply the take-down protocol will continue to be developed as creative shields against copyright owners who attempt to blame telcos or at least apportion blame. If copyright governance is viewed as a sword, digital rights management and telco governance possess several shields in their defence against aggressive copyright protectors. In a world of digitalization, laws are becoming infinitely harder to reconcile and copyright lobbyists have become more difficult to console because applying normative constructions of what constitutes a pirate is also proving difficult. The ontological assumption that a person who consumes illegally obtained media is prima facie in technical breach of the law is not enough to determine wrongdoing in a convergent digital arena. Epistemological considerations, in that consumption patterns are significantly more complex in the digital age, require a consideration of the duality between the positivist formal legal position (objective) and the legal reality that consumers participate in all sorts of modes of consumption (subjective) – irrespective of the strict legal position, and irrespective of whether they are willing or unwitting participants in illegal modes of consumption. Copyright laws and consumer patterns of consumption are dialectical because technological change determines the behaviour of consumers – not copyright governance.

A new era of Western media consumption

Drawing on Marx's dialectical materialism, if popular media's golden age was the twentieth century's age of mass communication and consumption, was the first decade of the twenty-first century the start a new age? Less than 100 years ago, talented musicians and authors toiled in sweatshop conditions to produce popular songs and ditties for sheet music publication and exploitation. These publishing houses flourished during the days of Tin Pan Alley (1890 to 1925) primarily because recorded music was not the predominant money-spinner (Wilk, 1976). In this setting, creators churned out songs and musicals for immediate performance, as well as sheet music for subsequent sale. For a relatively modest fee, the creators would assign their copyrights for regular writing income (as opposed to royalties), studio space and other overheads. Often, publishers and creators occupied entire buildings (hence the term 'sweat shop'). Mass production of affordable sheet music, for example, enabled consumers to perform in public places and spaces (as individuals or social groups).

Purchasing media such as sheet music for individual or public use was an early form of social media networking – word of mouth recommendations after having heard the song performed by others ensured the success of a particular song. Radio and television transformed popular media and became the cultural broadcasters, but it is interesting to note how Internet users as private individuals possess a desire to share popular culture without a gatekeeper. In this environment, publishers dominated output terms by way of copyright procurement. However, consumers dictated the *mode* of consumption, including any aesthetic quality attached to consumption in the absence a corporate cultural gatekeeper. Individuals were consumers making informed decisions about popular culture without being influenced by emerging technologies and conceptions of illegal consumption as a form of piracy. Consumers were free to choose – both in manner and form of consumption – because there were no intersubjective constraints.

When the precursor to the modern gramophone arrived, for the purposes of standardization and mass production of standardized flat records some 100 years ago, recorded professional performers were exploited by publishers and record companies, and popular broadcast media was born. Radio broadcasts were popularized in the early 1920s and what followed was the appropriation of mass culture by the corporation. Popular media (including the successive waves of formats) was subsumed under a broad corporate entertainment rubric within a very short space of time. As Chapter 3 sets out, the democratization of consumption in popular culture was lost.

The Internet has reignited our desire to reidentify with our own sense of self – self-worth, self-expression, as well as independence – in terms of cultural consumption. Piracy is a reflection of the politicization of consumption. Illegal consumption represents resistance against the inter-subjective nature of corporate control for some, or simply a mode of free consumption for others. The hospital staff in 1883 and the patrons in the Bournemouth hotel in 1933 (see Chapter 8) would certainly not consider themselves as being unrespectable for enjoying unlicensed and unauthorized performances.

Consumption of popular media is a complex process as varying levels of morality and immorality are attached, based on how consumers view the products. Therefore popular media consumption is associated with learned social interactions as cultural exchanges – irrespective of the legal consequences. Copyright law seeks to regulate this behaviour by *imposing* moral conditions. This is contrary to negative freedom and liberalism. Whatever the desire of the consumer, copyright in popular media is inherently a political issue. Consumption of popular media in the West cannot be understood without a substantive understanding of the political economy of copyright.

A short parable on copyright governance

Mickey Mouse's owner is indeed a powerful 'person'. According to *Fortune 500*, his corporate parents are the largest corporate popular media entertainment citizens in the US and the world (and the 65th largest US firm (Fortune Global, 2011)). Created in 1928, Mickey wanted to defy the laws of nature by not dying a natural death (as so many copyrights before him had). Indeed, he asked his parents to lobby Congress for extended life. The US Copyright Term Extension Act of 1998 granted Mickey his wish. Mickey can now live beyond the natural lifespan of any other copyrighted mouse (which was 14 years in the nineteenth century) for to up to 120 years (that is, to at least 2023). The legislation is known affectionately as the Mickey Mouse Protection Act (Lessig, 2001). Mickey's parents continue to lobby for copyright amendments. According to the Center for Responsive Politics (2011), Disney has allocated several million dollars over the past decade to influence the US government (perhaps for an even longer copyright protection period). The lobbying reports filed in 2009 pursuant to the Lobbying Disclosure Act 1995 reveal Disney as a most determined activist.

It seems that where Mark Twain (a natural person and original author) failed to influence government in order to improve protection against piratical publishers for his works for the benefit of his children, Disney (an artificial übermensch and übercopyright owner) has succeeded in preserving unnatural longevity for a cartoon character. Lobbying has proved successful, and it seems that it will be some time before Mickey Mouse is caught in a creative commons trap. In his 1882 denunciation of how copyright laws were being drafted in the US, Twain (2010, p. 96) asked, 'And who gets any real benefit out of it?' Not citizens and certainly not authors in his opinion. Balanced copyright governance, according to Twain (ibid., p. 97), can only be achieved when Congressmen who are not 'fools ... shall re-draft the copyright law ... pass it ... and by luck hit upon an interval when they chance to be out of idiots'. Twain's hyperbole aside, where the future of copyright in popular media remains uncertain, his criticisms of the legal and political economy of copyright governance regimes are still relevant in the twenty-first century.

Notes

1 Liberalism, Realism, Convergence, Consumption and Tensions between Technological and Legal Change

1. Copyright materializes from the core of a creator's labour process. Its original form fructifies from kernels of creativity (which might simply be described as Kern-copyrights). This book is concerned with copyright's transition to the more complex, corporatized commercial form extending to that of übercopyright status.
2. Western in this context generally means Western European and United States advanced capitalist nations (as opposed to developing nations, emerging economies, or nations historically or currently influenced by communist governments). Western nations possess governments that share either liberal or social democratic ideologies and values (or hybrids thereof), and provide a uniform approach to copyright management. Notwithstanding its lack of any clear liberal history, Japan is also included in the cluster of Western nations because its mode of advanced capitalist development (and subsequent corporate evolution) has been particularly Westernized. For the purposes of this book, Japanese citizens' attitudes and beliefs in terms of popular media consumption largely mirror those citizens where liberalism remains the dominant political ideology.
3. *Roadshow Films Pty Ltd v iiNet Limited (No. 3)* [2010] FCA 24 was affirmed on appeal in February 2011. This significant Australian case will be the subject of detailed examination in the following chapters as it is the first of its kind in the world to comprehensively assess several divergent statutory obligations vis-à-vis technological challenges.
4. By way of illustration, pop music is used to describe many popular music genres deemed to be commercially viable including (but not limited to) rock, heavy metal, alternative, punk, hip hop and electronic. In this book it is used to describe a mode of production as opposed to a style.
5. It is not suggested other popular (and informal) modes in non-Western cultures, as described by Manuel (1993) and Connell and Gibson (2003), are irrelevant. However, the scope of this book is limited to the dominant mode that is underpinned by Western notions of intellectual property rights (IPRs).
6. Traditional print media (namely books and magazines, and pulp fiction generally) might also be included in pleasure-driven pop culture (furthermore, e-books are becoming increasingly popular). The scope of this book is limited to audio-visual multimedia products that might be digitized and communicated for consumption.
7. See Pang's research (2006), which provides a comprehensive and compelling account of movie piracy in developing Asian nations and China. Similarly, the unprecedented copyright piracy in Russia and former Eastern bloc nations has also been discussed (see especially Peterson (2005)). The academic literature suggests that the attacks appear insurmountable in developing nations or nations with communist backgrounds.
8. For example, four music majors control in excess of 80 per cent of the global music market. Hollywood is the central repository for film and TV culture (Moran, 1993).

9. Shakespeare's works contain several references to liberal attitudes (for example, see reference to 'liberal villain' in *Much Ado about Nothing* (Act IV, Scene 1), and 'I will become as liberal as you; I'll not deny him anything' (*Merchant of Venice*, Act II, Scene II). Liberal villain can be used to describe a media pirate, while the quote from the *Merchant of Venice* epitomizes P2P download/upload culture. In Shakespeare's political play *Measure for Measure*, Locke's notions about freedom and individualism in a 'state of nature' are apparent – 'Liberty plucks justice by the nose' (Act I, Scene III). The common thread that binds these quotes is liberalism. Even in a literary context, liberal values are expressed as natural human tendencies.

10. Generally, these nations possess comparable legal systems within a liberal democratic framework. While other Western nations have to a large extent been shaped by a codified civil legal system within a social democratic political framework, the basic principles of copyright as espoused in the common law and other European jurisdictions have become universalized.

2 Global Governance: Regulation of Copyright Law and Policy in Popular Media Copyright Industries

1. Refer to Copyright (World Trade Organization Amendments) Act 1994.
2. An apt phrase coined by Counsel representing *iiNet*.
3. Due to privity of contract considerations and confidentiality provisions contained in most copyright agreements between private citizens, empirical evidence to support this proposition is difficult to obtain. However, cases support the proposition that corporations possess the relevant legal standing in litigation. Therefore copyright entrepreneurs – not the initial copyright owner – are represented in most proceedings.
4. Indeed, this High Court was particularly active in 1992 and used words and terms such as 'conflagration of oppression ... to dispossess, degrade, and devastate the Aboriginal peoples and leave a national legacy of unutterable shame' (per Deane J and Gaudron J at 95 in *Mabo v Queensland (No2)* 175 CLR 1).
5. During this time it was observed: 'Yet the International Copyright Act requires reciprocity. The Frenchman living in Paris ... may well sell his copyright in London' (*Some Remarks on the Law of Copyright*, p. 9). Politically and economically, the 1800s was very much a protected period. Despite issues concerning domestic procedures, in terms of harmonizing the overriding philosophy about the objectives of copyright laws, the dominant nations (namely Britain and France) were *ad idem*.
6. Compare the Broadcasting Legislation Amendment (Digital Television) Act 2006 (Cth) and Telecommunications Act 1997 (Cth) as amended. There is nothing simplistic about harmonizing legislative provisions for the purposes of a uniform digital agenda.
7. An examination of the most recent reprints (including subordinated legislation) of the Australian Copyright Act, the British Copyright Designs and Patents Act 1988 and the consolidated US copyright laws (Copyright Act 1976) reveals common that law jurisdictions do not recognize the term 'convergence'.
8. Consider the rationale behind Directive 2001/29/EC of the 'European Parliament and of the Council on the harmonisation of certain aspects of copyright and related rights in the information society'. EU members that are also members of

WIPO and WTO are expected to provide legal protection domestically through regulatory transposition in a timely manner and pursuant to the Directive. The Directive which essentially reflects the economic considerations of corporate citizens is a reflection of the international obligation imposed by WIPO treaties – thereby ensuring downstream harmonization on a formal level. This Directive may appear to have a narrow focus in that it is concerned with EU compliance issues, but given that the EU comprises more than one-half of the nations with the most powerful international copyright owners (the other dominant WIPO half – US and Japan – in any event have transnational interests in Europe), it is fair to observe the Directive is not only an upstream reflection of copyright governance for the bulk of EU WIPO members directly, but WIPO members globally. The thread that binds the international community in the copyright governance framework is transnational economic interests. WIPO serves to enforce and promote Eurocentric conceptions of copyright governance – which, historically, has always been the case.

9. For example, take Britain's Channel 4 television series *Shameless*. A Region Code 2 DVD of the series is freely available for purchase on the Australian online store Fish Pond, but Australia, for the purposes of DVDs, is artificially zoned as Region Code 4, notwithstanding that the products are identical in appearance and format. Yet the British Region Code DVD cannot be played using a Sony DVD player purchased in Australia. (The warning reads: 'This disc cannot be played. The region code is not correct.') However, a cheap Chinese DVD player, such as the Nu-Tech brand, conveniently plays all regional codes.

10. The appeal by the film industry was dismissed and the ISP was found not liable (see *Roadshow Films Pty Ltd v iiNet Limited* [2012] HCA 16).

11. Historically, this supports the contention that contractual terms and conditions in 'standard' film and music contracts have always been one-sided and onerous; and the power imbalance in terms of legal representation between creators and corporations is patently clear. Taking one historical snapshot as an example, in 1983 in the UK alone, Gordon Sumner (Sting) successfully sued Virgin Music for unfair contractual terms, and whilst he was not entitled to immediate reversion (he had to wait until 1990), his royalty rates substantially increased. A central allegation raised by Sting was ignorance of publishing deals and copyright law generally at time of signing. Another aggrieved artist, Gilbert O'Sullivan, also persuaded the English High Court in 1983 that his agreement was unfair (Clark, 1983, p. 163). Such legal developments led to unprecedented exploitation of authors, artists, performers and any persons capable of creating copyrightable works. Any cursory assessment reveals that corporate citizens are consistently represented by top-tier law firms whereas the bulk of copyright creators appear to be either self-represented or represented by pro bono lawyers assisting in arts law centres or less expensive and therefore less specialized firms. Eventually, Western jurisdictions throughout Europe, Britain, its Commonwealth nations and then, finally, the US gradually recognized the need for a minimum statutory rate in copyright streams for original copyright owners assigning their copyrights in perpetuity. However, it must be emphasized these are minimum compulsory statutory rates and are consistent with liberal democratic ideologies whereby individuals are free to choose how to conduct private business.

12. See especially *Elton John v James* [1991] FSR 397 and compare with *Panayiotou v Sony Music Entertainment (UK) Ltd* [1994] EMLR 229 (aka *George Michael and Sony*). Assignment from the first copyright owner to the entrepreneurial copyright owner is not the exception, but rather the norm.

13. A Dispute Settlement Body established at the request of the US (refer to WT/ DS362/7) to examine, inter alia, China's copyright governance deficits in the light of international copyright obligations.
14. See generally, P. Blecha's thorough history of banned bands and censored songs (in *Taboo Tunes*, 2004). Several transatlantic examples of censorship and destruction concerning modern pop music are provided. But perhaps the best example is the Anti-Nowhere League's prosecution in relation to the truly vulgar pop song 'So What'. Blecha (2004, p. 166) explains: 'After the police's record-seizing raids on label headquarters, the pressing plant, and distributor's offices, at trial the magistrates concluded that the song which had already sold a respectable 36,000 units – evinced a "tendency to deprave and corrupt" which resulted in the destruction of confiscated stock.' Most record sales analysts would agree that this release was commercially successful given the lack of major publicity and low interaction promotional costs (compare with the Sex Pistols who received major publicity as a consequence of the moral dereliction that was purported to have existed in the repertoires). The success of lewd ditty 'So What' is still evident when one considers the social media setting 30 years later. As at November 2011, over 820,000 consumers have listened to (and watched) the song on YouTube (www.youtube.com/watch?v=).
15. 'Is it necessary for a steel worker to put his name on a steel ingot that he produces in the course of his duty? If not, why should a member of the intelligentsia enjoy the privilege of putting his name on what he produces?' This was a popular saying in China during the Cultural Revolution (1966–1976), cited in W. Alford (1995, p. 56).
16. For example, the Rwandan Constitution of 2003 does not contain sovereign powers concerning copyright. Copyright governance is largely influenced through external affairs (Western-influenced rules and regulations). But in any event, it is argued that even if copyright powers were 'slipped' into a developing nation's constitution, they would constitute nothing more than a formal recognition to satisfy the more powerfully aligned WIPO and WTO members.
17. Refer to Chapter 8.

3 Corporate Control of Popular Media (and Culture): Competition Law and Policy in Popular Culture

1. *Australian Competition & Consumer Commission v Universal Music Australia Pty Limited; Warner Music Australia Pty Limited & Others* [2001] FCA 1800; and [on appeal] *Universal Music Australia Pty Limited; Warner Music Australia Pty Limited & Others v Australian Competition & Consumer Commission* [2003] FCAFC 193 (hereinafter referred to as the *ACCC* case).
2. When dominant corporations threaten smaller players with litigation (para. 77 of the *ACCC* decision), then such aggressive behaviour is cartel-like as is the coercive remark about 'favors' (para. 42). Indeed, s. 202 of the Copyright Act prohibits '[g]roundless threats of legal proceedings in relation to copyright infringement'.
3. For an examination of the microlabels/bedroom DIY phenomenon, see Cvetkovski, 2009/2005.
4. *Columbia Broadcasting System Inc and Columbia Record Club, Inc., Petitioners, v. Federal Trade Commission No. 16492, United States Court of Appeals Seventh Circuit June 26, 1969* (complaint made in 1962).
5. See *Re Applications by Australasian Performing Right Association* [1999] ACompT 3.

6. The literature often makes reference to the majors, generally meaning the entire industry. This is because they comprise up to 80–90 per cent of popular media ownership.
7. On 7 November 2003, BMG and Sony announced that they would enter into a joint venture to consolidate their recording interests. Similarly, EMI and Time Warner had also been negotiating expressions of interest for quite some time before Warner Group's announcement that it was to sell its entire music arm (publishing and recording) on 26 November 2003 to an independent consortium. In July 2004, Mi2N reported that the non-binding merger between Sony and BMG was approved by the EU's respective (national) regulatory bodies. Where there once was an exclusive club of five majors, there is now a club of four (see generally, *Five Eight* [23], 2003: 3 www.mi2n.com, and *Music & Copyright* (2003) No. 263 (November), London: Informa Publishing: 1–2, 12–13).
8. By way of background, LyondellBasell was formed by Access Industries' acquisition of Lyondell Chemical in 2007 (LyondellBasell Management Report (December 2007)). In 2010 it was described as the largest producer of polypropylene and related chemical compounds, and as '[having] the second global position in propylene oxide' (Bewley, 2010, p. 35). For further information about health and safety concerns, see Second Amended Petition (2008) as reported online by the socially networked Business and Human Resource Centre (at www.business-human-rights.org under Access Industries http://www.business-humanrights.org/Links/Repository/553436/link_page_view).

4 Copyright Developments in Popular Media: Doctrinal and Statutory Challenges

1. In his examination of *Grain Pool of Western Australia v Commonwealth* (2000), Barley (2003, p. 13) explains: 'Justice Kirby refers to Lawrence Lessig's book, *Code and Other Laws of Cyberspace*, as a general source of authority for a discussion of intellectual property and constitutional law. The joint judgment provides a qualified endorsement of the codified vision of the constitutional power regarding intellectual property. They seem to rely heavily upon historical accounts of intellectual property. By contrast, the judgment of Justice Kirby seems to adopt a transformative approach. He focuses upon the future developments of technology and science.' The nexus between the importance of constitutional rights from a human rights-based perspective in the judicial arena in terms of copyright governance and statutory interpretation is worth noting: 'The protection of intellectual property rights must be afforded in a constitutional setting which upholds other values of public good in a representative democracy' (per Kirby J at footnote 218 in *Grain Pool*).
2. ISPs' commercial imperatives centre around factors such as the financial benefits to customers, fast speeds, reliable streaming and the promotion of material, including popular media. These imperatives do not detract from ISPs' legal duties to provide reasonable help to copyright industries where possible.
3. At para. 162 of the Appeal decision, Emmett J observed:

> The effect of s. 14 of the Copyright Act is that if an act is done in relation to less than the whole of a work or other subject matter in which copyright subsists, there is no infringement unless a substantial part is involved. A feature of the BitTorrent System is that pieces obtained by a downloader are only fragments

of the whole Film. iiNet says that, in those circumstances, where only small, if regular, helpings are taken, there is no infringement (see *Ice TV Pty Limited v Nine Network Australia Pty Limited* (2009) 239 CLR 458 at [21]). iiNet says that, before there will be infringement in those circumstances, the whole or a substantial part of the relevant subject matter must be transmitted by someone. *That requires discrimination between members of the swarm who are iiNet users and those who are not. It must also involve discriminating between users in Australia and users who are not in Australia. iiNet contends that, once it is accepted that an iiNet user might obtain the whole of a Film by downloading, without sharing the same amount of data back into the swarm, it is not permissible to assume that, because the viability of swarms in a general sense relies on peers providing at least as much data as they take, the individual iiNet users detected sharing a single piece of a Film in fact had shared a substantial part of that Film.* iiNet says that there is no evidence in relation to any one act of transmission caused by individual DtecNet interrogations of individual iiNet users that constituted sufficient acts of transmission by the same user, being an iiNet user located in Australia, whereby a substantial part of any particular Film was transmitted. (emphasis added)

5   From Printing Press to Peer-to-Peer: Centuries of 'Modern' Media Piracy and the Social Urge for Legal and Illegal Consumption

1. G. Robertson, in Chapter 7, 'The Romans in Britain', in *The Justice Game*, provides another spectacular example of the interaction between allegations of obscenity, morality and Crown censorship over popular culture (at pp. 165–181). But the setting is Thatcher's 1980s and the Christian moral rights crusader Mary Whitehouse whose private prosecution (after petitioning the Attorney General) was eventually discontinued. No further evidence was offered – nor should have ever been offered in the first place (as the case probably fell outside the scope of prosecution guidelines).
2. Indeed, the US House Comm. on Commerce, H.R. Rep. No. 105-551, pt. 2, at 25 (1998) observed: 'the digital environment poses a unique threat to the rights of copyright owners, and as such, necessitates protection against devices that undermine copyright interests. In contrast to the analogue experience, digital technology enables pirates to reproduce and distribute perfect copies of works – at virtually no cost at all to the pirate. As technology advances, so must our laws.'
3. Australia's bonds to the UK are largely legally and socially intact. Despite recent trade developments involving South East Asia, it should not be forgotten that Australia did not enact its Australia Act until 1986 thereby abolishing the right to appeal from the highest court in Australia to the Privy Council in England. Doctrinal laws and statutes, parliament and the civil services were inextricably bound (and remain so to this day). In relation to copyright legislation this is particular evident.
4. 'It is proposed to hold another International Copyright Convention in September of this year [1886], and it is desirable that Her Majesty shall be empowered until then to enter into the International Copyright Union ... with the object of carrying out the provisions of the International Copyright Convention ... it is a matter of public interest. It arises in regard to whether Her Majesty shall enter into the International Copyright Union only on behalf of Great Britain, or also on behalf of the other Dominions of the Crown. It is thought that it will be well for the Empire

at large if we were to enter for the Colonies and India as well as for Great Britain ... Another very desirable provision has been introduced. It was found necessary to deal with the question of copyright between this country and the Colonies and the Colonies themselves. The House is aware that a British author publishing his work first in England has a copyright over the whole Empire ... to enter into this Copyright Convention; and I hope also that they will appreciate the spirit in which it has been introduced. (The Under Secretary of State for Foreign Affairs (Mr. Bryce, Aberdeen, S., *Hansard, HC Deb.*, 8 April 1886, vol 304, cc 1142-1144, Order for Second Reading).

5. For a lively discussion on the 'evil' of the Bubble Act, refer to the Attorney General's Speech at *HC Deb*, 2 June 1825, vol 13, cc 1018–1023.

6. The popular TV series *Boardwalk Empire* (copyright owned by HBO – the largest film subsidiary for Time Warner) spectacularly reflects this era of illegal alcohol consumption.

6 A Three-Front War on Piracy: Technological Protection, Legal Action and Education Programmes – *Null Bock Haltung?*

1. For example, the 'R4' card (mod-chip) was freely available for purchase at R4Card. com.au and WWW.R41-SDHC.COM, complete with instructions, forums and YouTube demonstrations about how to override the Nintendo DS and DSi anti-piracy software. Nintendo simultaneously commenced actions across the world (mainly in the West) with 800 actions across 16 nations (Le May, 2010). In Australia, distributor RSJ IT Solutions (along with its directors Patrick and James Li) was been ordered to pay Nintendo over AUD$500,000 (plus costs) for selling this video game piracy tool. As in Mr Burt's case, the terms were settled out court (however, an order was made). Patrick and James Li were clearly profiting from this enterprise. They were pirates – but then again so was the misguided Mr Burt. Nintendo's position is clear: 'The existence of piracy jeopardizes the strength of the video game industry overall' (as quoted in a report filed by Le May, 2010).

2. The Ten Commandments as set out in Exodus 20:1–17.

3. Blecha (2004, p. 45) asserts that Noebel blames Karl Marx for crimes against the moral fibre of consumers and the subsequent crimes perpetrated by today's youth caused by rock 'n' roll.

4. As *Napster, Kazaa, iiNet* and other comparable cases demonstrate, for many it seems that illegal consumption is 'morally permissible' as one descends down a 'slippery slope' of 'collapsing taboos' (Woods, 2000, p. 9). Woods (ibid., p. 117) argues: 'Taboos come in degrees, though not exactly on a scale of one to ten. At the high end we could expect to find the cannibalism taboo ... and almost another thing entirely – the prohibition in 1949, say, of homosexuality.' Now consider Woods' (ibid., p. 12) argument about human behaviour in the face of moral choice over legal boundaries: 'Some taboos prohibit what people in any event have little interest in or stomach for ... Others prohibit what lots and lots of people are keen to do and would do but for the prohibition.' If we adopt this observation for the current popular media setting, it is fair to suggest that symbiotic P2P consumers and pirates are united in their ambivalence to copyright laws and piratical conduct.

5. For a discussion on these developments, refer generally to an experiment involving ten copy-controlled CDs (Cvetkovski, 2005, 2009).

6. For a breakdown of actual interaction costs involved in CD releases, see Cvetkovski 2007.

7. The expression *Null Bock* generally is used pejoratively to mean 'don't give a damn', 'rat's' or 'shit' – about everything or anything. It is best used in a negative or derogatory sense.

8. www.youtube.com/results?search_query=Anti-piracy+parody&aq=f.

9. Moral responsibility is associated with an individual's understanding of what is right and wrong, irrespective of any legal responsibility. It is a fundamental liberal principle where although individuals behave in an atomistic way, and whilst they are willing to behave morally, they do not necessarily cooperate in a socially responsible way. Social responsibility is more of a positive liberty concept in that individuals collectively behave in a certain manner for the greater social good. There is a close connection between legal and social responsibility, but not necessarily between legal responsibility and moral responsibility about what is right and wrong.

10. www.wallettest.com provides the results of an interesting observational study and a fascinating survey of 100 people to support this observation, and my own lost wallet experiences seems to prove this act of honesty.

11. *Dans ce pay-ci, il est bon de tuer de temps en temps un amiral pour encourager les autres* ([b]ut in this country it is found good, from time to time, to kill one Admiral to encourage the others. Voltaire, in *Candide* (in Chapter XXIII) (a reference to the execution of Admiral the Hon. John Byng (refer to Little's version, available through the Gutenberg Project)). As many criminal law students and lawyers are aware, in its modern-day context this saying applies to parity in sentencing and proportionality where excessive ranges are sought, usually by the prosecution.

12. Examples of technology cases range from litigating against unauthorized public use (*Adelaide Corporation v APRA* (1928), *APRA v Jain* (1990) to music-on-hold (*Telstra Corporation Ltd v APRA* (1997) and ringtone downloads (*APRA Ltd v Monster Communications Pty Ltd* (2006)).

7 Occidental Failure: The Paradox of Transglobal Copyright Industries in Emerging Economies

1. This popular reference about limits to formal conceptions of equality is adapted from the following passage of the France's (1894, Book 1, Ch. VII, p. 53) book: 'The poor must work for this, in presence of the majestic quality of the law which prohibits the wealthy as well as the poor from sleeping under the bridges, from begging in the streets, and from stealing bread.'

2. Clearly, 'law-abiding' in the sense they have been permitted to enter a foreign nation with the relevant visa and are therefore deemed prima facie trustworthy international citizens. Indeed, the reality of market shopping was, surprisingly, mentioned in a recent episode of the popular Australian commercial television series *Getaway* (on the Nine Network (1 October 2011)). Reporting on the holiday destination Bali, the show host, Dermot Brereton, quipped 'so your shopping bag's full of dodgy DVDs and Bintang shirts'. Considering that Bali is the second most popular holiday destination (653,000 in 2010), the remark made by the presenter is worth noting, not so much because the statement was made, but because it is obvious and does not require corroboration; in other words, it is a trite statement. The popular Australian, politically active, folk band Redgum famously coined the phrase 'I've Been to Bali too' as a title to a song to suggest just how popular this destination is in many respects, including illegal activity: 'Bali t-shirts, magic mushrooms, Redgum bootlegs I've been to Bali too … going through Customs,

I've been to Bali too' (lyrics by Schumann of Redgum). The fact that Australians consume pirated goods in Bali is hardly a bold statement. It is not only reflected in popular culture, but is easily anecdotally validated by speaking to returned holidaymakers from Bali. Yet Australian Customs data show negligible seizures of 'bootlegs', and 'dodgy DVDs' (Australian Bureau of Statistics, September 2010).

3. Consider the US and Australia, each with a GDP of US$45,000 per capita (OECD, 2010).

4. These also include powerful and influential nations (but with comparably low GDPs, namely, China – GDP US$4,000; Russia – GDP US$10,400; and India – GDP US$1,200), and emerging but prominent nations such as Pakistan (GDP US$1,000), Thailand (GDP US$4,600) and Brazil (GDP US$4,600). See generally, the International Intellectual Property Alliance (IIPA), 2004.

5. Malaysia, per capita GDP – US$8,400.

6. Vietnam, per capita GDP – US$1,100.

7. Bulgaria, per capita GDP – US$6,300.

8. Afghanistan, per capita GDP – US$600; Iraq, per capita GDP – US$2,800. See Torrentfreak, 2010.

9. Macedonia, per capita GDP – US$4,400.

10. Anastasia, a Macedonian group of internationally acclaimed contemporary musicians, is an important music export and has collaborated with the critically acclaimed film director and writer Milcho Manchevski.

11. Mexico, per capita GDP – US$9,200.

12. The Legatum Institute has created a Prosperity Index that seeks to determine how prosperous a nation is, both qualitatively and quantitatively. 'The Index defines prosperity as both wealth and wellbeing, and finds that the most prosperous nations in the world are not necessarily those that have only a high GDP, but are those that also have happy, healthy, and free citizens' (Executive Summary of the Legatum Institute for 2011 (Legatum Prosperity Index, 2010)). The institute assesses some 110 countries and utilizes over 89 different variables to determine not only the economic growth for a nation, but also personal well-being for its citizens, in order to determine the overall 'prosperity' of that nation. As the Legatum Institute states on its website: 'The Index consists of eight sub-indexes; namely, Economy, Entrepreneurship & Opportunity (E&O), Governance, Education, Health, Safety & Security, Personal Freedom, and Social Capital' (http://www.li.com).

13. In Romania, the per capita GDP was US$11,755 in 2009.

8 The Nexus between Piracy and Legitimate Consumption: Social Networking, P2P File-Sharing and Consumer Empowerment

1. On the topic of consumers' private behaviours, I interviewed several music stakeholders and representatives as part of my doctoral thesis (Cvetkovski, 2005, pp. 128–129, references omitted).

> **Producer** argued that a downturn is evident partly because of the way the major labels primarily market prioritized artists that only have a short-term teen appeal. He explained music is 'thrust to the public more as wallpaper as opposed to a lifestyle or having any ideology'. Apart from that, both society and technology have changed within the context of an ever-widening leisure market. According to **Producer** 'the kid's are music smarter and won't put up the shit the majors

dish out'. This view is consistent with the notion that people want more value for money, that the current price structure is unfair, and that consequently people turn to other leisure products because (a) they refuse to pay high prices for music, or (b) they prefer to 'rip' the industry 'off' because it is free, rather than be 'ripped off' by what is perceived to be a powerful industry. **MarkExec** agreed: It's happening now – parents have invested money in computers and other hardware – the budget is really stretched – and most parents turn a blind eye to CD burning and downloads as it saves them money.

What the interviews showed is that there is a strong correlation between consumer loss of interest and feeling ripped off. Technology has created an avenue to express this resentment. These consumer responses highlight the complexity of music consumption.

2. Reference to the *Cavalier* story is found at p. 70 of Noebel's book, with authorship unattributed. But it is important to refer to the original source located at p. 37 of the magazine because the article in its entirety is written by music journalists Rudnick and Frawley and reflects more of an ode to liberalism than it does to any Marxist pretence.

3. Cursory views on forums associated with P2P sites (for example, BT Junkie) clearly indicate this type of cultural exchange (for example, 'Thanks uploader for sharing this as it is hard to obtain', and 'Please seed so that others may experience this wonderful show'). The forums are lively with retorts flung between members about the quality of illegal material vis-à-vis the risks taken by pirates 'risking their necks' (see generally, comments on sites at btsites.tk). The sheer volume of consumer indifference is most compelling.

References

ABC News (2012) 'Artist anger as Spotify launches in Australia', updated 23 May 2012, 11:14am AEST

Administrative Office of the United Sates Courts (2011) *2010 Annual Report of the Director: Judicial Business of the United States Court*, Washington DC: US Government Printing Office

Adorno, T (1962) *Introduction to the Sociology of Music*, New York: Seabury Press

Adorno, TW (1990) 'The Form of the Phonograph Record', *October* 55: 46–61

Adorno, TW and Horkeheimer, M (1979), *Dialectic of Enlightenment*, London: Verso

Advocates for Environmental and Human Rights (2007) *Industrial Sources of Dioxin Poisoning in Mossville, Louisiana: A Report Based on the Government's Own Data*, Louisiana: Subra Company and Mossville Environmental Action, Now

Akers, R (1994) *Criminological Theories: Introduction and Evaluation*, Los Angeles: Roxbury Publishing

Alford, W (1994) 'How Theory Does – and – Does Not Matter: American Approaches to Intellectual Property Law in East Asia', *UCLA Pac. Basin LJ* 13: 8–24

Alford, W (1995) *To Steal a Book is an Elegant Offense*, Stanford: Stanford University Press

Andrews, N (1997) 'The Logic of Late Capitalism Illustrated: MBO of Elders IXL', *Australian Journal of Corporate Law* 8:139–199

Ashenfelter, O and Jurajda, S (2001) 'Cross-Country Comparisons of Wage Rates: The Big Mac Index', October, Industrial Relations Section, Princeton University

Attali, J (1985) *Noise: The Political Economy of Music*, Manchester: Manchester University Press

Australia, House of Representatives Parliamentary Debates, *(Hansard)*, Hon. Nigel Bowen QC (Attorney-General), Second Reading, 'Copyright Bill 1968', No. 20, 16 May 1968, at 1527–1536

Australia, House of Representatives, Parliamentary Debates, *(Hansard)*, Mr Morrison (Minister for Science), Second Reading, 'Trade Practices Bill', 24 July 1974, No. 30 at 574–576

Australia, House of Representatives, Parliamentary Debates, *(Hansard)*, Hon. Daryl Williams AM QC (Attorney-General), First Reading, 'Copyright Amendment (Digital Agenda) Bill', 2 September 1999, No. 64 at 9748–9752

Australia (2012) *Convergence Review: Final Report*, Canberra: The Convergence Review Committee, Department of Broadband, Communications and the Digital Economy

Australian Bureau of Statistics (September 2010) 'Australian Statistical Trends, Holidaying Abroad', Canberra: Australian Government

Australian Copyright Council (1996) *Music and Copyright*, Bulletin 70, Sydney: Australian Copyright Council

Australian Customs and Border Protection Service (2010) *Annual Report 2009–10*, Canberra: Australian Government

Australian Institute of Criminology (2008) *Intellectual Property Crime and Enforcement in Australia*, Research and Publication Series No. 94, Canberra: Australian Government

Bakan, J (2004) *The Corporation: The Pathological Pursuit of Profit and Power*, London: Constable

Balio T (1996) 'Adjusting to the New Global Economy' in A. Moran (ed.) *Film Policy*, London and New York: Routledge

Barley F (2003) 'Patent Law and Plant Breeders' Rights' [2003] MUEJL 10(4): 1–45

Barnett, S (2004) 'Media Ownership Policies: Pressures for Change and Implications', Pacific Journalism Review, 10(2): 8–19

Bauxmann, P, Pohl, G, Johnscher, P, Strube, J and Groffmann, H-D (2005) 'Strategies for Digital Music Markets: Pricing and the Effectiveness of Measures Against Pirate Copies – Results of an Empirical Study', *ECIS 2005 Proceedings*, Paper 116, available at: http://aisel.aisnet.org/ecis2005/116

Bennett, A (2011) 'UN Criticises NZ's Three-Strike Piracy Law', *New Zealand Herald*, 7 June

Berlin, I (1969) 'Two Concepts of Liberty' in *Four Essays on Liberty*, Oxford: Oxford University Press

Bewley, L (2010) 'LyondellBasell's Exit Strategy', *chemicalweek*, May 10/17

Billboard (incorporating *Billboard.biz*) (1990 to 2011), New York: VNU Business Media

Birchall, S (2004) 'A Doctrine Under Pressure: The Need for Rationalisation of the Doctrine of Authorisation of Infringement of Copyright in Australia', AIPJ 15: 227–246

Bird, R (1983) *Osborn's Concise Law Dictionary*, London: Sweet & Maxwell

Blackshield, AR (1994) 'Reinterpreting the Constitution' in J Brett, JA Gillespie and M Goot (eds) *Developments in Australian Politics*, Melbourne: Macmillan

Blecha, P (2004) *Taboo Tunes: A History of Bands & Censored Songs*, San Francisco: Backbeat Books

Boje, D and Khan, F (2009) 'Story-Branding by Empire Entrepreneurs Nike, Child Labour, and Pakistan's Soccer Ball Industry', *Journal of Small Business and Entrepreneurship* 22(1): 9–24

Bourdieu, P and Eagleton, T (1991) 'Doxa and Common Life', *New Left Review* 191:111–121

Bourdieu, P (1984) *Distinction: a Social Critique of Judgment of Taste*, London: Routledge and Kegan

Bourdieu, P and Passeron, J-C (1977) *Reproduction Education, Society and Culture* (trans. Richard Nice), London: Sage Publications

Brandle, L (2011) 'NZ has Passed "Three Strikes' Legislation to Stamp Out Piracy. Will it Work?' *The Hook*, 3 May 2011, available at: musicmetwork.com

Braakman, A and Dutilh, N (1997) 'The Application of Articles 85 & 86 of the EC Treaty by National Courts in the Member States', July Report, Brussels: European Commission

Brewster, R (2011) 'The Surprising Benefits to Developing Countries of Linking International Trade and Intellectual Property', *Chicago Journal of International Law* 12: 1–47

Brown, A (1997) 'Let's All Have a Disco', in S Redhead, D Wynne and J O'Connor J (eds) *The Clubcultures Reader*, London: Blackwell Publishers

Burgess, GH (1989) *Industrial Organization*, Singapore: Prentice-Hall

Burnett, R (1995) *The Global Jukebox*, London: Routledge

Canterbury, E and Marvasti, A (2001) 'The US Motion Pictures Industry: An Empirical Approach', *Review of Industrial Organization* 19: 81–98

Center for Responsive Politics (2011), available at: www.opensecrets.org

Chappel, S and Garafalo, R (1977) *Rock 'n' roll is Here to Pay*, London: Nelson Hall

Chorvat, T and McCabe, K (2004) 'The Brain and the Law', *Phil. Trans. R. Soc. London* 359: 1727–1736

Clark, A (ed.) (1983) *The Rock Year Book*, London: Virgin Books

Clement, D (2003) 'Creation Myths: Does Innovation Require Intellectual Property Rights?' *Reason* March 34(10): 30–38 (quoting R Lucas at 35)

Connell, J and Gibson, C (2003) *Sound Tracks: Popular Music, Identity and Place*, London: Routledge

Copyright Convergence Group (1994) *Highways to Change: Copyright in the New Communications Environment*, Canberra: AGPS

Copyright Law Review Committee (1999) *Simplification of the Copyright Act 1968*, Canberra: AGPS

Copyright Office (1963) *Sixty-Fifth Annual report of the Register of Copyrights for the Fiscal Year Ending June 1962*, Washington DC: The Library of Congress

Crean, S (2000) 'Looking Back to the Future – Creators and Cultural Policy in the Era of Free Trade', *Journal of Canadian Studies* 35(3): 199–211

Cross, JC (2011) 'Mexico', in J Karaganis (ed.) *Media Piracy in Emerging Economies*, New York: Social Science Research Council

Curran, J (1991) 'Culturalist Perspectives of News Organizations: A Reappraisal and a Case Study' in M Ferguson (ed.) *Public Communication: The New Imperatives*, London: Sage

Cvetkovski, T (2005) 'The Political Economy of the Music Industry: Technological Change and the Political Control of Music', PhD Dissertation, The University of Queensland (published in 2009)

Cvetkovski, T (2007) *The Political Economy of the Music Industry*, Saarbrücken: VDM Müller

Cvetkovski, T (2009) *The Political Economy of the Music Industry: Technological Change and the Political Control of Music*, Saarbrücken: LAP Lambert Academic Publishing GmbH & Co. KG

Cvetkovski, T (2012) *The Political Economy of the Music Industry: Technological Change, Consumer Disorientation and Market Disorganisation in Popular Music*, Saarbrücken : AV Akademikerverlag

David, M and Kirkhope J (2004) 'New Digital Technologies: Privacy/Property, Globalization, and the Law', *Perspectives on Global Development and Technology* 3(4): 437–448

Dicola, P (2011) 'An Economic View of Legal Restrictions on Musical Borrowing and Appropriation' in M Biagioli, P Jaszi and M Woodmansee (eds), *Making and Unmaking Intellectual Property*, Chicago: The University of Chicago Press

Disney Worldwide Services Inc (2009) Lobbying Report filed with the US House of Representatives, US Senate, Federal Communications Commission and US Copyright Office

Dolfsma, W (2000) 'How Will the Music Industry Weather the Globalization Storm?' *First Monday* 5(5): 1–19

Dowd, DF (1979) 'Business as a System of Power' in R Quinney (ed.) *Capitalist Society: Readings for Critical Sociology*, Illinois: Dorsey Press

Dowling, S (2011) 'Maverick Pirate Party wins First German Seats', available at: www.smh.com.au/technology

Drahos, P (1998) *The Universality of Intellectual Property Rights: Origins and Development*, London: The University of London

Dunleavy, B and O'Leary, O (1987) *Theories of the State: The Politics of Liberal Democracy*, Basingstoke: Palgrave Macmillan

Dwyer, T and Uricaru, I (2009) 'Slashings and Subtitles: Romanian Media Piracy, Censorship, and Translation', *The Velvet Light Trap* 63: 45–57

Easley, RF (2005) 'Ethical Issues in the Music Industry Response to Innovation and Piracy', *Journal of Business Ethics* 62: 163–168

Eccleshall, R (2003) *Political Ideologies: An Introduction*, London: Routledge

Edenborough, M (1997) *Intellectual Property*, London: Cavendish Publishing

Edgely, M (2010) 'Criminals and (Second-Class) Citizenship: Twenty-First Century Attainder?' *Griffith Law Review* 19(3): 402–437

El-Agraa, A (2007) *The European Union*, Cambridge: Cambridge University Press

Electronic Frontier Foundation (2003–2005) *RIAA v. The People: Two Years Later*, available at: www.eff.org

Electronic Frontier Foundation (2007) *RIAA v. The People: Four Years Later*, available at: www.eff.org

Entertainment Software Association website, available at: www.theesa.com

EU website, available at: europa.net

European Commission (1997) Proposal for a European Parliament and Council Directive on the Harmonisation of Certain Aspects of Copyright and Related Rights in the Information Society (97/0359 (COD)

European Commission (2001) *Europa Press Release*, 'CD Prices', IP-01-1212, Brussels, 17 August 2001

Exposure Draft and Commentary: Copyright Amendment (Digital Agenda) Bill 1999, February 1999, available at: www.law.gov.au

Federal Trade Commission Decisions (1967) *FTC* July–December, Vol. 72: 112–219

Federal Trade Commission Press Release (2000) 'Record Companies Settle FTC Charges of Restraining Competition in CD Music Market', available at: www.ftc.gov/opa/2000/05/cdpres.shtm

Felson, M (1994) *Crime and Everyday Life*, Thousand Oaks: Fine Forge Press

Fenech, S (2010) 'Super Mario Video Piracy is no Longer a Game for James Burt', *The Courier Mail*, 9 February

Fenech, S (2010) 'James Burt to Pay Nintendo $1.5m for Illegal Uploading of New Super Mario Bros', *The Courier Mail,* 9 February

Ferrer, E (2011) *The Impact of Internet Piracy on the Australian Economy,* Sydney: Sphere Analysis

Fildes, N (2006) 'EU court judgment threatens EMI merger with Warner', *The Independent* (UK), 14 July

First, H and Shiraishi, T (2005) 'Concentrated Power: The Paradox of Antitrust in Japan', *New York University Law and Economics Working Papers*, Paper 11, New York: New York University

Five Eight: Music Business Insight (2003) 23 October, London: Frukt

Flew, T (2005) *New Media: An Introduction*, Oxford: Oxford University Press

Fornäs, J, Becker, K, Bjurström, E and Ganetz, H (2007) *Consulting Media: Communication, Shopping and Everyday Life*, Oxford and New York: BERG

Fortune Global (2011) *Fortune Global 500*, available at: money.cnn.com/magazines/fortune

Foucault, M (1991a) 'What Is An Author?' in P Rabinow (ed.) *The Foucault Reader*, New York: Penguin

Foucault, M (1991b) 'Complete and Austere Institutions' in P Rabinow (ed.) *The Foucault Reader*, New York: Penguin

Foucault, M (1993) 'Dream, Imagination and Existence' in K Hoeller (ed.) *Dream and Existence: Michel Foucault and Ludwig Binswanger*, New Jersey: Humanities Press

Fox, B (1998) 'Cheap Trick', *New Scientist*, 13 June: 10

Fox, B (2002) 'Why Copy Protection on CD is "Worthless"' *New Scientist*, 9 November: 9

France, A (1894) *Le Lys Rouge* [The Red Lily], e-book #3922, available at: ebookbrowse.com portal (and via Project Gutenberg)

Fraser, M (2010) 'UTS Speaks: National Content Network – Access Dig?' *AIPJ* 21: 56–72

Frith, S (1983) *Sound Effects: Youth, Leisure, and the Politics of Rock*, London: Constable

Frith, S (1986) 'Art Versus Technology: The Strange Case of Popular Music,' *Media, Culture and Society*, 8: 263–280

Frith, S (1988) *Music for Pleasure: Essays in the Sociology of Pop*, Cambridge: Polity Press

Furnham, A and Valgeirsson, H (2007) 'The Effect of Life Values and Materialism on Buying Counterfeit Products, *The Journal of Socio-Economic*, 36: 677–685

Garnham, N (1984) *Public Policy and Cultural Industries*, London: Greater London Council

Garnham, N (1990) *Capitalism and Communications – Global Culture and the Economies of Information*, London: Sage

Getaway (2011) Television Series, Nine Network: Brisbane (aired 1 October 2011)

Gibson, J (2011) 'Will You Go to Jail for Copyright Infringement?, University of Richmond School of Law, *Media Institute*, available at: mediainstitute.org (published online 25 May)

Gillespie, T (2011), 'Characterizing Copyright in the Classroom' in M Biagioli, P Jaszi and M Woodmansee (eds) *Making and Unmaking Intellectual Property*, Chicago: The University of Chicago Press

Ginsburg, J 'Essay: From Having Copies to Experiencing Works: The Development of an Access Right in US Copyright Law', (2003) 50 *Journal of the Copyright Society of the USA* 113

Glasbeek, H (2002) 'Shielded by Law: Why Corporate Wrongs and Wrongdoers are Privileged, *UWSLR* 6: 1–23

Glenny, M (1996) *The Fall of Yugoslavia*, Penguin: London

Goldman EA (2003) 'Road to No Warez: The No Electronic Theft Act and Criminal Copyright Infringement', *Oregon Law Review* 82: 369–432

Goldring, J (2008) 'Globalization and Consumer Protection Laws', *Macquarie Law Journal* 8: 79–101

Goldstein, P (1994) *Copyright's Highway: From Gutenberg to the Celestial Jukebox*, Stanford: Stanford University Press

Gomery, D (1986) *The Hollywood Studio System*, New York: St. Martin's Press

Gomez-Arostegui, HT (2010 'The Untold Story of the First Copyright Suit Under the Statute of Anne in 1710', 25 *Berkeley Tech. L.J.*: 1247–1349

Goold, M and Campbell, A (1998) 'Desperately Seeking Synergy', *Harvard Business Review*, September–October: 131–143

Groennings, K (2005a) 'Costs and Benefits of the Recording Industry's Litigation against Individuals', *Berkley Tech. L.J.* 20: 571–601

Groennings, K (2005b) 'An Analysis of the Recording Industry's Litigation Strategy against Direct Infringers', *Vanderbilt Journal of Entertainment Law and Practice*, Spring: 389–399

Gusfield, J (1981) *The Culture of Public Problems: Drinking-Driving and the Symbolic Order*, Chicago: The University of Chicago Press

Hanlon, J (1998) *European Community Law*, London: Sweet & Maxwell

Här är förhören med Pirate Bay-männen (Transcript of Record of Interview with the Men behind Pirate Bay) (5 February 2008), available at: www.*AvIDG*.se

Harrod, R (1958) 'The Possibility of Economic Satiety – Use of Economic Growth for Improving the Quality of Education and Leisure' in *Problems of United States*

Economic Development, Vol. 1, New York: Committee for Economic Development, 207–213

Hayden T and Kernaghan C (2002) 'Pennies and Hour and No Way Up', *The New York Times*, 2 July

Hausman, D (2008) *The Philosophy of Economics: an Anthology*, Cambridge: Cambridge University Press

Heindl, S (2010) 'LimeWire Found Guilty of Inducing Copyright Infringement', *Internet Law Bulletin*, 13 August: 4

Hesmondhalgh, D (2002) *The Cultural Industries*, London: Sage

Heywood, A (2002) *Politics*, New York: Palgrave

Hirsch, F (1977) *Social Limits to Growth*, London and Henley: Routledge and Kegan

IFPI (International Federation of the Phonographic Industry) website, available at: www.ifpi.org

IFPI (2011a) *Recording in Numbers*, London: IFPI

IFPI (2011b) *Digital Music Report*, London: IFPI

IIPA (2011c) 'Special 301: Historical Summary of Selected Countries' Placement for Copyright-Related Matters on the Special 301 Lists', Appendix D, issued 15 February 2011, available at: www.iipa.com/special301.

IFPI (2012) *Digital Music Report: Expanding Choice. Going Global*, London: IFPI

IIPA (International Intellectual Property Alliance) website, available at: www.iipa.com

IIPA (2004) 'Special 301 Report on Global Copyright Protection and Enforcement' (submitted 13/2/2004 and filed 17/2/2004), available at: www.iipa.com

Ilias, S and Fergusson, I (2011) *Intellectual Property Rights and International Trade*, CRS Report for Congress, Prepared for Members and Committees of Congress, Washington: Congressional Research Service

Index to Media 100 (2010) Ad Age DataCenter, available at: adage.com (subscription service)

International Labour Organization (2011) 'Wage Policies in Times of Crisis', *Global Wage Report*, Geneva: International Labour Office

Internet Archive website, available at: www.archive.org

The IT Crowd (2007) V2.0, TalkBack Thames (producer), Chanel 4 Television Corporation (distributor) (DVD format), available at: www.youtube.com/results?search_query=Anti-piracy+parody&aq=f

Jarvis, J (2009) *What Would Google Do?* New York: HarperCollins

Johns, A (2009) *Piracy: The Intellectual Property Wars from Gutenberg to Gates*, Chicago: The University of Chicago Press

Johnson, D and Turner, C (2006) *European Business* (2nd edn), London: Routledge

Jones, H (1961) 'Law and Morality in the Perspective of Legal Realism', *Columbia Law Review* 61(5): 799–809

Justinian Code From the Corpus Juris Civilis (trans. S Scott) (1932), Book IV, Title LIX, 'Concerning monopolies, unlawful agreements of merchants, the artificers or contractors, & the illegal & prohibited practices of bath proprietors', Cincinnati: The Central Trust Company

Justinian Institutes (1911) (trans. J Moyle) Book II, Title I.25–35, 'Of the different kinds of things', Oxford: Oxford University Press

Kafka, F (1998) *The Trial*, trans. Breon Mitchell, New York: Schocken

Kahan, D (1997) 'Social Influence, Social Meaning, and Deterrence', *Va. Law Rev.* 83: 349–395

Kaiser, A and Stouraitis, K (2001) 'Reversing Corporate Diversification and the Use of the Proceeds from Asset Sales: The Case of Thorn EMI', *Financial Management*, Winter: 63–102

Kaplan, B (1966) 'An Unhurried View of Copyright: Proposals and Prospects', *Columbia Law Review* 66(5): 831–852

Kaplan, B (1967) *An Unhurried View of Copyright*, New York: Columbia University Press

Karaganis, J (ed.) (2011) *Media Piracy in Emerging Economies*, New York: Social Science Research Council

Kaysen C and Turner DF (1959) *Antitrust Policy: An Economic and Legal Analysis*, Cambridge MA: Harvard University Press

King, H (2008) 'Corporate Accountability under the Alien Tort Claims Act', *Melbourne Journal of International Law* 9: 472–494

Kirby, M (Hon Justice Michael Kirby AC CMG) (2007) 'Computers & Law: The First Quarter Century', *New South Wales Society for Computers and the Law*, paper presented on 9 October 2007

Kopf, D, Boje, D and Torres, I (2010) 'The Good, the Bad and the Ugly: Dialogical Ethics and Market Information', *Journal of Business Ethics* 9: 285–297

Kovacic, W (2008) 'Competition Policy in the European Union and the United States: Convergence or Divergence in the Future Treatment of Dominant Firms?' *Competition Law International* October: 8–18

Kretschmer, M, Derclaye, E, Favale, M and Watt, R (2010) *The Relationship Between Copyright and Contract Law*, London: SABIP

Kretschmer, M, Klimis, G and Wallis, R (1999) 'The Changing Location of Intellectual Property Rights in Music: A Study of Music Publishers, Collecting Societies and Media Conglomerates', *Prometheus* 17(2): 163–186

Lawrence L (2001) 'Copyright's First Amendment', 48 *UCLA L. Rev.* 1057: 1057–1073

Leavis, QD (1933) *Fiction and the Reading Public* (1974 reprint) New York: Folcroft Library Editions

Lee, R (1982) 'An Economic Analysis of Compulsory Licensing in Copyright Law', *Western New England Law Review* 5: 203–226

Lee, S (1995) 'Re-examining the Concept of the "Independent" Record Company: The Case of Wax Trax! Records', *Popular Music* 14: 13–31

Leet, M (2004) *Aftereffects of Knowledge in Modernity*, Albany: State of New York University Press

Legatum Prosperity Index (2010), available at: www.prosperity.com

Lely, JM (1883) *Wharton's Law-Lexicon* (7th edn), London: Stevens and Sons

Le May, R (2010) 'Nintendo Looks to Sue More Aussie Firms', *Delimiter.com.au*, 19 February

Lessig, L (2001) 'Copyright's First Amendment', 48 *UCLA Law Rev.* 1056: 1057–1073

Lessig, L (2004) *Free Culture*, New York: Penguin Press

Locke, J (1967) *Two Treatises of Government* (2nd edn) ed. P Laslett, Cambridge: Cambridge University Press

Longhurst, B (1995) *Popular Music and Society*, London: Polity Press

Lyman, Peter (1995) 'Copyright and Fair Use in the Digital Age', *Educom Review* January/February: 33–35

LyondellBasell AF S.C.A (2008) *Management Report for the Year Ended 31 December 2007*, New York: Access Group

Madden, M and Lenhart, A (2003) 'Music Downloading', *File-Sharing and Copyright: A Pew Internet Project Data Memo,* Washington DC: Pew Internet and American Life Project, available at: www.pewInternet.org

Maffioletti, A and Ramello, G (2004) 'Should We Put Them in Jail? Copyright Infringement, Penalties and Consumer Behaviour: Insights from Experimental Data', *Review of Economic Research on Copyright Issues* 1(2): 81–95

Mandel, E (1975) *Late Capitalism*, London: NLB

Marron, DB and Steel, DG (2000) 'Which Countries Protect Intellectual Property? The Case of Software Piracy', *Economic Inquiry* 38: 159–174

Mason A (1986) 'The Role of a Constitutional Court in a Federation: A Comparison of The Australian and United States Experience', 16 *Federal Law Review*: 1–28

May, C (2000) *A Global Political Economy of Intellectual Property Rights: The New Enclosures?* London: Routledge

Manesh, M (2006) 'The Immorality of Theft, the Amorality of Infringement', *Stan. Tech. L. Rev* 5: paras. 1–110

Manuel, P (1993) *Cassette Culture: Popular Music and Technology in North India*, Chicago: Chicago University Press

Marcuse, H (1967) 'The Question of Revolution', *New Left Review*, September–October: pp. 1–5

Marron, D and Steel, D (2000) 'Which Countries Protect Intellectual Property? The Case of Software Piracy', *Economic Inquiry* 38(2): 159–174

Marx, K (1970) (first published 1857–1858) *Grundrisse*, New York: International Publishers

Marx, K (1977) (first published 1867) *Capital* (vol. 1), New York: Vantage Books

Marx, K and Engels, F (1976) (first published 1845–1846) *The German Ideology*, Moscow: Progress Publishers

Mazower, D (2000) *The Balkans*, London: Weidenfeld and Nicolson

McBride, S and Smith, E (2008) 'Music Industry to Abandon Mass Suits', *The Wall Street Journal*, 19 December 2008

McKeough, J and Stewart, A (1997) *Intellectual Property Australia*, Sydney: Butterworths

Melton, W (1991) 'An Examination of the Bootleg Record Industry and its Impact Upon Popular Music Consumption', *Tracking Popular Media Studies* 4(1) pp. 16–25

Mi2N (2011) 'New Research Highlighting Staggering Volume Of Traffic To Pirate Sites', 16 January 2011, at available at: www.mi2n.com/press

Mill, JS (1982) *On Liberty*, Harmondsworth: Penguin

Mill, JS (2004) *Principles of Political Economy with Some of Their Applications to Social Philosophy* (abridged edn) (ed.) S Nasen, Indianapolis: Hackett Publishing

MOJO Box , available at: www.boxofficemojo.com

Moohr, G (2003) 'The Crime of Copyright Infringement: An Inquiry Based on Morality, Harm, and Criminal Theory', *Boston University Law Review* 83(4): 731–784

Mook, N (2003) 'RIAA Sues 261 Including 12 Year Old Girl', available at: www.betanews.com

Moore, M (1998) *The Big One* (documentary), directed by and starring Michael Moore, produced by Kathleen Glynn, distributed by BBC and Miramax Films

MPAA (2004) 'Piracy, It's a Crime' (advertisement), available at: www.youtube.com/watch?v=HmZm8vN

Moran, A (1993) 'Terms for a Reader: Film, Hollywood, National Cinema, Cultural Identity and Film Policy' in A. Moran (ed.) *Film Policy*, London and New York: Routledge

Motta, M (2004) *Competition Policy: Theory and Practice*, Cambridge: Cambridge University Press

Murphy, M (1995) 'Publishing Agreements and Copyright Law', *QLSJ* October 25(5): 431–445

Music & Copyright (2004) No. 26 (September), London: Informa Publishing

Music & Copyright (2005) No. 264 (December), London: Informa Publishing

Music Industry News Network, available at: www.mi2n.com (subscription service)

Music Industry News Network (2011) 'YouTube Taps Rights Flow For Publishing Rights Management', 10 February, available at: www.mi2n.com

Navissi, F, Naiker, V and Upson, S (2005) 'Securities Price Effects of Napster-Related Events', *Journal of Accounting, Auditing & Finance* 20(2): pp. 167–183

Negus, K (1992) *Producing Pop: Culture and Conflict in the Popular Music Industry*, New York: Routledge

Nesdale, A (1980) 'The Law and Social Attitudes: Effects of Proposed Changes in Drug Legislation on Attitudes toward Drug Use', *Canadian J. Criminology* 22: 176–187

Nettleton, J, Hayne, K and Darmopil, S (2010) 'Copyright Infringement – Australia – Nintendo Settlement Gives Warning to Individual Copyright Infringers and Pirates – Unauthorised Wii Games Downloads – Watch Out for Copyright Infringement', *Addisons Focus Paper*, available at: www.addisonslawyers.com.au

Ngak, C (2011) 'Spotify Gets Sued for Patent Infringement', CBSNews (29 July 2011, 10:47 AM), available at: www.cbsnews.com/8301-501465_162-20085429-501465.html

Noebel, DA (1974) *The Marxist Minstrels: A Handbook on Communist Subversion of Music*, Tulsa: American Christian College Press

Nozick, R (1974) *Anarchy, State and Utopia*, Oxford: Blackwell

OECD (2010) 'National Accounts, Gross domestic product (GDP) StatExtracts for year 2010', available at: www.oecd.org

Office of Fair Trading (2002) 'Wholesale Supply Compact Discs', OFT391/2002, September, available at: www.oft.gov.uk/shared_oft/reports/consumer_protection/oft391.pdf

Opensecrets.com, Center for Responsive Politics, available at: www.opensecrets.org

Palmer, T (1989) 'Intellectual Property: A Non-Posnerian Law and Economics Approach', *Hamline Law Review* 12(2): 261–304

Pang L (2005) *Cultural Control and Globalization in Asia: Copyright, Piracy, and Cinema*, New York: Routledge

Pavlov, O (2005) 'Dynamic Analysis of an Institutional conflict: Copyright Owners against File Sharing, *Journal of Economic Issues* 3: 633–663

Peterson, DJ (2005) *Russia and the Information Revolution*, Santa Monica: RAND

Peterson, R and Annand, N (2004) 'The Production of Culture Perspective', *Annual Review of Sociology* 30: 311–335

Peterson, RA and Berger, DG (1990) 'Cycles in Symbolic Production: The Case of Popular Music' in S Frith and A Goodwin (eds) *On Record: Rock, Pop, and the Written Word*, pp. 140–159, London: Routledge

Petition Against a Bill to the Law Relating to Copyright (1800), First Reading in the House of Commons: *To the Honourable the House of Commons of the United Kingdom of Great Britain and Ireland. The Petition of Certain Authors, Publishers, and Booksellers of London, and Others* (Print No. 687250), London: T. Cadell (The Strand)

Points in Law and Equity (1792) London: Strahan and Woodfall

Posner, RA (1999) *Antitrust Law*, Chicago: The University of Chicago Press

Primo, N and Lloyd, L (2011), in J Karaganis (ed.) *Media Piracy in Emerging Economies*, New York: Social Science Research Council

Procopius (2004) The *Secret History of the Court of Justinian*, incorporating the *Justinian Code* and *Justinian Institute*, e-book #12916, available at: www.gutenberg.org

Project Gutenberg website, available at: www.gutenberg.org

RIAA (Recording Industry Association of America) website, available at: www.riaa.com

RIAA (2006) 'Music Rules! True Music Fans Play by the Rules' (poster format created by Learning Works), available at: www.music-rules.com/pdf.MusicRulesPoster.pdf

Redgum (1984) 'I've Been to Bali Too' (promo video), Lyrics by John Schumann, available at: www.youtube.com/watch?v=9toD_R6t1pI

Remarks on the Law of Copyright (188?), *19th Century Legal Treatises*, OCLC 264708179 and 64DD051 Ref. (unknown author and publisher)

Reuters (2007) 'Piracy Worked for Us, Romania President Tells Gates', *Washington Post*, 1 February

Ricketson, S (2001) 'Copyright' in T Blackshield, M Coper and G Williams (eds), *The Oxford Companion to the High Court of Australia*, pp. 152–154, Melbourne: Oxford University Press

Ringer, BA (1974) *The Demonology of Copyright*, New York: RR Bowker Company

RIP: A Remix Manifesto (2008) (documentary) Brett Gaylor (director) Eyesteelfilm/ National Film Board of Canada (produced by)

Robertson, G (1999) *The Justice Game*, London: Vintage

Rose, M (1993) *Authors and Owners: the Invention of Copyright*, Cambridge MA: Harvard University Press

Rousseau, J-J (1968) *The Social Contract*, tr. & intro M Cranston, Harmondsworth: Penguin

Rudd, BW (1971) 'Notable Dates in American Copyright', *Quarterly Journal of the Library of Congress*, April: 137–143

Rudnick, B and Frawley, D (1969) 'Music is the Revolution', *Cavalier*, 19(4): 37, 88

Schiller, H (1969) *Mass Communications and American Empire*, New York: A.M. Kelly

Schiller, H (2000) *Living in the Number One Country*, New York: Seven Stories

Second Amended Petition and Petitioners' Observations on the Government's Reply Concerning the United States Government's Failure to Protect the Human Rights of Rresidents of Mossville, Louisiana, United States of America (2008), Petition No. P-242-05, Inter-American Commission on Human Rights, submitted by Petitioners' Representatives: N Walker and M Harden (advocates for Environmental Human Rights), New Orleans

Sendy, J (1968) 'Democracy and Socialism', *Australian Left Review* 3: 8–16

Smith, A (1761) *The Theory of Moral Sentiments* (2nd edn) London: Millar

Soetendorp, R (2003) 'Music Piracy: Victimless Crime or Outright Theft?' transcript of online debate (14 February), *Make Sparks Fly*, available at: www.makesparksfly. com

Schwarzschild, M (2006) 'Keeping it Private', *The University of Queensland Law Journal* 25(2): 216–227

Sethi, SP, Veral, E, Shapiro HJ, and Emelianova, O (2011) 'Mattel Inc: Global Manu-facturing Principles (GMP) – A Life-Cycle Analysis of a Company-Based Code of Conduct in the Toy Industry', *Journal of Business Ethics* 99: 483–517

Sezneva, O and Karaganis, J (2011) in J Karaganis (ed.) *Media Piracy in Emerging Economies*, New York: Social Science Research Council

Shakespeare, W (1996) *The Complete Works of William Shakespeare*, Hertfordshire: Wordsworth

Schmitter, P (1974) 'Still the Century of Corporatism?' *The Review of Politics* 36(1): 85–131

Sherman, B (1997) 'Remembering and Forgetting: The Birth of Modern Copyright Law' in D Nelken (ed.), *Comparing Legal Cultures*, pp. 237–266, Aldershot UK: Dartmouth

Sherman, B and Bently, L (1999) *The Making of Modern Intellectual Property*, Cambridge: Cambridge University Press

Simpson, S (2002) *Music Business*, Sydney: Omnibus Press

Siwek, S (2010) *Video Games in the 21st Century*, Washington DC: Entertainment Software Association

Slater, JA (1939) *Pitman's Commercial Law*, London: Pitman

Smirke, R (2011) 'EU Extends Copyright Term To 70 Years', *Billboard.biz*, 12 September, available at: www.billboard.biz/bbbiz/industry/publishing/eu-extends-copyright-term-to-70-years-1005348552.story

Smith, A (1907) *The Theory of Moral Sentiments* (originally published 1759), London: Bell

Solomon, D (1999) *The Political High Court: How the High Court Shapes Politics*, Sydney: Allen & Unwind

Talfourd, T (1840) *Three Speeches Delivered in the House of Commons in Favour of a Measure for an Extension of Copyright – To which are added the petitions in favour of a Bill and remarks on the present state of the copyright question*, London: Edward Moxon

Tate, C (1995) 'Why the Expansion of Judicial Power?' in C Tate and T Vallinder (eds) *The Global Expansion of Judicial Power*, New York: New York University Press

The New York Times (1906) 'Twain's Plan to Beat the Copyright Law', 12 December

The New York Times (1908) 'Mark Twain turns into a Corporation', 24 December

The World Bank (2010) *GDP Statistics*, available at: worldbank.org

Torgler, B and Schneider, F (2007) 'What Shapes Attitudes Towards Paying Taxes? Evidence from Multicultural European Countries', *Social Science Quarterly* 88(2): 444–470

Torrentfreak (2008) 'The Pirate Bay Interrogations', available at: http://torrentfreak.com/the-pirate-bay-interrogations-080207/

Torrentfreak (2010) 'MPAA Worries about worries Pirating US Soldiers in Iraq' with embedded unclassified document released by Multinational Force Iraq entitled 'MNF-I Talking Points: Pirated Movies in Iraq', available at: torrentfreak.com/mpaa-worries-about-pirating-u-s-soldiers-in-iraq-100515/

Torres, A (1999) 'Unlocking the Value of Intellectual Assets', *The McKinsey Quarterly* No. 4: 28–37

Towse, R (1997) 'Copyright as an Economic Incentive', *Hume Papers on Public Policy* 5(3): 32–45

Tucker, KH (2002) *Classical Social Theory*, Oxford: Blackwell

Twain, M (1935) *The Complete Works of Mark Twain and Mark Twain's Notebook* (authorized edn), New York: Harper and Brothers

Twain, M (2010) *Who Is Mark Twain*, New York: HarperCollins

US House Commission on Commerce (1998) H.R. Rep. No. 105-551,Ppt. 2, available at: http://copyright.gov/reports/studies/dmca_report.html

Vallinder, T. (1995) 'When the Courts Go Marching In' in C Tate and T Vallinder (eds) *The Global Expansion of Judicial Power*, New York: New York University Press

Van Bael, I (2005) *Competition Law of the European Community*, Kluwer Law International: London

Veblen, M (1923/1954) *Absentee Ownership and Business Enterprise*, New York: Viking

Voltaire (1997) *Candide*, London: Penguin Books

Wan, H and Lu, M (1997) 'An Analysis of Chinese Laws Against Computer Crimes', *Journal of Global Information Management* 5(2): 16–21

Weatherall, K (2004) 'On Technology Locks and the Proper Scope of Digital Copyright Laws – *Sony* in the High Court', 26 *Sydney Law Review* 613–638

Wilk, M (1976) *Memory Lane: 1890 to 1925*, New York: Ballantine Books

Whale, RF (1970) *Copyright: Evolution, Theory and Practice*, London: Longman

Williams, D (2002) 'Structure and Competition in the US Home Video Game Industry', *The International Journal of Media Management* 4(1): 41–54

White, AL (ed.) (1987) *Lost in Music: Culture, Style and the Musical Event*, New York: Routledge & Kegan Paul

Wiseman, L (2002) 'Beyond the Photocopier: Copyright and Publishing in Australia', 7 *Media & Arts Law Review*: 299–314

WIPO, *Basic Notions of Copyright and Related Rights*, available at: www.wipo.int/copyright/en/activities/pdf/basic_notions.pdf

WIPO, *International Protection of Copyright and Related Rights*, available at: www.wipo.int/copyright/en/activities/pdf/international_protection.pdf

WIPO, Database of Intellectual Property, legislative texts, available at: www.wipo.int/tk/en/laws/tk.html

Woods, J (2000) 'Slippery Slopes and Collapsing Taboos', *Argumentation* 14: 107–134

World Trade Organization, WT/DS362/R, Dispute Settlement Board findings, available at: www.wto.org/english/tratop_e/dispu_e/cases_e/ds362_e.htm

www.opensecrets.orgs

Yar, M (2005) 'The Global "Epidemic" of Movie "Piracy": Crime-Wave or Social Construction?' *Media, Culture & Society* 27(5): 677–696

Yates, I (2004) 'Face the Music', *Internet.au* 99: 24–28, 80–86

Yu, P (2002) 'Four Misconceptions about Piracy', *Loy. L.A. Int'l and Comp L Review* 26: 127–150

Index

A&M Records, Inc. v Napster, Inc., 40, 45, 133, 137, 140, 165, 175, 188, 196, 224, 263
AACP (see Alliance Against Counterfeiting and Piracy)
absolutism, 6, 144, 153, 201, 211
ACCC case (see also Australian Competition and Consumer Commission)
ACCC v Universal Music Australia Pty Limited (trial), 92, 94, 99, 238
ACCC v Universal Music Australia Pty Ltd (appeal), 141, 168, 188, 243
access industries, 108–11, 202
Act for the Encouragement of Literature and Genius, 55, 151–2
Adelaide Corporation v APRA, 199, 274
Administrative Office of the United States Courts, 181
Adorno, Theodor, 16, 29
AFACT (see Australian Federation Against Copyright Theft), 69, 164, 179, 180, 184, 189, 192, 195, 206
Agreement between the UN and WIPO, 58, 59, 87
Agreement on Trade-Related Aspects of IPRs, 154, 213
Akers, Ronald, 185, 187, 189, 190
Alliance Against Counterfeiting and Piracy, 179
altruism, 46–8, 54, 63, 73, 82, 87, 143–4, 161–4, 217, 218, 248
AMCOS (see Australian Mechanical Copyright Owners Society)
anti-
  competition, 13, 26–7, 95–8, 104–6, 109, 116, 209
  corporate, 125
  monopoly, 112, 169
  piracy, 9, 45, 107, 154, 164, 168, 173–5, 179, 196, 213, 219, 220, 231, 246, 252, 258–60
  trust, 4, 13, 95, 98–9, 103, 106, 107, 144, 149, 211, 274

APRA (see Australasian Performing Right Association – also referred to as Australasian Performers' Rights Association)
APRA v Jain, 274
APRA v Monster Communications Pty Limited, 274
ARIA (see Australian Recording Industry Association)
Arista Records v Lime Group, 40
artificiality (see also façade), 13, 25, 64, 67, 70, 91, 109, 165, 200, 213, 217
Attali, Jacques, 23
Atari Europe S.A.S.U. v Rapidshare (see also GEMA v Rapidshare), 122
attitudes, 86, 125–6, 149, 160, 178, 188, 190–1, 180
Attorney-General, 71, 129–30
audio-visual technologies, 66, 174
Australian Bureau of Statistics, 115
Australian Capital Television v Commonwealth, 126
Australian Competition and Consumer Act, 95
Australian Competition and Consumer Commission, 89
Australian Constitution, 125–6, 141
Australian Customs and Border Protection Service, 205, 275
Australian Federation Against Copyright Theft (see AFACT)
Australian Industries Preservation Act, 95
Australian Institute of Criminology, 187
Australian Mechanical Copyright Owners Society, 69–70
Australasian Performing Right Association, 69–71, 77, 238
Australian Recording Industry Association, 69–70, 167, 238, 188, 231–2, 234
Australian Tape Manufacturers Association Ltd v Commonwealth, 157
authorization, 123, 128, 133–4, 139, 156–7, 184, 199, 237, 244

Printed and bound in the United States of America